Blue-Collar Conservatism

Politics and Culture in Modern America

Series Editors: Margot Canaday, Glenda Gilmore,
Michael Kazin, Stephen Pitti, Thomas J. Sugrue

Volumes in the series narrate and analyze political and
social change in the broadest dimensions from 1865 to
the present, including ideas about the ways people have
sought and wielded power in the public sphere and the
language and institutions of politics at all levels—local,
national, and transnational. The series is motivated by
a desire to reverse the fragmentation of modern U.S.
history and to encourage synthetic perspectives on social
movements and the state, on gender, race, and labor,
and on intellectual history and popular culture.

BLUE-COLLAR CONSERVATISM

Frank Rizzo's Philadelphia
and Populist Politics

Timothy J. Lombardo

PENN

UNIVERSITY OF PENNSYLVANIA PRESS

PHILADELPHIA

Publication of this volume was aided by a gift from Eric R. Papenfuse
and Catherine A. Lawrence.

Published by
University of Pennsylvania Press
Philadelphia, Pennsylvania 19104-4112
www.upenn.edu/pennpress

Printed in the United States of America on acid-free paper
1 3 5 7 9 10 8 6 4 2

Library of Congress Cataloging-in-Publication Data

Names: Lombardo, Timothy J., author.
Title: Blue-collar conservatism: Frank Rizzo's Philadelphia and populist politics /
    Timothy J. Lombardo.
Other titles: Politics and culture in modern America.
Description: 1st edition. | Philadelphia : University of Pennsylvania Press, [2018] | Series: Politics
    and culture in modern America | Includes bibliographical references and index.
Identifiers: LCCN 2018002986 | ISBN 9780812250541 (hardcover: alk. paper)
Subjects: LCSH: Rizzo, Frank, 1920-1991. | Philadelphia (Pa.)—Politics and government—
    20th century. | Conservatism—Pennsylvania—Philadelphia—History—20th century. |
    Populism—Pennsylvania—Philadelphia—History—20th century. | Mayors—Pennsylvania—
    Philadelphia. | Working class—Pennsylvania—Philadelphia—History—20th century.
Classification: LCC F158.54.R59 L66 2018 | DDC 320.5209748/11—dc23
LC record available at https://lccn.loc.gov/2018002986

For Beca

CONTENTS

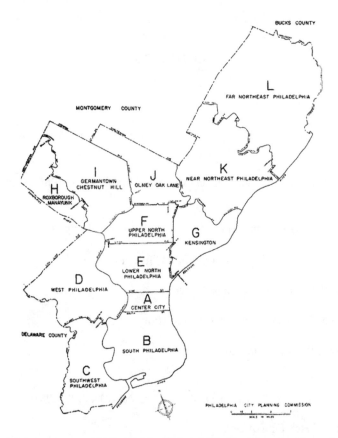

Figure 1. Sectional map of Philadelphia. Philadelphia City Planning Commission, population characteristics: 1960 and 1970, Philadelphia census tracts, 1972.

Blue-Collar Conservatism
and Frank Rizzo's Philadelphia

Frank Rizzo strode into South Philadelphia's crowded Columbus Square Playground with little fanfare. He had arrived to hear members of Philadelphia's American Federation of Musicians Local 77 give a free concert of Italian arias in honor of Columbus Day. Although he hoped to keep a low profile and said he was only there to celebrate his Italian heritage, the six-foot-two-inch-tall former police commissioner easily stood out in a crowd. Rizzo was also in the final month of his first campaign to become mayor of Philadelphia. The event quickly turned into a pro-Rizzo rally. Chants of "We want Frank!" drowned out the music as concertgoers clamored around the candidate. Longtime political reporter Sandy Grady said men cheered and women swooned at the sight of him. "These things just happen whenever Rizzo goes into an Italian American neighborhood," another reporter commented. Uncharacteristically humbled, Rizzo took the stage to insist the concert continue. When the show ended, Rizzo made a final stop at a nearby tavern. Surrounded by patrons sipping cold pints of Piels draft beer, he raised a toast to the hardworking men and women of South Philadelphia before heading out into the night. When Rizzo was gone, Sandy Grady took an informal poll of the bar's patrons, asking how he would fare in the election. Reflecting on the problems facing the city and the nation, one replied that Philadelphia needed "an 11th grade dropout" to straighten things out. "He'll win because he isn't a Ph.D.," barfly John Marzano continued. "He's one of us. Rizzo came up the hard way."[1]

Despite his warm welcome in South Philadelphia, Francis Lazaro Rizzo was one of the most controversial figures in the city's history. As a young man, long before his entrance into politics, the son of Italian immigrants dropped out of high school and followed his father's footsteps into the Philadelphia Police Department. He quickly earned a reputation as one of the toughest cops on the force. Rising through the ranks in rapid succession, he earned the department's highest post in 1967. As the city's top cop, Rizzo was fond of saying that the way to treat criminals was "scappo il capo," an Italian phrase he translated to "crack their heads." He earned a national reputation for his tough stance on crime, the heavy-handed tactics of his police force, and his openly hostile treatment of civil rights activists. Yet Rizzo claimed those methods were the reason that Philadelphia avoided the urban rioting that struck cities like Los Angeles, Detroit, or nearby Newark, New Jersey, in the late 1960s. While that won him little favor in African American communities or among liberals that decried his "Gestapo tactics," he became a hero to the white ethnic, blue-collar Philadelphians that demanded "law and order." Capitalizing on their enthusiasm, Rizzo used his police experience as a springboard for his first campaign for public office in 1971.²

Rizzo had been a longtime Republican until he switched parties to accept the job as police commissioner from Democratic mayor James H. J. Tate. Running his own mayoral campaign as a Democrat and the self-proclaimed "toughest cop in America," Rizzo scored an impressive victory when he became the first former police commissioner elected mayor of a major American city.³ He then polarized Philadelphia during his two terms in office. Rizzo split Democratic voters when he broke with his party to campaign for Richard Nixon in 1972. He maintained his base of support by opposing public housing, school desegregation, affirmative action, and other liberal programs that he and his supporters deemed unearned advantages for nonwhites. Although he alienated many Philadelphians with a series of scandals and controversial statements—most famously that he would "make Attila the Hun look like a faggot" when dealing with his political opponents—Rizzo remained incredibly popular among white ethnic, blue-collar Philadelphians. Their support helped him survive a strong challenge in the Democratic primary of 1975 and a recall drive in 1976, and almost succeeded in changing the city charter so that he could run for a third mayoral term in 1979. That effort only fell apart when an anti-Rizzo coalition mobilized after he told an all-white audience to "Vote White" for charter change.⁴ Still, Rizzo remained a hero to the blue-collar white ethnics that viewed him as "one of us" because they saw a bit of themselves in the immigrants' son who dropped out of high school and worked his way up to the highest position in Philadelphia.

Frank Rizzo was perhaps the archetypal example of late twentieth-century urban, white ethnic, populist conservatism and the quintessential "backlash" politician of the 1960s and 1970s. To his critics, Rizzo was little more than a villain. They saw him as an enemy to civil rights, a bully, a racist, a sexist, a homophobe, and a mean-spirited patriarchal figurehead of a regressive political order. He was all those things. But Frank Rizzo's politics and legacy were far more complicated than the caricature that emerges from his long record of outlandish behavior and offensive statements. More importantly, Rizzo's supporters never saw him as a villain. While Rizzo's critics have largely succeeded in writing his legacy, their grave depictions do not allow for a thorough understanding of the people who called him "one of us" or the politics they created and championed.[5] Frank Rizzo was loved as much as he was hated. The admiration he inspired among blue-collar white ethnics cannot be reduced to a simplistic backlash narrative.

This is not a biography of Frank Rizzo. Although his rise and fall is central to the story this book tells, other writers have more clearly detailed Rizzo's life and career.[6] Instead, this book uses Rizzo, his allies, and his city to examine broader changes in modern America. In addition to Rizzo, it is a book about the evolving politics of his blue-collar white ethnic supporters. Their abandonment of urban and New Deal liberalism is at the core of this book, but it is also about the long-standing blue-collar populism and political sensibilities that they created, developed, and maintained in the long postwar era. It argues that the resultant "blue-collar conservatism" arose from their mutually reinforcing promotion of law-and-order conservatism and selective rejection of welfare liberalism. While the racial upheavals of midcentury urban America were central to the rise of blue-collar conservatism, this book also shows how working- and middle-class white ethnics in Frank Rizzo's Philadelphia imbued their politics with blue-collar class discourses and identities.

The stories recounted herein are part of a larger whole that explain the United States' turn to the right in the late twentieth century. Yet the subtleties of the specific blue-collar politics presented call into question the traditional bifurcations of political history and political identity. Real people rarely fall into neat categories established by scholars and critics. The white, blue-collar supporters of Frank Rizzo steadily moved to the right over the course of the postwar decades. While they surely would have rejected the label "liberal" at the end of their political transformation, not all of them would have readily accepted the label "conservative." With few exceptions, the subjects of this book did not become conservative activists. Many blue-collar Philadelphians who began the postwar era in the Democratic Party shifted to the Republican Party by the 1980s, but not all of them. Shifting political affiliation is a part of this story, but many blue-collar whites remained in the Democratic Party and contributed to its subtle move to the right between the late 1960s and 1990s. This book's use of the term "blue-collar conservatism," therefore, is not meant to indicate a hard-set political ideology. Instead, the development of a specifically urban, blue-collar political sensibility examined in this book demands a reconsideration of the dichotomy between the right and left. Its ambiguities require a more nuanced conception of political categorization. They also demand the acknowledgement of categories that belie the strict polarization of traditionally understood liberal and conservative political identity.

The story of Frank Rizzo and his blue-collar supporters' shifting politics offers a window into these ambiguities and complexities in modern American working- and middle-class politics. While some of that story is tied to specific urban spaces, it is not a history limited to Philadelphia. It is true that some of the things Rizzo said and did would only make sense in his city. But he also shares an affinity with other big-city mayors like Sam Yorty and Richard Daley, as well as national figures like George Wallace, Richard Nixon, and Ronald Reagan. It is equally true that some of the events that led to Rizzo's rise and fall were indebted to the specificity of Philadelphia's structural, institutional, and political environment. Yet Philadelphia still offers an opportunity to draw broader conclusions about postwar urban America. It was the fourth-largest city in the country in the 1960s and 1970s. Philadelphia's size linked it to major metropolitan areas like New York, Los Angeles, and Chicago. Yet, due to its decentralized neighborhoods, its economic dependence on light industry and small-scale manufacturing, and, in many ways, its parochialism, Philadelphia also shared meaningful commonalities with smaller and midsized cities throughout the Northeast and Midwest. Its size may have made Philadelphia one of the nation's biggest cities, but its culture was often more analogous to cities like Cleveland, Pittsburgh, and Detroit. Perhaps more than many other cities, Philadelphia was representative of a large swath of the urban North. Furthermore, while Rizzo was one of the most transformative figures in this one city's history, he and his supporters were also representative of a much broader political realignment in postwar American history.

Historians have long argued that local politicians like Rizzo, Yorty, and Daley—or national figures like Wallace, Nixon, and Reagan—enjoyed the support of the "white ethnics" and the "white working class." Their work shows that many working-class whites felt alienated by liberalism, Black Power, feminism, and gay rights. They argue that urban working and middle classes found common ground in Rizzo's forceful rhetoric, Wallace's racist populism, Nixon's jingoistic enthusiasm, and Reagan's patriotic optimism. But the details of their ultimate conversion from New Deal liberalism to blue-collar conservatism remains clouded by broad brushstrokes.[7] With few exceptions, most accounts dismiss blue-collar whites as one-dimensional reactionaries. They are the foil in the standard narrative of the rise of civil rights and Great Society liberalism. On a national level, they are almost ubiquitously represented by the infamous 1970 "Hard Hat Riots" in New York City, when construction workers coordinated an attack on students protesting the Vietnam War just days after the massacre at Kent State University.[8] But white, blue-collar politics and their urban spaces were more complex. The eventual blue-collar embrace of conservative figures like Frank Rizzo was the result not only of resentment and fear, but also of careful engagement with the politics of the urban crisis in the 1960s and 1970s.

Marked by high rates of unemployment, shrinking city tax bases, fiscal shortfalls, rising crime, and, most dramatically, waves of urban uprisings, the American urban crisis was a turning point in modern United States history. It was both caused by and exacerbated a shift toward suburbanization, urban disinvestment, and deindustrialization that wreaked havoc on city school systems, job markets, and housing stock. It exposed the rampant inequalities in urban society that led to the expansion of movements for racial justice. At the same time, the urban crisis produced the spatial and political realignments that shaped modern American political culture.[9] Blue-collar white ethnics in Philadelphia and throughout the country were caught up in the many transformations wrought by the urban crisis. Their political transformation sprang from the economic instabilities and vulnerabilities, as well as challenges to the racial order. While blue-collar whites reacted to the crises around them, they were not simple reactionaries. Instead, they approached the interwoven politics of law enforcement, school desegregation, equal employment opportunity, and open housing in multifaceted and varied ways. Complex negotiations with the politics of the urban crisis remade white, blue-collar politics in the long postwar era and created Frank Rizzo's enduring blue-collar popularity.

The rise of blue-collar conservatism in Frank Rizzo's Philadelphia represents a shift in modern American political culture and urban history. As such, it prompts a reevaluation of several major themes in recent American urban and political development: the complexity and diversity of modern conservatisms, the function of class identity in modern American politics, the broader politics and influence of the urban crisis, and the centrality of urban spatial politics to American political development. These interjections show that Rizzo and his blue-collar supporters were more than transitional figures in the shift from liberalism to conservatism. They also prefigured some of the most significant developments in recent American political history.[10]

Conservatisms in Modern America

Accepted wisdom holds that the election of Ronald Reagan signaled a turn to the political right and the emergence of a new conservative era in the United States. Yet the earlier development of blue-collar conservatism has received scant historical attention beyond the once-dominant backlash narrative that suggested the white working and middle class abandoned the Democratic Party because of integration, Great Society programs, and the "excesses" of the late 1960s.[11] The roots of the backlash thesis lay in the 1968 Kerner Commission Report that blamed white racism for the urban uprisings that struck American cities in the mid-to-late 1960s. The backlash narrative put forward first by the Kerner Commission and promoted by a sympathetic media shaped the subsequent understanding of blue-collar whites in the urban crisis. But the familiar backlash narrative is misleading and overly reductive. It essentializes the reaction to urban disorder and fails to account for the subtle negotiations and realignments in urban space that equally contributed to changes in white, blue-collar politics. Parts of the backlash theory certainly ring true, but they still must be understood in the context of the myriad changes wrought by the urban crisis. In offering that contextualization, this book shows that the blue-collar conservatism that rose among Frank Rizzo's supporters was an understudied and qualified variant of modern populist conservatism.

Though an important shift in working- and middle-class politics, blue-collar conservatism was not a complete break from the New Deal liberalism that guided American, and especially urban, politics since the Great Depression. Forged by Franklin Delano Roosevelt, New Deal liberalism's rise and fall represents the central narrative in twentieth-century American political history. The fall of the New Deal welfare state had deep roots and the so-called New Deal coalition—the electoral alliance of urban white ethnics, African

Americans, and Southern whites that maintained American liberalism in the post-Depression era—was inherently unstable.[12] Yet it would be a mistake to conclude that existing tensions were solely responsible for its downfall.[13] Blue-collar defections from the New Deal coalition were not a foregone conclusion. Nor were they immediate. To the contrary, blue-collar whites' ultimate enlistment in the "Reagan Revolution" developed in the 1960s and 1970s. Their blue-collar conservatism combined an economic platform that appealed to a vulnerable working class with a "one of us" populism that rejected stuffy orthodoxy and elitism of all stripes, especially liberal elitism. The selective rejection of welfare liberalism chronicled in this book reveals both blue-collar white ethnics' deep antipathy toward American liberals and their desire to maintain key parts of the welfare state they created.

Relatedly, the backlash thesis's insistence that working-class antiliberalism and blue-collar conservatism stemmed primarily from the rise of culturally liberal forces—the civil rights movement, women's movement, and gay rights movement—obscures the perception of economic hardship that played a related and equally significant role in blue-collar Americans' reevaluation of their political allegiances. The politics of gender, sexuality, and especially race were intimately tied to economic motivators, but broadly conceived economic well-being—especially the feeling that blue-collar whites were on the losing end of a zero-sum game for limited urban and welfare state resources—formed a foundational prong of their political transformation. Blue-collar whites forcefully responded to perceived threats to their material welfare. While they were never as economically vulnerable as poor people of color, blue-collar whites still felt threatened by the economic and social disruptions of the urban crisis. Their political transformation was the result of a renegotiation of economic security, cultural identity, and political position in relation to a series of challenges to an established urban order.

The rise of blue-collar conservatism also represents an alternative to the concurrent development of conservative politics in middle-class suburban communities in the South and West.[14] While blue-collar conservatism shared a number of similarities with other conservatisms, several features make it distinct. Blue-collar conservatism had a religious foundation, for example. The majority of people discussed in this book were Roman Catholic. Although Jews and Protestants made up sizable minorities, Catholicity played a foundational role in the development of blue-collar conservatism by virtue of the ethnic and religious composition of urban spatial politics. Unlike the religious right that emerged concurrently, however, blue-collar conservatives held faith as one aspect of their politics, not a decisive feature.[15] As well, while blue-collar whites focused on broadly conceived economic issues, few shared foundational ground with libertarians and small-government activists that forged the New Right by putting their economic independence first among their political priorities.[16] Few adherents of blue-collar conservatism denied the federal or local government's right to tax or intervene in the modern economy. To the contrary, they accepted and welcomed it with important limitations and reservations. Nevertheless, blue-collar whites in urban centers like Frank Rizzo's Philadelphia still contributed to America's rightward turn. Their blue-collar conservatism offers evidence that modern conservatism was not strictly a Southern, Western, or even suburban phenomenon. Indeed, it shows that many conservatisms contributed to a nationwide rightward shift.

The white, blue-collar Americans in this book came to believe that liberal politics and state-guided economic development no longer benefited the white working and middle classes. As a result, they began selectively rejecting liberalism based upon culturally defined ideas of privilege and disadvantage. Their blue-collar conservatism emerged as a qualified conservatism. Its basis lay in a centrist acceptance of the welfare state and government intervention in the economy like urban renewal and state funding for education, provided the beneficiaries of these programs "earned" the right to government entitlements. Respect for "hard work" was central to blue-collar conceptions of earned rights, so blue-collar whites adopted a discourse that distinguished between deserving and undeserving, between those that earned what little they had and those that expected a "handout" from liberals. Their language of economic vulnerability, while real, masked the racial privileges that undergirded their selective rejection of liberalism. Nevertheless, a class identity and sense of blue-collar authenticity reinforced by "one of us" populism guided their engagement with liberal politics and policy-making. The culmination of this racially rooted but class-forward blue-collar conservatism not only reshaped urban and working-class politics, it became one of the most consequential, malleable, and appropriable political sensibilities in recent American history.

Class Identity and Color Blindness

A focus on the racial backlash elements of white, working-class antiliberalism has obscured the importance of class ideologies and identities. Social class as both a category of analysis and cultural identity mattered deeply in cities like

Philadelphia. Working- and middle-class Philadelphians drew comfort and commonality from others that shared their class experiences. Those commonalities resulted in a distinctly "blue-collar" cultural identity. Discussions of identity politics in the 1960s and 1970s typically refer to the movements that sought the recognition of multiculturalism in the United States. Social movements as varied as the black freedom struggle, Chicano movement, women's movement, and gay rights movement all used identity politics to challenge their exclusion from "normative America."[17] Working- and middle-class whites are either absent or appear as opponents of multiculturalism in these narratives. Yet working- and middle-class urban whites did engage a form of identity politics more focused on class and white ethnic roots than race, gender, or sexuality.[18] In cities like Philadelphia, blue-collar class identity was identity politics for working- and middle-class whites.

This blue-collar identity was more inclusive than typical notions of class. It was not limited by economic or occupational distinction. Instead, it was a cultural class identity indebted to a sense of blue-collar authenticity, an ethos based on the shared values of hard work, sacrifice, toughness, pride, and tradition. It became an identity claimed and defended by people from a wide economic strata, including those usually defined along a broad middle-class spectrum. The very fluidity of the blue-collar identity allowed whites who were economically working class to claim privileges of the white middle class while simultaneously allowing middle- or even upper-class whites to invoke the values associated with blue-collar authenticity. These categories transcended economic standing because upwardly mobile working-class whites could work their way up the social ladder to a higher class position, but remain culturally blue-collar. Frank Rizzo provides a case in point. Born into an immigrant family in a South Philadelphia row home, he maintained his blue-collar identity even after his wealth and political standing grew. In cities like Philadelphia—where blue-collar identity mixed with civic identity—a cultural populism that celebrated the working-class white ethnic reinforced the city's expansive class identity.

Additionally, by the 1970s, blue-collar identity politics became a means of obfuscating racial and gender discourses in debates over liberal programs like affirmative action, public housing, and school desegregation. While these class discourses were rooted in genuine economic anxieties and cultural identities, they were never separate from race and white privilege. Furthermore, the rhetorical privileging of blue-collar discourses did not mean that class supplanted race or gender. To the contrary, the celebration and promotion of blue-collar authenticity usually privileged a white and male cultural identity.[19] That is not to say that women were absent from blue-collar culture and politics. Wives and mothers were at the forefront of blue-collar battles over law enforcement, neighborhoods, and schools. Blue-collar culture celebrated feminine toughness and women assumed roles as protectors of blue-collar traditions and institutions. For both men and women, blue-collar authenticity and identity became tools of the working- and middle-class selective rejection of welfare liberalism. The politics of race, gender, and class were inseparable components of the emerging blue-collar conservatism, but blue-collar culture often foregrounded a white, male, working-class identity.

While complicating the backlash narrative common to accounts of working-class antiliberalism, this book also acknowledges that elements of racial backlash are true. Many blue-collar white ethnics in postwar Philadelphia were racist. They responded to the conflicts of the era through a defense of white privilege and white neighborhoods. While those reactions cannot account for the full spectrum of white blue-collar politics in the 1960s, 1970s, and beyond, those voices were nevertheless a key component in the development of blue-collar conservatism. Without excusing white racism, this book seeks a deeper understanding of it by tracing changing expressions of blue-collar racism over time. Racism among blue-collar whites was neither static nor monolithic. Their class conceptions and identities informed their conceptions of race, gender, elitism, and poverty, further complicating evolving ideologies. That blue-collar whites often based these beliefs in stereotypes and untruths indebted to a spatially segregated urban environment made them no less powerful. This book shows how blue-collar whites learned to change the way they discussed race, even in pursuit of the same racially restrictive policies.

The civil rights movement of the 1950s and 1960s altered racial discourses in the United States. After George Wallace's failed attempt to use a racially divisive campaign to win the presidency in 1968, race-baiting became politically taboo. Racist politics continued, but public appeals to white supremacy waned. In their place, coded language joined appeals to authenticity and meritocracy as replacements for race-baiting. This was true as much for urban, blue-collar whites as it was for candidates for national office. In Philadelphia, as in other urban enclaves, working- and middle-class whites turned away from the racial discourses that had previously shaped opposition to desegregation and liberal public policy. As in the Sunbelt South, where the language of middle-class meritocracy replaced explicit race-baiting among the suburban silent majority, blue-collar whites adopted color-blind discourses.[20] Yet urban, blue-collar whites' use of color-blind arguments differed in important ways. Whereas middle-class Southerners and neoconservative intellectuals extolled the virtues of meritocracy to dispute racially inclusive housing, education, and employment policies, working- and middle-class whites in cities like Philadelphia pointed to their blue-collar identities.[21]

Blue-collar identity championed pride, tradition, and hard work. Over the course of the long postwar era, Philadelphia's blue-collar whites invoked these values above all in their defense of neighborhoods, workplaces, and schools. First and often foremost, blue-collar pride suggested defensiveness, toughness, rootedness, and distinctiveness. "Proud" also became the principal means of describing blue-collar whites among outside observers. In such cases the term could be a positive descriptor of blue-collar culture—extolling hardscrabble, working-class values and a sense of civic identity, for instance— or it could be used as a Janus-faced compliment. When used as a substitute for stubborn, the implication was that blue-collar pride was foolish or misplaced. In its worst sense, pride could also be a stand-in for chauvinism or clannishness.[22] Nevertheless, both blue-collar whites and their chroniclers adopted this idiom as a means of describing and defending white ethnic, blue-collar Philadelphians. Intrinsically tied to this blue-collar pride was an equally passionate reverence for "tradition." Invoking working-class and white ethnic tradition became an important means of defending neighborhoods, schools, workplaces, folk customs, and culture. If pride described blue-collar character, tradition attempted to explain its origins. Finally, a loosely defined reverence for "hard work" was central to blue-collar culture. In blue-collar politics, hard work complemented pride and tradition by offering a discursive means of differentiation and exclusion. Furthermore, and most importantly, as blue-collar whites learned to avoid direct racial dialogues, they pointed to their pride in urban spaces and workplaces, their long-standing traditions, and veneration of hard work as a means of obfuscating race. Race became no less important to their politics, but blue-collar identity became a means of denying racist motivations.

Despite evidence to the contrary, Frank Rizzo and many of his supporters denied that they held any racial bias. They often rejected the most extreme strands of racial prejudice. They often minimized the extent of racial discrimination and the effects of structural inequalities. Many of them simply said race was unimportant to them. Some of them undoubtedly lied in order to avoid scrutiny. Others were genuinely color-blind, at least to the extent that race was not the sole or even primary motivating factor in their political actions. In any case, however, their color blindness was a function of their white privilege. White Philadelphians in segregated urban spaces normalized segregation. Their ability to claim race was unimportant to them was a result of their privilege to ignore it. It was a luxury nonwhites could never assume in the mid-twentieth century. Even though blue-collar whites denied their white privilege, ignoring it in this book would be irresponsible. Yet it would be just as irresponsible to ignore how powerfully that denial functioned in their political discourse and ideological change. Denialism played a critical role in the formation of working- and middle-class whites' class identity and their resultant blue-collar conservatism. What blue-collar whites said publicly and aloud mattered. Even when it hid deeper racial antipathies, the process of adopting class-based discourses led working- and middle-class whites to internalize the language they used. By relying on the self-affirming differentiation between earned privilege and unearned advantage, blue-collar whites made their class identity and ideologies a central part of their emerging blue-collar conservatism.

Blue-Collar Conservatism and the Urban Crisis

The rise of blue-collar conservatism, complete with discursive intricacies and cultural identities, was not born fully formed at any point in the long postwar era. It was not guided by a single movement or compulsion. Instead it was the cumulative result of two decades of wrestling with a worsening urban crisis characterized by a rise in crime and urban rioting, underfunded and inadequate educational infrastructure, widespread un- and underemployment, and a deteriorating urban core. The blue-collar shift to the right grew out of their engagement with the intricately interwoven politics of law enforcement, education, affirmative action, and housing. Each played an incremental and mutually constituting role in the reformation of blue-collar politics. The promotion of law enforcement conservatism and the selective rejection of welfare liberalism at the heart of blue-collar conservatism resulted from the complex interplay of urban crisis politics.

Calls for law and order became a potent political device in the 1960s. The popular campaigns against crime, disorder, and protest were instrumental in creating the "crisis of liberalism" and foreshadowing the conservative counterrevolution.[23] Instead of a top-down backlash led by national figures like Barry Goldwater, George Wallace, and Richard Nixon—or local ones like Rizzo—this book concentrates on the grassroots organizations and blue-collar cultural mobilization that supported the police and stricter law enforcement policies.[24] Despite urban police forces' growing reputation for brutality, blue-collar whites maintained a defensive culture of reverence for the police based on class commonality and the mutually reinforcing boundaries of race and urban space. The grassroots of law-and-order politics lay in the politicization of blue-collar whites' culture of reverence for the police.

It also lay with police officers. Police work was a blue-collar tradition and a central feature of blue-collar labor and politics. Any examination of blue-collar support for stricter law enforcement policy must also include police as political actors.[25] As such, this is also a story about police officers, their allies, and law enforcement politics. Police and their collective bargaining agent, the Fraternal Order of Police (FOP), were at the center of the politics of the urban crisis. The actions of Philadelphia police officers, along with their blue-collar supporters, led to the rise of Frank Rizzo and his brand of law enforcement conservatism. The politicization of police work in the 1960s led to the widespread advocacy of law-and-order politics, unfettered police action in the face of disorder, and harsher penalties for criminal behavior. The stricter law enforcement policies that Rizzo, the police, and blue-collar whites advocated became a constitutive branch of blue-collar conservatism. Just as importantly, it represents the deep roots of mass incarceration in modern America. The policies that led to the development of the largest prison system in the world were rooted in local and federal crime control efforts in the 1960s.[26] The case of Philadelphia shows that those policies rested on the explicit demand and tacit approval of the police and their blue-collar allies.

Law enforcement politics were inseparable from the racial politics of the urban crisis. Although most blue-collar supporters of the police denied that race played a role in their demand for stricter law enforcement, their efforts came in direct conflict with civil rights activists working for better police-community relations or protesting police misconduct. As a result, blue-collar conservatism developed reciprocally against the civil rights movement.[27] In addition to his police work, Rizzo's appeal grew out of the overlapping politics of neighborhood, workplace, and school integration. Rather than imagine the politics of law and order, education, affirmative action, and housing separately, this book offers a more holistic methodology because single issues cannot fully explain large-scale political transformation.[28] In Philadelphia and in urban contexts nationwide, the politics of crime, work, education, and neighborhood were interconnected and inseparable. Broader changes in urban politics emerged from the interrelated struggles over policing, housing, work, and education.[29]

Frank Rizzo notwithstanding, Philadelphia may still seem like an uneasy fit for a local history of postwar conservatism. American liberalism was an essentially urban development. Cities provided the impetus for the social and political reforms that laid the basis for a national liberal politics. They served as incubators for social reforms, economic philosophies, and the expansion of rights and privileges that were the hallmarks of American liberalism.[30] Philadelphia was no exception. The city had a rich progressive and reform tradition, especially in the immediate postwar era. Philadelphia was a city with a history of strong and progressive labor unions, civil rights activists, and other liberal institutions and organizations. It remains a city that has not elected a Republican mayor since 1948. But it was precisely the liberal Democratic regime established in Philadelphia's early postwar period that aroused blue-collar whites in the 1960s and 1970s. The structure and limitations of urban liberalism in postwar Philadelphia helped create the conditions that led to the later development of blue-collar conservatism.

Urban Space and Blue-Collar Philadelphia

The following chapters trace the development of blue-collar conservatism through a social and political history of white, working- and middle-class neighborhoods, workplaces, and institutions in post–World War II Philadelphia. Frank Rizzo left a powerful legacy in both Philadelphia and postwar America, but the roots of his influence and the broader politics they represented lay in the grassroots struggles over the city's labor markets, educational facilities, traditions, and especially, its urban spaces.[31]

Philadelphia's borders have remained the same since 1854, when the city consolidated surrounding boroughs, districts, and townships into Philadelphia County. Twentieth-century city planners then divided the city into several large sections based upon their geographic proximity to Center City— South, Southwest, West, Northwest, North, and Northeast Philadelphia.[32] But geographic boundaries alone cannot account for the distinctiveness of Philadelphia's urban spaces. Since the nineteenth century, waves of European immigration and African American migration, followed by increases in immigrants from Puerto Rico, Latin America, and Asia, helped populate the city. Patterns of settlement and restrictive housing arrangements created many unique inner-city neighborhoods characterized by race, ethnicity, religion, and class. In the early twentieth century, Irish ethnics populated most of West Philadelphia. There were Jewish and Irish enclaves in North Philadelphia. South Philadelphia was home to large numbers of Irish and Eastern European residents, as well as most of the city's Italian residents. African American newcomers settled in the crowded industrial districts immediately surrounding Center City. These diverse spaces earned Philadelphia a reputation as a "city of neighborhoods."[33]

By the mid-twentieth century, Philadelphia's neighborhoods were in a state of transition. Decades of immigration restriction and the two World Wars ended mass European migration and disrupted long-established ethnic residential patterns. At the same time, the lack of immigrant labor led to an influx of Southern blacks—part of the decades-long Great Migration—seeking employment opportunities and escape from Jim Crow. As African Americans moved into the city, white ethnics left their former enclaves for newer housing developments on the outskirts of the inner city. The result was a deeply segregated city.[34] The case studies that make up the heart of this book focus most intently on two of the most racially segregated areas in the postwar era, South Philadelphia and Northeast Philadelphia. Not coincidentally, those two large sections of Philadelphia provided Frank Rizzo with his largest base of support in the 1960s and 1970s.

One of the older sections of the city, South Philadelphia was primarily a working-class residential area after World War II. Row-home communities and old industrial structures continued to mark the landscape years after the onset of deindustrialization. With the residual effects of industrialization still visible, however, South Philadelphia retained a reputation as a section populated by skilled, ethnic, blue-collar workers, even after most of the industry had all but disappeared. These residents often chose to stay in their old neighborhoods—near their families, churches, and ethnic institutions—even after residents of other older sections of the city began to move out. Northeast Philadelphia, by contrast, was one of the newer sections of the city. Although the Northeast also became a part the city in 1854, the vast space north of Frankford Creek and expanding eastward along the Delaware River was sparsely populated until after the Second World War. Northeast Philadelphia followed a trajectory much closer to the development of suburban communities than urban areas. Most new residents of the Northeast were upwardly mobile blue-collar whites that could afford to move out of their older ethnic enclaves.[35] These were the spaces that produced and harbored blue-collar identity politics. Blue-collar pride and traditions first grew out of the tightly knit, ethnically and class cohesive inner-city neighborhoods found in areas like South Philadelphia and Kensington. Yet blue-collar pride and tradition were not limited to these urban spaces. As blue-collar identity expanded beyond the city's row-house neighborhoods into areas like Northeast Philadelphia, reverence for blue-collar pride and tradition moved with it into new urban and, eventually, suburban spaces.

Philadelphia's long postwar politics grew out of the restructuring of these urban spaces. The chapters that follow show how blue-collar Philadelphians defended their neighborhoods, workplaces, and space-based traditions through class-based definitions of privilege and disadvantage. The first part of the book traces the rise of law-and-order politics from the immediate postwar era to Frank Rizzo's promotion to police commissioner. While Rizzo was arguably the purest example of law and order translated into electoral politics, the spatial disruptions and social fissures of the two preceding decades created the structures that enabled his political career. Rizzo, above all, was a symbol. The politics he championed originated from the neighborhood residents that called for law and order. Law-and-order politics were not just the result of law enforcement policies, however. They were interlaced with the equally consequential urban politics of education, employment, housing, and equal opportunity. Because the slow rise of blue-collar conservatism must be contextualized in the postwar development of urban liberalism and civil rights, the narrative begins with the establishment of a municipal liberal consensus in the immediate postwar era before showing the multifaceted ways—from violence to accommodation to negotiation—that blue-collar whites rebelled against liberalism and sought to defend their traditions and institutions.

The second part of the book shows how Rizzo used his law-and-order credentials and "one of us" populism to position himself as the protector of blue-collar neighborhoods, traditions, and institutions from perceived attacks by liberals and civil rights activists. With Rizzo in the mayor's office, his blue-collar supporters enjoyed a rapid but fleeting ascendency in local politics and won a series of their battles over urban space. Their nominally color-blind, blue-collar populist politics guided their struggles over schools, housing, and affirmative action in the 1970s. As blue-collar clout began to fade, however, so too did their race-neutral discourses. At the same time, the politics of law enforcement came roaring back as the police department faced renewed charges of brutality, new challenges over equal opportunity hiring, and a series of violent confrontations with an obscure, mostly African

American back-to-nature collective known as MOVE. The combination of law enforcement and neighborhood politics caused the blue-collar political transformation to reach its culmination in the 1980s. By then, the long development of a populist politics based in the mutually reinforcing promotion of law enforcement conservatism and the selective rejection of welfare liberalism signaled broader influences and consequences for modern American political development.

Ultimately, this is the story of how white, blue-collar Americans came to see their interests more aligned with conservatives than with liberals. It is a history of accommodation, reaction, and resistance to local, state, and federal policies. It also explains one of the most consequential political transformations in modern American history. The turn toward the politics of relatability evident in Frank Rizzo's "one of us" populism became a central feature of national politics in the late twentieth century, especially on the social and cultural right. In the 1960s and 1970s, it was Rizzo's attacks on those that supposedly threatened blue-collar traditions that tapped into the deep wells of dissatisfaction with postwar liberalism among blue-collar whites. Although his supporters voted for Rizzo as a Democrat, his party affiliation hardly mattered. In 1970, when rumors circulated that he might make his first run for mayor, longtime Rizzo supporter and president of the Philadelphia FOP, John Harrington, said that "it wouldn't matter what ticket he ran on. He would have the backing of the silent majority that is fed up with permissiveness. A vote for Rizzo would be a vote for security."[36] Rizzo appealed to the "silent majority." He and his supporters helped hasten the end of the New Deal coalition. By the 1980s, pundits coined the term "Reagan Democrat" to describe the white, blue-collar supporters of populists like Rizzo. In Philadelphia, however, the press had already dubbed them Rizzocrats."[37]

PART I

From Liberalism to Law and Order

Philadelphia Neighborhoods

1. Logan Circle	29. Powelton	57. Fishtown	85. Tacony
2. Chinatown	30. Mantua	58. Kensington	86. Mayfair
3. Old City	31. Belmont	59. West Kensington	87. Oxford Circle
4. Society Hill	32. Mill Creek	60. Feltonville	88. Burholme
5. Washington Square	33. Haddington	61. Junianta	89. Fox Chase
6. Rittenhouse	34. Overbrook	62. Port Richmond	90. Rhawnhurst
7. Schuylkill	35. Carrol Park	63. Bridesburg	91. Lexington Park
8. Southwest Center City	36. Parkside	64. Andorra	92. Holmesburg
9. Hawthorne	37. Wynnefield	65. Upper Roxborough	93. Upper Holmesburg
10. Bella Vista	38. Wynnefield Heights	66. Roxborough	94. Torresdale
11. Queen Village	39. Spring Garden	67. Manayunk	95. Academy Gardens
12. Pennsport	40. Poplar	68. East Falls	96. Ashton-Woodenbridge
13. Wharton	41. Northern Liberties	69. Germantown	97. Pennypack Woods
14. Point Breeze	42. Francisville	70. Wister	98. Winchester Park
15. Grays Ferry	43. Fairmount	71. Morton	99. Pennypack
16. Girard Estate	44. Olde Kensington	72. East Mt. Airy	100. Bustleton
17. Packer Park	45. Ludlow	73. West Mt. Airy	101. West Torresdale
18. Whitman	46. Yorktown	74. Chestnut Hill	102. Morrell Park
19. Eastwick	47. North Central	75. Cedarbrook	103. Crestmont Farms
20. Elmwood	48. Sharswood	76. West Oak Lane	104. Millbrook
21. Paschall	49. Brewerytown	77. Logan	105. Modena Park
22. Kingsessing	50. Strawberry Mansion	78. East Oak Lane	106. Parkwood Manor
23. Southwest Schuylkill	51. Stanton	79. Olney	107. Mechanicsville
24. Cobbs Creek	52. Hartanft	80. Lawncrest	108. Byberry
25. Garden Court	53. Franklinville	81. Summerdale	109. Somerton
26. Cedar Park	54. Nicetown-Tioga	82. Northwood	
27. Spruce Hill	55. Allegheny West	83. Frankford	
28. University City	56. Hunting Park	84. Wissinoming	

Figure 2. Philadelphia neighborhoods. Philadelphia City Planning Commission, "Philadelphia: a city of neighborhoods," 1976.

CHAPTER 1

City of "Neighborhoods" and "Jungles"

In early 1957 investigative journalist Charles Shaw wrote an exposé about Philadelphia's "jungle," an area he described as running east from the Delaware River, north though parts of Kensington and North Philadelphia, and encompassing a large swath of the city's urban core. To research his story, Shaw accompanied police officers on their patrols. He claimed Police Commissioner Thomas Gibbons asked him to write the story to let people know what cops were up against. The term "jungle," Shaw said, came from Gibbons. Shaw relayed a story of destitution and decline, an area marked by blighted housing, a troublingly high crime rate, and a shamed population. Once a source of the city's industrial infrastructure, Shaw's "jungle" had joined the scores of midcentury American communities that had fallen into disrepair. Like the muckrakers of a half century earlier, Shaw told lurid tales of squalor and desperation. Unlike his Progressive-Era predecessors, however, Shaw had no interest in helping the denizens of Philadelphia's "jungle." He blamed them for their own poverty and called them drunks, thieves, and transients searching for instant gratification. Shaw's true concern was the threat his "jungle" posed to the rest of the city. "The jungle is Philadelphia's shame and sorrow, Philadelphia's greatest menace and Philadelphia's greatest challenge," he wrote. Although he invited his readers to see it for themselves, he made sure they knew "the jungle" was a place to avoid.[1]

Parts of Shaw's story rang false, however. The area he described did not sound like the blue-collar neighborhoods many Philadelphians knew. It especially baffled the working-class white ethnics that lived in those neighborhoods. Taking umbrage with the story, *Philadelphia Evening Bulletin* columnist Anne E. Hellyer revisited Shaw's "jungle" in search of the other side of the story. Instead of unkempt houses, she found block after block of neatly kept row homes lining well-swept streets. Instead of dejected derelicts, she

found proud, hardworking, and defensive residents of blue-collar neighborhoods like Kensington, Fishtown, and Port Richmond. Charles Shaw, she
said, had misjudged the powerful sense of pride they had in their homes.[2]

Neither Hellyer nor the white, blue-collar Philadelphians she interviewed
denied the reality of the city's "jungle." As many of them pointed out, however,
Shaw had misidentified it. He based his neighborhood boundaries on Philadelphia Police Division maps and included the entire Twenty-Sixth District
in his analysis. The North Central Police Division was one of the department's
largest. In addition to all of North Central Philadelphia, it included Kensington's river ward neighborhoods, parts of Fishtown and Port Richmond, as
well as the North Philadelphia neighborhoods of Brewerytown, North Penn,
and Strawberry Mansion. The borders that separated these neighborhoods
were never as fixed as police district boundaries. Indeed, it was these informal
borders that maintained Philadelphia's discrete communities and reputation
as a "city of neighborhoods." In pointing out Shaw's error, Hellyer and her
blue-collar sources claimed that "the jungle" strictly referred to the rundown
parts of North Central Philadelphia. Kensington, Fishtown, Port Richmond,
Brewerytown, North Penn, and Strawberry Mansion were separate neighborhoods, they said. Each was as distinct from the others as they were from "the
jungle." Together they were home to thousands of hardworking, white ethnic
homeowners. North Central Philadelphia was almost entirely populated by
African Americans, renters, and the unemployed. "We may be poor here,"
said a Port Richmond woman, "but we don't live in filth and crime. We are
clean, decent, God-fearing people."[3]

White, blue-collar residents of the Twenty-Sixth Police District roundly
dismissed their neighborhoods' inclusion in Shaw's "jungle." In disputing his
characterization, they were also quick to point out that they would defend
their neighborhoods from absorption. One "proud resident" of Brewerytown—where the shifting boundaries of North Central Philadelphia had
already initiated white flight from the neighborhood—said that his family
had lived there for years and they would not want to live anywhere else. "It is
a good neighborhood, friendly and decent," he continued. "It's not a jungle,
and we won't let it become one either." Proud blue-collar Philadelphians were
determined to resist any threat to their neighborhoods.[4]

Like Anne Hellyer, countless reporters and other observers of the urban
working class told the stories of proud residents of areas like Kensington,
Fishtown, Port Richmond, and others. The people Hellyer interviewed were

proud that they lived in the same neighborhoods that their parents and grand-parents had settled in. They were proud to provide the skilled labor for the factories and warehouses that still lined the neighborhoods' outer edges. They prided themselves on maintaining close-knit communities for generations. Parents were proud of the schools their children attended, which were often the same schools they had attended as children. Those that mortgaged their own homes took special pride in paying their own way toward homeowner-ship. Blue-collar pride was more than a statement of loyalty or self-respect, however. It also distinguished urban spaces and established exclusivity.[5] In the imagination of blue-collar white ethnics, white spaces were "proud neighbor-hoods" while black spaces were "urban jungles." Their protest against Charles Shaw was directed at his conflation of distinct urban spaces.

These distinctions were artificial and steeped in the history of racist hous-ing patterns and policies. In Philadelphia, as in cities throughout the urban North, "proud neighborhoods" and "urban jungles" grew together to erect the physical and social structures that shaped postwar politics. Both were products of the federal policies, local politics, and patterns of redevelopment that trans-formed urban space over the course of the twentieth century. Moreover, white, blue-collar neighborhood pride not only separated white and black spaces, it also led to the direct exclusion of African American residents from white spaces. Indeed, the jungle metaphor—long used to denigrate people of African descent as uncivilized or unfit for modern society—served as a reminder that the politics of neighborhood pride played out on deeply racialized terrain.[6]

Philadelphia's proud neighborhoods would carry all these implications with them when they became the center of blue-collar life and politics in the long postwar period. Defense of neighborhood was at the root of nearly every conflict that contributed to the transformation in white working- and middle-class politics in the 1960s and 1970s. Frank Rizzo, as both police com-missioner and mayor, drew his political strength from the city's blue-collar neighborhoods. The formation and fortification of these neighborhoods—and their symbiotic relationship with the so-called "urban jungle"—created the parameters that allowed for Rizzo's rise long before his law enforcement and political ascendancy. To be sure, the rise of Frank Rizzo and blue-collar conservatism were predicated on the postwar realignment of urban space.

Paradoxically, that realignment was indebted to a broader transforma-tion in Philadelphia's immediate post–World War II era, when urban liberals guided one of the most successful periods of reform in modern America. These reformers established a municipal liberal consensus based on commitments to "good government," city planning, and economic growth through private-public partnership. While harkening back to the Progressive Era's reliance on pragmatism and expertise, Philadelphia reformers also embraced the New Deal orthodoxy that had guided American liberalism since the 1930s.[7] Just as importantly, they came to municipal governance with an almost unprecedented dedication to civil rights policy-making and local government's responsibility to ensure equal opportunity. On a small scale, Philadelphia liberals recreated the New Deal coalition that had sustained the Democratic Party since the Great Depression and brought together the sometimes contradictory aims of good-government reformers, business leaders, intellectuals, civil rights activists, and organized labor.[8] Reformers birthed a period of immense promise. At the same time, however, they oversaw the re-creation of structural inequalities that transformed the city as much as their reforms. The gulf between the promises and limitations of urban liberalism established the politics of the urban crisis that shaped Philadelphia's long postwar period. The full emergence of blue-collar conservatism was still decades away, but the parameters on which it rose coalesced during the city's reform era.

Reform and the Promise of Urban Liberalism

Hundreds of thousands of Philadelphians toured Gimbels Center City department store in the late summer and fall of 1947. Drawn as usual by the chain's competitive prices and convenient location, they now came in droves to see one of the city's latest attractions, the City Planning Commission's "Better Philadelphia Exhibition." Together with the Chamber of Commerce and Citizens' Council on City Planning, the City Planning Commission (CPC) created the exhibit to showcase the promise of effective planning. The exhibition featured dioramas, aerial photograph maps, movies, cartoons, wall panels, and a built-to-scale model of Center City. Attendees viewed the planners' vision for rejuvenating the Central Business District and redeveloping the historic sites around Independence Mall. Plans also called for removal of an obsolete and unused Pennsylvania Railroad viaduct just west of City Hall, known locally as the "Chinese Wall." Outside of Center City, the Better Philadelphia Exhibition displayed plans for the highway system, the international airport, and large areas of still-undeveloped land in Northeast and Southwest Philadelphia. While the exhibit mostly focused on improving avenues of commerce and tourism, planners did not ignore the city's neighborhoods.

"Philadelphia has always been a city of neighborhoods," one planner said, so it was imperative for the exhibition to communicate how they would benefit.[9] Displays explained that city planning meant routing truck traffic away from residential areas as well as the creation of more recreation facilities, libraries, and community centers. It meant the removal of slum housing through substantial redevelopment and an expanded public housing program. Laying out their ideas in great detail, city planners drummed up support for a truly massive urban renewal program.[10]

The Better Philadelphia Exhibition was a resounding success. Nearly four hundred thousand people paid the one-dollar entrance fee to catch a glimpse at the promise of city planning. "The problem of new and improved public works was placed squarely before the citizens with price tags attached," reflected one city planner. "Indicative of the interest aroused by the exhibition," he continued, "60 per cent of the citizens attending replied 'Yes' to a question as to whether they would be willing to pay a little more in taxes in order to accomplish the improvements."[11]

Three years after the exhibition, Philadelphia's planning renaissance received a boost from an equally substantive political transformation. A group of business-oriented civic leaders united around the belief that the corrupt Republican machine that had ruled Philadelphia nearly unchecked for close to a century harmed the city's reputation and economic future. Forming the Greater Philadelphia Movement (GPM), the new organization backed reform-Democrat efforts to wrest power from the Republican Party and remake municipal government. Key to that project was the creation of a new city charter that would grant city government more autonomy from the state and curtail corruption.[12] The goal of charter reform was "good government," especially the removal of the city's notorious patronage system. Reformers wanted appointments based on professional qualification rather than political deal-making. The momentum from the Better Philadelphia Exhibition combined with GPM in 1951, when Philadelphians went to the polls and overwhelmingly approved a charter that established a strong mayoral government, limited the city council's power, expanded the civil service system, and empowered the City Planning Commission. Reformers not only created a new city government, they laid the groundwork for a municipal liberal consensus based on the mutually reinforcing dictates of expansive urban renewal and public-private cooperation for economic growth.[13]

The new city charter was the lynchpin of Philadelphia's municipal liberal consensus. The overall impact of charter reform was much broader, however.

When it went into effect in 1952, the new charter fundamentally altered city operations. It established a strong executive branch in the office of the mayor, which now included a managing director, director of finance, and a city representative with the authority to oversee new and vital aspects of municipal government. The charter put checks on the newly powerful mayor by demanding an annual audit by the city controller and including a provision for mayoral recall, but it nevertheless ensured that postwar Philadelphia politics would be focused on the mayor's office.[14]

Reform Democrat Joseph Clark, elected later in the same year that Philadelphians adopted their new charter, would be the first to use those expanded powers. Clark's longtime collaborator and mayoral successor, Richardson Dilworth, was elected district attorney in the same election. Although their personalities often clashed, Clark's and Dilworth's commitment to liberal reform overshadowed their differences and accentuated their similarities. Both were from wealthy backgrounds, educated in the Ivy League; and both found their way into politics after successful legal careers. Importantly, neither had any meaningful connection to the city's working-class neighborhoods. Dilworth had first run for mayor in 1947, but he ran headlong into the city's Republican machine. The electoral loss was only a minor setback. When Philadelphia's reform duo took aim at City Hall just months after voters approved the new charter, they captured the momentum of the Better Philadelphia Exhibition and Greater Philadelphia Movement. Clark, Dilworth, and a slate of Democrats won their electoral campaigns and began the process of remaking city politics.

Clark and Dilworth enshrined their place in the city's development by overseeing the implementation of the Better Philadelphia Exhibition's plans and the provisions of the city charter. The charter revamped city operations in a number of ways. It created ten new or restructured municipal departments under the supervision of the managing director, including the Departments of Public Health, Streets, Recreation, Public Welfare, Water, Public Property, License and Inspections, and Records. From the city's old Department of Public Safety, the charter created the newly independent Fire and Police Departments. The creation of an independent Philadelphia Police Department (PPD) modernized city law enforcement and brought it in line with that of most big city municipalities; but it also had broader consequences. By making an independent PPD, the new charter made the police commissioner a public figure on a par with the heads of other city agencies.[15] Following the charter movement's demand for the depoliticization of appointments, reformers and liberals advocated a strong police commissioner as a means of introducing more efficiency to city law enforcement and curtailing patronage. Yet the selection and retention of police commissioners became even more politicized under the charter, especially as the fear of crime and disorder became a top local issue. The city charter established the police commissioner as not just an effective administrator, but now also as a powerful player in city politics. In time, and much to the disappointment of liberals like Clark and Dilworth, Frank Rizzo would exploit this power more than any of his predecessors.

In addition to shaping Philadelphia's postwar municipal liberal consensus by remaking the executive branch, the charter also created or empowered new boards and agencies to work with the mayor. Of these bodies, none was more important than the City Planning Commission and newly created Commission on Human Relations (CHR), an agency tasked with overseeing and enforcing the charter's new equal opportunity policies. The CHR was indebted to the work of interracial civil rights activists in organizations like the Fellowship Commission and Urban League that had long sought municipal government oversight of equal opportunity policy. The agency took over the powers of Philadelphia's much-touted Fair Employment Practices Commission and expanded its purview to include fair housing, equal employment opportunity, and all manner of racial, ethnic, and neighborhood tensions.[16] The CHR retained a special position in city governance under mayors Clark and Dilworth. Both were part of the coalition that introduced a civil rights plank into the national Democratic Party platform in 1948. They maintained that commitment to civil rights when they returned to Philadelphia.[17]

In keeping with the reformers' emphasis on expertise and professional appointments, Joseph Clark enticed George Schermer to head the CHR. Schermer had years of experience in human relations and civic service. First working though New Deal initiatives and the Chicago Housing Authority in the 1930s, Schermer moved on to Detroit in the 1940s, where he spent twelve years serving or leading the Detroit Housing Commission, Federal Public Housing Authority, and Mayor's Interracial Committee. In the early 1950s, white Detroiters succeeded in ousting Schermer from the Mayor's Interracial Committee because of his affiliation with the liberal Americans for Democratic Action. Over twenty years of experience with race relations and a proven liberal record made Schermer a target in Detroit, but it made him a desirable commodity among Philadelphia reformers.[18] When Clark offered him the position, Schermer was especially impressed with the provisions of the city charter. He thought it put Philadelphia's commitment to civil rights "miles ahead" of any other city. Upon accepting the CHR's executive directorship, Schermer rounded out the final prong of Philadelphia's municipal liberal consensus. The commission also highlighted the fundamental limitations of the city's reform liberalism.[19]

Schermer's effect on this city began shortly after his arrival, as the CHR agents began investigating charges of discrimination in municipal employment. The agency scored an early success in 1955, when Wiley and Bertha Clark sought to become the first African Americans to move into a proud, blue-collar, largely Irish and Italian section of upper North Philadelphia. They were not looking to become a test case for residential integration. To the contrary, the Clarks only sought a home they could afford where their four children could play safely. Working as a car wash attendant and domestic servant, respectively, the Clarks borrowed three hundred dollars from a loan company to put a down payment on a small home near the intersection of Judson and Cambria Streets. The loan meant that they would have to sacrifice to pay their mortgage, so Wiley Clark personally undertook the repairs the home needed from eight months of lying vacant. As he began working on the house each evening after work he aroused the suspicions of his new neighbors. Rather than tell hostile neighbors that he had purchased the home, Wiley told them he was getting it ready for its new owner. An angry mob greeted the Clarks when they first moved into the house in August 1955. The next day Wiley returned from work to find his windows broken. While he went to contact the police, Bertha came home from work, saw the windows, and decided to wait outside for her husband. By the time Wiley returned with a police officer, Bertha had been surrounded by a screaming and spitting mob.[20]

George Schermer received word of the trouble around ten thirty at night and quickly put the CHR's interracial mission into action. Schermer and one of the CHR's African American community-relations experts met with the Clarks while two white Catholic CHR workers held a meeting with members of the predominantly Catholic community. White residents complained about Wiley Clark's alleged lie about owning the home and the house's appearance. Convinced that the Clarks would not take the same pride in their home as they did, the blue-collar residents of the Judson-Cambria area feared a drop in their property values. The CHR hoped to find a solution that would appease everyone, but the Clarks were ready to leave after their hostile welcome. Schermer feared that allowing the Clarks to leave in the face of white resistance would set a dangerous precedent. If the Clarks left, other white neighborhoods might use the same tactics to force newcomers out of their neighborhoods. The CHR had to convince the Clarks to stay and alleviate the concerns of their new neighbors. Schermer asked civil rights leaders to help orchestrate the creation of two community organizations, the Citizens Committee for Wiley Clark and the North Penn Civic Improvement Association (NPCIA). The CHR oversaw meetings between the two organizations that reached an accord. Civil rights organizations agreed to teach the Clarks how to be model homeowners in exchange for North Penn residents agreeing not to engage in panic selling. The Clarks finally moved their children into their new home in November 1955 and the CHR boasted that it had "stopped a race riot."[21]

The easing of tensions in North Penn highlighted the promise that urban liberal reformers offered postwar Philadelphia. Both the Clarks and the newly formed NPCIA proved willing to work with local government agencies and found a workable solution to the community's tensions. Early in the reform era, both blue-collar whites and African Americans remained willing to work with the city agencies that maintained Philadelphia's liberal municipal consensus. At the same time, however, the settlement of the Clark's housing dispute also hinted at the limitations of urban liberalism. As reporter Hannah Lees noted, the residents of North Penn never fully accepted the Clarks.[22] Moreover, the settlement of the situation forced the Clarks to tacitly admit that their hard work and pride in homeownership were less equal than their working-class, white ethnic neighbors. Blue-collar pride, as it was employed in disputes over neighborhood character, was a limited commodity that excluded outsiders as much as it celebrated insiders. And the Clarks' case was hardly isolated. The CHR regularly responded to similar housing disputes. Few shared the Clarks' limited happy ending. In the end, these housing disputes showcased the promise of urban liberalism while revealing its inability to fully address the structural underpinnings of urban inequality.

The municipal liberal consensus initiated by the new city charter ushered in an era of an unprecedented commitment to metropolitan growth and equal opportunity. Nevertheless, while the Clark and Dilworth administrations were as committed to civil rights as any municipal government in the nation, Philadelphia remained one of the most segregated cities in the United States. Despite their commitment to reform, pragmatic and piecemeal approaches to the problems facing the city rarely met high expectations. Just as important, Philadelphia's municipal liberal consensus was never as widespread as liberals hoped. The disconnect between reformers and the increasingly disillusioned civil rights community widened as liberal prescriptions for addressing urban conditions faltered. Likewise, a concurrent rift began developing between reform Democrats and the white, row-home Democrats that made up the other substantial portion of the local party's new political base. Segregated and separated urban spaces defined the chasm that led to broader divisions over race, class, and ideology.

Redevelopment and Limits of Urban Liberalism

The February 1958 issue of *Time* magazine ran a feature article on Philadelphia's urban renewal program. National attention was nothing new. Since sparked by the Better Philadelphia Exhibition, the city's planning and urban renewal agencies had become a model for national and international planning communities.[23] Like most coverage of Philadelphia's urban renewal, the *Time* article also praised the reform government that made such a vibrant planning program possible. Nevertheless, Mayor Richardson Dilworth agreed to speak with the magazine about "Philadelphia's New Problem." *Time* argued that plans to construct middle-income housing—designed to maintain the city's tax base by discouraging white flight and encouraging suburbanites to return—unintentionally created a more racially segregated city by pricing the poor and nonwhites out of new developments. Dilworth disagreed. He said the problem of residential segregation was not due to the city's urban renewal program, but resulted from suburbanization. He told *Time* that the suburbs were a "white noose" around the city's neck.[24]

Despite Dilworth's defense of urban renewal, *Time* still accused the city of perpetuating segregation. Dilworth was livid. He had personally helped establish the municipal government that put civil rights at the center of its reform agenda and took exception to the magazine's accusations. "Our program is based on the fundamental policy that Negroes must have the same opportunity to purchase homes and select where they want to live as any other Americans," Dilworth wrote the magazine. He assured its editors that African Americans in Philadelphia had every right to live wherever they desired. He again said the problem of racial segregation grew out of restrictive housing in the suburbs where "it is virtually impossible for a Negro family to purchase a new home." Philadelphia's problem, and that of urban America, lay not in attempts to keep higher-income whites from leaving, he continued. It was born out of the racial and class segregation created outside the city's borders. "That is why," he concluded, "it is essential to put an end to the white noose of the suburbs which is strangling our cities, and threatening our basic concepts of equality of opportunity."[25]

Dilworth was one of the first to employ the phrase "white noose." A few years later, when the United States Commission on Civil Rights repeated it in a Report on Housing, the "white noose" became a frequent liberal metaphor for metropolitan inequality.[26] Locally, after Levittown, Pennsylvania, erupted into violent protest when the first African American family moved into the suburb in 1957, Dilworth's "white noose" became a powerful indictment of the racialized housing patterns that marked metropolitan Philadelphia.[27] The mayor's use of the term signaled the progressive turn the city government had taken in the reform era. Yet *Time* magazine was not entirely wrong. Contrary to Dilworth's protest, many of the community development policies enacted by the City Planning Commission and Redevelopment Authority of Philadelphia (RA) reinforced or reestablished racial divisions in Philadelphia's housing markets, divisions that then extended into schools, workplaces, and culture of a city increasingly defined by its black and white spaces.[28] By shifting blame for residential segregation to the white suburbs, Dilworth pointed to a broader metropolitan inequality that exacerbated segregation throughout urban America. He also tried to deny urban liberals' culpability in maintaining Philadelphia's segregated spaces.[29]

Urban renewal was not just a key part of postwar Philadelphia's liberal municipal consensus, it was central to a much broader urban reform agenda throughout the United States and Western Europe.[30] In the United States, the Housing Act of 1949 set off urban renewal plans throughout the country and made the federal government a partner in the revitalization of the nation's cities. It made the goal of a decent home and safe environment national urban policy through home-loan mortgages, slum clearance, and an expansive public housing program. Because the law called for workable plans and citizen participation, it also encouraged the growth of city planning regimes to provide local influence and oversight over renewal.[31] Visionary city planner Edmund Bacon oversaw Philadelphia's urban renewal as the executive director of the City Planning Commission. The city charter further increased Bacon's reach by making the CPC responsible for creating annually updated comprehensive plans, zoning ordinances, and an annual capital program and budget. With expanded powers, Bacon and the CPC promised to transform Philadelphia's infrastructure, revitalize its neighborhoods, and initiate an era of urban and economic growth. But promises of rebirth also brought consequences that widened spatial and political divides. In Philadelphia, urban renewal represented the distance between the promise and limitations of urban liberalism more than any other reform.[32]

As in so many other cities, the results of Philadelphia's urban renewal were uneven. The rehabilitation of the Central Business District first imagined by the Better Philadelphia Exhibition became planners' first priority. When Richardson Dilworth appointed Center City magnate Albert M. Greenfield—known in elite parts of midcentury Philadelphia as "Mr. Philadelphia"—to chair the CPC in 1956, he offered a welcome complement to Edmund Bacon's executive directorship. Both Greenfield and Bacon looked first to the downtown district as a means of establishing a successful program. They reasoned that improving avenues of commerce and tourism would help maintain the city's revenue base, both through business taxes and the redevelopment of one of the city's historic downtown neighborhoods, Society Hill.[33] Greenfield's and Bacon's attention to Center City produced a number of successful results, including the creation of the Society Hill neighborhood, the removal of the "Chinese Wall," and the construction of the Penn Center office complex on its grounds. The efforts were not without controversy or broader consequences. As early as 1955, critics warned that the focus on the Central Business District meant that Philadelphia was failing to meet the housing needs of the rest of the city.[34] Nevertheless, the initial success of Center City's revitalization led planners to believe renewal would radiate outward to the city's residential neighborhoods.[35]

Unlike the comprehensive plans for New York, Chicago, and elsewhere, Philadelphia's renewal did not call for the wholesale demolition and clearance of large parts of the urban core. Instead, Edmund Bacon initiated a policy of clearance and rehabilitation of small project areas. When city planners undertook these conservation projects, they looked first to areas like South Philadelphia, where Frank Rizzo was born and raised. Although he moved to Germantown in Northwest Philadelphia shortly before joining the police force in 1943, he received his first promotion in 1950, to sergeant, in South Philadelphia's Thirty-Third Police District. In the 1950s, Frank Rizzo's South Philadelphia was a collection of tightly knit, white ethnic enclaves, most of them predominantly Irish or Italian. Despite long-established and relatively stable populations, these older neighborhoods still fell into decline. Edmund Bacon hoped the successful stabilization of potentially at-risk neighborhoods would demonstrate the value of urban planning outside the Central Business District.[36]

South Philadelphia also provided the opportunity to show white, blue-collar neighborhoods that urban renewal meant more than slum clearance.

For example, Southwest Philadelphia's Eastwick urban renewal project revealed the constitutive potential of urban renewal by creating a brand new community on largely undeveloped land.[37] More common, however, were smaller-scale projects that sought to prop up existing neighborhoods and reduce the risk of white flight. One of these projects, in a community not far from the confluence of the Schuylkill and Delaware Rivers, became the site of the postwar era's most contested fight over city planning, local control, affordable housing, and urban liberalism. By Rizzo's mayoralty it became a bitter and acrimonious controversy known as "the battle of Whitman Park."[38]

Badly deteriorating buildings pockmarked the still-unnamed community at midcentury. A 1957 Redevelopment Authority survey deemed over 4 percent of its residential structures substandard, as well as 8 percent of mixed use and 68 percent of its nonresidential buildings. But the area's population was stable. Its median income was slightly higher than the rest of South Philadelphia, $3,100 a year compared to a $2,890 citywide average. The majority of the residents worked blue-collar jobs as skilled craftsmen, operatives, and general laborers. Another large percentage worked in clerical positions and the service sector. A smaller number in professional and managerial occupations rounded out the community's adult workforce.[39] It was also one of the few predominantly white areas of the city not yet experiencing an exodus to the suburbs or Northeast Philadelphia. The CPC hoped that designating the neighborhood for urban renewal would encourage them to remain.[40] The neighborhood also included a small African American enclave near the community's perimeter, representing about 3 percent of the neighborhood's overall population. The highest percentage of black residency was along the area's eastern border in older and more run-down housing. City planners chose that site for the construction of a new public housing project. The RA then marked it for clearance. As in other clearance areas, relocation took precedence over rehabilitation and none of the area's African American residents remained in the neighborhood after displacement.[41]

The residents that remained not only welcomed the city's reforms and redevelopment, they actively worked with the City Planning Commission, requested additional projects, and recruited neighbors to participate in the community's renewal. In 1957, the community organized to request an upgrade to the city's conservation program. More comprehensive than other urban renewal projects, conservation combined public and private monies to preserve neighborhoods that planners deemed stable but threatened by blighting influences. "As representatives of civic associations, religious groups, and social agencies," area representatives pleaded, "we know that the people of our area both need and desire the improvements which such a program encompasses." They then promised to build a stronger community organization and encourage civic activity in pursuit of widespread neighborhood improvements like the removal of an unsightly junkyard, increased recreational space, and housing rehabilitation.[42]

For the area's blue-collar white ethnics, urban renewal promised wideranging improvements and changes to the community, not the least of which was giving it a new identity. Despite the city's reputation as a "city of neighborhoods," the area was still an unnamed 240-acre plot nestled between older industrial neighborhoods when the Redevelopment Authority designated it for renewal. Following official dictates to encourage citizen participation, the CPC originally coordinated plans with the Southwark Community Council, an organization representing a far larger section of South Philadelphia. After renewal began, and with planners' encouragement, residents created the Whitman Area Improvement Council (WAIC) as an organization separate from Southwark. They took the neighborhood's new name—Whitman—from the nearby and recently completed Walt Whitman Bridge. Along with the promise of enhancements to the structural quality of the community, urban renewal gave Whitman a name, a sense of neighborhood pride, and a mark of legitimacy in a city of neighborhoods.[43]

Nationwide, urban renewal left a legacy as a primarily destructive process. Areas like South Philadelphia's Whitman revealed the potential for urban renewal to be creative as well. For Whitman's residents, urban renewal meant the promise of structural revival and increased property values. Whitman's new identity also gave residents a fierce sense of place and pride in their community. Yet the different experience for the area's white ethnic and African American residents also highlighted the gulf between urban renewal's promise and limitations. Later, Whitman's successful renewal revealed how thoroughly the racial and spatial structures it produced remade blue-collar politics. On a different scale, a similar spatial transformation was also taking place in the city's largest and least developed section, Northeast Philadelphia.

Situated along the Delaware River and bordered by Bucks County to the north and Montgomery County to the west, Northeast Philadelphia was like no other place in the city and few others in urban America. Because of its size, city planners divided it in two halves named after their proximity to Center City, the Near Northeast and Far Northeast. Although the entire Northeast had officially been part of the city for a century, a series of creeks and large wooded areas effectively cut it off from the urban core. Pockets of industry along the Delaware River had helped create a score of small communities in the nineteenth and early twentieth centuries. Others arrived after public improvement projects brought paved roads and utility services shortly after the First World War. Until World War II, most Northeast Philadelphians lived in these long-established neighborhoods in the Near Northeast. The Far Northeast still had more farms and forested areas than residential spaces.[44] Edmund Bacon thought these lands held immense possibilities for the city's future. Where other older cities feared the twin problem of white and industrial flight to the suburbs or the union-weak South, Bacon thought the sparsely populated Northeast offered a solution few American cities were in a position to match.[45]

As a whole, the "Greater Northeast"—a collective term invented by boosters to unite the Far and Near Northeast—offered the city a commodity few cities as old or large could boast: space to grow. It was, as one reporter called it, "Philadelphia's last frontier."[46] For that reason, city planners, civic leaders, civil rights activists, and myriad other interested parties eyed the area as a place of promise. City planners were especially hopeful that the residential and commercial development of the Far Northeast would lessen the stress of the inadequate housing in older neighborhoods, encourage the retention of industry, and maintain the city's tax bases.[47]

The vast open space in the Far Northeast was especially attractive to the Philadelphia Industrial Development Corporation (PIDC), a quasi-public agency formed during the reform era to oversee industrial and commercial development projects. In the Far Northeast, they saw a salve against the potentially destructive forces of deindustrialization.[48] Working with the City Planning Commission, the PIDC orchestrated the relocation of nearly one thousand manufacturing plants to the Far Northeast. With space for more modern production facilities, where one-floor operations could replace multistory tenement-style factories, city planners brokered multiple deals to keep local businesses in Philadelphia. They ranged from light industries like the Budd Company, Yale and Towne, International Papers, and Crown, Cork, and Seal to large-scale food producers like Penn Fruit, National Biscuit, and Whitman Confections. In a little over a decade, about one-fifth of the city's industries relocated to the Far Northeast. By the early 1960s, seventy thousand blue-collar workers—about 20 percent of the city's industrial workforce—worked in Northeast Philadelphia's factories. As a result, Philadelphia and its working-class population weathered the problem of industrial flight and manufacturing job loss longer than cities like Detroit, Cleveland, and others in the emerging rust belt.[49]

With industrial relocation, city and economic planners turned a semi-rural city appendage into an indispensable part of the metropolitan economy. Edmund Bacon hoped to do the same with Northeast Philadelphia's residential spaces. The relatively empty spaces in the Far Northeast offered an almost blank canvas for the creation of new urban communities. Bacon did not want to recreate traditional Philadelphia neighborhoods in the Far Northeast, however. As early as the Better Philadelphia Exhibition, planners promised that new construction in the Far Northeast would preserve its sylvan character, respect its natural resources, and establish communities around existing wooded areas. Bacon also believed that cities should have distinct districts for living, working, and leisure, so his plans assured that there would be buffer zones between industry and new housing.[50] Bacon never had the power and influence over urban spaces that some of his contemporaries exercised in other postwar American cities. In Far Northeast Philadelphia, however, Bacon realized his fullest vision of urban design.[51]

Bacon's plans avoided the architecture and street design that characterized the rest of the city's neighborhoods. He envisioned a "multi-stellar" pattern, where cul-de-sacs and looping streets radiated from main thoroughfares. Even when plans included the traditional Philadelphia row home, as in the Morrell Park development near the city's northeastern edge, Bacon promised to reinvent row-home living. Bacon wanted to make a community of inexpensive row homes for wage earners in Morrell Park, hoping the new neighborhood would provide homes for laborers in the Far Northeast's growing factories. To allay concerns that row homes would disrupt the area's suburban environment, the CPC created new zoning designations and a new kind of row home for Morrell Park. Typical city blocks had homes tightly squeezed into a grid and houses that extended almost to the street curb. Bacon designed Morrell Park with blocks that included breezeways between every eleventh home, driveways that separated the house from the street, and backyards that formed the interior circle of the neighborhood's multi-stellar design.[52] Contrasting Edmund Bacon with the city's founder, one reporter said he implemented "imaginative city planning such as William Penn never dreamed of."[53]

When construction finished in 1959, Morrell Park was the largest planned residential community in Philadelphia and the most complete example of Edmund Bacon's city planning vision. It promised a bit of suburban living in the city. Morrell Park realtors used the suburb-in-the-city metaphor to their

Figure 3. Morrell Park row homes, circa 1960. Courtesy of Special Collections Research Center, Temple University, Philadelphia, PA.

advantage. Increased space was one of the foremost lures of the new neighborhood. Realtors not only touted the more open space of the Far Northeast, including an expansive and federally protected wooded area called Pennypack Park, but also the greater space within individual homes and properties. The homes in Morrell Park all featured three or four bedrooms, spacious kitchens and dining rooms, and backyard space.[54] Builders also offered an alternative to one of the most pressing spatial problems of the automobile age. Architects designed all new housing in Morrell Park with garages below the living space of the home, a feature unknown in most inner-city neighborhoods. A personal parking space was not only a solution to a pressing concern of older, working-class neighborhoods, but also a symbol of upward mobility.

Success in Morrell Park set off a wave of construction in Far Northeast Philadelphia. Bacon's updated row-house design and single, detached homes proliferated in new and nearby neighborhoods like Academy Gardens, Parkwood, Holme Circle, Winchester Park, Byberry, Bustleton, Somerton, and Torresdale. Within a decade, the Far Northeast was home to several distinct, contiguous neighborhoods and over a half million people. Combined with the Near Northeast, which experienced a concurrent population boom, the Greater Northeast practically became its own city. It occupied forty-eight square miles of territory. It was home to about one-fifth of the city's population, making it larger than Newark, New Jersey, and almost twice the size of Miami, Florida. If it had been a separate city, Northeast Philadelphia would have been the third largest in Pennsylvania. Spatial advantages and the allure of upward mobility attracted residents to Philadelphia's fastest growing area.[55] Like the beneficiaries of South Philadelphia's urban renewal, furthermore, Northeast Philadelphia's political future would be shaped by the restructuring of its urban space in the reform era. In the decades to come, both South Philadelphia and Northeast Philadelphia would give Frank Rizzo his most enthusiastic support.

Predominantly white, blue-collar areas like South Philadelphia's Whitman and Northeast Philadelphia's Morrell Park received the benefits of city planners' and urban liberals' expansive visions. But the overall promise of Philadelphia's urban renewal was limited. Although the CPC and RA worked closely with local citizens to maintain the institutions that held close-knit communities together, displacement was an unavoidable part of urban renewal. To cope with dislocations, the city established a Relocation Bureau within the RA to oversee the rehousing of those displaced by urban renewal. Reformers efforts were incapable of overcoming preexisting structures of inequality, however. Due to long-established patterns of migration and settlement, close to 50 percent of the city's African American population lived in designated renewal areas. Edmund Bacon also adopted a policy based on the immediate removal of the most blighted areas. He hoped successful rehabilitation in the most needed areas would create a beachhead for expanding renewal efforts. As in Whitman, however, the immediate result was that slum clearance disproportionately affected African Americans. Even with the liberal reformers' commitment to equal opportunity, urban renewal still earned the pejorative "Negro Removal."[56]

The establishment of Philadelphia's renewal and relocation programs also coincided with the rapid growth of Philadelphia's nonwhite population. Between 1950 and 1960, the city's African American population increased by 41 percent, only a 9 percent drop from the height of black migration during World War II. Some settled in older African American sections of South and West Philadelphia, but the vast majority—around 207,000—concentrated into areas of North Central Philadelphia that whites had only recently fled for the suburbs or Northeast Philadelphia. As a result, North Philadelphia challenged South Philadelphia's old Seventh Ward as the center of black life in the city. Made famous at the turn of the century by W. E. B. Du Bois's study *The Philadelphia Negro*, the old Seventh Ward had remained an area of heavy black settlement sandwiched between Center City and the working-class Irish and Italian enclaves of South Philadelphia. In the late 1950s, however, the Redevelopment Authority targeted the area for renewal and forced over two thousand African American families to relocate.[57] Due to opposition from areas like the Far Northeast, the Relocation Bureau resettled the vast majority of them in North Philadelphia. Because slum clearance was also a part of North Philadelphia's renewal, both the relocated and newly arrived African Americans found themselves squeezed into dense communities with limited housing options or pushed into public housing. Urban renewal made North Philadelphia the center of the city's emerging urban crisis.[58]

The Reverend Leon H. Sullivan was one of many African Americans to make their way into North Philadelphia in the postwar years. Upon his arrival in 1950 to pastor North Philadelphia's Zion Baptist Church—a position he used to launch a crusade for civic and economic rights, eventually leading to the creation of his Opportunities Industrialization Center in 1964—he began taking note of the changes taking place around him. He remembered seeing the single homes that working- and middle-class whites used to live in, now turned into apartments and tenements retrofitted to accommodate more families. He saw blocks of "For Sale" signs where blue-collar whites used to live. "I had never seen so many dilapidated houses, row upon row, in my life," he wrote.[59] Making matters worse, while Philadelphia had built over 150,000 new homes in the 1950s, only 1,022 were available to African American families.[60] But poor housing was only a fraction of the problems besetting North Philadelphia. The industrial relocation that led to Northeast Philadelphia's rise had an inverse effect on North Philadelphia, as the factories that had employed the area's white working-class population for generations shifted production. A persistent and mutually reinforcing racial segmentation in the city's labor market combined with North Philadelphia's deteriorating housing conditions to establish it as an area of spatially concentrated poverty.[61] It also reinforced the popular perception among blue-collar whites that North Philadelphia's "jungle" was to be scorned and avoided.

Blue-collar white ethnics in so-called "proud neighborhoods" pointed to the same conditions as Leon Sullivan when they fretted about the city's expanding "jungle." In the communities adjacent to North Philadelphia, especially in parts of Kensington and South Philadelphia, blue-collar neighborhood pride both championed blue-collar, white ethnic traditions and turned those traditions into a means of defense and differentiation from African American newcomers. Likewise, the promise of Northeast Philadelphia was never just about space and class. It was also promised racial exclusivity. Fearing a loss of profits, private developers refused to sell to African Americans. As a result, over 90 percent of Northeast Philadelphia's postwar population explosion was white. Richardson Dilworth was not wrong when he argued that racial and economic segregation resulted from restrictive suburban housing policies, but he failed to acknowledge that Philadelphia's "white noose" did not begin at the city limits. Indeed, reform liberals' urban renewal helped create and maintain Philadelphia's "proud neighborhoods" and "urban jungles." For blue-collar whites, urban renewal and redevelopment fortified the spatial boundaries that cultivated the political evolution of blue-collar identity and culture.

"Proud Neighborhoods" and Blue-Collar Culture

The planning and reuse of land in Northeast Philadelphia led to a postwar population growth that was nothing short of remarkable. While the city as a whole lost about seventy thousand residents in the 1950s, the Greater Northeast gained about one hundred thousand. Most of them were white working- and middle-class Philadelphians that could afford to move out of older ethnic enclaves. Class differences played a powerful role in determining where they settled. Working-class white ethnics usually moved into the older, formerly industrial neighborhoods in the Near Northeast or into row-home communities like Morrell Park. Upwardly mobile and middle-class transplants tended to move into the single-family homes closer to the suburbs. Despite these differences, Northeast Philadelphia became an area where blue-collar families could buy a home and see themselves melding into the middle class. Just as important, because geographic contour and limited transportation infrastructure kept the area cut off from the urban core, the Greater Northeast cultivated a sense of separateness from the rest of the city. In 1961, eight years after the removal of Center City's "Chinese Wall," a resident of the Far Northeast's Bustleton neighborhood told a neighbor about the success of urban renewal in Center City. "Someday," he reportedly told his neighbor, "I must go to Philadelphia and see what they've done."[62]

Northeast Philadelphia's growth, especially in the Far Northeast, was far more indebted to the work of the city planning establishment and reform era municipal government than residents' sense of separateness suggested. Nevertheless, Greater Northeast residents shared a palpable distinctiveness from the rest of the city. Residents of the predominantly working-class and Polish Catholic enclave of Bridesburg in the Near Northeast, for example, took pride in the fact that their neighborhood was different from the city. One of the Near Northeast's older neighborhoods, Bridesburg was bounded by the Delaware River to the east, Frankford Creek to the north and west, and cut off from the city by the raised tracks of the Pennsylvania-Reading Railroad to the south. The neighborhood held onto its identity as a distinct township over a century after its official consolidation into the city. "This isn't Philadelphia," one local civic leader said. "This is Bridesburg."[63] The statement became an unofficial neighborhood slogan.

Northeast Philadelphia's sense of separation from the city helped create a distinct social and political culture that even newcomers to the Greater Northeast quickly adopted and adapted to their old neighborhood traditions. It often gave way to an adversarial, and occasionally hostile, relationship with city planners and City Hall, especially when city services, education facilities, and transportation failed to keep up with population growth. Northeast Philadelphia was not alone in breeding hostility toward city leaders. The culture of Philadelphia's blue-collar neighborhoods contrasted powerfully with that of city planners like Edmund Bacon, civic leaders like George Schermer, or liberal reformers like Joseph Clark and Richardson Dilworth. Although the city's white working- and middle-class communities overwhelmingly voted for political reform and liberal politicians throughout the 1950s, they shared little in common with those at the forefront of Philadelphia's planning and reform revolutions. Clark and Dilworth, for example, both came from wealthy, well-connected families. Dilworth, in particular, acted distant and disinterested when viewed from the neighborhoods. Throughout his career, Dilworth found large and small ways to alienate the residents of blue-collar districts like South Philadelphia, Kensington, and the river ward neighborhoods in the Near Northeast. The entire reform cohort appeared as out-of-touch elites that could not understand blue-collar culture and values. Clark and Dilworth represented real political reform and their liberal municipal consensus was a significant change in the city's political culture, but they maintained the stodgy WASP elite culture that had long been the widespread image associated with Philadelphia's civic identity.[64]

Blue-collar neighborhoods, by contrast, were overwhelmingly populated with working-class Roman Catholics. They lived and worked differently than city leaders. For longtime and new residents alike, blue-collar neighborhoods were institutions that insulated, preserved, and protected values and traditions. These neighborhoods housed the schools, places of worship, and social clubs that created close-knit communities. Residents of blue-collar neighborhoods sometimes romanticized their communities and overstated their cohesiveness, especially when they felt under attack. Nevertheless, they did live, work, pray, and play together. It was in these neighborhoods that blue-collar whites built and maintained traditions like community organizations and folk customs. These neighborhoods housed and sheltered institutions like schools and labor unions. These traditions and institutions fostered blue-collar culture and identity. In the ensuing years, blue-collar whites treated the communities they built like treasured possessions worthy of defense from any potential threat to home or livelihood.

Work in these neighborhoods came in many forms. Employment in the factories and light industries that maintained the city's manufacturing base was common. Increasingly, the retail businesses that made up Philadelphia's growing service sector provided another avenue of employment. Municipal employment was another viable option. The most treasured positions were those provided by the city's exclusive labor unions, especially in the building and construction trades. White-collar workers also found their place in blue-collar communities, provided that they maintained the cultural expectations of the neighborhood. "Hard work" was paramount in blue-collar neighborhoods, especially when it came to judging inclusion and authenticity. After work, adults shared barstools and work stories at the corner tavern or, in warmer months, relaxed with neighbors on the front steps. In the crowded row-house neighborhoods of South Philadelphia, Kensington, and the Near Northeast, marble or concrete stairs leading from the sidewalk to the front door were an architectural necessity, but they also served an important cultural function. They were informal gathering places for impromptu neighborhood meetings of all sorts, from daily gossip to weightier matters about the fate of the community and city. They were where the families went to feel the cool air when the house got too warm and reinforce communal relations with their neighbors. In these neighborhoods, both work and home provided the spaces needed to build and maintain a distinct blue-collar culture.[65]

Blue-collar culture was not only neighborhood oriented, it was also family focused. Parents frequently sent their children to the same schools and brought them to the same churches they had attended when they were young. Although they might not be outright discouraged, children were rarely expected to seek a formal education beyond high school. Many parents expected their children to follow in their footsteps. For working-class fathers, one of the few privileges they looked forward to bestowing upon their sons was entry into an apprenticeship program with a union. As incomes rose, blue-collar Philadelphians joined postwar Americans everywhere that looked to fulfill both wants and needs. Families with the means looked forward to taking annual vacations "down the shore" or "up the mountains," as Philadelphians referred to the drivable resort destinations in southern New Jersey or the Pocono Mountains. As blue-collar Philadelphians celebrated the lifestyles they achieved in the 1950s, work, home, school, and culture all fed into the defensiveness that defined postwar neighborhood politics.[66]

As in blue-collar neighborhoods throughout the city, most new residents of Northeast Philadelphia were homeowners. Mortgaging a new home was not always the easiest decision, but it was an investment in the future. Homeownership offered another source of pride in both home and neighborhood. Margaret Moran, for example, was new to Northeast Philadelphia in the 1950s. She and her husband had moved between white working-class neighborhoods near Kensington and North Philadelphia before settling into Mayfair in 1950. The house the Morans purchased was smaller than their previous homes, but the neighborhood was preferable. "It was different surroundings," she remembered. "People were different. Everything was different about it."[67] She explained that she felt her family had moved up the social ladder by moving to Mayfair. It seemed cleaner than Kensington and the other areas she lived. In order to afford their mortgage, Margaret Moran followed the detailed savings and payment program provided by the Federal Housing Authority. Because of the sacrifice that came with moving to Mayfair, Moran knew her family was vulnerable. It was hard work, she thought, but well worth it to have escaped the cramped inner city for the more middle-class surroundings of Northeast Philadelphia.

By the late 1950s and early 1960s, as thousands of families like the Morans moved into newer neighborhoods, Philadelphia's blue-collar culture and traditions moved with them. Northeast Philadelphians' incomes may have been a little higher, their homes a bit bigger, and their neighborhoods less densely packed, but they retained row-home customs and values in their more suburban and middle-class environment. Northeast Philadelphia neighborhoods were less likely to identify with a single ethnic group, but a white ethnicity remained a central feature of blue-collar culture in new neighborhoods. Some older neighborhoods in the Near Northeast even held on to real and symbolic ethnic identities—like the largely Polish Bridesburg neighborhood or the Irish enclave in Mayfair—but the children and grandchildren of European immigrants created numerous multiethnic white neighborhoods.[68] Their surroundings were new, but the culture they shared was reminiscent of the proud blue-collar neighborhoods that still characterized row-house neighborhoods throughout Kensington and South Philadelphia.[69]

Neighborhood pride drew on an emergent sense of blue-collar authenticity that championed a "work-your-way-up" ethos and a mythic white ethnic heritage based on European immigrant roots, sacrifice, and self-improvement. As a result, expressions of blue-collar neighborhood pride often took on a defensive and exclusionary position. Neighbors resented encroachments on their communities. The belief that outsiders and newcomers would not take the same pride in their home and environment was a common refrain of neighborhood protectionists, especially when the proposed newcomers were from different racial backgrounds.

Kensington and South Philadelphia were often the first choice for nonwhites attempting to escape areas of spatially concentrated poverty. Since so many white ethnics had relocated to the Northeast, there was an increasing stock of housing available. Those that remained became even more defensive. The belief, reinforced by the real estate industry, that nonwhite neighbors would create either a dangerous or an economically unsound environment tapped directly into blue-collar vulnerability. They warned that integration would lead to white flight from the neighborhood, thereby causing surrounding property values to fall. Despite a Commission on Human Relations education campaign to dispel such rumors, the belief that black residency lowered property values became a paramount fear. For economically vulnerable blue-collar whites, the threat of lowered property values was real, despite its basis in fear, misinformation, and racism. Few blue-collar whites disputed the notion that nonwhite neighbors would lower property values. They were too protective of the class status that homeownership bestowed.[70]

Fear of falling property values complemented preexisting hostilities toward racial and ethnic minorities. When the mutually reinforcing politics of race and class met on blue-collar neighborhood streets, white residents often responded to the presence of unwanted newcomers with violence. In 1960, the CHR highlighted six episodes where white resistance to nonwhite neighbors led to minority families vacating their homes. In one instance, the Fernandez family leased a second-floor apartment in Fishtown from the proprietors of a grocery store on the first floor. The family was Portuguese, but because José Fernandez was dark skinned his neighbors presumed he was African American or Puerto Rican. After three days of crowds stoning their building, the Fernandezes left in fear. Similarly, when the African American Harris family rented a home in Kensington, whites enlisted the police to dispute the Harris's rental agreement. Their home had a sheriff's notice on the front door and, when confronted, the Harrises could not produce documents proving rightful occupancy. Their white neighbors had the police escort them from their home until they could prove they were not trespassing. The Harrises provided the proper documentation, but the community still threatened further action. Against CHR wishes, the Harrises decided that the neighborhood was unsafe for their children and left.[71]

Blue-collar whites that did not relocate to Northeast Philadelphia dug in for protracted fights against integration. These incidents foretold the volatility that housing disputes would play in Philadelphia's long postwar period. They also suggested another structural barrier to integration that troubled George Schermer and the CHR. The police seemed unwilling to make examples of white mobs. Instead, Schermer thought the police too closely followed a policy of letting hostile crowds settle down on their own. He was especially worried that the failure to disperse crowds or make arrests encouraged white residents or, worse, signified police sympathy with the protesters.[72] Schermer recognized a growing division between Philadelphia's white and black residents and their relationship to municipal agencies. For African Americans, the CHR became a trustworthy source for the redress of grievances. For blue-collar whites, it was the police. That division, as much as any other in segregated Philadelphia, would have profound consequences for the rise of Frank Rizzo and the emerging politics of the urban crisis.

As the blue-collar neighborhoods nearest North Philadelphia proved hostile to nonwhites, civil rights leaders and municipal agencies looked to the spacious environs of Northeast Philadelphia. They hoped that the opening of the Greater Northeast would ease the pressure on the crowded inner city. In fact, the Northeast was home to a number of new housing concepts, including one of the nation's first planned integrated communities in Morris Milgram's Greenbelt Knoll and an experimental mutual-ownership community known as the Pennypack Woods Home Ownership Association.[73] Both were testaments to the promise that Northeast Philadelphia represented to equal opportunity housing activists. Private housing developers, however, had different ideas. They made it clear that new homes in the area would not be available to nonwhites. When builders and realtors began selling homes in Morrell Park in 1959, they readily admitted to discriminating against African Americans. Testifying before the CHR because African American home seeker Andrew Nix had been denied an application for a newly built Morrell Park home, realtor James D. Scully said that white home buyers frequently asked if the development would be racially mixed. He further testified that they would not purchase a home if African Americans were permitted to purchase in Morrell Park. But, Scully insisted, Nix's application denial "had nothing to do with his race." Instead, Scully testified that it was "the economics involved" that led to the decision.[74] Morrell Park home builders echoed Scully, saying it would have been "economically unsound" to sell to African Americans.[75]

Because the upwardly mobile white ethnics eyeing new construction in Northeast Philadelphia would not purchase a home in a racially mixed area, builders and realtors claimed that they could not risk their investments on African American homebuyers. When the CHR responded by initiating a program to allow African Americans to move to the Northeast, the Philadelphia Northeast Realty Board (PNRB) protested that it was a violation of what voters had in mind when they approved the new city charter. Instead of easing racial tensions, the PNRB accused the CHR of "blatantly pitting one group against another." They said they did not condone restrictive housing, but they worried that introducing unwelcome residents into Northeast Philadelphia would increase racial animosities and exacerbate the housing problem. As a result, they said they were duty bound to their investors and customers to maintain Northeast Philadelphia's exclusionary housing market.[76]

For blue-collar white ethnics, Northeast Philadelphia included the tacit promise that it would remain all white. African Americans were not so quick to give up on the promise of Northeast Philadelphia, however. Leon Sullivan recognized that the Northeast offered an escape from the crowded communities he ministered to in North Philadelphia. In 1963, he issued a statement saying there were five hundred African American families prepared to move to Northeast Philadelphia. Although Sullivan admitted that the number was an exaggeration, his proclamation sent a wave of consternation throughout the area's blue-collar neighborhoods. Sullivan prompted the formation of several new neighborhood organizations and solicited a response from the *Northeast Times*, a regional newspaper that claimed the mantle as the voice of the entire area. A proponent of the idea that the Northeast was fundamentally distinct from the rest of the city, the *Northeast Times* defended the area against charges of racial discrimination. The editorial board insisted on their support for the desegregation of public accommodations and sympathy for "public equality." But, while claiming to disagree in principle, they also supported a community's right to "private segregation."[77] The newspaper's invocation of the doctrine of freedom of association reflected Northeast Philadelphians' most common approach to integration. The argument offered a defense of the status quo while maintaining a nominally color-blind discourse and rhetorical support for equal opportunity. Defending freedom of association allowed the *Northeast Times* and area residents to separate themselves from overtly racist arguments against housing integration without advocating desegregation.

For African Americans, private realtors and private resistance to integration in Northeast Philadelphia created a new barrier to quality affordable housing. City planners, however, hoped public housing could fill the void. A robust public housing program administered through the Philadelphia Housing Authority (HA) was an essential part of the city's urban renewal program. City planners and housing activists viewed public housing as a means of compensating those displaced by urban renewal and fostering integration.[78] Significant public housing projects were a part of the early planning for the new neighborhoods in the Northeast as well as rehabilitated neighborhoods like Whitman in South Philadelphia. In each instance, however, the HA faced stiff resistance from white residents. Through negotiations with city planners, Whitman community leaders pressured the city to change original plans for a high-rise housing complex and delayed construction on any public housing for over a decade. Northeast Philadelphia neighborhoods were even more successful. Residents fought the construction of apartments, public housing, or anything they thought would change the character of their neighborhoods in the Lower Northeast's Oxford Circle and Far Northeast's Summerdale neighborhoods.[79] Faced with firm opposition, the HA retreated from most plans to build new public housing in predominantly white neighborhoods. Instead, most new public housing construction took place in the already high-density areas of North and West Philadelphia.[80]

As early as 1957, the CHR found that public housing as a means of integration was failing.[81] The prospects for such a program only grew worse in the 1960s. Indeed, controversies over public housing—like the burgeoning battles in Whitman and another in Morrell Park—produced the two most protracted housing disputes in the long postwar era. As a result, the area white Philadelphians knew as "the jungle" continued to grow, fostered by white resistance to integration and liberal reformers' policy and planning limitations. Together, they left limited viable housing and employment options for low-income people of color. The result was a city deeply divided, racially, spatially, and conceptually. Much as in the cities of Chicago, Detroit, and others in the urban North, the lack of either affordable private housing or effective public housing helped fortify the contrast between Philadelphia's "proud neighborhoods" and "urban jungles."[82]

The fortification of Philadelphia's racial and spatial divisions coincided with the end of the city's reform era. Richardson Dilworth resigned the mayoralty in 1962 to pursue an ultimately unsuccessful run for governor of Pennsylvania. His successor, James H. J. Tate, assumed the mayoralty from his position as president of the city council. He represented a sharp break from Clark and Dilworth. Tate was a Democrat, but he had long drawn political support from the city's exclusive labor unions and blue-collar neighborhoods. As city councilman and mayor, he continued to live among his constituents in a modest row home in an all-white working-class neighborhood in lower North Philadelphia.[83] In a short time, Tate made clear which side of the local Democratic coalition he was on when he dismissed George Schermer's proposal to enforce nondiscriminatory hiring on city contracts with the powerful unions in the Building and Construction Trades Council. Schermer resigned his post in protest. Liberals and civil rights leaders flooded the mayor's office with letters denouncing the end of the reform era.[84]

Tate's mayoralty represented a shift in the city's political culture, but the politics of the urban crisis that led to the rise of blue-collar conservatism and shaped Philadelphia's long postwar period were cast in the reform era. It began with the promise of reform, revitalization, and a better city through urban liberalism. But the municipal liberal consensus that attempted to forge a coalition of business interests, blue-collar whites, and African Americans left a legacy of half-kept promises and urban division. Planning and redevelopment regimes reinforced or created racial divisions that extended from housing to schools and workplaces. Separate cultures fostered by spatial division shaped new structures of privilege in white, blue-collar neighborhoods while inspiring a shift in civil rights activism toward a more confrontational quest for equal opportunity and urban power. The disparity was stark. In 1964 it reached its explosive tipping point.

CHAPTER 2

Grassroots Law and Order

Robert Wells radioed a hurried "assist-officer" plea to police headquarters on a steamy Friday night in late August 1964. The African American police officer's partner, white patrolman John Hoff, had just been attacked by a man later identified as James Mettles. Immediately before the attack, the two officers had responded to a report of a stalled vehicle in the middle of a busy intersection in a densely populated African American neighborhood in North Central Philadelphia. When Wells and Hoff arrived at Twenty-Second Street and Columbia Avenue around 9:30 p.m. on August 28, they found Rush and Odessa Bradford inside the stopped vehicle, intoxicated, and arguing with each other. After failing to get the two to leave the intersection, Hoff attempted forcibly to remove Odessa Bradford. A crowd gathered to watch the altercation. Mettles emerged from the crowd and struck Hoff as he struggled with Rush. Wells made his call for backup as the crowd grew. His hurried distress call was the first of more than fifty similar calls made by Philadelphia police officers that night.[1]

Bricks and bottles rained down from nearby rooftops as Wells and Hoff attempted to wrestle Odessa Bradford and James Mettles into a police wagon. Reinforcements temporarily dispersed the crowd, but a rumor soon spread through the neighborhood that a white police officer had beaten and shot a pregnant woman. Angry crowds began throwing stones and debris at arriving police cars. Before long, a large throng headed toward the neighborhood's business district, breaking store windows and looting shops along the 2100 and 2200 blocks of Columbia Avenue. More than six hundred police officers soon made their way to the area, where Police Commissioner Howard Leary and Deputy Commissioner Frank Rizzo commanded the response. Representatives of the city's Commission on Human Relations (CHR) arrived shortly thereafter. Though they worked alongside the police as well as community and civil rights leaders, CHR efforts to get people to leave the streets and return to their homes failed. Following Commissioner Leary's riot control plan, the police kept the trouble contained to a relatively small part of North Philadelphia, but did very little to stop the looting. The plan worked, mostly. Looting and vandalism continued, but the police prevented the rioting from spreading beyond nearby Ridge Avenue. Nevertheless, Frank Rizzo was enraged. He thought Leary's plan prohibited the police from restoring order. When he confronted the commissioner, Leary told him to follow the plan. Rizzo later said it was the closest he ever came to disobeying a direct order.[2]

The next day, August 29, the CHR called a meeting of area civic and religious leaders to formulate plans to restore calm. Around one hundred community leaders unanimously agreed to petition the mayor and police to use whatever force was necessary to restore law and order. They also established teams to circulate through the area to quiet specific trouble spots. Meanwhile, Mayor James H. J. Tate rushed back from his vacation home at the New Jersey shore. He ordered a riot proclamation on Saturday afternoon, calling for a curfew covering a much larger part of North Philadelphia than the riot-torn area around Columbia and Ridge avenues. Howard Leary assigned fifteen hundred more officers to enforce the proclamation and prevent the riot from spreading. Rizzo commanded them, insisting that he remain on the streets rather than in the mobile command center that Leary established near Temple University.[3]

Following Tate's proclamation and Commissioner Leary's riot plan, police and community leaders worked to reestablish order. It took them another full day to completely quell the uprising. All told, the disturbance lasted nearly three days. Two people had been killed and 339 wounded, including 100 police officers. The police made 308 arrests, charging 200 with burglary, 30 with breach of the peace and rioting, and 78 with violating the mayor's curfew. The city estimated the riot caused more than three million dollars' worth of property damage. There had been 170 businesses in the immediate area on Friday evening. Only 52 remained on Sunday night.[4]

The riot in North Philadelphia was part of a larger trend in American cities in the 1960s.[5] It was the result of, and reaction to, the inequalities built into the city's postwar revitalization and the failures of its municipal liberal consensus. Similar scenes occurred in other urban areas in the coming years—most notably in the Watts section of Los Angeles, in Detroit, Michigan, and in nearby Newark, New Jersey—when seemingly minor police actions triggered uprisings in predominantly poor and working-class African American neighborhoods. When New York City's Harlem erupted just a month before Columbia Avenue, it marked the unofficial beginning of the "long, hot summers" that so brutally encapsulated the nadir of the American urban crisis. In Philadelphia, the Columbia Avenue Riot marked a turning point in the city's racial politics and law enforcement policy-making. It shattered the liberal postwar era's myth of racial progress.[6] Combined with other clashes between police and African Americans in Philadelphia and across the nation, the uprising and the debate over its meaning became a touchstone for problems facing the city in the years to come. It also hastened a move to an even more militant push for equal rights in the urban North while amplifying the clamor for "law and order."[7]

The mutually reinforcing rise of black militancy and law-and-order politics were central to the racial, cultural, and political terrain of 1960s urban America. In Philadelphia, the popularity of law-and-order politics directly led to the rise of Frank Rizzo. He received two promotions in response to the rise of law-and-order politics—first to deputy commissioner then to police commissioner—which sent him on the course that led to his mayoral victory. Before his ascendancy, however, the politics of law and order grew out of a grassroots reaction to crime and the politics of law enforcement. In Philadelphia, the rise of law-and-order politics derived from the politicization of a culture of reverence for the police that was indebted to the mutually reinforcing politics of race, space, and class commonality.

White reverence for police officers intensified when civil rights leaders turned their attention to police procedures, police-community relations, and, especially in Philadelphia, police brutality. In response, a mid-1960s campaign led by police officers' collective bargaining agent, the Fraternal Order of Police (FOP), helped rally supporters and defenders of the police department. The FOP found ready allies in Philadelphia's white, blue-collar neighborhoods, where a powerful sense of shared blue-collar culture united these neighborhoods with the workforce that made up the Philadelphia Police Department. Together, the efforts of the FOP and their allies in the city's white, blue-collar neighborhoods forced city officials and the police department to abandon law enforcement liberalism and promote law-and-order conservatism.

While the FOP's defense of police officers easily coincided with racist fears of civil disorder and black criminality, they also made appeals based upon the cultural politics of class. The blue-collar commonality between police officers and the broader white working class provided a wellspring of grassroots support for stringent law enforcement. Police work was a blue-collar job and tradition, often passed down generation to generation. White police officers also shared the blue-collar identity that developed in the city's white working- and middle-class neighborhoods. Most rank-and-file police officers fit somewhere into a lower-middle- to middle-class economic class category. But even those higher up on the chain of command and pay scale remained culturally blue-collar, provided that, like Frank Rizzo, they "worked their way up." Most importantly, police officers were a model of the cultural traits and shared values associated with blue-collar identity, especially those that were white and male.[8] As a result, few people in blue-collar Philadelphia could claim blue-collar authenticity more than police officers.

The white, blue-collar defense of the police was also a defense against the loss of a racialized and gendered blue-collar tradition. Although many of them claimed that racism played no part in their support of the police or calls for law and order, the culture of reverence for the police that spurred that support arose from the racial politics of segregated metropolitan space. Despite claims to the contrary, race played a central role in the blue-collar defense of the police and the blue-collar conservatism it helped engender. Furthermore, the Columbia Avenue Riot may have led to a more forceful blue-collar defense of the police, but the patterns of police-community relations that shaped differing cultural attitudes toward the police developed long before August 1964. How people in racially and spatially distinct areas of the city viewed the police department as an institution and a municipal agency, as well as how they interacted with individual police officers, determined the deep divisions over the politics of law enforcement. These divisions also fueled the debate over the urban crisis, the revolt against law enforcement liberalism, and the grassroots origins of law-and-order politics.

Urban Space and Police-Community Relations

The Columbia Avenue Riot served as a flashpoint for the reassessment of police-community relations, but it was hardly the first incident in North Philadelphia to divide citizens over the proper role of police power in a democratic society. In late October 1963, just ten months before the August 1964 uprising and only a few days before the 1963 mayoral election, white patrolman John Tourigan shot and killed a twenty-four-year-old African American man named Willie Philyaw for allegedly stealing a watch from a North Philadelphia drugstore. Police claimed that Philyaw had attacked Tourigan with a knife. But witnesses testified that Philyaw was incapable of running from the officer, much less attacking him, because he was a "cripple and an epileptic."[9] Eyewitnesses claimed that Tourigan shot Philyaw as he tried to flee. An angry crowd viewed Tourigan's actions as representative of the poor police-community relations that plagued North Philadelphia for years. Later that night, a small group took out their frustrations on area businesses and police officers. Though on a much smaller scale than the following August, they looted stores and threw bricks at oncoming police.[10]

Unlike the Columbia Avenue Riot, the disturbances after the Willie Philyaw murder were quelled relatively quickly by community leaders and police. Moderate civil rights leaders and liberals quickly distanced themselves from the looting, but maintained that a history of police brutality had created mass resentment in areas like North Philadelphia. They took the opportunity to press for reforms in law enforcement policy and procedure, but showed their willingness to work within the structures of municipal government.[11] Younger, often more militant activists were less inclined to see the value of reform. Representatives of the Philadelphia chapter of the Congress of Racial Equality (CORE) were initially willing to work with the city, but withdrew from the Mayor's Citizens Advisory Committee on Civil Rights in protest when the committee met to discuss police-community relations in the aftermath of the Philyaw shooting. CORE representative Edward Hollander called the committee a "tool of the white power structure." Younger civil rights activists already began distrusting liberal promises.[12]

Even more than CORE, the most militant reaction to the shooting of Willie Philyaw came from the recently elected president of the Philadelphia chapter of the National Association for the Advancement of Colored People (NAACP), Cecil B. Moore. Outspoken and brash—he often bragged about his heavy drinking and referred to himself as "the boss" of North Philadelphia— Moore's forceful rhetoric appealed to a growing segment of the community that began losing faith in working through traditional avenues of power. His more confrontational approach to the quest for racial equality found its most welcoming audience among younger black men. At the helm of the Philadelphia NAACP, Moore was often at odds with the civil rights moderates and the liberal establishment in Philadelphia. He was a constant critic of Mayor Tate and the Commission on Human Relations, but he saved his most biting critiques for the police. In time, Frank Rizzo became a frequent target. For

Moore, Willie Philyaw's death was further evidence of the harmful policies the police department foisted on North Philadelphia.[13]

When the police department suspended Officer Tourigan to conduct an internal investigation, the shooting and suspension elicited an entirely different reaction from Philadelphia's blue-collar neighborhoods. While African American residents were outraged at what they considered the lack of investigatory vigor, many blue-collar whites were outraged that the city performed any investigation at all. Letters of protest poured into the mayor's office.[14] Several accused the Tate administration of forcing the police department to conduct the investigation for political purposes or to appease the demands of civil rights leaders. One specifically charged Tate with investigating the shooting only "to gain the Negro vote in the next election" before asking how "can the Negro gain the respect he wants" when they "preach disrespect for the police of Philadelphia."[15] A woman from the Near Northeast, who quizzically signed her letter "A Phila. Democrat?" told the mayor that his campaign slogan should not be "A vote for Tate is a vote for Kennedy" but rather "A vote for Tate is a vote for Cecil Moore."[16] Another woman from Logan, an upper North Philadelphia neighborhood in the middle of a rapid racial turnover, asked what the other course of action anyone expected the white officer to take when attacked by an assailant with a knife. Her willingness to believe Tourigan's recollection of events rather than eyewitnesses illustrated blue-collar Philadelphians' faith in police officers and reflected the fact that policing in white, blue-collar neighborhoods rarely resembled policing in North Philadelphia. She also expressed a desire to keep policemen safe when she asked how people "expect[ed] men to risk their lives to protect the people of this City, if their superiors don't stand behind them in a crisis?" Like several other angry letter writers, she threatened to leave the Democratic Party if they continued "playing politics" with the police department.[17]

The white, blue-collar women that wrote to Mayor Tate assumed an important role in the cultural politics of law enforcement. Most people in the 1960s considered policing a "man's job" and the blue-collar veneration of police officers highlighted a special regard for masculine toughness. Women were not excluded from this cultural trait. Very few of them became police officers, but women exhibited their blue-collar toughness by assuming a protective role. The politicized culture of reverence for the police included blue-collar women's efforts to safeguard the police from external or political attack. In 1963, with an election just days away, the Tate administration did not take their letter-writing campaign lightly.

The mayor had built his earlier city council career on the support of white ethnic, blue-collar Philadelphians. Tate completed Richardson Dilworth's term in office when the reformer resigned to run for governor of Pennsylvania. In 1963, Tate sought to win his own mayoralty. As the first Irish Catholic mayor of Philadelphia, he knew that white ethnic Roman Catholics living in blue-collar neighborhoods still made up a significant majority of his political base. Tate turned to his blue-collar supporters to help him ward off a tough challenge from the reform wing of the local Democratic Party in the primary election. Tate also believed in finding political compromises, so he began making overtures to African American communities as well. His campaign rested on his ability to maintain a difficult balancing act between his white, blue-collar base and the African American communities that also made up Philadelphia's Democratic majority. His ability to do so helped him win a narrow victory over his Republican challenger.[18]

Tate made concessions to both segments of his shaky coalition after the election. When liberal Police Commissioner Howard Leary announced that the police department ruled the shooting of Willie Philyaw a justifiable homicide, Tate recommended a full reinstatement for John Tourigan. He also supported his police commissioner's decision to hold a series of meetings with civil rights and community leaders designed to dispel the negative reactions coming from the black community.[19] Tate then ordered a shake-up in the police department and announced the promotion of several new deputy commissioners. He first promoted Richard T. Edwards to deputy commissioner in charge of community relations, making him the first African American deputy commissioner in the Philadelphia Police Department. Edwards had a long record of working to build bridges between the police and the African American community, especially in North Philadelphia. His promotion was a sign that the city was willing to seriously consider establishing a better police-community relations program. In exchange, however, Tate named Frank Rizzo deputy commissioner in charge of uniformed officers.[20]

Rizzo had risen steadily through the ranks of the police department since 1943, when he followed his father's footsteps into police work at the age of twenty-three. His career trajectory was partly indebted to his work ethic, but doors opened along the way because of his father's connections and reputation. Starting out as a beat cop, Rizzo passed the civil service exam for sergeant in only eight years and earned a promotion to acting captain less than two months later. After serving as lieutenant in South Philadelphia's Thirty-Third Police District, Rizzo received his first command post in

West Philadelphia's Sixteenth District, where the area's predominantly African American residents began complaining about his policing shortly after his arrival. Within months Rizzo received a reassignment and promotion to command the Nineteenth District in Center City. On the way toward his promotion to deputy commissioner, Rizzo earned a reputation by taking on vice and illegal gambling, especially for cracking down on underground clubs and coffee houses that had become hotspots of the city's homosexual community in the 1950s.[21] Although he was little known outside the precincts he worked and commanded, Rizzo earned accolades from his superiors and esteem from those familiar with the city's law enforcement personnel. His tough approach to police work earned him the nickname "the Cisco Kid" after the popular television cowboy. Perhaps the greatest compliment paid to Rizzo during his ascent came from his fellow officers. He was widely known as a "cop's cop."[22] His promotion to deputy commissioner after the shooting of Willie Philyaw was a signal to his fellow blue-collar officers that the mayor was not going to bend toward the critics.

The reactions that followed the shooting of Willie Philyaw illustrated how racially and spatially distinct parts of the city developed different attitudes toward municipal institutions like the police department. The reorganization of urban space in the postwar era reinforced separate cultures. Civil rights activists and African American leaders viewed the police as the sum of its whole, as an institution with a record of damaging effects on their communities. As white police officers in predominantly black neighborhoods tended to see residents as potential criminals and viewed civil rights activism as a threat, residents came to fear and resent the police.[23] In addition to brutality and harassment, young black men in particular reported frequent detentions for unspecified offenses and unofficial practices like "turf dropping," where police would drive African American suspects into white neighborhoods and leave them there, outnumbered, to fend for themselves among the white youths. While turf dropping worked both ways—it was not an unheard-of punishment for white youths—it was primarily a means for police to flaunt their authority while simultaneously reinforcing the racial and spatial boundaries of segregated Philadelphia.[24] Practices like turf dropping reinforced the belief that police in African American neighborhoods were not there to protect the residents.

Like African American communities, blue-collar white neighborhoods viewed the police in ways indebted to the intense segregation in postwar Philadelphia. More frequently in white neighborhoods, police officers were

not simply "the police," but friends, neighbors, and family. In addition to bas-
ing their support for the police on the bonds of kin and community, moreover, they denied that any racialized deviation in police-community relations
existed in different parts of the city. They also refused to accept that police
brutality warranted significant changes in law enforcement policy because
police simply did not treat their communities the same way they treated African American neighborhoods. Few supporters of the Philadelphia police in
the 1960s ever experienced the police-community relations typical in African American neighborhoods, and the relative tranquility of their neighborhoods reinforced their faith in and trust of police officers. Defenders of the
police further accused those who drew attention to a racialized system of
law enforcement of artificially invoking race, and those who attempted to
redress these inequities of playing politics with the police department—a city
agency they felt should rise above the compromises and petty deal-making of
municipal politics.

Some of the most forceful defenses of the police and denunciations
of their detractors came out of the largest and most segregated section of
the city, Northeast Philadelphia. In addition to the more upwardly mobile
working- and middle-class whites that jumped at the chance to purchase the
recently built homes in neighborhoods like Morrell Park, a large percentage
of the Northeast's new residents were police officers. Official police department policy and local ordinances encouraged blue flight to the Northeast.
The department prohibited any officer below the rank of captain from living
in the communities they policed. Although the policy ran counter to modern
law enforcement theories that suggested police-community relations would
be improved by increasing intimate relations between officers and the areas
they policed, the department thought daily close contact with neighbors and
friends would diminish an officer's ability to do their duty.[25] While the Northeast was larger than any other part of the city, it also had fewer police districts,
so fewer officers were barred from living in the area. As well, a city ordinance
dictated that all city employees, including police officers, had to live within
the city limits. As they were kept from living in the communities they policed
and prohibited from moving to the suburbs, purchasing a home in Northeast
Philadelphia was the closest white police officers could come to the middle-
class American dream without leaving police work behind. The police officers
that relocated and became members of their new communities developed
many of the relationships that became the basis of the culture of reverence
for the police.[26]

Assuming its self-appointed role as the voice of the Greater Northeast in the early 1960s, the *Northeast Times* began defending police against accusations of police brutality made by "the Negro Press." In a reference to the *Philadelphia Tribune*, the largest African American newspaper in the city and a frequent critic of the police department, the *Northeast Times* editorial pages attacked the other newspaper for crying brutality in the case of another white officer acquitted in the shooting death of a North Philadelphia bystander. Drawing on the blue-collar veneration of "hard work," the *Times* editorial board defended the officers by explaining the difficulty of police work. "These men are constantly being called upon to face death and injury and nobody thinks much about it," the paper said. "It's their job."[27] In another editorial defending the police against charges of police brutality, the paper said that "the job of a policeman is to maintain order on his beat and to prevent criminals from molesting decent citizens. The policeman should be free to beat up a hoodlum with a night-stick and to shoot to kill, if necessary." Much as the *Northeast Times* had done when defending freedom of association in housing, they denied race should be a factor in community policing. Instead, the editorial board claimed that the real problem was the "general tendency to drag the Negro question into all discussions on any subject."[28] In addition to trivializing the concerns of African Americans, the *Northeast Times* became an early adopter of a discourse that invoked the difficulty of police work as a pretext for potentially extralegal behavior.

While the *Northeast Times* voiced the concerns of a growing portion of Northeast Philadelphia residents, community organizations rallied behind their friends on the police force. In June 1963, the Northeast Federation of Community Councils (NFCC) gathered area leaders to draft a resolution encouraging the state legislature to pass a pending bill that would make an attack on a police officer a felony. The bill sat before the legislature because of the efforts of Philadelphia highway patrolman and president of the State Fraternal Order of Police, John J. Harrington. The NFCC responded to Harrington's request that sympathetic citizens support the bill. When the Pennsylvania legislature passed it, the new law provided an early victory for defenders of the police and provided John J. Harrington with a valuable lesson. Even with the new law, however, the NFCC still worried about protecting police officers in the line of duty. In a letter to the mayor, community representative Patrick Geraghty said he was distressed to learn that several police officers had been injured in a skirmish with "integration demonstrators" at a school construction site because they were under orders not to carry clubs or guns for their own defense.[29] The rumor was false. Stories of unarmed police officers in dangerous situations were a common misconception.[30] The NFCC, more importantly, was part of a growing faction of white Philadelphians putting pressure on the city to protect the police. It signaled more than respect for the law. It was in this protectionist impulse for culturally similar police officers that the politics of law and order found their most powerful grassroots proponents.

The rising voices to protect and respect the hard work of police officers in Northeast Philadelphia did not acknowledge the reality of policing in other parts of the city. Years of poor relations between the community and the police in predominantly African American areas like North Philadelphia created a culture that viewed police officers less like protectors and more like enforcers of a white power structure. It was a sentiment not limited to Philadelphia. In 1965, Senator Robert Kennedy told *Time* magazine that "there [was] no point in telling Negroes to obey the law. To many Negroes the law is the enemy."[31] Civil rights leaders still viewed the police as an institution that could be changed, however. In addition to equal job and housing opportunities, Philadelphia's civil rights community aimed their efforts at changing local law enforcement policy. Those efforts received a renewed urgency after Willie Philyaw's murder.

African American community leaders wanted to ease the tensions that created poor police-community relations, but they were cognizant of the debilitating impact crime had on their neighborhoods. Those who were more likely to live with the threat of crime demanded effective law enforcement as forcefully as white supporters of the police, but they also wanted the police to treat innocent residents with dignity and respect. The West Philadelphia–based Philadelphia Council for Community Advancement (PCCA) made those twin goals clear in 1963. The PCCA presented the city with a plan for a model police district and community education program for North Philadelphia. Hoping to prove that proper police education and training could produce better relations with the black community, the PCCA wanted to make officers familiar with the communities they served.[32] They wanted officers educated in criminal and constitutional law. To open avenues of communication between the police and the community, the PCCA proposed that officers visit schoolchildren in their classrooms, make use of free television and radio services, and meet with parents to encourage active discussions about youth and crime. The model police district also included plans to have PCCA staff help communities find legal services in cases of police abuse. The PCCA hoped reforming the police department and educating local residents would effectively address the problem of police-community relations in North Philadelphia.[33]

Other organizations proposed similar plans. The North City Congress (NCC) and CORE formed a joint committee to deal with youth gangs and juvenile delinquency. CORE even brokered a truce between the major North Philadelphia gangs.[34] In response, the Tate administration began plans to create a Citizens Advisory Committee on Youth that would include both organizations. Police Commissioner Howard Leary accepted a proposal issued by Cecil B. Moore to station NAACP lawyers in North Philadelphia police precincts to oversee arrest procedures and protect the civil rights of the accused. In response, Moore called Commissioner Leary "the most enlightened police man in America."[35] On the eve of the Columbia Avenue Riot, community leaders and civil rights activists believed that a new era of policing based in common understanding and civilian oversight was not only possible, but forthcoming.

Their enthusiasm was short lived. Howard Leary's cooperation with community leaders formed the basis of his law enforcement liberalism and held out the promise of real reform to police procedure. But faith in his liberal approach to law enforcement was not widespread. The Fraternal Order of Police and their white, blue-collar allies opposed reforms to local law enforcement policy. They feared liberal law enforcement policies would endanger their neighborhoods and put rank-and-file officers at risk. Their efforts to safeguard the police found renewed traction after August 1964, when Howard Leary's modest law enforcement liberalism seemed to imperil officers in the line of duty.

Riot and Response

Late at night on August 29, 1964, deep into the second day of the Columbia Avenue Riot, the *Philadelphia Inquirer* received an anonymous telephone call from someone identified only as "a beleaguered city police sergeant." Claiming to have been working the riot area, the officer called the newspaper to explain how the city had restricted the police from controlling the situation. "His embittered statement reflects the feeling of many policemen trying to fight a 'war' under extraordinary circumstances," the *Inquirer* editorialized before printing a transcript of the officer's report. The sergeant told the newspaper that patrolmen received orders not to use their pistols and that their

nightsticks were to be their only weapons. He complained that the procedures in place had put area businesses and police officers in danger. "We try
to defend citizens and their property and even our own men," he explained,
"yet we have nothing to help ourselves." Without identifying him directly, he
clearly implied that Howard Leary's riot control plan prevented the police
from restoring order. He added that he had been a police officer for fifteen
years, but stated that "If I knew of a better way to make a living, I'd leave
the force—and I'm not the only cop that feels this way." Concluding with a
statement that simultaneously reflected the growing resentment to the liberalization of law enforcement and questioned the strictures placed on police,
he asked, "If they want us to do a job why do they tie our hands?"[36]

The unidentified police officer offered a critique of local law enforcement
policy that reached well beyond the city's uniformed forces. Many white,
blue-collar Philadelphians already expressed fears that police were woefully
ill prepared for the job they had to do on a regular basis, let alone a full-scale
riot. His anonymous testimony of the limitations placed on police in North
Philadelphia framed their debate over the proper way to deal with crime and
civil disorder. Similar complaints from police officers and their blue-collar
allies led to the advocacy of unfettered police action in the face of disorder
and harsher penalties for criminal behavior.

Their complaints and advocacy notwithstanding, the police kept the
Columbia Avenue Riot relatively short, fairly well contained, and less cata-
strophic than the rebellions that struck other American cities in the 1960s.
Civic leaders from nearly all quarters commended the police department's
work. Liberals and civil rights and religious leaders heaped praise on the
mayor for the way the police handled the disturbance.[37] Even James Williams,
chair of the Philadelphia CORE and a critic of the police department, com-
plimented the police for containing it to a small area. Attempting to make the
best of the situation, Williams hoped that "a new police-ghetto relationship"
could start in the wake of the uprising.[38] Community and civil rights leaders
joined liberals in pointing to the city's ability to quickly control the riot with
limited loss of life and property damage as proof that the system that they
had helped put in place functioned properly. Together they hoped to foster
something positive in the aftermath of tragedy.[39]

While praise for the ways the police handled the riot was widespread
among white liberals, other civil rights leaders expressed different views of
its causes and management. Cecil B. Moore drew attention to the poverty
in the area and blamed the police for creating a volatile situation through

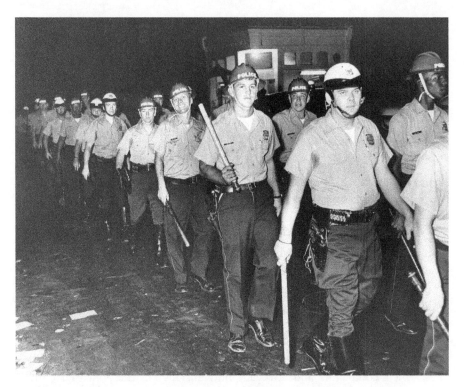

Figure 4. Police get in line and prepare to contain the Columbia Avenue Riot, 1964. Courtesy of Special Collections Research Center, Temple University, Philadelphia, PA.

years of abuse in black communities. Issuing a statement saying that police acted with "vindictive racial bigotry," he insisted that they only acted with self-discipline because they were so greatly outnumbered.[40] Moore's criticism found a receptive audience among residents that had long ago learned to distrust the police, and he became a symbol for a larger shift in civil rights activism. But he also became a target for those that believed the city capitulated to militants, especially among Columbia Avenue business owners.

While many residents that inhabited the space in the immediate riot area praised the restraint shown by police, several business owners felt they had not done enough to protect their property. The largely Jewish shopkeepers that owned the looted store fronts along Columbia Avenue were the first civilians to express concerns over the riot control plan. They felt targeted because of their faith and ethnicity.[41] Although interviews with area residents suggested that the rioters' motivations were more antiwhite than specifically anti-Semitic, the merchants were not entirely wrong. Anger toward them stemmed from the fact that they owned businesses in the community without residing in it. Residents believed that store owners overcharged and exploited African American customers.[42] As a result, the only shop fronts that remained untouched after the riot were those that displayed signs declaring black ownership. Police touring the area found one undamaged toy store with a sign proclaiming "This is a Negro business." An undamaged delicatessen carried a sign reading "This is a colored place." Although the rioters did not spare all black-owned businesses—a taproom and an unoccupied building were damaged—those clearly identified as African American–owned fared better than white-owned businesses.[43]

Area business owners remained worried about the area's police protection months after the uprising.[44] The police department had assigned two patrolmen to each square block in the weeks immediately following the riot, but in December 1964, Columbia Avenue Business Men's Association (CABMA) representative Sydney Orlofsky demanded more. Although they requested specially trained police officers that would not exacerbate residual tensions, they still wanted police to make more arrests for anything resembling criminal behavior. The CABMA merchants especially wanted police to disperse large groups at street corners, taprooms, and pool halls. They also expressed concerns about community ill will toward the police and their businesses. Orlofsky suggested distributing posters throughout the neighborhood promoting respect for the police. They also told police about a number of barroom tabloid newsletters that allegedly fostered animosity toward the merchants.[45]

The CABMA insisted on a more stringent law enforcement system that would reinforce restrictions on the space accessible to the neighborhood's African American residents. They saw the solution to the area's problems in an increased police presence and stricter punishment for offenders. Liberal Jewish activists were concerned about some of their suggestions. Organizations like the city's Anti-Defamation League, Fellowship Commission, Jewish Labor Committee, and Jewish Community Relations Council (JCRC) were at the forefront of Philadelphia's liberal–civil rights alliance. Jewish liberals had spent years cultivating relationships with African American leaders and working for civil rights initiatives, including reforms in law enforcement policy. North Philadelphia's Jewish merchants caused them to question how the uprising would affect Black-Jewish relations, a bond they believed essential to progressive politics in the city.[46] In addition to merchants that feared the police had not done enough to quell the disturbance in a timely manner, they heard from some that suggested that the police should have used dogs, fire hoses, tear gas, and gunfire to stop the rioting. Although the JCRC determined that poverty, joblessness, and housing conditions were the root causes of the uprising, they also concluded that the resentment and potential for overt hostility would continue until they found a way to dispel the distrust coming from both sides.[47]

While liberals like those in the JCRC condemned the riot, they also saw it as an opportunity to initiate educational and job training programs designed to alleviate poverty.[48] To a growing number of Philadelphians, however, the liberal prescriptions for alleviating the conditions in North Philadelphia sounded too much like rewarding criminals. Kowtowing to the rioters would not ease community tensions, they said. Only stiffer penalties for criminals and an abandonment of law enforcement liberalism had the ability to confront the urban crisis. Joined by increasingly vocal supporters of the police, they hastened the rise of law-and-order politics.[49]

Department policy forbade police offers from expressing their own dissatisfaction with the handling of the uprising. Those that did, like the "beleaguered city police sergeant" that telephoned the *Philadelphia Inquirer*, did so anonymously. Even the usually outspoken Frank Rizzo kept his criticisms quiet until years later. As deputy commissioner in charge of the uniformed division, Rizzo had the ear of the department's rank and file. He and the police on the ground were especially angered by the orders not to stop the vandalism or use their weapons unless directly threatened. The dispute opened a rift between Rizzo and Howard Leary that never healed.[50] With police officers' criticisms anonymous or quieted, others emerged to defend them. Overwhelmingly, these defenses repeated the criticism that the city and Commissioner Leary had "tied the hands" of police officers. The two main sources of this defensiveness were the Fraternal Order of Police and their allies in the city's white, blue-collar neighborhoods.

The FOP was one of the only means of public redress and protest available to police officers. Yet, early on, few officers viewed the organization as anything more than "something you just do." White rank-and-file officers questioned the FOP's effectiveness and admitted that they maintained their memberships to attend social functions or the meeting hall's taproom. The FOP also had a reputation as being "all white." Even when they joined the organization, African American police officers reported that they rarely used the meeting hall and felt unwelcome at social gatherings.[51] Shortly after the

Columbia Avenue Riot, however, the organization shifted focus in ways that made white, blue-collar officers reconsider the effectiveness of police unionization. FOP president John J. Harrington originally praised the city's action and publicly thanked the Tate administration for its leadership during the riot, but quickly changed his tune. Only recently elected to the FOP presidency, Harrington became one of the most vocal critics of law enforcement liberalism and a cheerleader for the return to law and order. In addition to criticizing efforts to restrict police action, he also rejected liberal assertions that pointed to ghetto conditions in North Philadelphia as a cause of the uprising. Issuing a press release just days after the calm returned to Columbia Avenue, Harrington said it was not poverty, lack of opportunity, or poor police-community relations that led to the rioting. Instead, he insisted that "the main reason for this tragedy was the utter lack of respect for the police and the laws they must enforce."[52] Harrington helped turn the FOP from a social organization and an obligation to an advocacy union working for the interests of the city's uniformed officers.

A "typical Irish cop," as his fellow officers called him, John J. Harrington was a sergeant in Highway Patrol and resident of blue-collar South Philadelphia. Like so many other Philadelphia police officers, Harrington's path into police work was a family tradition. His father was a retired patrolman, his uncle a sergeant, and his brother a lieutenant. Equally opposed to all "anti-American" protests and disruptions—from civil rights to the Vietnam War—Harrington claimed to give voice to the police officers that could not publicly challenge their superiors.[53] After serving as the president of the Pennsylvania FOP, the twenty-four-year veteran ran for president of Philadelphia's FOP Lodge 5 in March 1964. Harrington pointed to his record as head of the Pennsylvania State FOP, where he used his position to press for legislation granting law enforcement officers additional benefits and protections. As a labor leader, Harrington ran his campaign for the Lodge 5 presidency on the principle of collective bargaining and the promise to negotiate a lower retirement age and wage increases. As a representative of an increasingly frustrated police force, Harrington promised to rebuild respect for law enforcement officers in Philadelphia.[54] He said he wanted a new image for the Philadelphia police, one that would put their officers on a par with internationally known police forces like Canadian Mounties, Scotland Yard, and the Federal Bureau of Investigation. "We're just as good, but nobody knows about us," he told a rally of supporters. His boasting was unrealistic, but as he reiterated throughout his campaign, building "respect for the policeman" was his greatest goal.[55] With a margin of victory of 2,340 to 1,426, Harrington clearly tapped into a deep well of discontent among the city's uniformed officers. As a vocal and politically active police officer, furthermore, Harrington paved the way for Frank Rizzo's shift from law enforcement to politics. Within a few years Harrington also became an early champion of Rizzo's law enforcement conservatism as an alternative to Howard Leary's law enforcement liberalism.

Harrington used the media in a manner unlike any of his predecessors. Although the press often quoted him in an effort to embarrass and expose the politicization of the police department, his over-the-top statements found an audience among rank-and-file police officers and blue-collar Philadelphians alike.[56] Outspoken and energetic, Harrington also suggested that police officers explain the difficulty of their jobs and their need for greater support to their civilian friends, family, and neighbors. His call to renew respect for police officers became one of the most oft-repeated elements of the city's law-and-order campaigns. Harrington's demand for a more vigorous support of the police department, a less "permissive" criminal code, and harsher punishments for criminals found a welcoming audience among those who identified and sympathized with the city's blue-collar police force.[57]

After Harrington and the FOP, the most passionate denunciations of the Columbia Avenue Riot came from the city's white, blue-collar neighborhoods. Many suggested that the police should have responded to the violence with an equal show of their own violence. Some spoke about their fear that the riots threatened their own homes. "Not only were we worried the riot might spread," wrote one woman, "but we were also aware of the fact that the police were standing by watching the colored steal." Condemning Commissioner Leary's plan to contain the riot without stopping the looting and vandalism, she asked "What would happen to me if I were to break into a store, steal merchandise and run when the police told me to stop?" She was confident that the police would have shot at her. As did other respondents, she also spoke as if personally victimized by the restrictions placed on police during the riot.[58] Another woman from the Near Northeast told the mayor that policemen should not have to stand by and watch such vandalism, unable to perform their duty. She also expressed a growing feeling that the Tate administration and the police department bent to the whims of civil rights activists. "If those rioters had been quelled and rioters arrested in the beginning without the thoughts of consequences coming from the NAACP or CORE, we may not have witnessed the other two nights of vandalism, lawlessness and downright disregard for the law," she said. "Civil rights makes it possible for all to receive a fair chance," she added. "But it certainly does not allow for or permit people to take the law into their own hands and knowingly abuse and break it."[59] The two blue-collar women assumed their dual roles as defenders and protectors of the police. They both made a point to denounce new programs to support the poverty-stricken area around Columbia Avenue. Like John Harrington, their solution was greater respect for law and order.

The belief among blue-collar whites that Commissioner Leary forbade police to use their weapons in order to appease civil rights activists was part of the widespread misinformation that emerged in the wake of the uprising. Many false rumors also claimed that the police department intentionally sent officers into the riot area unprepared and unable to control the rioting. City and law enforcement officials pointed out that the rumors stemmed from misconceptions regarding common police procedures. Despite efforts to curtail the rumors, the belief that Leary prevented the police from restoring order contributed to a wider belief that law enforcement liberalism made the city unsafe.[60] When *U.S. News & World Report* ran a story about the Columbia Avenue Riot in September 1964 and reprinted the complaint made in the *Philadelphia Inquirer*, a deluge of angry letters from across the country flooded Mayor James Tate's office. Several of them accused James Tate and Howard Leary of "tying the hands" of the police.[61] Soon thereafter, supporters of Republican presidential candidate Barry Goldwater included the unidentified patrolman's testimony in their racially charged campaign film "Choice." The national news coverage and Goldwater campaign film linked critics of Leary's law enforcement liberalism to a broader conservative campaign that blamed President Lyndon Johnson's Great Society for spiking crime rates in the mid-1960s.[62] In fact, Johnson responded to the uprising in Harlem by saying that the overriding issue was the preservation of law and order. Over the next few years, the president initiated a series of programs designed to bring federal aid to urban police departments under the rubric of his War on Crime. It soon became clear that both liberals and conservatives agreed that the solution to urban unrest was stricter policing.[63] By the end of 1964, James Tate buckled under the pressure. In response to the complaints that the police did not handle the Columbia Avenue Riot with enough force, his administration made a full turn toward the politics of law and order.

After the Columbia Avenue Riot, clear lines emerged between the advocates of law enforcement liberalism and police department reform and those that favored law-and-order conservatism. Civil rights leaders, militant and moderate alike, joined liberals in an attempt to thwart the police department's shift in law enforcement policy. On the other side of the divide, the Fraternal Order of Police led a broader blue-collar effort that demanded stricter law enforcement and greater protection for police officers. Their new target was a city agency created during Philadelphia's reform era for the explicit purpose of providing civilian oversight of the police and giving citizens a means of redress for allegations of police misconduct, the Police Advisory Board. Among FOP leadership and blue-collar whites, it was the most hated agency in Philadelphia law enforcement. The fight for the survival of the Police Advisory Board ultimately led to the abandonment of law enforcement liberalism and the primacy of law and order.

The Fraternal Order of Police and the Police Advisory Board

"Second Class Citizens," screamed the front page of the March–April 1965 issue of the *Peace Officer*, the Philadelphia Fraternal Order of Police Lodge 5's official newsletter. "It is amazing in this era of Civil Rights," it began, "that our citizens and City officials fail to recognize the plight of the Policeman in this regard." The *Peace Officer* compared the struggles of police officers to the ongoing civil rights movement. Appropriating equal rights discourse, the article cited the denial of the right to strike as evidence of the "shackles" on the "Civil Rights of Policemen." While the article recognized the public safety issues involved with a police labor strike, it argued that police officers needed a better means to collectively bargain for higher wages. More importantly, it claimed the lack of an appeals process for complaints against the police enraged officers and threatened their safety. Citizens of Philadelphia had a means to bring complaints against the police in the Police Advisory Board. Police, the article cried, had no such appeals process. Asking what the citizens of Philadelphia would think if they knew about the "rights denied to Policemen," the *Peace Officer* closed by reassuring the FOP that "President Harrington is not taking it sitting down" and that he "is taking the fight for the rights of the policemen directly to the public by means of every media publicity."[64]

Established during the city's reform era, the Police Advisory Board (PAB) was the culmination of years of effort by organizations like the Fellowship Commission's Committee on Community Tensions and the Philadelphia Chapter of the American Civil Liberties Union. These organizations that wanted civilian oversight of police procedures and a means to redress accusations of police brutality found an ally in Richardson Dilworth, who thought the board would curtail police corruption as well. When Dilworth founded the originally named Police Review Board by executive order in 1958, it became the first agency for civilian review of a municipal police department in the United States. Given the responsibility to investigate, hear, and determine the validity of charges of misconduct against police officers, the board worked with the police commissioner and other city officials in an attempt to create an effective city policy against police misconduct.[65] Like many of the initiatives that grew out of the reform era, however, the PAB reflected the faith liberals had in their ability to address the city's problems while showcasing their failure to fully provide the means to solve them.

The board defined misconduct broadly, including accusations of mistreatment, abusive language, false arrest, unwarranted use of force, unreasonable search and seizure, as well as the denial of civil rights or discrimination because of race, religion, or national origin. Board members had limited authority, however. They could hear citizens' complaints against the police and recommend nonbinding disciplinary action to the police commissioner, but they had no authority to enforce their decisions.[66] As a result, the PAB never fully satisfied civil rights activists that wanted an agency with the authority to prosecute police misbehavior. Furthermore, the PAB rarely ruled against police officers. In the seven hundred cases brought before the PAB between its founding in 1958 and its suspension of activities in 1966, when the FOP filed a lawsuit against it, the board only recommended disciplinary action against twenty-four officers.[67] Sociologists Joseph D. Lohman and Gordon E. Misner further doused enthusiasm for the board. They brought national attention to the PAB in 1966 when they focused on Philadelphia's continued police-community relations problems in their two-volume report for the President's Commission on Law Enforcement and Administration of Justice. Confirming the fears of civilian review proponents nationwide, they called the PAB underused and ineffectual. Lohman and Misner concluded that budget cuts and a lack of advertising limited the PAB's efficacy. Their full report called attention to the limitations of liberal law enforcement reforms not only in Philadelphia, but throughout urban America.[68]

Despite criticisms, liberals lauded the board for its potential to provide a needed safeguard for the innocently accused. They also defended the principle of civilian review by claiming it would protect police officers by reducing the number of unfounded charges made against the force. Early on, the PAB won widespread support. Mayor Tate said the agency served an important function to protect both police and the public. Police Commissioner Howard Leary likewise approved of the board. He worked closely with its members and argued that it promoted the kind of good police-community relations that were the centerpiece of his law enforcement liberalism. Members of the PAB pointed to Philadelphia's comparatively low crime rate as evidence that it served its function well. Beyond Philadelphia, the PAB became a model for similar civilian review boards in Rochester, New York, and New York City. Liberals and civil libertarians across the country pointed to the city's adoption of the board as an ideal means for improving police-community relations in heavily African American areas.[69]

While the framers of the PAB intended it to serve as a means of public redress for all Philadelphians, African Americans and civil rights leaders used the board most frequently. NAACP lawyers handled the first case ever brought before the Police Review Board as well as the first that resulted in disciplinary action against a police officer.[70] While they recognized the board's shortcomings, civil rights activists still defended it vigorously. African Americans especially worried about police brutality and misconduct. Responding to the complaints they heard from constituents, a special committee of the local NAACP delivered an impassioned plea elucidating the need for a civilian review process along with a list of illustrative cases of police abuses they handled on a regular basis. In one, two black teenagers reported that police arrested, detained, and beat them without pressing any formal charges against them. Two others charged police officers with hospitalizing them for minor transgressions. One light-skinned woman reported that two patrolmen stopped her and asked what she was doing in a "colored neighborhood." The officers detained her and charged her with intoxication without testing whether or not she even had one drink. As the NAACP explained, many suspects went uncharged of any crime. Others were guilty of minor traffic violations, public drunkenness, or alleged trespassing. Most of them committed no crime beyond a breach of the unwritten laws protecting the city's unofficial spatial boundaries. The NAACP wanted stiffer penalties for officers found guilty of these abuses, arrest records destroyed in cases of improper arrest, as well as officers trained in dealing with diverse citizens. They said a stronger Police Advisory Board was the only agency capable of making sure the police could not act with impunity.[71]

While the most forceful defenses of the PAB came from civil rights activists, they were not alone in supporting the civilian review process. Others pointed out that in addition to curbing police abuses, civilian review could also protect police departments from the widespread perception of police corruption. In June 1965, Lyndon Johnson's attorney general and Philadelphia native Nicholas Katzenbach explained the necessity of civilian review to an interviewer from *Look* magazine. He specifically mentioned Philadelphia as a city that needed such an agency. "The public's faith in the integrity of local law enforcement must also be built up," he said. Unlike others that made similar claims, however, Katzenbach did not point to a general decline in respect for authority. Instead, he worried about how the perception of corruption affected the image of local police departments. He said civilian review and oversight ensured the integrity of the local police system, especially in places like Philadelphia, where he said "half the people [in the police department] are on the take." After a public outcry over his accusation, Katzenbach clarified that he did not think half of Philadelphia police officers were corrupt, but that a civilian review process could alleviate perceptions that corruption was widespread.[72] Like many liberals across the country, Katzenbach viewed civilian review as a means both to monitor and to protect the police.

In spite of its widespread support, limited authority, and record of restraint, the Police Advisory Board remained a controversial agency. Police officers worried that criminals could abuse the board and the FOP soon emerged as its biggest critic. Early 1960s FOP president Maurice O'Leary expressed the feelings of many police officers when he simply said civilians should not have the right to judge policemen.[73] When his boisterous, media-savvy successor John J. Harrington ran for the FOP presidency, he made opposition to the PAB a centerpiece of his platform. Determined to take the fight against the board beyond the FOP meeting hall, Harrington asked sympathetic civilians to support the police and pressure the city to disband the PAB. "The whole idea of the Advisory Board will tend to have a demoralizing effect upon our policemen, who are trying to protect the law-abiding citizen," wrote one Northeast Philadelphia resident. His words neatly echoed those of Harrington and other FOP officials. "There is no widespread brutality, discrimination, etc., by our police force to warrant such a committee," he continued. Like many residents of the Northeast and other white, blue-collar neighborhoods, he denied that police misconduct was a problem worthy of systemic reform.[74]

By July 1964, John Harrington began accusing the PAB of encouraging the harassment of police, depleting the FOP treasury because of the officers it represented legally, and depriving the public of police protection. Criticizing the board's "stepped-up program of trials against policemen," Harrington further said that the PAB hampered morale on the force and made it more difficult for officers to do an already difficult job. He also charged that the board put police officers in "triple jeopardy" because criminal charges against a police officer would mean a trial before a magistrate, action by the police department's internal trial board, as well as an appearance before the PAB. Harrington never addressed the concerns of those that worried about trusting the department to discipline its own. Instead, he relied on the alleged psychological effects the board had on the men on the force. He further played on the already prevalent fear of crime he helped foster by suggesting that the PAB robbed citizens of police protection.[75]

By the mid-1960s, the campaign against the civilian review process had gained momentum in other cities and the support of high-profile national figures. Following the release of a report on the 1964 urban riots, Federal Bureau of Investigation (FBI) Director J. Edgar Hoover blamed civilian review boards for "pillorying" policemen. By 1966, New York City's civilian review board was under attack from the city's Patrolmen's Benevolent Association.[76] Hoover and the Patrolmen's Benevolent Association blamed civilian review for hindering the police response to riots and worsening the lawlessness of the urban crisis. In Philadelphia, John Harrington said the Police Advisory Board had become "a sounding board for those who would flout law and order" and blamed a lack of respect for the police for causing the urban uprisings.[77] Marking the termination of his first year as FOP president, however, Harrington was happy to report that the PAB was barely functioning because citizens had voiced their resentment against it. Because of their collective action, he said, the FOP had "instilled a little back bone" in policemen, so that "when he makes an arrest he does so with confidence that he has done the right thing and will be backed by the Lodge and the Police Department and does not need an attorney for himself when he stands the defendants before a Magistrate or Court."[78]

In August 1965, Harrington took his police force advocacy nationwide. The Philadelphia Lodge 5 brought the largest delegation to the national organization's convention in Pittsburgh, where John Harrington sought the presidency of the national FOP. He secured an upset victory by only twenty-nine votes. During his acceptance speech, however, Harrington won over the rest of the FOP members in attendance. He praised Los Angeles police chief William H. Parker for his handling of the rioting in Watts, calling him "one of the greatest police administrators in the world." He also championed the use of more forceful police procedures, including the use of more police dogs in confrontations with civil rights protestors.[79] Harrington's forceful rhetoric won him the admiration of law enforcement personnel nationwide and a broader platform for his law-and-order politics. In Philadelphia, his growing clout gave him leverage against the Police Advisory Board and the Tate administration.

James Tate initially responded to Harrington's criticisms of the PAB by repeating the liberal argument that it equally protected uniformed personnel against accusations of brutality. He once pointed out, for example, that in the year since its founding, the board threw out far more charges against the police than it recommended for disciplinary action. As he often did with controversial issues, Tate tried to find a middle ground in the PAB dispute. But John Harrington's campaign soon became too strong to mediate and the mayor could no longer afford to be on the wrong side of the newly powerful and influential FOP president. For Tate, making concessions to Harrington became an absolute necessity as he began eyeing reelection. He knew that if he stood a chance he needed to secure his base of white, blue-collar supporters. Tate tried to appease the FOP by appointing two retired police officers to the PAB, but none of his efforts at reaching a compromise satisfied his critics.[80] Unable to placate the FOP and their allies, Tate's support for the Police Advisory Board steadily dwindled.

Tate was not alone in his shrinking defense of the PAB and the process of civilian review. By the mid-1960s, the other two civilian review boards in urban America were facing similar attacks. The campaigns against the PAB and the boards in Rochester and New York were part of a larger reaction to the philosophy of civilian review and law enforcement liberalism. Early in 1966, after a court ruling invalidated the Rochester board, PAB chair Mercer Tate (no relation to the mayor) called the ruling evidence that "the full force of conservative police thinking throughout the entire United States is now directed against the Philadelphia Board."[81] Then, just as the tide of public opinion and political support was turning against the civilian review process, the PAB lost one of its last voices of support from within the police department. In 1966, Police Commissioner Howard Leary accepted an offer to take over the top position in the New York Police Department.[82]

Support for the PAB dwindled and Harrington recognized that the pendulum was swinging away from law enforcement liberalism. Even so, he continued to lay all the problems facing the police department at the feet of the Police Advisory Board. Morale was at an all-time low and the department was having trouble recruiting new officers because of the board's restrictive policies, he said. Policemen felt "handcuffed" by the board. In a reversal of the accusations usually leveled at the police, he said, "Minority groups don't fear arrest. They spit and curse officers and refuse to obey laws because they know policemen can't arrest them. In some instances, they strike policemen, knowing the officers won't strike back for fear of being charged with brutality."[83] His harsh rhetoric clearly reflected the feelings of white, rank-and-file officers. In April 1966, he easily won reelection to the local FOP presidency by a nearly three-to-one majority. For Harrington, the reelection was a mandate to continue his effort to abolish the Police Advisory Board locally, and the entire process of civilian review nationally. Emboldened by his victory, the already outspoken Harrington went on the offensive in the press and at various speaking engagements around the country.[84]

In July, while serving as president of the local and national FOP, John Harrington retired from the Philadelphia Police Department in protest. He said he was "fed up" because "you can't do police work anymore." In addition to the problems with the PAB, Harrington cited recent Supreme Court decisions—like *Miranda v. Arizona*—that "shackle" police as reasons for his retirement.[85] While Harrington was the only high-profile police officer to actually resign his position, others in the FOP made similar threats. Testifying against the PAB, Philadelphia FOP secretary Virgil Penn said it was humiliating for policemen to face charges from people with criminal records. Penn claimed he forbade his sons from joining the police force because of the board's actions, threatening to end a long-honored blue-collar tradition of sons following their fathers into police work.[86] Harrington's public resignation and the threat that others would follow suit drew even more attention to his crusade against the PAB.

The political grandstanding surrounding Harrington's public resignation notwithstanding, retiring also allowed him to continue his speaking engagements and concentrate on the court case the FOP had filed against the PAB. Harrington told a New Jersey FOP convention that civilian review boards were following in the footsteps of fascist dictators. "Hitler destroyed the police power in Germany," he said. "Mussolini did the same."[87] A month later, while testifying against the PAB in court, he made a similarly erroneous claim that police officers only stopped the rioting on Columbia Avenue after receiving assurances that the PAB would not investigate their behavior. Using his own resignation as evidence, he said that the PAB made police officers second-guess themselves and hesitate in life-or-death situations. That, he claimed, was the reason he quit the force. He then drew a comparison to Rochester, New York, the only other municipality with a citizen's advisory board in 1964 and also the city behind Philadelphia with the second worst rioting that year.[88]

Invoking the public's fear of urban rioting, Harrington cleverly but deceptively linked the city's civilian review process with the loss of personal safety and the worsening urban crisis. Harrington's claims that the PAB emboldened criminals, however, were not borne out by the facts. The police department's own FBI-based report on "Crime in the Nation" listed Philadelphia as the major American city with the lowest rate of crime in the country. While, nationwide, crime was on the increase, the percentage of homicides, robberies, aggravated assaults, burglaries, and auto theft actually went down in Philadelphia.[89] Liberals saw the city's comparably lower crime rates and concluded that the PAB was an effective organization and that Leary's law enforcement liberalism worked. Reflecting on the department's findings, PAB chair Mercer Tate called Harrington a "demagogue of the first order with no regard for the truth" who rode to national prominence "on a platform of imaginary and inflammatory fear."[90] He also contradicted Harrington's testimony about the Columbia Avenue Riot, explaining that no city official told Harrington the police would not face investigation for their behavior.[91] Neither Mercer Tate's defense of the PAB nor Philadelphia's crime rate mattered. Harrington's tough talk found a receptive audience in blue-collar Philadelphia. He had won in the court of public opinion and he was beginning to win the FOP's court case against the Police Advisory Board.

Liberals, civil rights leaders, and civil libertarians tried to save the PAB, but their testimonies failed. In March 1967, Judge Leo Weinrott declared the police department had the right to discipline its own officers and that the FOP had brought forth ample evidence that the board impaired police work and lowered morale on the force. He ruled Richardson Dilworth's executive order creating the PAB violated the city charter.[92] Advocates of civilian review hoped to convince Mayor Tate to work for a new board, but by 1967 Tate recognized that his greatest political strength lay with John Harrington and the blue-collar Philadelphians that demanded he stand behind police. The mayor made a similarly calculated decision when he promoted Frank Rizzo to acting police commissioner in the middle of his campaign for reelection.[93] The following November, shortly after Tate won reelection in a campaign that largely turned on questions of law and order and included his campaign promise to retain Rizzo as police commissioner, the mayor finally declared that the city would not make any effort to save the Police Advisory Board. Echoing John Harrington, Tate said it had become a "sounding board" for any and all complaints against the police.[94] The court's ruling and Tate's abandonment of the Police Advisory Board ended Philadelphia's experiment with law enforcement liberalism.

The August 1964 uprising on Columbia Avenue was both the culmination of years of poor police-community relations in North Philadelphia and a harbinger of the end of law enforcement liberalism in the city as a whole. Later efforts to reform police culture and police-community relations in North Philadelphia failed. The overwhelming defensiveness coming from the Fraternal Order of Police and their allies in Philadelphia's white, blue-collar neighborhoods stopped even modest proposals for liberal approaches to law enforcement. They also forced James Tate to turn to the politics of law and order midway through his first full term as mayor. The pressure from grassroots supporters of the police also paved the way for the rise of Frank Rizzo, who built upon his increasing clout and the preexisting culture of reverence for the police to become one of the most pivotal figures in the city's history.

The police and their blue-collar supporters ushered in an era of law-and-order conservatism with Frank Rizzo at the helm. By the late 1960s, as Rizzo's image as the salvation of blue-collar Philadelphia emerged, his role as a big-city police commissioner with higher political ambitions also made him de facto protector of the city's white, blue-collar traditions. His ascendancy to local power stemmed from the grassroots efforts of the FOP and their blue-collar allies. Their movement to create strict protections for the police and rid the city of more liberal law enforcement policies established the popularity of law-and-order politics. Greater respect and protection for police officers would continue as a popular position and a cornerstone of local law-and-order politics. The culture of reverence that intensified in response to the Columbia Avenue Riot, civil rights protests, and rise of black militancy remained a central facet of the emerging blue-collar conservatism. Through it all, blue-collar Philadelphians maintained a defense of what they considered a blue-collar tradition. They adopted a similar defense when they perceived that civil rights activists targeted their traditional neighborhoods, folk customs, and schools.

CHAPTER 3

"This Man Is the City's Salvation"

Giordano Scopinich was like many blue-collar Philadelphians. Born into an immigrant family in 1924, he attended Philadelphia public schools before enlisting in the army and serving in the Second World War. Scopinich married the love of his life while on leave from basic training and together they raised three children after he returned from his service. With GI Bill funding, Scopinich attended technical school and trained for his lifelong career as a draftsman. By his own admission, Scopinich's life was unremarkable. "I am not a President, a King, or a Religious leader," he wrote, "[they have] biographers, historians, and others to record their presence on earth."[1] So Scopinich wrote a memoir for his children and grandchildren; to give them a way to take stock of his life and accomplishments. Most of his unpublished autobiography was devoted to his wife and their sixty-year marriage, including a litany of love letters, poems, and other tokens of his deep affection for her. Only one other "demanding mistress" competed with the attention he gave his wife. With great detail and tender memory matched only by the descriptions of his relationship with his wife and family, Scopinich recalled his participation in the New Year's Shooters and Mummers Day Parade.[2]

Throughout most of Philadelphia's long postwar era, Scopinich played accordion in the string bands that marched in and provided the soundtrack to Philadelphia's annual New Year's Day tradition. Belting out "Oh Dem Golden Slippers"—the official theme song of the Mummers Parade—with the Greater Kensington String Band and later with the Polish American String Band, Scopinich helped maintain one of the oldest working-class, white ethnic folk celebrations in the United States. Mummery was a family, neighborhood, and ethnic affair. Sons followed their fathers into the parade tradition. New Year's associations and clubs divided into Shooters, Fancy Brigades, and String Bands that represented neighborhoods and ethnic associations. Throughout the year, these clubs created elaborate performances in preparation for the New Year's Day festivities. On parade day, they would begin in South Philadelphia, where many of the clubs were located, and march north along South Broad Street to City Hall. Shooters—garish clowns toting parasols and dressed in bright colors—started the parade with their trademark strut. Next, decked out head to toe in sequins and feathered plumes, the Fancy Brigades and String Bands completed the urban carnival with choreographed performances for bragging rights and city-sponsored prize money. Few major American cities hosted anything comparable to the Mummer's Parade. For men like Giordano Scopinich the parade was much more than an annual tradition. "Mummers are a form of society within a society," he explained, "with a structure and a language all their own, a language that does not necessarily communicate to everyone."[3]

Mummery was one of the most important and long-established blue-collar traditions in Philadelphia. By the 1960s, however, it had come under attack from civil rights organizations. The Mummers and New Year's Shooters Association, the organization that oversaw parade rules, barred all women and nonwhite men from participating. Since ethnic, family, and neighborhood associations determined club membership, the annual parade remained an entirely white event. Segregation was not civil rights activists' main concern, however. Far more troublesome was the long tradition of Mummers donning burnt cork and performing in blackface.[4]

Neither the wearing of blackface in the parade nor outrage over its use was new in the 1960s. Blackface Mummers dated back to the late nineteenth century, when minstrel shows were at their height in the United States. African Americans repeatedly tried to stop the practice. In the mid-1950s, the city orchestrated a compromise whereby blackface minstrels would be allowed to march in the parade, provided they did not "intentionally mimic, mock, or portray any race, creed or religion." The compromise never satisfied civil rights leaders, especially the younger, more militant activists that gained wider influence in the 1960s. Led by the city's chapter of CORE, they demanded a permanent ban on the "insulting, outmoded, and uncalled for practice" that the city sanctioned through parade funds, street space, police protection, and prize money. Civil rights groups did not trust the Mummers Association to self-regulate the parade. Even if Mummers officials barred blackface, they said, the organization could not control the actions of all the individuals involved. Those working to end blackface in the parade demanded the municipal government assume responsibility. Finally, in December 1963, city officials responded to the demands and imposed a ban on blackface per-formance just weeks before the parade.[5]

Both the Mummers and their many supporters protested. "If the wearing of this make-up is detrimental," queried one newspaper editorial, "then why not go all the way? Ban all the Indian costumes and make-up. Ban yellow paint and Far East divisions to avoid offending the Chinese and other orientals [sic]. Ban Russian and Polish themes. Ban Irish derbies and shillelaghies [sic]." If the city were to proceed with the ban, the editorial suggested, "the New Year's Parade will be nothing more than a group of men and boys marching four-abreast, wearing business suits, no music, no color, no nothing. Just a long and tedious march."[6] The city did maintain the ban, but inclement weather delayed the event until the fourth of January. While only a few Mummers blackened their faces when the parade reconvened, string bands marched silently through the African American sections of South Philadelphia. Their revelry resumed as they arrived at Center City, but the show remained subdued. Afterward, how-ever, when the marchers made their way to a stretch of Second Street in the Pennsport neighborhood of South Philadelphia for the unofficial but tradi-tional continuation of the parade—known locally as "Two Street"—blackface Mummers reappeared. As night fell on Two Street, a cry came from the crowd: "The Democrats own Broad Street; we own Second Street."[7]

With the city's failure to enforce the ban in 1964, the controversy reignited the following year. National CORE representative Louis Smith reported that members of his organization were prepared to descend on Philadelphia to carry out demonstrations if the city did not assure that both the main parade route and the post-parade festivities were free of blackface. Adding another element to the already tense situation, the 1965 Mummers parade would be the first televised nationally. Not wanting the city embarrassed, Mayor James Tate again ordered a blackface ban.[8] The Mummers and New Year's Shooters Association warned that the "spirit of mummery will eventually die" if the city enforced the ban. Other supporters said that blackface was not intended to offend. Mummers said the mayor's order robbed them of their right to mimic and satirize. Black-faced minstrelsy, they claimed, was "steeped in tradition."[9]

The city upheld the ban over the protests. In time, the blackface tradition died out. Despite the dire warnings of the Mummers and their supporters, men like Giordano Scopinich carried on the parade, making it grow and thrive. Nevertheless, the controversy over keeping blackface a part of the parade festivities demonstrated how fiercely white, blue-collar Philadelphians defended their cherished traditions from threats, both perceived and real.

Philadelphia's New Year's tradition has few direct corollaries in modern America, but the controversy over the Mummers Parade illustrated a broader blue-collar response to the changes and challenges wrought by the modern civil rights movement in the urban North. Participants and supporters of the Mummers greeted protests against the use of blackface in the parade with a mix of ignorance, indignation, and confusion. As civil rights activists targeted other so-called traditions, no one response encapsulated the blue-collar reaction. In some cases, blue-collar whites responded with the virulent racism common to the backlash narrative. On other occasions, blue-collar Philadelphians met challenges to their long-held traditions with moderation and "color-blind" defenses of their institutions. One element that unified the varied reactions was a feeling that traditions were under attack. Together, these reactions indicate how strongly blue-collar whites responded when accused of maintaining segregated cities in the urban North.

Blue-collar whites had normalized the racial and spatial boundaries that sustained segregation. When presented with challenges to it, their defensiveness indicated just how invested they were in the maintenance of those boundaries and how much segregation shaped their perspectives on race, class, and urban politics. Their specific means of defending blue-collar institutions—like folk customs, neighborhoods, and public schools—showed how varied and complex their motivations could be. When the Mummers and their allies claimed that the use of blackface in the parade was inoffensive, they expressed a denial of racial motivation common among blue-collar attempts to defend segregated traditions they internalized as normal. Filtering reactions to these challenges through the perspective of tradition enabled blue-collar whites to maintain that theirs was not an effort to deny equality or rights to nonwhites, even when they responded with vicious or violent racist expressions. Blue-collar Philadelphians reacted similarly when they wondered why African American families would want to move into all-white neighborhoods or why educational activists sought school system reforms to promote integration. They greeted transgressions against what they considered normal with suspicion, hostility, and sometimes violence. As important, the mid-1960s controversies over all-white institutions directly led to Frank Rizzo's emergence as the unequivocal protector of Philadelphia's blue-collar traditions.

Rizzo's ascendancy through the police force and increasing popularity among blue-collar whites was a direct result of the challenges waged by civil rights activists. As civil rights leaders increasingly demanded local and national government action to force change, and liberal politicians and policy-makers responded, blue-collar whites felt beset on all sides. They found their salvation in a figure that vocally and physically promised to defy challenges to their traditions. But it was the defense of blue-collar traditions that created the political space that Frank Rizzo eventually filled. Blue-collar whites elevated Rizzo to the position of blue-collar savior and in the process highlighted the spatial battles that led to the rise of blue-collar conservatism. Their fiercest defense of blue-collar tradition occurred when challenges hit closest to home: the city's all-white, working-class neighborhoods.

Kensington Against the World

In early October 1966, Lillian Wright began moving into a small row home near the intersection of Coral Street and Cumberland Avenue in the Kensington section of Philadelphia. Wright had excitedly signed the lease for the modest home because of its inexpensive rent. She had high hopes that the nearby schools would prove suitable for her three children. But Wright and her family were the first African American residents in that part of Kensington, a large section of the city still overwhelmingly populated by working-class white ethnics. Although her realtor warned Wright about moving into the neighborhood, she thought the affordable rent and close schools were worth leaving her home in North Philadelphia. She received unwelcoming stares from her new neighbors almost immediately after she arrived with a moving van early Sunday morning, October 3. Later that day, a small group gathered at the corner of Coral and Cumberland to watch the Wright family move in. Wright said that she heard a man's voice shout "Niggers are moving into that house." After unpacking, she decided to take her children and spend the night with a family member.[10]

News of the move-in quickly spread throughout the neighborhood. By nightfall, the small group of onlookers turned into an estimated two hundred noisy and agitated people. Eggs, rocks, and bottles were flung from the crowd and broke the front windows of the small row home. Police arriving on the scene reported young people shouting "Negroes get out" and cheers going up from the crowd every time another projectile crashed into the house. While the police eventually dispersed the crowd, they made only two arrests. The unruly crowd sparked the first of five increasingly hostile nights of rioting over the prospect of integrating the neighborhood.[11]

Lillian Wright conferred with Cecil B. Moore the following day. Despite the harassment, she decided to return to her new home. Reunited with her estranged husband Leon Wright, the couple stated that they had no intention of leaving. That night, another crowd gathered near their home. Anticipating trouble, the police stationed additional officers throughout Kensington. Reinforcements kept the rowdy crowd at a safe distance from the Wrights' house, but nearly five hundred angry residents took over the intersection of Coral and Cumberland. Once again, they threw bottles, bricks, and random debris, injuring two police officers. Police restored order a few hours later, but kept arrests down to ten adults and seven juveniles. The next morning, after the Wrights' first harrowing night in their home, representatives of the local NAACP brought the family groceries and other provisions. State police and FBI agents also arrived to monitor the situation. That evening the police department called upon Reverend Joseph A. McCloskey, pastor of the nearby Visitation BVM Roman Catholic Church, to help calm the crowd. "I know some of you belong to the Visitation Church," he said when he appeared before them. He asked parents to remove younger children from the intersection and "all of the Catholics" to go home. The crowd responded with boos and catcalls. Someone hurled a brick that struck a police officer standing next to the priest. Despite Father McCloskey's pleas, the community's anger showed no sign of abating.[12]

The situation reached its lowest point the following evening, when demonstrators marched outside the Wright's home for the fourth night in a row. A crowd of about four hundred gathered to watch. The mostly young protesters carried Confederate battle flags and homemade signs mimicking the language used by civil rights activists, including slogans like "We Shall Overcome Niggers" and "White Power." They twice burned crude effigies of African Americans while chanting "burn nigger burn." The watching crowd booed every time the police made an arrest. When teenagers climbed on top of parked cars and began throwing bottles at police, adults in the crowd took it upon themselves to calm the young protesters. The police allowed one man to use their sound truck to inform the rioters that residents had retained an attorney in an effort to legally force the Wrights out of the neighborhood. Another man grabbed the loudspeaker to address the crowd. "I don't want niggers in Kensington," he said. "Neither do you. Everybody wants to get rid of them," he continued. "Niggers get things done by picketing. We can, too, but it's got to be orderly. Let's march!" He then led a group of two hundred toward the intersection of Coral and Cumberland, but police would not allow them to pass the Wrights' home.[13]

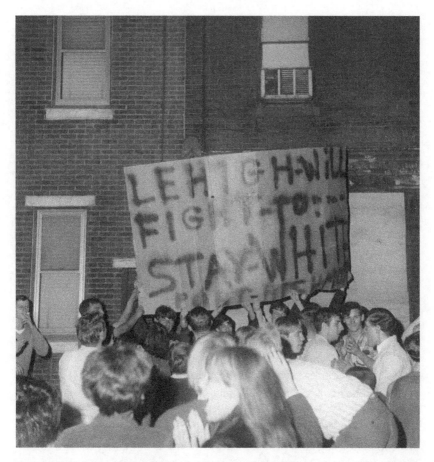

Figure 5. Kensington rioters mass near Lillian Wright's home. Along with signs that read "White Power" and "We Shall Overcome Negroes," the rioters here carry a sign reading "Lehigh Will Fight to Stay White," 1966. Courtesy of Special Collections Research Center, Temple University, Philadelphia, PA.

Representatives of local civil rights organizations arrived to offer their services to the Wrights a little before midnight. They also protested the city's failure to bring an end to the rioting. Open-housing and religious leaders expressed their concern over the city's slow response. The local Student Nonviolent Coordinating Committee (SNCC) denounced the "kid-glove treatment" police used when dealing with the white protesters. "We do not condone police brutality in any instance," SNCC said in a statement to the press. But, they continued, if police responded to disturbances in African

American neighborhoods with force, then "they should take the same type of action in the white streets of Kensington."[14] The police department finally responded to civil rights leaders the following night, assigning more than four hundred policemen to the area. After five nights of rioting, peace finally returned to Kensington.[15]

After the initial incident, the police department assigned plainclothes officers to monitor the area. For the next few days, the police mingled with area residents and collected interviews about the Wrights. While a small minority of Kensington residents were willing to accept the family into their neighborhood, most of those interviewed by the police were hostile to the move. At a taproom at the intersection of Kensington Avenue and Cumberland Street—about three blocks away from the Wrights' home—plainclothes police overheard patrons complaining that the "hullaballo [sic] had started too late and that it should have started when the Puerto Ricans moved into the area." At another tavern, a few residents identified as members of the Kensington String Band—participants in the annual Mummers Parade—talked about donning blackface and marching on Kensington Avenue.[16] Two years earlier, white participants had claimed that they could not see how blackface could be deemed racist. Now, with the first African Americans moving into an all-white neighborhood, whites discussed wearing blackface in a terrorist campaign to remove the Wright family from Kensington.

The Kensington Riot immediately drew comparisons to the Columbia Avenue Riot. In contrast to the uprising in North Philadelphia, however, the Tate administration took days to issue a statement on Kensington. Civil rights and housing activists accused the mayor of not doing enough to protect the Wright family and African Americans moving into formerly all-white neighborhoods.[17] Once calm returned to the area, the city's Commission on Human Relations (CHR) hoped to recreate the success they had a decade earlier by trying to develop a community organization in Kensington to encourage interracial dialogue. White Kensingtonians responded with animosity and obduracy. The CHR had to admit that they were too understaffed and ill equipped to handle an area the size of Kensington. Without the proper staff and facing resistance, CHR representatives failed to establish an effective response to the tensions in Kensington.[18]

After five nights of rioting, Kensington became the epicenter and a powerful symbol of Philadelphia's "white backlash." The residents' refusal to cooperate with city agencies was indicative of the area's reputation for proud traditions and stubborn self-reliance. It also represented a prime example of

the indefinite boundaries of the city's neighborhoods. As Kensington was situated northeast of Center City, city planners and residents alike had long
included the area as part of the Near Northeast. By the mid-1960s, however,
as more and more upwardly mobile blue-collar Philadelphians moved to the
Far Northeast, the unofficial border of the "Greater Northeast" moved with
it. Older areas like Kensington, which was too big to be a neighborhood in
a definite sense, became a section of the city in and of itself. In the popular
imagination and in city planning maps it ceased to be a part of the Northeast.
It was more ethnic and decidedly more working class. It no longer fit with
the middle-class quasi-suburban ambitions and self-perceptions of Northeast
Philadelphia. Instead, Kensington became an object of scorn, marked as "low
class" by middle-class Philadelphians that now lived in tract homes instead
of row houses. They considered Kensington a step down the economic ladder
from their own white enclaves.[19]

By 1966, Kensington was not just a section of the city, but an area imbued
with a powerful sense of white, working-class place. Sandwiched between
Center City, North Philadelphia, and the Near Northeast, the area was predominantly populated by lower-income white ethnics. Before October 1966,
Kensington's biggest claim to fame and historical significance had been
another riot, in the 1840s, when anti-Catholic rioters burned churches and
houses in response to the influx of Irish immigrants. The long-simmering
hostilities between Catholics and Protestants dissipated over the course of
the following century and a new image emerged. During the heyday of Philadelphia's industrial might, Kensington billed itself as the "Workshop of the
World." In the early decades of the twentieth century, it teemed with garment factories and other light industries. Kensington then became a center of
immigrant working-class life in Philadelphia. By the 1960s the area was home
to the largest percentage of first, second, and third generation white ethnics
in the city, and their lives were rapidly changing.[20]

Kensington as a whole was in a state of decline. The once strong center
of hosiery and textile manufacturing fell victim to changing fashions and the
pursuit of cheap labor in the union-weak South. While industrial relocation
and the construction of modern factories in the Far Northeast during the
city's reform era was an overall boon to Philadelphia's industrial infrastructure, Kensington joined North Philadelphia in bearing the brunt of the city's
economic and planning changes. Its mills and factories began leaving or shutting down in the early postwar era. Kensington's infrastructure was crumbling
as well. Its air was polluted, its crime rate was rising, and its school buildings

were among the oldest in Philadelphia.[21] Upwardly mobile residents were not alone in seeking an escape. A once thriving business district along Kensington's main thoroughfare steadily lost customers to suburban shopping centers and large retail outlets in Northeast Philadelphia. Area business leaders worried that a further decline in business volume would result in vacancies and, as a consequence, lead to an inevitable decline in the property values. "At worst," warned the president of the Kensington Business Men's Association, "the ultimate result can be another blighted area in the City of Philadelphia."[22]

By the time Lillian Wright and her family moved into Kensington, some of the dire warnings made by the business community had come to fruition. Many of the area's row homes were in various states of disrepair and much of the area showed signs of creeping blight. Residents complained about a lack of city services and recreation facilities. Many felt they had been ignored by the city for years. Their most frequent complaints were that city spending and rehabilitation efforts favored the nearby African American sections of North Philadelphia and that city planners focused more of their attention on their burgeoning neighbors in the Far Northeast. More than a decade since the start of Philadelphia's urban renewal renaissance, many Kensingtonians began feeling left behind by the liberal city rehabilitation system or caught in the middle between North Philadelphia's "jungle" and Northeast Philadelphia's suburban landscape. Residents feared that the crime, gangs, and poverty they associated with North Central Philadelphia were inching into Kensington. In fact, since the 1950s, the unofficial boundary that separated all-black North Philadelphia from all-white Kensington had moved six blocks east. The northern parts of Kensington acted as a spatial and social buffer between the lower-income African American residents of North Philadelphia and the more upwardly mobile white residents of Northeast Philadelphia. By the mid-1960s, Kensington was literally in the middle of Philadelphia's racial and class tensions.[23]

After October 1966, urban sociologists and social workers pointed out that conditions in Kensington were only marginally better than the conditions that led to the disturbance on Columbia Avenue two years earlier. Some, like sociologist and Regional Director of the American Jewish Committee Murray Friedman, argued that the poverty and poor human services in white areas like Kensington were just as severe as they were in African American areas, but liberal politicians did not pay the same attention to white urban poverty. Friedman pleaded with social workers and intellectuals to see the Kensington Riot as more than "the misguided behavior of a bunch of bigots." He insisted that reformers needed to understand the causes of white rioting as much as they needed to understand the rioting in Watts or North Philadelphia.[24]

Friedman observed that Kensington bore striking similarities to North Philadelphia. Sixteen percent of the families living in the Coral Street area immediately adjacent to the Wrights' home had incomes below the poverty level. Friedman said that white anxiety was a result of their watching African Americans, a group just below them on the economic ladder, receiving public attention and sympathy, to their own detriment. While Friedman sympathized with the Wrights and condemned the action of Coral Street residents, he hoped the Kensington riot would cause reformers to "look up from our concentration on the problems of Negroes" and "begin to pay some attention to needs of other disadvantaged groups in our society." As he argued, the need to understand events like the Kensington Riot was essential because the "civil rights progress has been stalemated in many parts of the country because the groups who are resisting so vigorously have been largely ignored."[25]

The riot in Kensington brought the realities of lower-income whites' hostility to integration into sharp relief. But the area also offered a snapshot of the complexities of backlash politics as well as the varied ways working-class white ethnics encountered the civil rights era. In the mid-1960s, local journalist and author Peter Binzen spent two years conducting interviews, visiting schools, and observing the broader community for his classic study *Whitetown, U.S.A.*, a profile of Kensington and its residents. "Like Harlem and Watts," Binzen wrote, "Kensington is filled with bitterness, but this is a case of white rage." Describing the residents, he went on: "It is home for a hundred thousand proud, irascible, tough, narrow-minded, down-to-earth, old-fashioned, hostile, flag-waving, family-oriented ethnic Americans."[26]

Despite the physical and economic condition of their neighborhoods, residents of Kensington had a reputation for being fiercely proud. When used by journalists like Peter Binzen, pride also meant stubborn and chauvinistic. As in previous housing controversies, Kensington's blue-collar pride was never a solely innocent expression of pride in place. It also functioned as a means of reinforcing racial and spatial segregation. Reflected in the popular slogan "Kensington Against the World," area residents expressed their anger at the encroachment of poor nonwhites as well as their frustration with what they considered the benign neglect of local liberals and elites. When the *Philadelphia Inquirer* ran a story in August 1964 about an educational pilot program to increase the reading ability of working-class Kensington schoolchildren, it called Kensington a "slum" with "underprivileged" children. According to the *Inquirer*, "Upon reading the story, Kensingtonians arose in proud and righteous wrath."[27] Many refused to admit the problems that existed in their neighborhoods. Their protests notwithstanding, education was not a priority for many Kensingtonians. Few residents finished formal schooling and less than 2 percent of the population completed college. Kensington's children usually opted to follow their parents' footsteps into blue-collar, skilled trade, or union jobs.[28] For most area residents, their small homes and tight-knit communities were all they had worth defending from perceived threats. They considered protracted defenses of their homes and neighborhoods a defense of their only real economic asset. They were objectively more privileged than working-class African Americans, but Kensingtonians and other blue-collar Philadelphians still felt vulnerable in a changing urban environment.

While they complained about a lack of recreational facilities and neighborhood deterioration, Kensington residents generally spoke favorably of their communities. When Peter Binzen asked residents of Fishtown—a large, slightly higher-income blue-collar neighborhood in southeastern Kensington—why they remained attached to their neighborhood, one responded that he liked Fishtown "Because it's all white. Because it's friendly and all white."[29] Almost all of Binzen's interviewees stated a vigorous opposition to the integration of their neighborhoods, but most of them also qualified their remarks. Perhaps, they said, they would be willing to accept "decent Negroes" as neighbors. Police investigators found similar attitudes among Kensington residents in the immediate aftermath of the October 1966 riot. Many said that they would not mind black families living near them "if they were decent." Others echoed fears that the presence of an African American family meant that more would move in, and that the area would automatically become "another Ghetto."[30] When discussing potential African American neighbors, blue-collar whites in Kensington and Fishtown made clear distinctions between the hardworking "good ones" and those that created slums and drove down property values.[31] One woman recalled going to school with an African American girl that everyone liked. But, she countered, "when you hear one is moving into your block all you can picture is the wild ones." Like other working-class whites, she was willing to be tolerant when she personally knew a "good Negro," but resorted to racial stereotypes when resisting integrated housing.[32]

Kensington and Fishtown residents reflected widespread beliefs in white, working-class neighborhoods. Their depictions of African Americans stemmed from the normalization of segregated space. They used the differentiation between good and bad African Americans to justify their own racism and ignore their own privilege—the privilege not to be held responsible for the actions of others. In order to obfuscate their discriminatory feelings toward potential neighbors, blue-collar whites in areas like Kensington and Fishtown used class distinctions as rhetorical qualifiers to explain who they were and were not willing to share urban space with. Their statements rested on long-standing racist stereotypes about the broader African American community, stereotypes that grew out of the culture of segregation that affected the white working class throughout the country's segregated urban spaces. Their admission that they would be willing to live near African Americans if they kept their homes as they did exemplified the subtle and complicated ways that working-class whites dealt with the changes of the civil rights era. At the same time, however, as if to discursively reassure themselves that they need not worry about actually having black neighbors, a group of Fishtown residents told Binzen that "decent colored" preferred to stay with their own kind. Segregation had become so normalized that to transgress it was itself evidence that an African American was not worthy of living in a white neighborhood.[33] One woman, who uncommonly admitted to being "prejudiced," said she hoped she did not live to see African Americans move into Kensington. She just could not even understand why African Americans would want to live in such an area. "Why would a colored person want to come out and move into a block with all whites?" she asked. She would "never in a million years" move into an all-black neighborhood, no matter how nice and inexpensive the house was.[34]

In late October 1966, Kensingtonians defended their neighborhood from the perceived threat of African American encroachment. Thereafter, the Wright family experienced continued harassment. Rocks and eggs were thrown at their home, their windows were broken, and insults were hurled at them. They lived in fear for most of the winter and rarely let their children leave the house. After six months, the environment became too toxic. Leon Wright said he still believed in his family's right to live in the neighborhood. He also would stay if he were alone, he added. For his children's sake, however, he had to look for a new home. In March 1967, the Wrights moved out of Kensington. The previously all-white neighborhood became all white again. "The whites who live there have won," remarked *Philadelphia Inquirer* columnist Joe McGinnis. It took six months, but they chased the Wrights out of Kensington. "And when it finally subsided," McGinnis wrote, "it was clear that Philadelphia is the City of Brotherly Love all right, but only if that brother is white."[35]

Economic resentment and racial backlash figured heavily in the politics of white, blue-collar communities like Kensington. Over time, as these communities renegotiated their place in the changing urban system and reassessed their protest strategies, opponents of integration tempered their speech and leaned on ostensibly "color-blind" defenses of traditions. No single set of behaviors can describe the blue-collar response to desegregation in cities as large and complex as Philadelphia. When civil rights activists and educational reformers targeted public schools, for example, white parents waged a far more restrained effort to resist integration.

Defending Traditional Education

In May 1965, about 125 white parents staged a demonstration outside the board of education administration building at Twenty-First Street and the Benjamin Franklin Parkway in Center City Philadelphia. "Neighborhood schools for neighborhood children," they shouted. Under the direction of the Parents and Taxpayers Association of Philadelphia (PAT), representatives of several parents' organizations gathered to protest the student transfer program the school board initiated at the beginning of the school year. After the PAT filed a suit to block the busing, head of the organization Joseph J. Frieri said the board had "succumbed to pressure from radicals" when they accepted the transfer system. "They are sacrificing one man's rights for the benefit of another," he continued. The PAT charged that the only purpose of the program was to "effect racial distribution and dispersion under the guise of eliminating crowded school conditions."[36] When given an opportunity to present their demands to a school board representative, the parents said that busing was "wasteful, hazardous and time consuming." The head of the PAT said that it would be more desirable if the board built new schools closer to children's homes.[37]

White parents' organizations like the PAT vehemently protested the proposed changes to the Philadelphia public school system. They accused educational reformers and liberals of trying to destroy one of the foundations of their communities: the neighborhood school. Most white parents had themselves grown up attending schools near their childhood homes and they wanted the same for their own children. They had also attended extremely segregated schools. Yet, with some notable exceptions, most of the parents that protested efforts to integrate Philadelphia's public schools refrained from explicitly calling for the maintenance of traditionally segregated education. They did, however, oppose efforts to alter the school system in ways they thought had no educational value beyond integration. Their efforts to maintain traditional neighborhood schools put them in direct conflict with civil rights activists and educational reformers that had worked to overhaul the public education system for decades.

A majority of students in Philadelphia public schools—57 percent and growing—were African American. By 1964, furthermore, three out of every four African American children attended segregated public schools, as did two out of every three white children.[38] Although segregation was not legally mandated in Pennsylvania, segregated housing patterns created schools that reflected the racial composition of city neighborhoods. As a result, schools in North and West Philadelphia were predominantly African American. Those in the Northeast were overwhelmingly white. Even in South Philadelphia, where African Americans represented just over half of the public school students, 92 percent of black students attended schools that were 85 percent or more nonwhite. Schools attended by majority nonwhite students were overcrowded, understaffed, and ill equipped to educate their students. Furthermore, the need for more schools in developing areas of Northeast Philadelphia grew as more middle-class whites relocated. Despite the school district's stated objective to build new schools in areas that could serve both white and black populations, all-white Northeast Philadelphia presented the most difficult challenge to integrated education.

There was no need for the legal enforcement of segregation. The postwar realignment of urban space effectively segregated the school system as it did the neighborhoods. Segregated schools were another reflection of the normalization of segregated space. Indeed, as one city Community Renewal Program stated, "All efforts to construct an integrated school system are severely restricted by the high percentage of Negro pupils and the segregated pattern of housing."[39] For civil rights activists, promoting integrated education was not enough. In the mid-1960s they adopted the position that quality education and integrated education were one and the same. Philadelphia liberals agreed. Under pressure from civil rights leaders, educational reformers, and government bodies, the Board of Public Education adopted policies meant to foster integrated schools.[40]

Philadelphia's school board first made desegregation an official policy in 1959. As school desegregation became national policy in the wake of the

Supreme Court's *Brown v. Board of Education* decision, city, metropolitan, and regional planners sought a variety of implementation plans. Little Rock, Arkansas, famously adopted a "controlled minimum" plan to achieve token integration. Charlotte, North Carolina, and other Southern school districts turned to color-blind neighborhood schools to undo the vestiges of their Jim Crow school systems before turning toward a student transfer program. Massachusetts's Racial Imbalance Act of 1965 set a precedent for school districts outside the South by mandating a busing solution to segregated schools.[41] Much like desegregation efforts elsewhere, the difficult process of producing an integrated education plan in Philadelphia created controversy. After years with few results, reformers began to question the board's willingness to cooperate with others seeking the same goals. In 1963, a committee tasked with studying the technical aspects of school desegregation charged the board with deliberately obstructing efforts to implement a workable plan. The Educational Equality League, Urban League, and Philadelphia NAACP advocated busing to reduce overcrowded schools and foster integration. They also promoted a number of vast changes to the Philadelphia public school system.[42] Floyd Logan, head of the Educational Equality League, had worked to eliminate discrimination in the public education system for over a decade. He helped forge alliances with liberals, civil rights organizations, and educational reformers that pressured the city to take affirmative steps toward integrating public schools.[43] Logan became the driving force behind civil rights activists' efforts to force the board of education to enact a desegregation policy by any means necessary, including busing.

Just before the start of the 1964 school year, the mayor's Citizen's Advisory Committee on Civil Rights considered a plan that would have added three thousand additional students to the thirteen thousand that already rode buses to school. While the committee agreed that the plan represented a workable means to foster integration, they worried about opposition from white parents, especially in Northeast Philadelphia.[44] Their concerns were correct. Parents and community organizations from the Northeast protested the plan and threatened mass demonstrations against the board of education if they implemented any reforms that included busing.[45] Although many white parents agreed that African American students should have access to equal educational opportunities, they opposed policy changes they thought would risk their own children's educational experiences. Even many of those who agreed with the idea of integrated education in principle worried that the goal was not worth risking "quality education." The racial politics of student busing were undeniable. Throughout urban America advocates of integrated education backed student transfer programs designed to foster student diversity. Busing was a well-known strategy to enforce racial integration. Nevertheless, many white parents, especially those in blue-collar neighborhoods, denied that race was a motivating factor in their opposition to busing. Overwhelmingly, however, parents in the Northeast supported the maintenance of neighborhood schools and advocated a return to separate but equal.

In response, the mayor and the city council refused to sanction the committee's program. James Tate and City Council President Paul D'Ortona—both initially elected from blue-collar sections of the city—forced the committee to draft a new plan that would preserve traditional neighborhood schools.[46] Tate and D'Ortona bent to the power of the neighborhood school concept. But, as educational reformers argued, in a neighborhood school system the quality of the school depended on the quality of the neighborhood. Disinvestment in working-class African American neighborhoods invariably led to poor quality schools.[47] For activists like Floyd Logan, integration was a means of not only fostering intergroup understanding, but, more importantly, achieving educational equity. Viewing the commitment of the school board, mayor, and city council to neighborhood schools as a commitment to segregated education, Logan resigned his post on the Citizen's Advisory Committee on Civil Rights.[48]

At the same time, reaction to the announcement from white parents was negative and immediate. Across the country, no other potential school policy wrought as powerful a reaction among whites as forced busing. In Southern cities like Atlanta and Charlotte, postwar student integration plans fostered decades-long controversies. Among Northern cities, Boston most famously engaged in the most protracted battle over student transfer programs.[49] Philadelphia was like most urban districts, where the burden of busing most often fell to African American students and their families, but white parents protested student transfer plans nevertheless. Even when parents were willing to admit that something needed to be done to alleviate overcrowding, white parents still opposed most busing plans. In many instances, racist stereotypes about African American children's willingness or ability to learn marked much of the opposition. Some parents also expressed concerns that integrated education might lead to intermarriage.[50] White parents' most oft-repeated fear, however, was the possibility the school board would implement a "reverse busing" policy, sending white children into predominantly African American neighborhood schools. In an attempt to placate white parents, the school board explicitly stated that its policy would not include reverse busing.[51] Still, white parents' fears of sending their children to other, non-white areas invoked broader anxieties about the breach of the city's unofficial boundaries. Even the term reverse busing spoke to the normalization of seg-regated space. The use of the directional signifier "reverse" subtly acknowl-edged that segregation created separate spaces for different races. In white sections of Philadelphia, the defense of blue-collar traditions like the neigh-borhood school also helped maintain informal racial barriers.

Despite their official policies, both the city and the school board proved unwilling to commit fully to public school desegregation in the early 1960s. But the City of Philadelphia was under pressure to desegregate its schools. After a state Human Relations Commission investigation found widespread and systematic segregation, Mayor Tate had little choice but to follow the state's directive. He made changes in the school board's composition to com-ply with the state. In addition to appointing several new members, Tate nom-inated former mayor and longtime liberal reformer Richardson Dilworth for president of the board of education. Dilworth had maintained a high level of civic engagement since his failed campaign for governor in 1962. He remained especially concerned with the public school system. Dilworth served as a con-sultant or board member to several civic, community, and educational orga-nizations, including the Philadelphia Council for Community Advancement (PCCA) and the Citizens Committee on Public Education (CCPE). When Tate tapped him to head the board of education in 1965, Dilworth resigned his other posts and brought a genuine commitment to educational reform and integration. Although few of their ultimate goals were fully met, Dilworth's board of education represented a real effort to achieve educational equality.[52]

Under Dilworth, the new board was willing to consider drastic changes and experimentation to reduce overcrowding and foster integration. The board's proposed plan included the adoption of magnet schools, specialized centers, redistricting, and the construction of new facilities. At the heart of the board's proposal was the implementation of a K4-4-4 school system. Pub-lic schools in Philadelphia functioned on a K3-3-3 system, whereby pupils attended elementary schools that held kindergarten through sixth grade, fol-lowed by three years of middle school and three more in high school. The K4-4-4 plan shifted students' attendance to kindergarten through fourth grade in an elementary school, fifth through eighth grades at middle school, and ninth through twelfth grades in high school. The architects of the plan hoped that restructuring the school system would alleviate the stress on overcrowded schools by spreading the pupil population across district boundaries. The city's Commission on Human Relations endorsed the K4-4-4 plan as a positive step in helping achieve an integrated school system. Chairwoman Sadie Alexander said the plan would provide "the most meaningful integrated experience possible for the children in every one of our schools." She approved of the K4-4-4 plan because it provided for more kindergarten and preschool classes. It would also "bring together children from a wider range of backgrounds at an earlier age."[53] The Philadelphia Federation of Teachers, civil rights organizations, and educational reformers joined the CHR. At the same time, however, the plans to reorganize public schools angered many parents, especially those with children in the experimental districts chosen to implement the K4-4-4 system.[54]

The plan faced its stiffest opposition from Home and School Associations (HSA), parents' groups that organized at each Philadelphia public school. The Philadelphia Home and School Council (PHSC), the body that governed the collective HSAs, took a middle ground position on the K4-4-4 change. They did not endorse it, but neither did they immediately reject it. They wanted the program tested in an area of the city receptive to the idea before the board implemented it citywide.[55] Individual HSAs, however, especially those in predominantly white neighborhoods, opposed the K4-4-4 plan because it was untested, or because they thought it had no educational value beyond promoting integration. They especially opposed any potential busing plans and some threatened that forcing small children to attend school in different parts of the city would exacerbate the problem of middle-class flight to the suburbs.[56]

No HSA representative testified against integration as a goal, but rather against the means to achieve integrated schools. Some even claimed to support integrated schools as long as their own children could continue attending schools in their own community. Many expressed fears of being unable to retrieve their children in case of an emergency or illness. Some claimed children would lose the influence of the home if forced to attend school outside their neighborhood. The HSAs mostly wanted the school board to concentrate on fixing deteriorating conditions in existing schools before embarking on such extensive reforms.[57] The litany of concerns presented by the HSAs covered a wide range of topics, but they all reflected the two most prevalent and mutually reinforcing objections. First, HSAs feared that the school reorganization plan threatened traditional schools. Second, and relatedly, they repeated their opposition to changing the school system in order to foster integration. The blue-collar parents in the HSAs never publicly stated that their goal was to maintain a segregated school system. The race of the school-children played no part in their conclusions, they said. Instead, they adopted arguments that favored promotion of traditional neighborhood schools over the explicit denunciation of integrated education. The rationale created an outcome similar to the false dichotomy between de jure and de facto seg-regation. By advocating neighborhood schools over desegregation, white parents were able to deny that racial preference or the protection of white privilege was present or inherent in their advocacy of traditional educational standards. In doing so they reinforced another of the multiple structures that maintained segregated urban spaces and segregated schools. Their adoption of a "color-blind" rhetoric nevertheless fortified racial segregation.

A typical blue-collar response to the school board's reorganization plan came from Mildred Poole, the president of the Disston Elementary Home and School Association in Tacony, an entirely white neighborhood in the Near Northeast. Like many parents in Northeast Philadelphia, Poole claimed that the good neighborhood school was the reason her family remained in Tacony. She argued that the school board was subjecting Northeast Phila-delphia parents to untested changes "for no other reason than to foster inte-gration," a goal she did not think was worthy in and of itself. She further felt there was little need to improve the city's schools beyond maintaining the physical conditions of the buildings. "I find it hard to believe any school in this city is as bad as I have read," she said. "Nor will I ever believe they were neglected because they were in Negro neighborhoods." She then implored the school board to "start giving some thought to white children."[58] Poole expressed opinions that were common among blue-collar whites who were unable or unwilling to look beyond the borders of their own familiar spaces. Her refusal to acknowledge the problems of schools and neighborhoods out-side her own was a product of the normalization of segregated space. Poole's argument highlighted the cultural impact that the informal segregation of urban space had on blue-collar whites. It also drew attention to the growing disconnect between Northeast Philadelphia and the rest of the city.

Elements of that disconnect ran throughout the controversy over school reorganization and desegregation, especially as it turned to the question of bus-ing. Complicating matters, the Eighth School District that covered most of the Greater Northeast was geographically larger than any other district in the city. The Northeast's population growth far exceeded the expectations of city plan-ners and educational leaders. One of the most significant misjudgments was the number of new schools needed to accommodate the growing population. The Robert B. Pollock Elementary School, for example, quickly became inadequate to serve the needs of its growing Far Northeast neighborhood. While parents requested an addition to the school, the board of education offered a temporary solution by supplying portable trailers for the 1965–1966 school year. The portables would not provide enough space for the following school year. Against the opposition of the parents, the board of education considered busing as a solution to the twin problems of overcrowding and segregation.[59]

Parents in the Northeast did not think the Central School District could adequately attend to the needs of such a large and distinct section of the city. Additionally, many parents in Northeast Philadelphia felt left out of the organizational structure of the PHSC and ignored by the board of education. When the board of education held community meetings on potential changes to the school system, including the introduction of crosstown busing, it planned on including District Eight in a meeting to be held at Girls High School in Olney, which would create a travel burden for many Northeast parents.[60] As a result, some of the most vehement protests against the K4-4-4 plan came from the Northeast. "We want our children in our neighborhood where they belong," said Marion Blum of the Clara Barton Elementary School HSA. According to the school board's plans, her children would have to attend school outside their Juniata neighborhood in the Near Northeast.[61] The Mayfair HSA compared the Task Force program to a "communal system so necessary to sustain Socialism and Communism."[62] In 1966, the president of Northeast Philadelphia's school district HSA resigned from the Home and School Council because she felt it did not adequately represent the Northeast and that it ignored the feelings of parents in the eighth district.[63]

The Neighborhood School Association (NSA) emerged as the strongest organized opponent of the K4-4-4 system and other attempts to integrate the public schools. Billing itself as "non-partisan, non-sectarian, and non-ethnic," the NSA declared itself "against busing of children and for better materials and more schools instead."[64] The NSA said city agencies like the CHR and Citizens Commission on Civil Rights disregarded their concerns on busing. They accused the school board of intentionally defying the wishes of parents in the Northeast. They vowed in turn to defy changes in the school system that required their children to travel outside their own community and started a letter-writing campaign designed to rally white parents against the K4-4-4 plan. Parents reminded the board of education that they bought their homes because of their proximity to good neighborhood schools. Their

rhetoric echoed opposition to school busing in other cities, notably in Charlotte, North Carolina, where middle-class white parents engaged in a homeowners' rights campaign to defeat a similar student transfer program.[65]

In 1966, the Neighborhood Schools Association began distributing literature at Home and Schools Association meetings. They targeted meetings taking place at Philadelphia High School for Girls in the Olney neighborhood in
Upper North Philadelphia. Olney was in the midst of racial turnover and sat
in the Seventh School District, which the board of education targeted for the
potential transfer of students through busing. More importantly, the board
held all of its HSA meetings for parents with children in Northeast Philadelphia schools at Girls High. By targeting Northeast Philadelphia schools, the
NSA hoped to lure more white working- and middle-class parents into the
struggle to maintain the neighborhood schools system.[66] Northeast Philadelphia parents formed the backbone of the antibusing movement that would
figure heavily in the politics of education for the next decade.

Organized parents groups like the Neighborhood Schools Association
and Parents and Teachers Association never acknowledged the racial barriers
erected by the maintenance of a neighborhood school system. Neither did
they publicly rally in support of racially segregated education. Instead, they
protested the potential racial integration of public schools on grounds that
highlighted their attachment to their traditional models of public education.
As desegregation activists and educational reformers began gaining the support of liberals—especially in Richardson Dilworth's board of education—the
battles over Philadelphia's public schools continued into the late 1960s and
1970s. By then, however, many of the proponents of traditional neighborhood schools had found hope in the newest protector of blue-collar tradition,
Frank Rizzo. While Rizzo was no stranger to those familiar with the police
department, he became the de facto champion of citywide blue-collar politics after a series of encounters with militant civil rights organizations and
their attempts to challenge white privilege in public schools and other long-
established Philadelphia institutions.

Civil Rights and the Rise of Frank Rizzo

By the mid-1960s, civil rights leaders had already taken aim at a number of
Philadelphia's symbols of white privilege. Their latest target was Girard College, an all-white boarding school for orphaned boys in the heart of all-black

North Philadelphia. Girard College looked like a fortress, with high white walls protecting expansive grounds and mansion-like structures from the surrounding neighborhood. It was an architectural manifestation of African Americans' exclusion from the city's white power structure. When Martin Luther King Jr. visited Philadelphia in 1965, his first appearance was outside the Girard wall. Like other efforts to integrate all-white institutions, moderate civil rights leaders worked through the court system to integrate Girard College. By the mid-1960s, however, Cecil B. Moore began a direct-action campaign to integrate the boarding school. Between May and December 1965, Moore's daily marches and impassioned speeches outside Girard College drew the ire of white Philadelphians. They also brought Moore into regular confrontation with the Philadelphia police, and especially their increasingly visible Deputy Commissioner Frank Rizzo. The Girard College protests cemented Moore's role as the leader of militant black Philadelphia. They also secured Rizzo's reputation as the face of the police, and by extension, blue-collar politics in white Philadelphia.[67]

The segregation of Girard College stemmed from the last will and testament of nineteenth-century Philadelphia banker and financier, Stephen Girard. His century-old will mandated that the boarding school remain open exclusively to white orphaned boys. Confounding Girard's will, governance of the boarding school passed to the City of Philadelphia through a semipublic Board of City Trust. The municipal government maintained a segregated facility. As a result, local civil rights activists began taking aim at Girard's will shortly after the 1954 *Brown v. Board of Education* decision. The Board of City Trust, however, turned control over to an independent board made up of school alumni, thereby circumventing the court's decision by making Girard College a private institution. Cecil B. Moore then began organizing protests outside the Girard wall. The militancy of Moore's protests also led to far more confrontational encounters with Frank Rizzo and the Philadelphia police.[68]

Rizzo never publicly condemned the racial integration of Girard College. He always framed his response to the protests in terms of his duty to uphold law and order. Nevertheless, as Rizzo repeatedly clubbed young African American protesters outside the Girard wall, the deputy commissioner made his loyalties clear to both sides of the dispute. A confidential memorandum to Mayor Tate on the "Philadelphia Negro Situation," based on conversations with black clergy, said that the Girard protests led to "widespread negro feeling that Deputy Commissioner Frank Rizzo hates negroes."[69] When the Girard protests spilled out in front of the State Office Building at Broad and

Spring Garden Avenues because Tate was meeting Governor William Scranton, the picketers specifically targeted Rizzo. A scuffle between the police and the protesters left Rizzo with a bloodied hand. He stayed on the scene and the image of an injured yet resilient Rizzo began cementing his reputation in blue-collar Philadelphia. FOP president John Harrington asked the mayor to award Rizzo a commendation and called him "an outstanding example of one of our best policemen."[70]

It took another three years and another Supreme Court ruling before the trustees of Girard College admitted the first African American child. The protesters eventually won their battle against a mighty symbol of white privilege. In the process, however, they helped spur the rise of one of the greatest protectors of white privilege the city would ever know. Rizzo's public presence at the Girard College protests caused his reputation to reach new heights in white, blue-collar Philadelphia. Over the next few years, Frank Rizzo began making his indelible mark on the City of Brotherly Love.[71]

Frank Rizzo's rise was inextricably tied to the growth and increasing militancy of the civil rights movement as well as the liberalization of law enforcement and internal politics of the Philadelphia Police Department. Rizzo was well known to those within the department by the 1960s, but for many Philadelphians, the Girard College protests were the first formal introduction to the deputy commissioner. Already known as a "cop's cop," Rizzo was well respected by the blue-collar officers under his command.[72] His promotion to deputy commissioner in charge of uniformed personnel in 1963 made him even more popular among his fellow officers. Within the department, he had a reputation as one that would look out for the men under his command, even if that meant siding against his superiors. In fact, Rizzo often clashed with his superiors, especially Police Commissioner Howard Leary. Rizzo, a high-school dropout, resented the police commissioner's higher educational background and liberal approach to law enforcement. Where Leary preferred trying to build police-community relations, Rizzo wanted the police to be more assertive. He was furious at Leary's handling of the Columbia Avenue Riot, the Girard College protests, and other instances that Rizzo considered a capitulation to the demands of civil rights leaders like Cecil B. Moore.[73] Rizzo's reputation for taking on his superiors to protect his own officers resonated strongly with blue-collar Philadelphians who maintained the culture of reverence for the police. Combined with his confrontations with desegregation protestors taking aim at segregated neighborhoods and schools, Rizzo emerged as a fierce protector of white, blue-collar tradition.

After the Girard College protests, Rizzo became an early candidate for police commissioner when Howard Leary accepted an offer to take over the top position in the New York Police Department (NYPD). New York's Harlem experienced a similar uprising the month before Philadelphia's. As in North Philadelphia, years of poor police-community relations was a contributing factor in Harlem's explosion. New York's mayor John Lindsay was impressed with the way Leary commanded the Philadelphia police through various civil rights protests. He also hoped Leary could bring his emphasis on building connections between the police and poor communities of color to New York. Leary could not turn down an opportunity to lead the NYPD.[74] His departure was not unwelcome in Philadelphia. John Harrington and Frank Rizzo's push for law and order was in full swing. Leary was the figurehead of Philadelphia's brief experiment with law enforcement liberalism. He also stood in sharp contrast to the blue-collar officers that made up the police department. While Leary remained a favorite among liberals and civil rights organizations, the rank and file cheered his departure.[75]

The search for his replacement then sparked a new front in the battle for the future of the city's law enforcement. Mayor Tate wanted police department veteran Edward J. Bell for the position. Bell, like many of Tate's choices, was an attempt at compromise. Bell represented a middle ground between the conservatism of John Harrington and Frank Rizzo and the liberals that still favored a police commissioner with a record and background like Howard Leary. Bell was not the choice of Tate's own advisory committee, however. Made up of civic, legal, religious, law enforcement, and civil rights leaders, the advisory committee feared promoting from within the department. Instead, they consulted law enforcement experts in the International Association of Police Chiefs and the Federal Bureau of Investigation before inviting seven officers to interview for the position. After an exhaustive search, the committee nominated Bernard L. Garmire, the chief of police of Tucson, Arizona. Garmire had nearly thirty years of experience of policing in Indiana, Wisconsin, and Arizona, twenty of it in an administrative capacity. He had studied modern law enforcement at Indiana University, the Indiana State Police Academy, Chicago University, and the Federal Bureau of Investigation National Academy.[76] But the Tate administration saw Garmire as too much like Howard Leary at a time when the tide of law enforcement politics was turning toward Frank Rizzo's law and order. Tate's enduring quest for political compromise led him to ignore the advice of his advisory council and appoint Edward Bell the new police commissioner.[77]

In August 1966, while Commissioner Bell was vacationing, Tate named
Rizzo acting police commissioner. Rizzo refused to let his first chance commanding the entire department go to waste. He orchestrated a series of raids
against the city's chapter of the Student Nonviolent Coordinating Committee.
The local chapter had publicized and protested police abuses during the Girard
College protests. SNCC national chairman Stokely Carmichael had begun
calling for "Black Power" and regularly protested police action against the civil
rights demonstrations. Rizzo claimed that an informant told police that the
local SNCC chapter were stockpiling arms and preparing for an assault on
police, but the raid was politically motivated. Rizzo wanted to end the Black
Power presence in Philadelphia before it started. The police raided four homes
in North Philadelphia and found a few sticks of dynamite. Amid claims that
the police planted the explosives, Rizzo charged four local SNCC leaders with
plotting to blow up Independence Hall. Rizzo had them arrested and held on
$50,000 bond. The charges and hefty bond drew the attention of the national
organization. Stokely Carmichael came to Philadelphia and denounced "racist
Rizzo." He promised continued protests. Carmichael emboldened the deputy
commissioner, who made a series of statements promising to get tough on
protesters. The cases against the arrested members of SNCC eventually failed,
but the damage had been done. SNCC faltered in Philadelphia and Rizzo's reputation mushroomed. He became a national figure, probably the most famous
second in command of a police force in the United States.[78]

James Tate, whose administration had already taken a turn toward the politics of law and order, realized Frank Rizzo's value, especially with reelection
pending. In May 1967, shortly after he defeated another challenge from the
reform wing of his party, Tate announced that Edward Bell had taken ill and
resigned his position. The mayor named Rizzo acting police commissioner,
adding that he would have a "free hand" in running the police department.
Rizzo's promotion sent shockwaves through the city's civil rights community, who interpreted it as a direct attack. Civil libertarians likewise worried
that Rizzo's overzealousness was cause for alarm. Even if his actions were not
racially biased, they complained, his reputation for toughness with all sorts of
protestors raised questions about his motivations.[79] Tate's decision was strategic, however. He had already severed most of his ties with the reform wing
of the local Democratic Party. In 1967, an additional threat to Tate's political
future also lay in the city's young district attorney, Arlen Specter. When Specter won the Republican Party's nomination for mayor, he became the local
party's first viable candidate since the dawn of Philadelphia's reform era. The

popular prosecutor's promise to restore law and order became the center-piece of his mayoral bid. James Tate turned to Frank Rizzo. For the remain-der of the 1967 campaign, Tate promised to retain the popular commissioner and insinuated that Specter would replace him. The election hinged almost entirely on Frank Rizzo and the politics of law and order.[80]

In the weeks leading up to the election of 1967, civil rights and Black Power activists held a series of rallies at predominantly African American schools in support of Cecil B. Moore, who launched his own third-party cam-paign for mayor. At the same time, younger activists were organizing black students. For months, they held workshops and rallies on black pride, black history, and Afro-centrism.[81] While James Tate campaigned for reelection, Rizzo monitored the rallies at the schools. Not content with the administra-tive work that went along with being police commissioner, Rizzo was often out front commanding the response to the specific demonstrations, clashing with young protesters and students. The largest occurred on November 17, 1967, just days after Tate won one of the closest elections in the city's history.

On November 17, African American students staged a protest at the board of education administration building in Center City Philadelphia. Inspired by local civil rights and Black Power activists, the students demanded more black teachers, the inclusion of African American history to the curriculum, and permission to celebrate their African heritage by wearing traditional clothing. By noon, over 3,500 students had arrived at the board of educa-tion building. Superintendent Mark Shedd and board of education president Richardson Dilworth invited a handful of the protest leaders to meet with them to discuss their demands. Shedd and Dilworth were open to the dis-cussion. Both championed integrated education and supported the intro-duction of black history to the curriculum.[82] But while Shedd and Dilworth attempted to negotiate a peaceful settlement to the protest inside the school board administration building, Rizzo and police arrived intent on restor-ing order outside. When two boys climbed on top of a parked car, witnesses claimed Rizzo said "Get their black asses!" before leading the charge into the demonstration.[83] The police began attacking the young protesters. Crit-ics, including Mark Shedd, later called the events that transpired outside the school board building a "police riot."[84]

Liberals and civil rights leaders were quick to denounce the actions of the police. Rizzo and his blue-collar supporters, however, said the school board protest was evidence of the breakdown of law and order in the schools.[85] Blue-collar whites believed Rizzo had defended the public schools from the demands of Black Power activists. His reputation as the protector of blue-collar tradition was sealed. It also merged with his law-and-order persona. He received numerous petitions and signs of support from the city's blue-collar neighborhoods, including a seventy-foot-long petition and holiday greeting signed by "the people of Kensington and Fishtown," thanking him for his actions at the school board demonstration. Several of the petitions demanded that James Tate retain the police commissioner despite the pressure from liberals and civil rights leaders.[86] In response, Tate kept his campaign promise and officially reappointed Frank Rizzo. One woman told the mayor that his decision "converted me from a died-in-the-wool [sic] Republican to a 'Tate' Democrat."[87] Another supporter, identified only as "One Who Wants to Save Philadelphia," told the mayor that he should do everything in his power to make sure Rizzo had whatever he needed, because "This man is the city's salvation."[88]

After the police department justified the action taken at the school board demonstration as a proper way to uphold law and order, the North Philadelphia–based North City Congress (NCC) challenged the department's assertions by comparing the events of November 1967 with those in Kensington in October 1966. "When faced with the same kind of 'provocative behavior' by a large mob of white Kensington residents who gathered a year ago to protest to the move of a Negro family to their area," the NCC charged, the police "were much more restrained and polite and did not feel called upon to use such extreme force." Comparing accounts from local newspapers, the NCC showed that similar behavior took place at both riots: youngsters climbing on cars, damage to windows, resisting police, throwing projectiles, and injuring police officers. Pointing out that the Kensington rioters were in many ways more lawless and provocative than the students at the board of education, the NCC squarely blamed Frank Rizzo for the violence.[89]

Rizzo's reputation as a protector of white privilege was not lost on civil rights activists. When James Tate named him police commissioner, he cemented a new era of white, blue-collar politics in Philadelphia. For those who felt as if their neighborhoods, schools, and traditions were at risk, Rizzo became the answer to their problems and the protector of their blue-collar traditions and values. In the late 1960s, they continued looking to Rizzo as further challenges arose from civil rights activists, liberals, and city planners.

CHAPTER 4

Philadelphia Plans

Not since the Columbia Avenue uprising of August 1964 had an event in Philadelphia aroused white anger like the student demonstration at the board of education administration building on November 17, 1967. In the days immediately following the protest, Richardson Dilworth sorted through what he called "literally hundreds of anonymous, hysterical, denunciatory letters."[1] Others that defended the students or school board received similar letters that were threatening, viciously racist, or both.[2] The letter writers were furious that administrators agreed to meet with the protest leaders. Many of them demanded their resignation. They blamed the introduction of new programs and progressive pedagogies for emboldening the students. Worst of all, they worried that the public schools had ceased enforcing discipline. City Council President Paul D'Ortona even said that the meeting between administrators and protesters showed a lack of "respect for law and order in our schools."[3] Through all the outrage, an overarching accusation emerged: liberals and elites on the school board were responsible for the protests. Almost all of them blamed Richardson Dilworth and the superintendent of public schools, Mark Shedd.[4]

The superintendent was already wildly unpopular among white parents. The Harvard PhD was a nationally recognized expert on progressive educational philosophies. He had successfully implemented a desegregation plan as superintendent of the Englewood, New Jersey, public school system before taking the job in Philadelphia. Richardson Dilworth recruited Shedd because he valued his experience combating segregation in a Northern school district. Shedd was more than a champion of integrated education, however. The superintendent pushed experimental education and progressive disciplinary tactics. He also agreed with many of the demands made by the African American students. He encouraged curriculum changes that emphasized black history and sought more African American teachers. Shedd even allowed Cecil B. Moore to hold rallies at public schools.[5] With Dilworth's backing, Shedd's proposals sought compliance with Pennsylvania's public school integration mandate, but his plans met stiff opposition from white parents that feared the loss of their neighborhood schools. Few were implemented successfully.[6] Nevertheless, his attempts to change the public school system and accommodate African American students drew the ire of blue-collar whites.

Shedd and Dilworth defended their decision to meet with the protest leaders as a means to bring a peaceful end to the demonstration. Shedd also insisted that the protest was not the unruly riot the police and media had labeled it. Instead, Shedd placed the blame for the violent outcome entirely on the heavy police presence. Dilworth joined Shedd by directly blaming Frank Rizzo for the violence.[7] Taking stock of the criticism he received, Shedd put the white reaction to the school board demonstration and his educational policies in the context of the worsening urban crisis. He said that white Philadelphians had developed a "preoccupation, almost an obsession, triggered by the riots of the last two or three summers, for law and order, safety, for protection of rights and property." He hoped that education and a "return to reason" would ease the tensions created by the recent disorder.[8] Dilworth called for Rizzo's removal.

Dilworth and Shedd's education reforms already made the two men unpopular in blue-collar neighborhoods. After criticizing Rizzo and the politics of law and order, however, they became targets of white resentment.[9] One petition commending Frank Rizzo for his action in the demonstration denounced the criticisms made by Dilworth and Shedd. "These officials should have been more concerned with who they allow to speak to the children in our schools and why these children were not in school where they belonged," it stated. "These children should be in school learning to respect the law instead of violating it by damaging other citizen's property," it continued. Hundreds signed the petition as it circulated through the white, blue-collar neighborhoods of Northeast, South, and Southwest Philadelphia. It blamed the student demonstration on "the negligence of the school board and Mr. Dilworth."[10]

The school board demonstration and its aftermath made the connections between the politics of law and order and education starkly clear. By attacking Mark Shedd and Richardson Dilworth, blue-collar Philadelphians held two progressive reformers responsible for the public school crisis. Dilworth,

the once great urban liberal and former mayor, had helped to usher in Philadelphia's era of good government. Liberals still lauded him. By the late 1960s,
however, blue-collar Philadelphians not only blamed Dilworth for the problems in the public schools, they held him and fellow liberals responsible for
the worsening urban crisis.

The attacks on Shedd and Dilworth were not isolated. They were part of
a much larger white, blue-collar revolt against the liberals, elites, and "do-
gooders" that attempted to address the inequities in urban education, employment, and housing. By the late 1960s, blue-collar whites concluded that liberal
efforts to create equal opportunity in blue-collar schools, job markets, and
neighborhoods intentionally put them on the losing end of a zero-sum game.[11]

The blue-collar revolt against liberalism brought together the politics of
education, equal employment, and equitable housing. Against the backdrop
of the urban uprisings that hit American cities and Frank Rizzo's forceful
response to street crime, the blue-collar response showed that the politics
of education, affirmative action, housing, and law enforcement were directly
and inextricably linked. The revolt also marked an important shift in blue-
collar politics. Before embracing populist conservatism, blue-collar whites
rejected urban liberalism by targeting reformers and planners. No single issue
forced blue-collar antiliberalism to the fore. Indeed, it was the confluence of
these politics in the late 1960s that initiated the blue-collar rejection of liberal
politics. This shift, however, was not a complete break with the liberal policies that had guided politics in Philadelphia since the 1950s and much of the
nation since the 1930s. To the contrary, in battles over Catholic and public
schools, the integration of the construction industry, and city planning, white
working- and middle-class Philadelphians sought to redirect liberal policies
toward their own needs and interests. When those efforts failed, blue-collar
whites found new solutions in Frank Rizzo's aggressive, "one of us" populism.
Blue-collar antiliberalism in the late 1960s was a turning point toward the
emergence of blue-collar conservatism in the 1970s.

The Urban Crisis and Urban Education

By the late 1960s, the crisis of urban education reached beyond Philadelphia's public schools. Across metropolitan Philadelphia more than 275,000
students attended Catholic schools, making the Archdiocesan School District of Philadelphia the second largest in the United States. To meet growing

demand, the archdiocese opened five new elementary schools in the 1960s, one in Philadelphia and four in the surrounding suburbs. Beginning in 1963, a new Catholic high school opened in the Philadelphia suburbs every year through the end of the decade. Archbishop Ryan High School for Boys and Archbishop Ryan High School for Girls opened in the Far Northeast in 1966.[12] In South Philadelphia, more school-age children attended Catholic schools than ever before. The growth of Philadelphia's Catholic school system signaled school parents' desire for religious education, but also their desire to keep their children close to home. More than 90 percent of South Philadelphia parents told a surveyor that they sent their children to parochial school because they wanted them to attend a neighborhood school through the eighth grade.[13] For parents in South and Northeast Philadelphia, Catholic schools were religious institutions, traditions, and neighborhood alternatives to the public school system.

Catholic schools were not immune to the problems that beset the public schools. Although the Archdiocese of Philadelphia criticized the city's segregated public schools, they failed to acknowledge that Catholic schools were just as segregated. The archdiocesan parish system linked elementary schools to churches that served the surrounding Catholic community. After finishing elementary school, Catholic school students attended high schools fed by their surrounding parishes. Because Catholic parishes were parts of segregated neighborhoods, Catholic schools reflected those segregated demographics. Catholic schools in West and North Philadelphia were almost entirely African American or Puerto Rican. South Philadelphia, Kensington, and the Near Northeast still had ethnic parish schools that primarily catered to Italian Catholics, Irish Catholics, and Polish Catholics. The Catholic school system grew fastest in Northeast Philadelphia and the suburbs, but those schools remained exclusively white. As a result, Catholic schools mirrored the racial makeup of the public schools. Racial composition was not the only reason Catholic parents sent their children to parish schools, but parish segregation created a school system sometimes more segregated than public schools. In South Philadelphia, a busing program made public schools more integrated than Catholic schools.[14]

Many liberals and civil rights leaders began viewing the insularity of the archdiocesan school system with suspicion, but blue-collar Catholic parents avoided controversies over desegregation by invoking the primacy of religious and ethnic tradition. Journalist Peter Binzen suggested that more than faith and ethnicity guided Catholic parents. Binzen argued that Catholic schools gave parents the discipline they believed public schools lacked. With only a hint of hyperbole, he compared the type of order upheld in Philadelphia's Catholic schools—including the wearing of uniforms and the inculcated respect for authority—to Soviet elementary schools he visited in Moscow and Leningrad. Binzen's exaggeration notwithstanding, discipline was a cherished hallmark of Catholic education. He also pointed out that discipline and ethnic composition made Catholic parents fiercely proud of their "Catlicks," as Binzen mimicked the working-class vernacular for the city's Catholic educational facilities. He said blue-collar whites reveled in comparing the failing public schools to their superior "Catlicks."[15]

As with blue-collar neighborhood pride, the blue-collar Catholic pride in parish schools signaled both differentiation and exclusivity. But pride could not forestall the crises that struck the Catholic schools in the late 1960s. Unlike the challenges faced by public schools, those facing Catholic education did not come from the perceived threat of integration or student protest, but from increasing financial burdens. The archdiocese maintained tuition-free education longer than many other major Catholic school systems, mostly funded from the church collection plate.[16] By the early 1970s, however, an archdiocesan-sponsored but independent Advisory Committee on the Catholic Schools found that Philadelphia parishes operated at a net deficit of $1.2 million. Catholic elementary and high schools added another $997,000 shortfall. By the end of the 1960s, the combined cost of the parishes and school system caused the archdiocese to operate at a $2.2 million deficit.[17] Poor and working-class parishes relied on fundraisers like community bingo games to keep their schools afloat, but financial burdens forced a decline in enrollment. Prior to the 1967–1968 school year, the archdiocese reduced the number of students accepted into their high schools because they could not meet their financial needs. Many Catholic parents became resentful, especially because their tax dollars aided the public schools their children did not attend.[18] The archdiocese and blue-collar Catholic parents concluded that the future of Catholic education in Philadelphia depended upon securing tax-funded state aid for parochial schools.[19]

A series of doctrinally and socially conservative cardinals oversaw the archdiocesan school system for most of the twentieth century. They had been distrustful of state interference in Catholic schools and wary of public education's influence over their institutions.[20] By the 1960s, however, the Catholic school financial crisis forced the archdiocese to seek a cooperative relationship with the public board of education. More importantly, Catholic administrators began modest efforts to secure state aid for parochial educa-tion. In 1965, the Pennsylvania legislature established a program that pro-vided parochial school students with transportation on public school buses. It was a small step, but the archdiocese cheered the law for its potential to help thousands of non-public-school students. That same year, the federal Elementary and Secondary Education Act of 1965 included provisions to provide non-public-school students with limited educational benefits and programs. The Philadelphia Archdiocese and Catholic parents recognized the limits of these legislative steps, but viewed their passing with anticipation and prayed they would survive challenges to their constitutionality.[21]

By 1967, several efforts to create a system of public support for parochial schools had made their way to the Pennsylvania state legislature. In June, Martin P. Mullen, a Democratic state representative from Southwest Philadel-phia, introduced a bill into the Pennsylvania General Assembly that proposed a state Nonpublic School Authority with the power to dispense public funds to private schools.[22] Despite a growing distrust of liberal policies, sections of the city with heavy Catholic populations rallied behind the bill. Support was especially strong in Northeast Philadelphia. During the debate over the Mullen Bill, a *Northeast Times* editorial called the aid to nonpublic schools a necessity given the number of non-public-school students in the city and the escalating costs that threatened these institutions.[23] Organizations like Citi-zens for Educational Freedom, which was especially strong in the Northeast and the surrounding Bucks County suburbs, pressured state lawmakers to pass the bill. By the end of the year, as the Mullen Bill awaited the signature of Governor Raymond Shafer, Philadelphia area Catholic churches organized petition drives and collected parishioners' signatures after Sunday Mass. Over one hundred thousand Catholic parents sent telegrams to the governor asking him to sign the Mullen Bill. The vast majority of them were from the Philadelphia area. The efforts worked. In 1968, Pennsylvania became the first state in the nation to grant public funds to nonpublic schools.[24]

Despite the efforts of Catholic parents, state aid to nonpublic schools faced heavy opposition. Even modest efforts to secure state funding for non-public schools met resistance from liberals, civil libertarians, and advocates of the separation of church and state.[25] Liberal and Jewish organizations led the opposition to the Mullen Bill. Liberal Jewish activists like those in the Jewish Community Relations Council, Jewish Labor Committee, and Anti-Defamation League feared the Mullen Bill would undermine the constitu-tional prohibition against the establishment of religion. They were joined by

Protestant clergy who feared that public support of parochial schools would encourage the proliferation of nonpublic school systems and weaken financial support for public education. Civil rights activists and educational reformers raised the possibility that state funding for parochial schools would lead to "separatist schools" that would perpetuate segregation.[26] Executive director of the Philadelphia Urban League, Andrew Freeman, specifically argued that the bill would result in a more segregated public school system because it would encourage more parents to send their children to private schools.[27]

Measures like the Mullen Bill would ostensibly have benefited all parochial schools, but its intended beneficiaries were Pennsylvania's Catholic school districts. Opponents of the bill therefore directed many of their critiques at the archdiocesan school system. When the Mullen Bill became law, the same organizations worked for its repeal. Catholic parents felt they had won a small victory in their efforts to maintain traditional parish schools, especially in the working- and middle-class parishes that bore the brunt of the financial crisis. That the main opponents of state aid for parochial schools were liberals was not lost on blue-collar Catholics. As the passage of the Mullen Bill turned into a protracted battle over the state funding of religious education, they came to view liberal challenges to its constitutionality as a deliberate attempt to cripple their educational institutions.[28] Meanwhile, white public school parents held board of education liberals responsible for the outbreak of student protest and the breakdown of law and order in the schools. When they again targeted Richardson Dilworth and Mark Shedd, they joined their Catholic counterparts in blaming liberals for the mutually reinforcing crises in urban education.

Shortly after the student demonstration at the board of education, about fifty white mothers with children in South Philadelphia (Southern) High School threatened to hold their own sit-in at the board's administration building. The mothers claimed they were afraid for their children's safety. Periodic gang activity and racial hostility had plagued Southern since the early 1960s, including two stabbings, a shooting, and multiple fights between black and white students.[29] The mothers demanded stricter discipline, the installation of electronic surveillance devices, and an added police presence. They also called for the removal and banishment of "detrimental outside influences," a reference to the militant civil rights leaders that had addressed students before the school board demonstration. When African Americans demanded a larger role in governing the school system, white parents in South Philadelphia and other blue-collar areas worried about the growth of Black Power activism in the schools.[30] The women that demanded police in Southern High connected their protest against disorder and black militancy in the schools to broader concerns about the urban crisis. Like their counterparts in fights over neighborhood integration or law enforcement policy, these mothers reestablished their role as protectors of blue-collar traditions and expanded the blue-collar revolt against liberalism.

Southern High's proximity to the far more troubled Bok Vocational High School compounded parental safety concerns. Less than a mile from Southern, Bok was one of the board of education's three technical high schools. Most students in these schools traveled from other neighborhoods to take industrial training classes. Typically, boys took classes in traditionally blue-collar skills like automotive maintenance, sheet-metal work, welding, and machinery while girls learned dressmaking, industrial sewing, or nursing. With a selective admittance, these schools offered the most comprehensive occupational training programs available in the public school system. Bok was the city's most successful school for providing African American students with vocational training. Its troubled reputation stemmed not from problems within the school building, but from tensions between students and the surrounding neighborhood. The student body was 95 percent African American, but the school was located in an all-white, primarily Italian American neighborhood.[31]

Administrators at Bok wanted an integrated student body and attempted to recruit from the surrounding area, but received few applications for entry. In fact, Bok typically received fewer applications from South Philadelphia students than the area's two Catholic high schools. According to the school board, Bok suffered from a poor image. White parents were unwilling to send their children to a school with predominantly black pupils. Counselors in Bok's feeder schools rarely suggested that white students apply.[32] As a result, most of Bok's students traveled from neighborhoods in West and North Philadelphia. They then had to pass through a hostile white neighborhood to get to school, where residents accused African American students of travelling in large groups, using foul language, and damaging property. The students spoke of feeling like outsiders. "It's kind of scary when you have to move through a place like South Philly by yourself and everybody hates you and you know it," said a Bok student from West Philadelphia. "Even the little kids would stop and stare at us like we was some kind of animals, 'cause their mammas would tell them we was animals."[33]

Racially motivated incidents between neighborhood youths and the Bok students had marred the community since the early 1960s, but diminished

considerably by middecade. In the lead-up to the school board demonstration, however, protest organizers targeted Bok students and large numbers of
them participated in the event. Neighborhood residents feared the influence
of Black Power advocates and the possible resumption of hostilities. The tensions between the students and the neighborhood reached their highest point
after October 2, 1968, when a group of black youths stabbed a white student
from Bishop Neumann Catholic High School, located just a few blocks from
Bok. Although the youngster arrested for the stabbing did not attend Bok,
the incident led to a series of violent confrontations between the neighborhood residents and Bok students. White residents harassed Bok students as
they made their way through the neighborhood. Black students retaliated
by attacking the few white students in Bok. The school ended classes early
because of the severity of the fighting. On the night of October 8, a crowd of
angry whites marched on a nearby police station, demanding Bok's closure.
The police responded to blue-collar requests by stationing extra patrols in the
area. The next day, black students from Southern attempted to join students at
Bok in a show of solidarity, but police blocked their path. When the schools
let out, police tried to shuffle Bok students onto waiting buses, but many of
them refused and asserted their right to pass through the white neighborhood.
Along their way, more fights broke out between white and black youths.[34]

After a week of minor skirmishes, white parents organized a demonstration against Bok. They demanded that the school board stop the admission of
African American students or close the school entirely. Nearly seven hundred
area residents packed the school's auditorium for a meeting with Commission
of Human Relations Chair Clarence Farmer and Police Commissioner Frank
Rizzo. The attendees shouted down Farmer, chanting "Close down the school
or we'll burn it down." Others announced their support for presidential candidate George Wallace. The crowd cheered when Rizzo took the microphone,
even though he explained that his police would not tolerate disorder from
either white or black students. Rizzo was in his element, however. The South
Philadelphia native was hardly more popular anywhere else and he knew how
to raise the audience's ire. He told them that his power was limited and that
the situation escalated because of Richardson Dilworth and Mark Shedd's
inaction. Still bruising from when the two top education officials blamed
him for the violence outside the school board administration building, Rizzo
rarely let go of a grudge. He told the crowd that he invited Dilworth and
Shedd to attend the meeting, but they refused. In fact, Dilworth was vacationing in South America and Shedd was meeting with another white community

organization. Rizzo's mistruth fed the blue-collar revolt against liberalism. In time he would harness it to make the shift from law enforcement to politics. In the meantime, Mark Shedd issued an order to close Bok for the remainder of the week.[35]

Governor Raymond Shafer prepared to send the Pennsylvania National Guard into South Philadelphia when Shedd announced that Bok would reopen for classes on Monday, October 15. Local residents, however, wanted Bok closed permanently. On the day before classes resumed, over one thousand whites spent almost five hours marching through South Philadelphia. The ad hoc committee that staged the march made a series of demands of the school board, including making Bok a predominantly white school and assigning security guards to patrol the halls. Led by a sound truck, the leaders of the march urged neighbors to join the protest in explicitly racial terms. "We need you as long as you are white," came the call from the truck. "We don't care if you're Polocks or Jews. We want whites!" Asking residents to overcome ethnic and religious divisions, the protest organizers appealed to South Philadelphians' shared whiteness. When organizers presented a teenage girl they claimed had been attacked by Bok students, they started chanting "We want white power." Trying to calm white parents, Mark Shedd issued a statement asking for cooperation and understanding, but he could not negotiate with the protesters. Like Rizzo, most of them continued to blame his leadership for fostering the public school crisis.[36]

Sympathetic politicians stoked those fears as the Bok crisis spread beyond South Philadelphia. A Northeast Philadelphia city councilman told an assembly that the violence around Bok provided evidence against the school board's proposed busing program for the Northeast.[37] Others began using the Bok crisis to argue for the superiority of neighborhood schools. In a meeting between white and black community leaders that finally started bringing the demonstrations in South Philadelphia to an end, one white resident stated that the trouble never would have started if Bok had catered to local high school students. "If the school had only served the kids from South Philly, we wouldn't have this trouble now," he said.[38] Two weeks later, Mayor Tate declared he would take action to end the protests, but further fueled blue-collar resentment by accusing the board of education of "falling flat on their faces" and "having extremists agitate the children in the auditoriums of the schools."[39] The mayor finally brokered an agreement with the school board that put more security guards in the school and sought to create a racial balance in Bok's student population.[40]

The crisis at Bok showed how much blue-collar white ethnics conflated the liberal governance of the board of education with the rise of African American protest in the schools. Some believed that Richardson Dilworth purposely caused the disorders to get revenge on the neighborhood for opposing a political proposal he made when he was mayor. "Dilworth hates South Philadelphia because we fought his plan to charge $40 to park your car in front of your home," said one local resident. "He's been getting even with us ever since," he continued. "He keeps putting more Negroes in the schools."[41] While misguided, the man's conspiratorial description of Dilworth's motives spoke to a broader belief that liberals intentionally targeted blue-collar neighborhoods. A resident of Northeast Philadelphia made a similar claim when he stated that "Dilworth and Shedd are bound and determined to turn the schools over to Negroes."[42] Whether they blamed liberals for seeking political revenge or for kowtowing to the demands of militant civil rights leaders, the same sense of victimization undergirded their outrage. Many were also convinced that gains for African Americans came at their expense.

Dilworth and Shedd became proxy targets for a broader revolt against urban liberals. In 1968, they embroiled the board of education in another controversy affecting blue-collar whites when they prohibited two local labor unions from using Bok's facilities for their apprenticeship training programs. Shedd and Dilworth banned the International Brotherhood of Electrical Workers Local 98 and Sheet Metal Workers Local 19, two member unions of the city's powerful Building and Trade Union Council, for failing to meet a federal mandate to increase the number of nonwhites in their apprenticeship programs. By attempting to force the unions to comply with federal guidelines, Shedd and Dilworth thrust the school board headlong into the fight over the so-called Philadelphia Plan, one of the nation's first affirmative action programs.[43] Liberals and civil rights leaders cheered their actions, but the unions decried interference with their hiring and recruiting practices. Joseph Burke of the Sheet Metal Workers told Dilworth that he should confine himself to the business of education and warned the board not to adopt "this vicious, arbitrary, costly, impractical, unfair and useless plan."[44] The contest over the Philadelphia Plan represented a second battleground in the blue-collar revolt against liberalism. Dilworth and Shedd showed that it was intractably tied to the crises in education. They also convinced blue-collar Philadelphians that liberals wanted to destroy another valued tradition: their union jobs.

Urban Employment and Blue-Collar Labor

Andy Plant was a painter in the construction industry. He lived in a blue-collar section of Fishtown with his wife and children, where he fought for neighborhood schools and against the implementation of a student busing program. Along with his home and schools, Plant counted the benefits of his union job as a mark of his blue-collar values and economic standing. Building-trades unions were cherished institutions. Plant believed the security of his union job, like the security of neighborhoods and schools, was under attack from liberals and civil rights leaders. He further claimed that African Americans did not want equal treatment. They want "better than what you got." He said the enactment of the Philadelphia Plan made white workers resentful of blacks on the job. In the construction industry, he continued, "niggers used to be nice, they did things you wanted them to, you could be friendly with 'em. Now with all this crap that's come around, they're surly. They'll talk back to you. They won't do what you want, and that kind of stuff." Liberals and civil rights organizations also made his boss afraid to fire black workers for poor performance, he said. "They don't want what you want," Plant repeatedly said of black workers. "They want more than you want."[45]

Few white union men expressed their opposition to the Philadelphia Plan as candidly as Andy Plant. Yet as the controversial employment program began affecting Philadelphia-area work sites, it engendered a similar resentment for liberals and civil rights activists. Conceived in 1967, the Philadelphia Plan was the first fully formed affirmative action program in the United States and the blueprint for federal affirmative action nationwide. It gave definition to the phrase "affirmative action" by requiring federal contractors to establish goals and timetables for hiring African American apprentices in the Philadelphia building trades in order to increase minority representation in building and construction unions.[46] The plan was bitterly opposed by the Building and Trades Council of Philadelphia (BTC). The unions argued that outside oversight of their training practices would infringe upon their autonomy and hard-fought labor rights. On the other side, civil rights leaders claimed federal action was necessary to stop rampant discrimination in the building-trades unions. Their liberal allies further said that the jobs program would stem the tide of the ongoing urban crisis. In the late 1960s, the politics of equal opportunity hiring, the urban labor market, and the urban crisis came together in the debate over the Philadelphia Plan.

Organized labor gained an increasingly influential position within city government in the postwar era. Forged during the Clark-Dilworth years, Philadelphia's labor-liberal alliance was a cornerstone of the city's reform era and one of the strongest progressive coalitions in the nation. No administration, however, was friendlier to labor than that of Mayor James H. J. Tate. Under Tate's mayoral administration, unions gained tremendous influence over city politics, policies, and agencies. He sought the counsel of organized labor and appointed labor leaders to most boards and commissions.[47] James J. O'Neill, president of the Building and Construction Trades Council and a dominant force in the Philadelphia branch of the American Federation of Labor-Congress of Industrial Organizations (AFL-CIO), sat on the City Planning Commission. Edward F. Toohey, president of the Philadelphia AFL-CIO, took positions on the boards of the Philadelphia Industrial Development Corporation, the Philadelphia Port Corporation, and the Philadelphia Anti-Poverty Action Committee. At several union meetings, furthermore, Tate told enthusiastic audiences that "Philadelphia will be known as a union town" as long as he was mayor. In return for his patronage, Tate could count on tens of thousands of union men and women, as well as union fundraising, to help advance his political career.[48]

Tate also insisted that the city use union labor for all public work. The BTC, representing over forty thousand members and the most powerful labor group in the Philadelphia AFL-CIO, reaped the benefits of this close relationship with city government. They also remembered when that was not the case. For many unionists in Philadelphia, especially older members and officials, the lean working years of the Great Depression remained a not-so-distant memory. Edward Toohey, AFL-CIO Philadelphia Council president and an opponent of the Philadelphia Plan, came into the building trades as a plasterer in the 1920s. He vividly remembered when work was sporadic and seasonal. "The Building Trades were then under a siege of widespread unemployment," he said of his early years as a trade unionist.[49] High-paying union jobs were only a recent development. Like blue-collar neighborhoods that feared reductions in property values, union leaders like Toohey feared losing an institution that maintained working-class stability. Organized labor remained wary of any policy that threatened their newly acquired position of influence and privilege in city government and the local labor market.

The relationship between the mayor and his labor allies began to strain when civil rights leaders pressured Tate to confront discrimination in city building projects. Local chapters of CORE and the NAACP staged a series of high-profile demonstrations at his home and mayoral office. In response, the city's Commission on Human Relations (CHR) initiated an inspection program to oversee compliance on public and private construction sites. Additionally, the CHR reviewed apprenticeship training programs conducted through the joint apprenticeship training boards in the construction trades. Because the building-trades unions remained resistant to liberal oversight over union procedures, the CHR concluded that failure to comply with nondiscrimination regulations was an intentional effort to maintain racial exclusivity.[50]

While the Building Trades Council was one of the more powerful units in Philadelphia's labor movement, they did not represent all organized labor in the city. Several unions were integrated, led by African American activists, and worked for civil rights unionism.[51] The building trades, however, became a target of civil rights activists for reasons both symbolic and economic. Construction work represented what it meant to be a "blue-collar worker" in urban America. There was a prestige among the "Hard Hats," as they were popularly known. They were the skilled labor that built and maintained urban environments. Construction work bestowed honor among those who did it. Their work was difficult, and as such, "manly." Building-trades unions also championed principles of hard work, tradition, and family. Familial and ethnic ties were often a prerequisite for entry into apprenticeship programs. Similar to other Philadelphia blue-collar traditions that came under scrutiny in the 1960s—like the police department and the Mummers Parade—the building trades were overwhelmingly white and male. Asked later about the homogeneity of the building trades, Joseph Burke of the Sheet Metal Workers said that no African Americans ever came looking for work. "I never said no to a Negro," he said. But, he admitted, "We didn't go out looking for them either."[52] For civil rights activists seeking full citizenship in a country that privileged men's earning potential, construction jobs meant earning respect in a nation that privileged male breadwinners.[53]

Along with police work, few occupations symbolized blue-collar identity and authenticity more than construction. The building trades also offered the added benefit of some of the highest wages available to skilled, working-class male breadwinners. Public works construction was one of the healthiest segments of the economy. Federal, state, and municipal governments spent more than $17 billion on Philadelphia-area construction projects in the mid-1960s. Even as Philadelphia lost manufacturing jobs in the 1950s and 1960s, the blue-collar workforce remained strong because federal protections and urban renewal programs changed the nature of construction work. Unlike Edward

Toohey's recollections of leaner times, massive federal spending made construction work more readily available. Millions of federal dollars pouring into construction projects in the five-county Philadelphia area assured the building-trades unions that employment would remain steady for the foreseeable future. These unions had also won several battles for the maintenance of prevailing wages and fringe benefits on all federal building projects. Along with the cultural capital that came with construction work, liberal federal and municipal policies made construction one of the most secure and lucrative blue-collar employment options in the city.[54]

The building trades' ascendency in local municipal and cultural politics made them a glaring example of discrimination in the urban labor market. Discriminatory hiring was not limited to these unions, but the benefits of federal and municipal protections, high wages, and steady employment made the virtually all-white building trades a symbol of the impediments to equal opportunity. Furthermore, these trade unions had earned a reputation for discrimination. When, in 1963, the Philadelphia Council AFL-CIO, working with the city's Commission on Human Relations, tried to establish a committee of building trades and industrial unions to work on problems of racial integration, the BTC threatened to resign from the local AFL-CIO. Philadelphia's AFL-CIO placated the building trades by abandoning plans to establish the commission.[55] The BTC's threats foreshadowed the arguments they would use against the Philadelphia Plan. Despite the very low rates of nonwhite membership in the skilled trade unions, the council adamantly denied that any of their training practices were discriminatory.

The unions' insistence on their color-blind training practices hid the deeper patterns that created and maintained occupational segregation. In addition to selective apprenticeship recruitment among neighborhood, ethnic, family, and religious groups, labor contracts allowed the building trades to control all hiring procedures. Training their apprentices ensured quality of work and proper skill level for all workers. It also helped the unions maintain their advantageous place in the Philadelphia labor market. Controlling apprenticeship programs gave the unions control over the labor force. New apprentices had to go through proper union channels before attaining journeyman status and becoming full-fledged union members. With no oversight of the training practices, the unions were free to hire new workers as they saw fit. Usually, that meant new apprenticeship positions went to relatives, close acquaintances, and neighborhood friends. Some required that new apprentices have union sponsors, which ensured that friends and relatives were the first to gain entry into the training programs. Though they denied it was intentional, their control over training guaranteed that their unions remained exclusively white.[56]

Whether or not the building trades' hiring practices were the result of outright discrimination, their emphasis on their own color-blind recruiting practices hid the ways that structural inequalities maintained strict segregation in construction work. The intense segregation of the city's working-class neighborhoods helped create the labor pool that the unions chose to train. Since the building trades recruited from within their own neighborhoods and families, few nonwhite workers were able to crack the unions' hiring practices. As in school segregation, urban space determined Philadelphia's skilled labor market. But the normalized structure of residential segregation allowed the building trades to argue that their hiring practices were the result of ordinary living patterns instead of discriminatory practices. Urban spatial separation and tradition permitted unions to call themselves color-blind and their apprenticeship programs merit based.

White unionists ignored how residential segregation affected their pool of apprentices, but civil rights leaders did not. The pressure they put on local and federal governments began getting results. John F. Kennedy and Lyndon B. Johnson established the national policy and legal foundations for affirmative action in the construction industry. Kennedy's Executive Order 11114 banned discrimination on all construction projects built with federal money and Johnson's Executive Order 11246 created the Office of Federal Contract Compliance (OFCC) to enforce nondiscrimination clauses in federal building contracts. Most significantly, Title VII of the landmark Civil Rights Act of 1964 outlawed discrimination in both public and private employment.[57] The Johnson administration then implemented a series of experimental hiring programs in St. Louis, San Francisco, and Cleveland, before turning to Philadelphia in 1967. Instead of directly focusing on the unions, administration officials in the Federal Executive Board (FEB) put pressure on Philadelphia-area contractors to integrate their workforces. The FEB targeted several critical trades and specific unions with the worst track records for minority hiring. Although the unions in question represented just 4 percent of Philadelphia's 225,000 union members, these were also the highest-paid workers in the city's trade unions. Just as importantly, these seven trade unions—electricians, sheet-metal workers, plumbers, roofers, structural ironworkers, steamfitters, and elevator constructors—were made up of prototypically blue-collar workers scheduled to work on every federal construction project in the city.[58]

The federal Philadelphia Plan applied to all contracts of more than $500,000. The OFCC made building contractors provide evidence that they would employ nonwhite workers in all phases of the work. If they were unable or unwilling to prove the employment of a representative number of minority workers, their contract would be offered to the next lowest bidder. By placing the responsibility for meeting the hiring goals on the contractors rather than the unions, however, the Philadelphia Plan upset the building trades' long-standing recruitment practices. According to earlier labor contracts, unions retained the right to manage and recruit the workforce through a union hiring hall. Typically, union members worked on a job until it was finished. When a project ended, they would go back to the hiring hall until another position opened up. The unions considered seniority, length of time out of work, and possession of the requisite skills when determining placements. Although some unions claimed that nonunion members could seek work at the hiring halls, they only deemed individuals that had gone through the union apprenticeship programs as qualified.[59] With little to no minority representation in the unions, the hiring hall practice effectively barred African Americans from construction work. The Philadelphia Plan targeted contractors in order to sidestep union hiring hall practices.[60]

The building trades saw the maneuver as an attack on established labor rights like seniority and workforce management. The Building Trades Council immediately announced their opposition to the Philadelphia Plan, calling it unworkable and an unconstitutional use of federal power. Abraham E. Freeman, lawyer for the Operating Engineers Local 452, said the government did not understand the union's hiring practices. "This union has always encouraged Negroes to attend training schools and register for apprenticeship jobs," he continued. "The hiring-hall set up . . . is the best guarantee for Negro representation in all jobs."[61] Each time the BTC forwarded a color-blind argument against the Philadelphia Plan, however, they reinforced the very structures that created and maintained segregation in the construction industry. Because the hiring hall system favored prior union membership, African Americans and other nonwhites who had not broken into the apprenticeship programs remained locked out. Recognizing the limits of traditional recruitment practices, the FEB suspended over $19 million in federal building construction and almost $97 million for federal highway construction in

May 1968. Building contractors had little choice but to comply with the Philadelphia Plan. Most sought to increase minority representation on their jobsites, even if that meant using nonunion labor. BTC business manager James Loughlin threatened walkouts for the use of nonunion labor.[62]

In April 1968, tensions reached a fever pitch at the worksite for the new US Mint facility in Center City. Federal officials threatened to shut down the $37.7 million project and gave the McCloskey and Company building firm one week to comply with regulations or lose the job. Within days, McCloskey announced a plan to increase the number of African Americans working at the mint by inviting black electricians to take journeyman qualification exams. More than twenty members of the International Brotherhood of Electrical Workers Local 98 walked off their jobs when two nonunion African American electricians reported for work.[63] Union representatives were furious. Henry Formosa and Bernard Katz, Local 98's business manager and lawyer, issued a statement denouncing "the almost unbelievable action of the Federal Government" and called the Philadelphia Plan a "direct perversion of the country's dedication to opportunity regardless of race, color, or creed." They vowed that the "combination of racial discrimination and outright union-busting which the Philadelphia Plan represents will not go unchecked." Echoing Formosa and Katz, the Pennsylvania State Building and Trades Council announced their opposition to the plan. Similarly, the state BTC framed its argument in terms of traditional labor rights, calling the Philadelphia Plan a "union-busting, anti-civil rights movement which violates all the principles of trade unionism in America."[64]

In the meantime, the building-trades unions tried to regain control of their apprenticeship programs. After lengthy debate, the BTC approved a measure to recruit more African American apprentices through "voluntary affirmative action." Although one African American delegate reported that opposition to the new measure was based in "unfounded fears that under it locals will become all black," the council approved the action by a vote of seventy to thirty. A few weeks later, Mayor Tate held a meeting between white and black labor leaders to iron out the details. Labor and management organizations agreed to apply for a $58,000 grant from the Department of Labor to finance a new outreach program. It did not come without significant pressure from civil rights organizations, city government, and federal agencies—nor did it quiet the objections of union workers like Andy Plant—but the building trades took a first step toward integrating their unions. In practice, however, voluntary affirmative action had little effect. Union hiring hall practices continued to disadvantage African Americans in construction work. The building trades attempted to placate the federal government, but showed liberals and civil rights leaders that voluntary actions were not enough to combat blue-collar protectionism.[65]

Shortly after the unions adopted voluntary affirmative action, federal bureaucrats dismantled the Philadelphia Plan. Because it did not include a quota system—which the Civil Rights Act of 1964 prohibited—the program violated federal contract rules by not fully disclosing minimum requirements. Lyndon Johnson, preoccupied with the Vietnam War and having already announced his decision to not seek reelection, failed to intervene. Philadelphia civil rights organizations and their liberal allies remobilized. Activists staged protests at worksites and liberals raised the specter of urban rioting if the Plan was not revived.[66] Indeed, affirmative action policies were never far removed from the fears of urban disorder. In Philadelphia, James Tate faced reelection the same year as the Philadelphia Plan's announcement. He gave nominal support to the Plan, but worried about alienating blue-collar voters. Trying to balance the competing factions of his electoral base, he made Frank Rizzo police commissioner. Tate's bargain helped him win the election, but Rizzo's promotion drove a deeper wedge between liberals and labor. Three years after Tate's victory, Rizzo ran his own campaign for mayor on the twin promises of law and order and opposition to "special privileges" for nonwhites, a clear reference to the affirmative action programs that white, blue-collar unionists fought against.[67]

In the meantime, liberals did not trust the building trades to voluntarily desegregate. As a result, the Commission on Human Relations instituted its own Philadelphia Plan and civil rights organizations pressured the board of education into denying the building trades the use of public school facilities.[68] When the fate of federal affirmative action fell to Richard Nixon in 1969, liberals successfully engaged the politics of the urban crisis to convince a law-and-order-oriented Nixon administration that affirmative action could be a bulwark against urban disorder. In June 1969, Nixon's Department of Labor unveiled its Revised Philadelphia Plan.[69] The new Plan avoided the question of quotas by instituting percentage ranges for minority recruitment rather than required number of minority hires. The Revised Plan stated that gradual increases in those ranges would take place over a three-year period until minority participation in the construction industry matched the area's overall population. The Revised Plan also took pressure off contractors by allowing them to make "good faith" efforts toward hiring goals. The building trades, however, continued to see the Revised Philadelphia Plan as a means to break their unions.[70]

In late August, assistant secretary of the Department of Labor, Arthur Fletcher, the highest-ranking African American in the Nixon administration, arrived in Philadelphia to hold hearings on the Revised Plan. For three days, Fletcher heard arguments from civil rights leaders, representatives of city government, and academics who spoke in favor of the Philadelphia Plan. Yet two BTC representatives gave the longest testimony of the hearing. BTC attorney Bernard Katz repeated familiar arguments at length: that the unions did not exclude on the basis of race, that new apprentices needed to go through the proper union apprenticeship training, and that the plan would force the building trades to put unqualified workers at construction sites.[71] Fletcher was unmoved. After the hearings, the Department of Labor and the Office of Federal Contract Compliance moved to finalize the Revised Plan. By September, Secretary of Labor George Shultz announced the full implementation of the nation's first affirmative action program.[72]

The building trades continued to oppose the Philadelphia Plan, but they realized they had little choice but to accept the new way of conducting their operations when the Supreme Court refused to hear a case against the Philadelphia Plan in 1971. "I guess we'll just have to live with the plan," lamented Thomas Magrann.[73] Within a few years the Philadelphia Plan served as the basis for affirmative action on all federal hiring projects. Magrann and the BTC might have learned to live with the plan, but not without opening a rift between liberals and building-trades unions. They continued to hold liberals responsible for attempting to break their union and for forcing unwanted regulations on their apprenticeship programs. To the unions, the Philadelphia Plan was another in a long line of liberal attacks on blue-collar institutions.

When policy-makers responded to civil rights activists' demands to address inequalities in the local labor market, they attempted to provide liberal solutions to the urban crisis. Liberals at the local and federal level undertook similar efforts to address a number of social disparities. By the end of the Great Society era, planners in Philadelphia recognized that economic handicaps were not limited to occupational discrimination but intimately tied to other structural barriers. "Lack of housing, overcrowding and excessive rents limit the Negro's ability to move freely in pursuit of job opportunity," said one planning report. "Because of the close relationship between housing and employment," the report continued, "and also because poor housing, poor educational opportunities, and poor environment affect the social as well as the economic life of the Negro family, housing problems have become a primary factor in the struggle for equality."[74]

Urban Planning and Blue-Collar Neighborhoods

Despite the decline of reform politics in the early 1960s, the other half of Philadelphia's reform era continued its influence throughout the decade. City planning and urban renewal remained central to the city's growth and revitalization. Edmund Bacon and the City Planning Commission (CPC) continued their grandiose plans for a more livable city. Northeast Philadelphia continued to grow under Bacon's direction. South Philadelphia remained a center of urban revitalization. By the late 1960s, Philadelphia's city planning establishment and urban renewal systems had received widespread recognition.[75] Nevertheless, city planners' grand schemes rarely succeeded in alleviating the conditions in the inner city. Furthermore, the negative effects of urban renewal, like relocation, almost exclusively affected the nonwhites and the poor. As a result, civil rights organizations made equitable and successful urban renewal a priority. In 1966, the Tate administration responded by tasking the Fellowship Commission with creating and staffing the city's official Citizens' Committee on Minority Housing. City government charged the committee with studying the city's urban renewal program and proposing solutions for a more successful process. Finding a city in the midst of widespread resegregation, the committee's report concluded that existing housing laws were inadequate. They instead advocated stronger government policies to combat discrimination and segregation in the city's housing market. Following the release of the report, civil rights organizations and housing-focused liberals agreed that the city needed to expand its public housing program.[76]

By the late 1960s, many Philadelphians had lost faith in the possibility of public housing. The widely held fear that housing projects bred crime and blight, or that they perpetuated poverty, added to the program's tarnished reputation. Nevertheless, housing reformers continued working on behalf of an improved program. They advocated the construction of low-rise housing that would fit in aesthetically with surrounding neighborhoods, reduce the cramped space, and provide a safer environment for children. Working with city planners, they hoped to eliminate the stigma associated with public housing while creating an alternative to homes on the private housing market that few low-income Philadelphians could afford.

Although the Tate administration followed the groundwork laid by Clark and Dilworth, the 1960s revival of public housing was not merely a continuation of the liberal policies of the previous administrations. It also resulted from the confluence of the civil rights and housing movements that worked together to secure housing for low-income African Americans. Tate's housing officials also realized that private housing and building industries were ill equipped to provide adequate shelter for all of Philadelphia's low-income families. Because the private building industry could not limit the cost of new construction enough to provide affordable housing, the city assumed responsibility for rehabilitating abandoned and derelict structures for new public housing.[77] Aided by economic boom and federal subsidies for housing construction, the Philadelphia Housing Authority (HA) scheduled several new developments and planned major renovations for existing projects. Promotional brochures touted the plans and featured idyllic illustrations of well-maintained and architecturally modern homes. Tree-lined streets and shared common space illustrated a safe and welcoming atmosphere. The city also recruited administrators from the housing reform movement and implemented their recommendations. With federal funding, liberal housing reformers and the HA produced a sense of possibility reminiscent of the early days of public housing.[78]

Despite the housing authority's liberal boosterism, the promise of public housing rarely coincided with the realities of administering a citywide program. Idyllic depictions of public housing rarely reflected the reality of life in the projects. Living quarters were cramped and subject to random inspection by social workers; and residents had little input on HA policies. While the HA had a stated commitment to integrated facilities, most of the city's public housing was thoroughly segregated. Indeed, public housing had a reputation as undesirable "black housing."[79] The Tasker Homes bordering South Philadelphia's Grays Ferry neighborhood reinforced the negative qualities associated with public housing. In 1949, a decade after it opened, the HA heralded the Tasker Homes as one of the city's best housing projects and proof that public housing could work. By the late 1960s, however, the Tasker Homes were in deplorable condition. Residents complained of overcrowded and outdated facilities. The HA's modernization program was not enough to fix the problems, they said. Worse, residents called the development an "island of fear" because of the threat of robberies and violent crime.[80]

Conditions at the Tasker Homes contributed to the problems of select-
ing sites for new construction. Housing reformers and civil rights activists
warned that putting public housing in already impoverished or African
American neighborhoods contributed to ghettoization. But white work-
ing- and middle-class communities revolted when planners proposed the
construction of new public housing in their neighborhoods. In March 1971,
South Philadelphia's small, blue-collar Whitman neighborhood erupted in
protest over the beginning of a public housing project on the edge of their
predominantly white community.[81]

Before the public housing controversy, the neighborhood had benefited
from the extensive urban renewal and city planning. Urban renewal gave
the area its name and identity in the 1950s. By the 1960s the newly formed
Whitman Area Improvement Committee worked closely with the CPC and
redevelopment authority to secure further improvements. In part, their commitment to working with the city led the CPC to designate Whitman for
conservation.[82] Whitman's conservation plan called for extensive improvements and building projects, including several blocks of new private housing,
a regional playfield, a new shopping center, and the public housing project.
A federal grant in excess of $3.6 million made Whitman the largest conser-
vation area in the city and commenced expansive improvements. Whitman
homeowners enthusiastically jumped at the chance to make improvements
to their homes and spruce up their neighborhood. By the mid-1960s, 387
families in Whitman had received federal and local aid to rehabilitate their
homes. The city rewarded Whitman residents with participation citations
and Edmund Bacon publicized the community's story as an example of effective city planning. For Whitman residents, liberal city and federal spending
meant structural improvements and increased property values.[83]

Despite benefiting from liberal spending, and although plans for Whitman
Park had been in development for over a decade, local residents fiercely fought
the introduction of low-income public housing into their neighborhood of
homeowners. Beginning in March 1971, Whitman residents began protesting
construction by climbing on top of bulldozers and blocking work crews. They
continued protesting the site until work stopped in late April.[84] Resident Betty
Volkman explained what was at stake in the community's protest, explicitly
couching her appeal in the community's blue-collar pride, hard work, and tradition. "We are a proud people," she wrote, "our entire life revolves around our
friends, neighbors and our children." Invoking the community's deep roots,
she continued, "Our ancestors worked long and hard—and only through

PERSEVERANCE have we maintained a 'moderate' standard of living." But, she went on, "Because of over-taxation; many of us are now struggling on the border lines of independence." Volker said that low-income housing "could very easily DEMORALIZE our entire country and destroy the financial structure of our cities" and introduce "high crime" to Whitman. "Scores of uneducated, low-income (and some just plain lazy) people are constantly moving into the Philadelphia area," she said. "Will the taxpayers be responsible for furnishing homes for these people too?" she asked. She ended her letter by demanding the federal government end its public housing proposal and asking other blue-collar communities to join Whitman's protests.[85]

Similar protests did occur when construction crews began working on the Morrell Park housing project in the Far Northeast. In both Whitman and Morrell Park, residents blamed liberals and city planners for "forcing" public housing into their neighborhoods. The fights against public housing in South and Northeast Philadelphia highlighted the growing revolt against the city planning regime that had led the city's postwar rejuvenation. Within a few years, the two contests became the city's most acrimonious conflicts over the politics of liberalism, city planning, and desegregation.[86]

New public housing plans were one cause of the blue-collar revolt against city planning. The redevelopment of urban space was another, especially in Northeast Philadelphia. Addressing the lack of resources and housing in the Northeast had long required some of the CPC's most inventive plans. But as population growth outpaced development, the area presented a difficult challenge for city planners. As with controversies about overcrowded schools in the Northeast, residents complained about a lack of recreational facilities and city services.[87] Transportation remained especially troubling to blue-collar Northeast Philadelphians. Samuel and Nancy Sullivan, for example, moved to Morrell Park in 1960. They had lived in Frankford, a blue-collar neighborhood adjacent to Kensington, but wanted a new home with more outdoor space for their children. Their $10,900 home presented an affordable alternative for a Bell Telephone Company employee and his stay-at-home wife. Yet the suburban feel of Morrell Park was not without challenges. "We were told by people in City Hall that after we got four hundred families up here we would get better transportation service," Sullivan told a reporter in 1961. "There are now more than a thousand families up here and the service is no better. If anything, it is worse."[88]

The city remained sensitive to the needs of the growing and generally more prosperous residents of the Far Northeast. City planners pledged the construction of new facilities and reserved lands for recreation sites. By the time they were complete in the late 1960s, Northeast Philadelphia had more designated open and recreation spaces than every other section of the city combined. Yet that was rarely enough to quell a rising sense of discontent among area residents who believed city planners and the municipal government ignored the Northeast at the expense of poorer and nonwhite communities.[89]

The combination of racial homogeneity, spatial openness, and feeling of neglect from city government resulted in a sense of social, cultural, and political separateness. In the late 1960s, this separate identity caused Northeast Philadelphians to fight nearly every effort to connect the area to the rest of the city, even transportation infrastructure that had long been part of the area's planning. The necessity of those improvements became even more apparent as the area's population boomed. By the early 1960s, the city had planned two freeways to connect Northeast Philadelphia to the rest of the city, the so-called Northeast Freeway and Pulaski Expressway. The latter was renamed in an effort to appeal to the many Polish Americans that lived in Bridesburg and Port Richmond, two areas that would bear the brunt of early construction.[90] Additionally, the CPC included plans to extend the Broad Street subway system into the Northeast. Business leaders in the Northeast Philadelphia Chamber of Commerce enthusiastically backed the plans and residents cheered the solutions to their transportation woes. By the mid-1960s, however, as plans moved closer to implementation and construction threatened to displace residents and disrupt communities, blue-collar Philadelphians turned against city planners.

The planned freeways and subway extensions suffered repeated delays as city planners and area civic leaders failed to agree on specific routes. Many had come to appreciate the suburban quality of their communities. Both newly transplanted Northeast Philadelphians and longtime residents resisted any effort to disrupt their suburb-like space. By the early 1970s Northeast Philadelphians were building new organizations and mounting demonstrations in opposition to the freeway and subway plans. In February 1971, five hundred turned out to oppose a bill that would have commenced construction on the Northeast Freeway and subway extension. Eight hundred more protested the Pulaski Expressway the following September.[91] When picketers took to the Roosevelt Boulevard—Northeast Philadelphia's main thoroughfare—to protest the Northeast Freeway, they engaged an emerging discourse that suggested their tax dollars were keeping the rest of the city afloat. "Need Tax Money?" read one placard, "Why Demolish the Source?"[92] Increasingly angry protestors continued mounting ever larger demonstrations against highway construction, culminating in a one-thousand-person protest in March 1972. After years of obstruction, the city finally cancelled plans to construct the highways and extend the subway system in 1973.[93]

Northeast Philadelphia residents fought and won their battles against the whims of supposedly misguided city planners. Northeast Philadelphia's suburb-like development led residents to believe they shared more in common with the suburban communities just outside the city's borders. By the early 1970s, their sense of separateness from the city turned to resentment as the belief that Northeast Philadelphians paid more than their fair share of the city's tax burden grew.[94] Discussing the city's political and planning leaders, a twenty-nine-year-old mother of two daughters declared that "at election time they want your vote, at tax time they want your dollars, but nothing else. The poor have welfare, the rich have money. What have we got?"[95]

Northeast Philadelphians protested not only their taxes, but also accusations that the "lily white" Northeast was a refuge for racists. In response to questions about changing neighborhoods, Jeanette Tomar of the Oxford Circle neighborhood in the Near Northeast said her neighbors would be very unhappy to see the area's racial composition change. "Neighborhoods that have changed have big problems," she said. "It sounds like you're strictly a bigot if you oppose change. But it's really out of fear—fear of what has happened in every neighborhood that has changed." Her specific fear was of a drop in housing prices if a "lower class element" moved into the neighborhood. The same was true of school busing, she said. "It's not white children mingling with black students per se, but the matter of safety that parents worry about." Tomar wrestled with the implications of her own argument, but held tight on her neighborhoods' position on housing and busing. "It's very hard," she finally said, "trying to be somewhat liberal while still keeping your balance and analyzing why these things are happening."[96]

The tangible result for African Americans in Philadelphia was the reification of strict spatial boundaries. But Tomar, her counterparts in Northeast Philadelphia, and many others like them in urban America began expressing their experience in the segregated metropolis through the language of class and safety rather than race. Race still concerned Northeast Philadelphians, but a class-based discourse offered a new means of expressing similar sentiments. As further white working- and middle-class Philadelphians adopted similar class-based arguments, they signaled a turning point in their politics to a more consciously blue-collar politics.

In early June 1970, African American students at another school—Olney High School near the border of the Near Northeast and North Philadelphia—staged a sit-in in protest of disciplinary measures taken by the board of education after a series of racial conflicts. The disorders sent another wave of outrage through blue-collar Philadelphia, especially when Mark Shedd agreed to meet with the protesting students as he did in November 1967. In fact, Shedd had taken a harder line on school discipline, but his concession to the students angered Olney parents nonetheless. Many called for his ouster.[97] Helen Wiley, an angry parent from Olney, wrote to Richardson Dilworth to excoriate the school board president and former mayor for all the trouble he and other liberals had caused the city. But, she added, she once supported him. Wiley told Dilworth that she "rang door bells and vigorously campaigned for you and Mr. [Joseph] Clark in 1951" but because of liberal policies in the 1960s she "campaigned just as diligently against Mr. Clark" in his 1968 bid for reelection to the US Senate. She said that Dilworth and company had sacrificed the principles of good government and fairness that originally brought them to power in exchange for "integration and liberalism." Before telling Dilworth that she had sold her home and planned to move to Florida to escape Philadelphia, Wiley told Dilworth that the city would be better off if he and the other "do-gooders" had never come along.[98]

Helen Wiley's anger at liberals like Richardson Dilworth and Mark Shedd was typical among blue-collar Philadelphians in the late 1960s and early 1970s. The belief that liberals had failed them or cast them aside fueled a broader revolt against the reform and city planning regime that had guided the city's development since the 1950s. In fact, partly because of angry, blue-collar obstruction, many of the liberal policies of the late 1960s did fail. Dilworth and Shedd admitted that full integration of the school system was impossible. The Philadelphia Plan did not satisfy the desires of civil rights leaders who wanted a fully integrated construction industry, and the building trades did not end their discriminatory recruiting practices. Public housing became one of the most contested issues of the 1970s. Liberalism did not just fail in the 1960s, it was actively defeated by blue-collar Philadelphians that protested every liberal policy they viewed as an attempt to destroy their cherished institutions.

Yet many blue-collar whites benefited from and cheered liberal plans like urban renewal and federal spending for construction. They also attempted to redirect liberal politics toward their own ends in the drive for state aid to parochial schools. That willingness to accept and demand certain aspects of welfare liberalism pointed to a central facet of their emerging blue-collar conservatism. In the debates over affirmative action and public housing, blue-collar whites rejected entitlement spending and legislation based upon culturally defined ideas of privilege and disadvantage. As the lines of disagreement hardened into the 1970s, they differentiated the right to entitlements by making the clear distinction between hard work and handouts. They deserved the benefits of the welfare state because they had worked hard to get where they were. Nonwhites and the poor, they said, depended on handouts from liberals. The blue-collar frustration with liberals, city planners, and "do-gooders" foreshadowed that political evolution.

Late 1960s Philadelphia also laid bare how interwoven urban education, equal employment opportunity, and equitable housing were with the politics of the urban crisis. Almost all of the city's reforms in the mid-to-late 1960s, from urban renewal to the construction of new public housing units; from efforts to desegregate public schools to negotiating with student demonstrators; from confronting discriminatory union practices to endorsing federal equal opportunity employment schemes were justified in terms of the need to stem the tide of the urban crisis and prevent further disorder. Equally entangled with those issues were the triumphant politics of law and order, encapsulated in Philadelphia by Frank Rizzo. As he made the transition from police commissioner to mayor, he became a personification of the blue-collar revolt against liberalism that started with the grassroots politics of education, employment, and housing.

PART II

The Rise of Blue-Collar
Conservatism

Figure 6. One of the most famous photographs ever taken of Frank Rizzo. He stands at the Tasker Homes public housing project with a nightstick protruding from his formal wear, 1969. Courtesy of Special Collections Research Center, Temple University, Philadelphia, PA.

CHAPTER 5

"He's One of Us"

Shortly after Frank Rizzo took over as the city's top cop, *Philadelphia Magazine* ran a lengthy profile of the new police commissioner. Greg Walter, the article's British-born author, was carving out a career as one of the city's most rigorous investigative journalists. In the early 1970s he earned a reputation for taking on the municipal government and the city's powerful institutions, including corruption in the police department. Like many white Philadelphians in 1967, however, he was still enamored with Frank Rizzo. His glowing portrait of the commissioner offered a flattering introduction to the "the greatest cop Philadelphia ever had." Walter introduced readers to Rizzo's familial and ethnic roots, tracing his parents' immigration from Calabria before settling in an Italian enclave in South Philadelphia. His father, Ralph Rizzo, first took a job as a tailor before joining the police force, where he remained a patrolman for forty-one years. Walter stressed how hard the senior Rizzo worked to provide for his family and imbue his children with a strong sense of right and wrong. He taught his son from an early age that there were two kinds of people in the world, "the goodies and the baddies." Rizzo biographer S. A. Paolantonio argues that young Frank was closer to his mother, Teresa, who stayed home and took care of four sons until she died in 1941, but Walter failed to mention her by name. Instead, Walter said Rizzo's father was his greatest influence. It was Ralph Rizzo that convinced Frank to join the police department a few years after he dropped out of high school.[1]

Frank Rizzo's increasingly visible role in the protests of the mid-to-late 1960s made him a public figure, yet most people only knew Rizzo the cop. Few knew Rizzo the person. Greg Walter's profile served as introduction to Frank Rizzo's broader life story. Readers learned that Rizzo's hard-knock childhood and ability to judge between "the goodies and the baddies" shaped his rise through the police department. Combining the story of Rizzo's background with the exploits that established his reputation—busting illicit Center City coffee houses that were known meeting places for beats, hipsters, and homosexuals in the late 1950s, standing on the front lines of the Columbia Avenue Riot, and confronting Cecil B. Moore at Girard College, among others—Walter explained how Rizzo applied the white ethnic, blue-collar lessons he learned growing up in South Philadelphia to law enforcement. Rizzo was not content to sit behind a desk, Walter explained, because he knew the value of hard work. That ethic not only made him a great cop, it won him the loyalty of his fellow officers. "Rizzo was a cop's dream come true—the poor kid from an Italian neighborhood who started walking a beat and 24 years later was made commissioner," Walter wrote. "Rizzo didn't make it because he was an egghead," he continued. "He made it because he was a tough cop who has never hesitated to jump into a brawl against the most enormous odds." Most of all, Rizzo stood up for the police under his command, and that endeared him not only to rank-and-file police, but also to the legions of blue-collar Philadelphians that maintained the culture of reverence for the police.[2]

Greg Walter was the first to link Rizzo's blue-collar upbringing to his rise through the police department. His profile foreshadowed the "one of us" populism that Rizzo parlayed into a political career four years later. In addition, Walter allowed Rizzo to put forward a related narrative that also became a key part of the evolution of blue-collar politics. Despite what critics said, Rizzo insisted he was no racist. "If there's one thing I'm not," Rizzo told Walter, "it's against somebody because they are a Negro or an Irishman or anything else. Hell, I'm an Italian. I've known a lot of good Negro cops." Walter went to great lengths to reaffirm Rizzo's color-blind enforcement of the law, claiming that the only people Rizzo hated were criminals. His racist reputation was only due to ill-informed civil rights advocates and "irresponsible elements of the Negro press," Walter said. Rizzo's expressions of color-blind law enforcement were emblematic of the white, blue-collar engagement with race in the late 1960s and 1970s. Like Rizzo, blue-collar Philadelphians learned that the civil rights movement had changed the way people publicly discussed race. As explicit expressions of prejudice became less acceptable, Rizzo and his supporters adopted a nominally color-blind discourse based upon the defense of blue-collar tradition and identity. Increasingly, blue-collar Philadelphians claimed their support for the police—along with their opposition to school desegregation, affirmative action, and public housing—had nothing to do with race or civil rights.[3]

The attributes credited to Frank Rizzo in *Philadelphia Magazine*—a work-your-way-up ethos, a masculine sense of toughness, and a veneer of color-blind politics—defined the blue-collar populism that triumphed over reform-era, "do-gooder" liberalism in the 1970s. Over the next few years, until he resigned the commissionership to run for mayor of Philadelphia, Rizzo bolstered his reputation as an icon of these newly resurgent working-class cultural politics and foreshadowed the blue-collar populism that defined his political career.

Frank Rizzo began fashioning his public image from the moment he accepted the position as police commissioner. As outlined in Greg Walter's article, Rizzo's background was not unlike that of many white, blue-collar Philadelphians. It reflected a firm attachment to white ethnic and urban neighborhood tradition and began creating Rizzo's status among blue-collar whites as "one of us." As long as Rizzo had allies in the local media he had a hand in maintaining his own public persona. While it was partly a shrewd politician's carefully constructed image, it also grew out of Philadelphia's blue-collar identity politics. Rizzo's ability to tap into those identity politics allowed him to withstand years of well-deserved scrutiny and criticism. As commissioner, he was never short of detractors that labeled him a racist or denounced the "Gestapo tactics" of the police under his command. Rizzo remained especially unpopular among African Americans who viewed his rise as a threat to the still-vulnerable gains they had made in the previous two decades. Rizzo survived politically because his "one of us" populism made him a hero to the white ethnic, blue-collar Philadelphians that believed they were on the losing end of the equal opportunity politics of the 1960s.[4]

Rizzo's ability to relate to working- and middle-class Philadelphians became his greatest political strength. Even though it was indebted to the widespread anger blue-collar whites directed toward liberals and the civil rights movement, his popularity represented more than a backlash against the politics of the previous two decades. Rizzo was also an affirmation of the blue-collar culture that prized a bottom-up work ethic and ethnic traditions. As exemplified by Rizzo, blue-collar authenticity relied on an almost mythic sense of white ethnic self-sufficiency and the dichotomy between "hard work" and "handouts."[5] Real or imaginary, it was a powerful argument for blue-collar whites that felt they had been shortchanged by policies like school desegregation, affirmative action, and public housing. Although Rizzo's blue-collar populism was indelibly tied to the racial politics of equal opportunity, he actively avoided public race-baiting. Most often, as in his interview with Greg Walter, Rizzo denied the accusations of racism that followed him throughout his career. Instead, he relied on his "one of us" populism that, while ostensibly color-blind, still communicated the racial connotations of blue-collar identity politics. Rizzo's self-touted Italian heritage provided him with one means of the politicization of blue-collar identity. His career in the police department provided the other.

Rizzo's police work simultaneously reinforced his blue-collar identity, his law-and-order credentials, and the racial politics of both. For the blue-collar Philadelphians that maintained a culture of reverence for the police, Rizzo was an especially effective police commissioner. He oversaw the police department during the worst years of the urban crisis. He personally appeared at most newsworthy crimes and offered a running commentary on criminal justice in Philadelphia and across the nation. His commissionership confirmed his role as a crusading savior of the city to those that conflated the rise of black militancy with the liberals they blamed for endangering their traditions and institutions. Rizzo's actions communicated the racial politics of law enforcement in the late 1960s even when he spoke of color blindness. They also captured the gender politics of his blue-collar populism. Not only was police work still male dominated in the late 1960s, but Rizzo projected an ultramasculine image. As police commissioner, he contrasted his masculine toughness against the supposed threat of the Black Power movement.[6] As a mayoral candidate, he positioned himself as the masculine alternative to the supposedly effete liberals who let the city fall into the grip of the urban crisis. In addition to the racial subtext of Rizzo's law enforcement reputation, the law-and-order politics that shaped his "one of us" populism were fundamentally gendered as well.

"The Toughest Cop in America"

On June 12, 1969, Frank Rizzo was an honored guest at a black-tie dinner at the Bellevue Stratford, one of Center City's finest hotels and a regular meeting spot for political deal-making. Nearly all proverbial back room deals in Philadelphia Democratic politics took place at the posh Bellevue Stratford. Mayor James Tate owed his 1967 reelection to Rizzo's popularity, so he invited him to meet and mingle with the city's Democratic power players. Rizzo donned a tuxedo and prepared for an evening of hobnobbing with the people that could help him transition from law enforcement to politics. Midway through the dinner, however, an aide informed him that a near riot was underway at the Tasker Homes public housing project in South Philadelphia. Located adjacent to the working-class, white ethnic Grays Ferry neighborhood, the Tasker Homes had been the site of hostility for years. Grays Ferry neighbors thought the housing project bred crime and blight. The poor, mostly African American residents of the Tasker Homes became frequent targets of local white youths. Rizzo leapt into action when he heard an incident was under- way. He immediately left the glitz and glamour of the Bellevue Stratford and headed to South Philadelphia. When he arrived, he grabbed a police officer's nightstick and hastily shoved it into the cummerbund of the tuxedo he was still wearing. He then approached the white youths that had been throwing rocks and bottles at the housing project. Rizzo convinced them to go home. It would not be the last time that the Tasker Homes and surrounding neigh- borhood erupted in violence, but for the time being, Rizzo helped restore an uneasy calm.[7]

Photographers had grown accustomed to following the police commis- sioner, so they were on hand to witness the fracas in South Philadelphia. The next morning, their photographs graced the front page of every Phila- delphia newspaper and soon spread across the country. The photographs of the tuxedo-clad police commissioner, nightstick protruding from his formal wear, standing on the front lines of a potential disaster, became some of the most famous images of Frank Rizzo's career. Rizzo, the pictures seemed to convey, personally stopped another riot.[8]

Few images could have done more to further Rizzo's reputation than the photographs taken at the Tasker Homes. They probably did more to secure his political future than any meeting at the Bellevue Stratford could have. Rizzo's growing legion of blue-collar supporters believed that the police com- missioner and his brand of law enforcement made the city safe. To them, little else mattered. Rizzo represented security in a city and country that increas- ingly appeared to be succumbing to lawlessness. In the late 1960s and early 1970s, blue-collar Philadelphians looked to Rizzo and his law enforcement tactics as the antidote to the urban crisis.

Rizzo did represent a clear break with the recent leadership of the police department. He intentionally made himself a larger public figure than pre- vious commissioners. It was no accident that photographers were on hand to capture his exploits at the Tasker Homes. In part, Rizzo's antics and out- spokenness made him a newsworthy story waiting to happen. Rizzo was also very media savvy. One of his most influential supporters and confidants was Walter Annenberg, the media mogul owner of both the *Philadelphia Inquirer* and *Philadelphia Daily News*. Annenberg not only ensured that his newspapers regularly featured the commissioner, but he insisted that Rizzo receive positive coverage. When *Inquirer* journalist Joe McGinnis wrote a series of scathing articles about Rizzo shortly after his promotion to commissioner, Annenberg's editorial page condemned their own columnist. That relationship changed when Annenberg sold the papers to the Knight-Ridder company in 1969. Following editorial changes, Rizzo's friendly relationship with the press waned and often became antagonistic. By then, however, Rizzo had already used the local press to craft his public image.[9]

Rizzo's governance of the police department also marked a sharp contrast with his predecessors. Since the 1950s, the police department had been racked with internal dissension due to fear of disciplinary reprisals for aggressive or shoddy police work. Rizzo's predecessors sought to establish better police-community relations as a means of reducing crime. Howard Leary even gave tacit approval to the Police Advisory Board (PAB). Rizzo fully repudiated law enforcement liberalism and said police should have the right to perform precisely the kind of procedures the PAB was meant to curb, including the unwarranted right to stop and search suspected criminals. Foreshadowing a centerpiece of law enforcement conservatism nationwide, Rizzo specifically advocated "stop and frisk" practices. "Once in a while we violate someone's rights," Rizzo admitted, "but by and large the community is behind us."[10] John Harrington, the still-influential president of the Fraternal Order of Police, credited a drop in the city's major crime rate to Rizzo's leadership. "I attribute this to two people," Harrington said, "to Mayor Tate and Commissioner Rizzo because both have done so much to raise the morale of the police department." There had been few major disturbances in Philadelphia, he continued, because Rizzo would allow police to "treat riots with a firm hand."[11]

Evidence suggested that Rizzo's tactics were effective. A 1968 Federal Bureau of Investigation (FBI) report named Philadelphia the major American city with the lowest major crime rate in the nation. The report also said Philadelphia was the only city of the nation's ten largest where the incidence of rapes, aggravated assaults, larcenies, and automobile theft declined.[12] That the city's declining crime rate coincided with Rizzo's first year as police commissioner was not lost on the people of Philadelphia. Mayor Tate and law enforcement officials claimed that the statistics were a rebuff to critics that pointed out the often heavy-handed tactics of Rizzo's police force.[13] Not all of the credit belonged to Rizzo, however. His police had stopped small incidents from escalating. Rizzo introduced emergency curfews, mobile response teams that allowed for quick reaction times, and other, more controversial measures—like the purchase of military-style armored personnel transports that his critics labeled "tanks"—that allowed the police to handle tense situations relatively well. But the general drop in the crime rate had multiple sources. In fact, the crime statistics were suspect. The police department supplied the FBI with the raw numbers and critics accused Rizzo of inaccurately reporting major crimes in order to artificially lower the city's crime rate. More importantly, the statistics ignored community anticrime efforts. Clergy and community groups in high-crime areas like North and West Philadelphia took direct action to make their communities safer.[14] The North City Congress brokered a truce between rival gangs and started a police-community relations program that orchestrated meetings between the community and police until Rizzo ended it. African American community efforts to address urban crime never garnered the same attention as the get-tough police commissioner.[15]

Rizzo refused to share credit for reducing crime because the same organizations that worked for community anticrime efforts also concluded that nothing would be done about police brutality while Rizzo led the police department. Police brutality remained an especially high concern in African American communities. While accusations of excessive force were nothing new, Rizzo was uniquely unresponsive to complaints against the police department.[16] Although he never condoned police brutality, he flatly denied it was a systemic problem. He dismissed clear examples of police abuse as the actions of a few bad officers or the overreaction of civil rights organizations.[17] Rizzo made it clear that his police department would not actively investigate allegations of misconduct. As a result, a brief but ultimately unsuccessful effort to reinstate the Police Advisory Board emerged among liberals and civil libertarians, but the widespread support of Rizzo's policing hampered any effort to reestablish the agency. Even under pressure from former liberal allies, Mayor Tate refused to support efforts to revive the board.[18]

African American communities resented the lack of attention from the police department and city government. Rizzo's intransigence provoked a renewed, more militant response to police brutality, which included the rise of the Black Panther Party in Philadelphia. In the few years since their founding in Oakland, California, the Black Panthers had become the most emblematic Black Power organization in the United States. Their revolutionary image—including brandishing guns, wearing paramilitary garb, and warning of urban warfare with police—was especially attractive to young black men. Many young African Americans saw Frank Rizzo's law enforcement administration as the Black Panther critique of the police playing out as predicted. The growth of the small local chapter was a direct result of Rizzo's law enforcement policies in black communities. After its founding in 1969, both their challenge to the authoritarianism of Rizzo's police and the appeal of their revolutionary rhetoric caused the local party to grow. Although they were neither the only nor the most influential Black Power organization in the city, the reputation of the armed, militant Black Panthers preceded the relatively small Philadelphia chapter, making them seem more threatening to police who also associated the rise of black militancy with the supposed leniency of liberals and elites.[19]

Though small, the Philadelphia Black Panthers attracted the attention of the wider Black Power movement. Impressed with the local chapter's community organizing, national Panther leadership chose to hold a Revolutionary People's Constitutional Convention in Philadelphia. Organizers planned to hold the meeting at Temple University in early September 1970 and hoped to bring together various factions of the Black Power movement, white New Left, and radical anti–Vietnam War movement. It would also mark original party founder Huey Newton's first public appearance since his conviction for murdering a police officer was overturned. White Philadelphians viewed the convention as a threat to the city's safety and evidence of the need for Rizzo's law enforcement. Rizzo made it a personal and professional goal to stop it. In late August 1970, a week before the scheduled meeting, Rizzo found the pretense for quashing both the Revolutionary People's Convention and the Philadelphia Black Panther Party.[20]

On Saturday, August 29, 1970, two police officers at a Fairmount Park guardhouse in West Philadelphia were ambushed and shot, allegedly by a gang of black militant gunmen. One of the police officers survived badly wounded. The other died at the scene. Rizzo ordered a sweep of the area. Police found one suspect and a cache of weapons and explosives at a house two blocks from the crime scene. Rizzo warned that the police were under siege even before the bloody weekend came to an end. The following night two cops were shot in a patrol wagon not far from the prior night's shooting. In Southwest Philadelphia, two more officers made what they thought was a routine traffic stop but happened upon two men wanted for bank robbery. They opened fire on the police officers as they approached the car. Both survived, but were critically wounded. One of them was Thomas J. Gibbons

Jr., the son of the 1950s police commissioner that gave Frank Rizzo his first promotion. Fuming, Rizzo said the two nights' shootings were the work of a "band of organized revolutionaries." In fact, the shootings were unrelated, but four police officers still lay dead or wounded after the course of one weekend.[21] White blue-collar Philadelphians rallied around the police as outraged neighborhood organizations declared their support for Rizzo and "all actions taken against the perpetrators of this recent indecency against the designated protectors of our laws." Most of them, like Rizzo, blamed the Black Panthers.[22]

There was no link between the Black Panthers and the murders. But Frank Rizzo equated black militancy with violence against the police. With his influence among most white Philadelphians, he had little trouble justifying swift and decisive action. He immediately ordered raids on Black Panther headquarters in North Philadelphia, West Philadelphia, and Germantown. Police exchanged gunfire with Panthers during the raid in North Philadelphia and confiscated guns, ammunition, and literature from the other locations. After removing the Panthers from their North Philadelphia headquarters, police officers forced them to strip naked at gunpoint to make sure they were not concealing more weapons. Photographers on hand snapped pictures of the Panthers with their hands against a brick wall and stripped of all their revolutionary appearance. Like the picture of Rizzo with the nightstick in his cummerbund, the photograph of naked Black Panthers was on the front page of every Philadelphia newspaper the next day and soon in news outlets across the country. Although Rizzo was not present for the strip search, he gained the praise and bore the brunt of the criticism in ensuing controversy over the photograph.[23]

The police raids were the beginning of the end for the Black Panthers in Philadelphia. The Revolutionary People's Convention still went on, but under intense police surveillance. Little resulted from the subdued event. Within a few years, the Philadelphia Black Panthers were defunct. The internal politics of the Black Power movement were just as responsible for the demise of the Black Panthers as the police repression.[24] Among white, blue-collar Philadelphians, however, it once again appeared that Frank Rizzo had personally stopped another threat to law and order. To no small degree, the appeal of the Black Panthers was their ultramasculine image. When the police publicly stripped them bare, they also stripped them of their revolutionary manhood. Frank Rizzo and the police represented an overtly masculine response to the urban crisis. His toughness and unwillingness to compromise in the face of crime and disorder were qualities that endeared him to blue-collar whites that prized the same traits. By forcing the Black Panthers to strip naked, Rizzo's police asserted their own white, blue-collar manhood over militant, black manhood. Time and again, moreover, Rizzo's successes lent credence to the claim that his heavy-handed methods kept Philadelphia safe.

Rizzo's policing was the manifestation of law-and-order politics put to action. It represented not only a break from the city's law enforcement liberalism, but the beginning of a much larger turn toward a more punitive criminal justice system. As commissioner, Rizzo started a campaign against the "lenient" judges and law enforcement personnel that allegedly put the public and police force in danger. Rizzo again traded on his own toughness and masculine image by contrasting his more punitive philosophies against those that "coddled" criminals. He argued that judges' compassion for criminals was misplaced and that crime had changed too much to allow liberal sentencing to continue. "Crime today is too frequent, too violent, and too brutal," he told a luncheon gathering of the Justice Lodge of B'nai B'rith. Even as Rizzo admitted that crime was rooted in poor housing, inadequate schools, and unemployment, he argued that until "experts" came up with a better solution, police and their allies needed to push for a disciplinary retribution system that would imprison criminals instead of seeking noncarceral forms of criminal justice.[25]

Rizzo was not alone in his belief that criminal courts had gotten "too soft." Joining him in a grassroots effort to promote a more punitive criminal code and rid the criminal justice system of lenient judges were the most ardent supporters of the police: their wives. Just as the FOP spoke for police officers that were discouraged from openly campaigning for political causes, police wives became a voice for rank-and-file police. They told of their daily fears that something terrible would happen to their husbands while trying to provide for their family. Policemen were not just cops, they reminded. They were husbands, fathers, loved ones, and breadwinners. Police wives humanized their husbands and the danger they faced in a difficult profession. For blue-collar whites already sympathetic to the hard work police officers performed, police wives' testimonies reinforced the culture of reverence for the police that fed the desire for both law and order and a harsher criminal justice system.[26]

More than reminding Philadelphians of the risks their husbands took in the line of duty, police wives also began organizing for criminal justice reform. Marie Ann Mackley and Bonnie Whalen founded Police Wives and Interested Citizens for Action (PWICA) in 1968. Their catalyst was the death of Patrolman William Lackman, an officer killed on the job in October 1968 by an ex-convict free on bail. Their target were Philadelphia criminal court judges that offered lenient sentences or probation instead of hard jail time for criminal offenders.[27]

PWICA drew strength from their emotional appeals for the protection of their husbands and sought to rally sympathetic Philadelphians around the threat posed by politicians and lenient judges. When Councilman David Cohen announced that his office would accept complaints against the police in lieu of the no-longer-active Police Advisory Board, Mackley and Whalen initiated a letter-writing campaign in support of the police. They received over two thousand letters in support of the police and stricter prison sentencing. After their successful mail drive, they sought to turn the public's attention to the lenient judges that endangered their husbands. They took specific aim at Herbert S. Levin, a common pleas judge with a reputation for offering probation instead of jail time. Mackley and Whalen called him the most lenient judge in Philadelphia. His decisions to release criminals on probation or offer light sentences, they said, put their husbands in danger. Although Levin defended his use of probation by pointing out that the rates of recidivism were lower among probationers than among those released from penitentiaries, PWICA's campaign against him brought the issue of punitive law enforcement policy to more Philadelphians.[28] They used their campaigns against Levin and Cohen in order to promote their primary goal of rallying support for stricter sentencing and bail reform. Drawing comparisons to the complaints normally leveled at the police, Mackley said that people always heard about police brutality, but they never heard about the "civilian brutality inflicted on police." The media reported the treatment of the Black Panthers in 1969, she said, but needed to be reminded about the police officers killed in the line of duty. The police had become "walking targets," she said, and "present laws are too liberal." Although police wives could not legally remove Levin from the bench until he faced reelection in 1976, they made sure they publicized his reputation as a "do-gooder" judge that "coddled" criminals. They also caught the attention of Frank Rizzo, who praised the women for trying to keep both his police force and the city safe.[29]

Frank Rizzo's popularity and the culture of reverence for the police showed that blue-collar cultural politics championed masculine toughness as a virtue. Yet the police wives offered an example of the complex gender dynamics involved in blue-collar culture and political development. Women who had organized for neighborhoods and schools had already assumed roles as protectors of blue-collar values. Police wives' efforts to safeguard their husbands

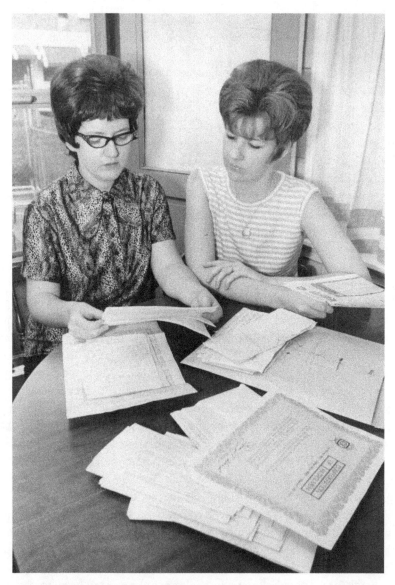

Figure 7. Marie Ann Mackley and Bonnie Whalen of Police Wives and Interested Citizens for Action sort through letters supporting their efforts to safeguard the police and enact stricter prison sentencing, 1970. Courtesy of Special Collections Research Center, Temple University, Philadelphia, PA.

not only reinforced women's roles as protectors, they signaled women's capacity for a brand of blue-collar toughness that rested easily alongside the promotion of masculinity. They also showed that Frank Rizzo alone was not responsible for the shift to law and order in the late 1960s.

Rizzo had an indelible impact on law enforcement in Philadelphia. But all he accomplished would not have been possible without widespread support for the police officers under his command. The culture of reverence for the police among white, blue-collar Philadelphians reinforced and condoned Rizzo's behavior. His power and prestige rested upon their tacit and explicit approval. Likewise, the turn toward a more punitive system of criminal justice was not only the result of autocratic figureheads like Rizzo. Rather, the turn to harsher sentencing and the resultant carceral state, like the politics of law and order, depended on widespread approval. Blue-collar whites that demanded a more punitive criminal justice system prepared themselves to accept later changes in carceral policy. The development of the American carceral state rested on decades of support for more punitive policies.[30] In the meantime, Rizzo engaged the popularity of those law enforcement politics in order to further his own career. By the end of 1970, the support he received from white blue-collar Philadelphians set the stage for his transition to local politics. On February 2, 1971, Rizzo informed Mayor Tate that he was resigning as police commissioner in accordance with the rules set by the city charter. He then announced his intention to run for mayor of Philadelphia.[31]

"Rizzo Means Business"

Frank Rizzo did not make appearances in predominantly African American sections of Philadelphia during his 1971 campaign for mayor. Instead, his advisers wagered that he could win the election with only the support of white, blue-collar neighborhoods. Following his campaign manager's advice, Rizzo spent most of the campaign in white neighborhoods, especially in Northeast and South Philadelphia, while allowing his opponents to woo black voters in North and West Philadelphia. Rizzo relied on his tough-cop image and "one of us" populism to court voters that appreciated his background and personality. Reflecting the way blue-collar Philadelphians identified with Rizzo, one supporter offered him the following slogan for his mayoral campaign: "Vote for Rizzo—Think of Yourself for a Change."[32]

Rizzo possessed a genuine ability to connect with his constituents. His own cultural identity played heavily in his identification with blue-collar whites. As a candidate, he often talked about his humble roots and his childhood in a South Philadelphia row home. It was both a carefully constructed image and a reflection of Rizzo's blue-collar authenticity. Rizzo also buttressed his political appeal by engaging all the issues that had aroused blue-collar whites in the 1960s. He promised that he would not allow city planners to disrupt stable neighborhoods and swore an end to the city planning regime as it existed. He said he would not allow the construction of public housing in any community that opposed it. As a Roman Catholic, he promised that he would work to safeguard state funding for parochial schools. Rizzo's campaign offered a repudiation of urban liberalism as well as a direct challenge to the politics of city planning, education, and affirmative action. Combined with his "toughest cop in America" image, Rizzo's "one of us" populism appealed directly to blue-collar identity politics. Rizzo's campaign took the late-1960s blue-collar revolt against liberalism and began the process of turning it into blue-collar conservatism.

Rizzo's populist politics complemented his law-and-order reputation. For example, he railed against permissiveness in public schools and promised to reinstate tougher disciplinary measures. He also vowed that one of his first official acts would be to fire Mark Shedd, the superintendent of public schools. It was an authority the mayor did not actually have—Rizzo's rhetoric was often more bluster than substance—but the promise resonated with the blue-collar parents that fought Shedd's reforms and desegregation plans. Although Shedd had already begun implementing new disciplinary procedures, he remained wildly unpopular among blue-collar parents. He became an easy target for Rizzo, who blamed him—and by extension, all liberals—for the "complete lack of discipline in the schools." With an exaggeration that soon became a hallmark of his public statements, Rizzo vowed to oust Shedd from his position within "three seconds" of assuming the mayoralty.[33] In that context, the multiple meanings of Rizzo's official campaign slogan, "Rizzo Means Business," easily translated to his blue-collar supporters. He not only promised economic prosperity, but would also handle with a firm hand the liberals, do-gooders, protesters, and criminals that threatened blue-collar traditions and institutions.

Rizzo's campaign slogan was a masterstroke of double meaning that allowed voters to project their own politics into his campaign. The flexibility of "Rizzo Means Business" also meant he could avoid explicit race-baiting. Instead, Rizzo avoided interacting with African Americans and used his blue-collar identity to mask overt appeals to shared whiteness. "Rizzo Means Business" presented the candidate as the forceful alternative to the effete liberals, intellectuals, and planners. He was the tough cop that understood what it took to keep the city safe because he had patrolled the streets before working his way up. He touted his blue-collar background as evidence that he would not disrupt blue-collar neighborhoods or neighborhood schools. For blue-collar whites, "Rizzo Means Business" also meant that he would secure all they sought to protect in the last decade and initiate new political direction for the city.[34]

When Rizzo first announced his intention to seek the Democratic nomination for mayor, he vowed that he would be the candidate of the political center. "Here and now," Rizzo said at the press conference, "I publicly disavow extremism of the left and extremism of the right. I come as a candidate appealing to the broad middle ground of the electorate."[35] In the contest for Philadelphia's Democratic nomination, however, Rizzo clearly represented the social and cultural right. To his left was William Green III. Green was the son of a former member of congress and longtime Democratic Party leader. William Green Jr.'s untimely death in 1963 cut short a rising political career that insiders assumed would end in the mayor's office. His son took on the family mantle and quickly became the top choice and last hope for the reform wing of the local Democratic Party. He received enthusiastic endorsements from Joseph Clark and Richardson Dilworth, the local chapter of Americans for Democratic Action (ADA), and several other liberal groups. But Green could not capture the loyalty of the Democratic power structure and his association with reform-era liberalism killed his chances in blue-collar neighborhoods.[36]

Green's candidacy was the last gasp of Philadelphia's old liberal reform era. When the campaign failed, it opened the door for the creation of a new liberal-progressive political coalition represented by Hardy Williams, the Democratic candidate to Green's left. Williams was a prominent member of the Black Political Forum, a West Philadelphia–based political organization focused on community organizing and placing African American representatives in state and local government. Williams had no real chance of capturing the nomination. In fact, unsubstantiated rumors circulated that the Rizzo campaign secretly funded Williams so he would siphon black votes from Green. Williams denied the stories. His campaign represented black political empowerment. Williams ran a protest campaign against the rightward shift in the Democratic Party represented by Rizzo and the lethargy of

reform liberalism represented by Green. It was also part of a strategic evolution in local black politics that started building alliances at the community
level in the hope of creating a coalition capable of challenging the reigning
Democratic power structure. Williams's 1971 candidacy failed, but it helped
lay the groundwork for a local movement that would eventually remake Philadelphia politics.[37]

When Rizzo won the Democratic nomination, he confirmed a broader
shift in white, blue-collar politics and a rightward swing within the Democratic
Party. Activist liberals were left without a candidate. Organizations like the
Fellowship Commission and ADA waged a campaign to stop Rizzo's momentum. Richardson Dilworth resigned the presidency of the school board to
campaign against him.[38] But the Rizzo campaign used his unpopularity among
liberals to his advantage. One campaign advertisement listed the liberals who
opposed Rizzo's candidacy—including Richardson Dilworth, Mark Shedd,
and several prominent members of the ADA—and countered that "only the
people want Rizzo."[39] The advertisement contrasted liberals with blue-collar
Philadelphians. Following that strategy, Rizzo also discredited his critics by
attacking their privileged backgrounds and upper-class social standing. He
was not entirely wrong. The vast majority of ADA members were affluent and
well educated. Dilworth grew up wealthy. Shedd had a Harvard doctorate. By
contrasting "the people" with Dilworth, Shedd, and the ADA, Rizzo invoked
blue-collar identity as a means of curbing the power of so-called liberal elites.

These Philadelphia liberals had been loyal Democrats, but they could
not support Rizzo. Nearly every liberal organization in the city endorsed his
Republican opponent. But the local Republican Party had floundered since
the reform era of the 1940s and 1950s. Many voters still associated Republicans with the corruption and graft of the pre-reform era. In the years since,
they only once put forward a mayoral candidate with any real chance of winning, when District Attorney Arlen Specter ran for mayor on a law-and-order
platform in 1967. Although he posed a threat to James Tate, the mayor took
the law-and-order issue away from Specter by promoting Rizzo. Republicans
approached Specter about running again, but he refused to run against the
former police commissioner. The Republicans' only chance at victory was to
fan the fears of a Rizzo mayoralty and appeal to the alienated liberals and
reformers.[40] They nominated Thacher Longstreth, president of the Philadelphia Chamber of Commerce and self-proclaimed "Main Line WASP." Like
the liberals that endorsed him, however, Longstreth never had a chance in
white, blue-collar Philadelphia. Even when Longstreth clearly bested Rizzo

in policy proposals and public debate, he could not shed his patrician image. The Rizzo campaign capitalized on this weakness and charged that "Longstreth does not care about the working man."[41]

Rizzo's campaign not only made appeals to the "working man," he also counted organized labor as one of his most enthusiastic constituencies. Labor unions were a central part of the city's Democratic coalition and Rizzo made his support for organized labor clear. "I'm tired of hearing that unions go too far," he said at one event. "Thank God we have unions," he continued, before reminding his audience that Thacher Longstreth represented big business and owned three homes. Like his attacks on liberals, Rizzo used his own blue-collar background to contrast himself with his wealthy Republican opponent. In fact, both candidates were one-time union members. Longstreth joined the American Federation of Television and Radio Artists when he worked as a sports announcer in the 1950s. Rizzo, in addition to his membership in the Fraternal Order of Police, had joined the United Steelworkers of America when he briefly worked at Philadelphia's Midvale Steel Works after dropping out of high school. When it came to union supporters, Longstreth simply could not compete with Rizzo's blue-collar authenticity.[42]

Not all organized labor supported Rizzo. The Negro Trade Union Leadership Council and Jewish Labor Committee thought he threatened the labor-liberal alliance that had long worked for union rights and racial equality.[43] But Rizzo appealed to the factions in organized labor that still resented liberals' efforts to desegregate their unions. When Longstreth endorsed the Philadelphia Plan, Rizzo declared his inalterable opposition to affirmative action; and the powerful building-trades unions enthusiastically endorsed him. The vast majority of Philadelphia unions followed suit. Near the end of the campaign, as Thacher Longstreth made inroads among disaffected liberals and African Americans, outgoing Mayor Tate campaigned for Rizzo at union halls. Still a favorite among labor leaders, Tate told crowds that Rizzo would be "the greatest labor mayor" in the city's history. "We made this a union town," Tate reminded his audiences, "and Rizzo will help keep it that way."[44] By Rizzo's own estimate, he secured over 90 percent of the union vote. Although prone to exaggeration, he was not far off. With the vast majority of organized labor in his camp, Rizzo secured the blue-collar vote.[45]

Rizzo's greatest strength was in the blue-collar neighborhoods that identified with his candidacy. From the South Philadelphia tavern where Rizzo made an impromptu Columbus Day appearance just weeks before the election, reporter Sandy Grady received a full account of the candidate's blue-collar popularity. By virtue of showing up to a local watering hole and engaging with its patrons, Rizzo displayed his ability to connect with the city's blue-collar voters. "Rizzo showed me something tonight," said Al Maz, the bar's owner. His regular customer John Marzano even more pointedly captured the reason so many blue-collar neighborhoods looked to Rizzo as their salvation. From their barstools, Marzano's compatriots nodded along as he explained the difference between Rizzo and Longstreth: "He's one of us. Rizzo came up the hard way. He hasn't got three million dollars like Longstreth."[46] In addition to his "toughest cop in America" image, Rizzo possessed a blue-collar authenticity that could not be matched in areas like South Philadelphia.

Longstreth's ability to court liberals and willingness to campaign in African American communities gave him a fighting chance against Rizzo's popularity in white, blue-collar neighborhoods. Despite a day's worth of driving rain on election day, Philadelphia's voter turnout was the highest since 1935.

Figure 8. South Philadelphia welcomes Frank Rizzo home as he campaigns for mayor, 1971. Courtesy of Special Collections Research Center, Temple University, Philadelphia, PA.

In the end, Rizzo's "one of us" populism proved enough to secure a victory in a very close election. The results upset traditional voter demographics and belied national trends, as all but one of the city's predominantly African American wards went to Longstreth. But Rizzo swept Northeast Philadelphia, South Philadelphia, and every white, blue-collar neighborhood in between. His largest margins of victory were in Whitman's ward in South Philadelphia and the working- and middle-class neighborhoods in Northeast Philadelphia. Overall, Rizzo won thirty-five of the city's sixty-six wards. He beat Longstreth by a count of 394,067 to 345,912.[47]

Rizzo's campaign was not about ideas or policies. In fact, many of Rizzo's proposals were unworkable or not within the power of the mayor. Some reporters questioned whether he truly understood the position.[48] Instead, the election turned on the power of Frank Rizzo's "one of us" populism. When Rizzo won the election, it was a win for all the blue-collar Philadelphians that felt wronged by liberalism and civil rights advances. They saw Rizzo as the antidote to the urban crisis. But resentment alone did not lead them to Rizzo. He was also an affirmation of their blue-collar identity. Rizzo celebrated his white ethnic heritage and his working-class background. His electoral victory represented a triumph of blue-collar culture because Frank Rizzo identified with it. White ethnic, working-class Philadelphians saw him as one of their own. His victory not only represented a broader shift in white, working-class politics, it also signaled a cultural shift in a city whose civic identity began to reflect Rizzo's blue-collar populism. Philadelphia's blue-collar white ethnics had long been overshadowed by a civic reputation as WASP-y and stodgy. Rizzo's victory established a new image as a blue-collar city.[49]

"We Are Now a Blue-Collar City"

Frank Rizzo's reputation as Philadelphia's no-nonsense police commissioner thrust him into the national spotlight. His election to mayor cemented his standing as a symbol of the city and its civic identity. Nationally syndicated comic strip artist Garry Trudeau made that connection explicit in August 1972, when he set a series of his popular comic *Doonesbury* in Philadelphia. The three-part series was part of a larger storyline that followed characters Mike Doonesbury and Mark Slackmeyer on a cross-country road trip to the Republican National Convention in Miami. Making their way via motorcycle and sidecar, the duo stopped in Philadelphia en route to Florida. The first panel in the series found Doonesbury and Slackmeyer asking a bystander for directions to the Philadelphia YMCA before being confronted by a hulking figure with a slick of black hair in the comic's second panel. Armed with nightstick in his left hand and a rifle in his right, the figure towered over Doonesbury and Slackmeyer, saying, "I'll give you some directions, hippie! You get this junk heap out of my city or I'll beat your brains out! Got it?" As he walked away, a stunned Slackmeyer turned to ask "Who was that?" of the bystander offering him directions. "The mayor," he responded.[50]

Since *Doonesbury*'s creation in 1970, Trudeau's widely read strip had come to epitomize countercultural-inspired satire. A favorite among liberals, Trudeau's biting wit pulled few punches when lampooning public figures. Rizzo was no exception, especially in the second strip set in Philadelphia. The comic opened with a disheveled and unshaven Slackmeyer sitting at a diner counter with a cup of coffee. From out of frame a voice yelled, "Hey! You! I thought I told you to get out of town." Standing over Slackmeyer in the next panel, Trudeau caricatured Rizzo's blue-collar accent and mannerisms when he had the character ask, "What you still doin' in Phillie, Boy?" Slackmeyer responded, "Gee, I'm sorry, sir, I didn't think you were serious. After all, I'm a fellow Italian American." Rizzo, noticeably cheerier in the next panel, exclaimed, "You Are?! Well, now, that's different. Yup, that's a very different kettle of fish!" A smiling Rizzo settled in next to Slackmeyer in the final panel. Laying his hand on Slackmeyer's shoulder and finishing the gag, Rizzo said, "I thought you were a Hippie or a Negro or somethin'!"[51]

Trudeau never identified Rizzo by name in the three-day series. It was unnecessary. The humor in the *Doonesbury* series rested on the mockery of Rizzo's reputation for brutality and bigotry, at least when the strips ran nationwide. When the second strip ran in Philadelphia, the *Philadelphia Evening Bulletin* edited the final frame to say only, "I thought you were a Hippie or somethin'!" By editing the punchline the *Bulletin* softened the criticism against the mayor and reiterated Rizzo's carefully crafted public color blindness.[52] As the nationally syndicated version of the comic attested, however, Rizzo was never able to dissuade liberal critics from his racist reputation. The final strip in the series, furthermore, played on Rizzo's other popular well-known characteristic: his ethnic pride. It followed Doonesbury and Slackmeyer as they left the city. Slackmeyer, telling Doonesbury of the evening he spent with the mayor the night before, said that he turned out to be a "pretty nice fellow." The two went to Rizzo's house, he said, where they shared a home-cooked meal, wine, and stories about the "old country." The mayor even signed Slackmeyer up as an honorary member of the Philadelphia Italian Anti-Defamation League. "All of which is no mean feat for a Jewish boy," Slackmeyer quipped in the final panel, bragging of his ability to fool the mayor.[53]

Doonesbury showed how much Rizzo had come to represent the city in the public imagination. The strip featured no other identifiable figures or landmarks. If not for Rizzo, there was nothing to identify the setting as Philadelphia in the final two strips. In *Doonesbury*, Rizzo became a stand-in for the entire city. Moreover, the Frank Rizzo caricatured in the comic was the embodiment of blue-collar Philadelphia and its connotations. The weapons Rizzo carried in the first strip reflected his toughness and inflexibility. His unpolished vernacular reinforced his up-from-the-streets image. White ethnic heritage mattered deeply to the character. The fictional Rizzo was an exaggeration, but he captured an image that represented both the mayor and his city. It was especially representative of the blue-collar Philadelphians that felt they finally had a mayor that truly represented them, who they considered "one of us." They supported Rizzo throughout his political career, and through a series of challenges and controversies, because they saw him as one of their own.

Blue-collar Philadelphians wrote to Rizzo constantly. The sheer amount of mail his mayoral office received was astounding. People wrote to Rizzo to express their admiration, to inform him of local issues that mattered to them, or even to ask him to act on state or national issues—like capital punishment and abortion—that were beyond his control. Letters encouraging Rizzo to run for governor of Pennsylvania started filling his mailbox as early as 1972. Yet blue-collar Philadelphians did not just write to Rizzo as a politician. They also sent him mountains of fan mail and well wishes. Birthday and holiday greetings piled up year after year. They sent him postcards from family vacations. His wife, Carmella Rizzo, intentionally kept a low profile and refused a public role of any kind, but still received Mother's Day greetings from adoring strangers. Time and again, letter writers included personal anecdotes, telling Rizzo how they had met him at a campaign rally or how he had once helped a relative. Most times, they received a letter from the mayor thanking them for writing and telling them that he remembered them. Of course, it would have been impossible for Rizzo to respond to every letter and recall so many minute details. More than likely a staff member responded to the letters and maintained a personal touch. But it worked. Each letter reinforced the feeling that Rizzo not only represented blue-collar Philadelphia, but was a part of blue-collar Philadelphia.[54]

Italian Americans were especially proud of Rizzo. In 1972, a letter from South Philadelphia's Loretta Crea exemplified the kind of mail Rizzo regularly received. Crea began by telling Rizzo how much she admired him and thanking him for helping to end a labor strike at the Delaware River Port Authority, where her husband worked. The reason for her letter, however, was to let Rizzo know how sorry she was about the criticism he received. It was unfair, she said, and clearly based on his Italian ancestry. "I find that people will attack you in my presence because they know that I am of the same Italian heritage that you are," she told Rizzo. She identified with Rizzo and it mattered deeply that she could see Rizzo as one of her own. "You have given people like myself a great deal of hope," she concluded her letter. "I sincerely hope that you continue on the pattern you have set in front of yourself thus far." Like so many others, Crea received a personal response from the mayor's office.[55] To white ethnic, blue-collar Philadelphians like her, Rizzo was more than a mayor, he was like a friend and neighbor. When scandal plagued his administration, letter writers reminded Rizzo that he still had their support.

Rizzo's first term in office was riddled with controversy. The scandals ranged from frequent verbal gaffs and poorly timed media appearances to much more serious allegations of misappropriation of federal funds and using the police to spy on political enemies.[56] At times, the scandals veered toward the cartoonish, as when, in 1973, Rizzo publicly failed a polygraph test administered immediately after vouching for its veracity. Democratic Party rival Peter Camiel had accused Rizzo of using the police department as a personal spy ring and offering bribes to reward the mayor's friends. Local newspapers initiated investigations into corruption in City Hall and *Daily News* editor Rolfe Neill challenged Rizzo, Camiel, and deputy mayor Phillip R. T. Carroll to take lie detector tests. All three agreed. Before taking the test, Rizzo famously said, "If this machine says a man lied, he lied." Rizzo and Carroll failed. Camiel passed.[57] But Rizzo's blue-collar constituency refused to believe any of the accusations and steadfastly stood by their mayor. One said that her faith in Rizzo was "now stronger than ever" and another said Rizzo had been "baited by the lousy liberal press bastards."[58] Likewise, when a disastrous appearance on the nationally televised *Lou Gordon Show* ended with Rizzo storming out of the interview after being presented with evidence of widespread police corruption under his watch, blue-collar Philadelphia came to his defense. Most of them blamed "the biased media" who were out to get "the working peoples' mayor."[59] When accusations swirled about Rizzo's misappropriation of public funds to build a multimillion-dollar mansion, his supporters wrote off the accusations as mere rumors. Many of them thought Rizzo had earned his "dream house" and congratulated the mayor on its purchase, even after evidence proved his administration had misused public funds to construct the house.[60] Throughout his first term and most of the 1970s, there was little Rizzo could do to jeopardize the loyalty of white, blue-collar Philadelphia.

While Rizzo maintained enormous popularity in blue-collar Philadelphia, his controversial mayoralty divided the city and the local Democratic Party. He continued his criticism of the civil rights movement and publicly fought with liberals. He alienated Democrats when he endorsed Richard Nixon's reelection in 1972.[61] Rizzo considered the president a personal hero and called him the greatest president in American history. The respect was mutual. Nixon considered Rizzo essential to his urban strategy and welcomed the endorsement from across party lines. Rizzo then made a spectacle of his support for the president and opposition to George McGovern. When Rizzo held a press conference to publicly endorse Nixon for reelection, he carried with him a rubber chicken pinned with a "McGovern for President" campaign button. He also presented Nixon with a Zippo cigarette lighter featuring an illustration of popular cartoon dog Snoopy saying "Fuck McGovern."[62] Rizzo seemed to go out of his way to insult and antagonize liberals. They, in turn, assumed a defensive position. Liberals and civil rights activists regrouped and began forming a new political coalition capable of challenging Rizzo's blue-collar appeal. For the time being, however, they were overwhelmed by a city and nation that welcomed Rizzo's brand of blue-collar politics. Richardson Dilworth called it an "unfortunate period," the "Reign of the Hard Hat," and the "persecution of intellectualism."[63]

Liberals like Dilworth saw the rise of Frank Rizzo and the blue-collar cultural populism it represented as a dangerous deviation from the politics of the postwar era. They interpreted the success of figures like Rizzo and Nixon as a fluke guided by the politics of resentment and backlash. In many ways, Rizzo did owe his victory in 1971 and his unrelenting popularity to the blue-collar resentment of liberalism and the civil rights movement. But Rizzo also reaped the benefits of a widespread cultural populism that celebrated working-class aesthetics in the early 1970s, both locally and nationally. He represented more than political success. His election was proof that blue-collar whites had overcome the challenges of the 1960s. They saw Rizzo's good fortune as their own because they saw themselves in the mayor. Rizzo was proof that Philadelphia had become a "blue-collar town."[64]

For working-class white ethnics, the late 1960s were an era of embattled blue-collar traditions and institutions. The rise of blue-collar cultural populism in the 1970s celebrated their working-class authenticity. Popular politics, popular culture, and a vast array of popular entertainments celebrated the blue-collar cultural populism. Throughout the 1970s, television programs like *All in the Family* and popular movies like *Dog Day Afternoon* celebrated blue-collar protagonists.[65] Nationally, this blue-collar revival reinforced an image of the working class as narrowly white and primarily male. In Philadelphia, the popular and political culture combined to create an idealized civic identity, an urban manifestation of blue-collar culture represented by Frank Rizzo and his blue-collar authenticity. Television's cantankerous blue-collar stereotype Archie Bunker would have felt perfectly at home in Frank Rizzo's Philadelphia.

The reality of an increasingly multicultural working class and struggling economy contradicted the blue-collar optimism represented by Rizzo-era cultural populism. Movements for racial inclusiveness forced federal and local policy changes that ended white men's exclusivity in blue-collar employment. As police wives and neighborhood school mothers proved, blue-collar culture was neither wholly nor exclusively male. Economically, moreover, Philadelphia no longer fit the blue-collar label. Like many American cities, a loss of manufacturing jobs sapped traditional blue-collar jobs. The federal spending that led to record levels of construction jobs in the 1960s subsided in the sagging 1970s economy and put a once-secure blue-collar job into steady decline. Simply put, the blue-collar cultural ascendency did not change the reality of blue-collar economic decline. Even as Rizzo signified a triumph of blue-collar identity politics, his administration oversaw the reinvention of Philadelphia's economy. Despite his conservative rhetoric, Rizzo's mayoralty did not dismantle urban liberalism on a local level. His team of talented economic advisers worked to attract new industries and established policies that helped make the city a center of the health care and pharmaceutical industries.[66] Ironically, Philadelphia's blue-collar reputation emerged just as it was in the midst of transition to a more white-collar and service-sector economy. The city maintained its reputation as a "blue-collar town" partly because of Rizzo's image and partly because popular culture in and about Philadelphia in the 1970s reinforced that civic identity.[67]

Philadelphia celebrated its white ethnic, blue-collar traditions long before the 1970s. The annual Mummer's Parade remained a staple of white ethnic heritage and a yearly celebration of the city's blue-collar culture. By the 1970s, moreover, the previous decades' controversies had largely disappeared as Mummers clubs observed the ban on blackface that marred the parade in the 1950s and 1960s. Even so, Mummers clubs still banned the participation of nonwhites and women, thereby reinforcing the representation of blue-collar cultural identity as predominantly white and male. More importantly, the Mummers signaled a continuity between the beleaguered blue-collar culture of the 1960s and the celebration of blue-collar cultural populism in Frank Rizzo's 1970s. The emerging celebration of blue-collar culture maintained the implicit racial and gender politics. Often, the racial and gender connotations of blue-collar culture in the 1970s surpassed that of the earlier era and began remaking the city's civic identity.[68]

No medium cemented Philadelphia's reputation as a blue-collar city more than professional sports. Philadelphia had long been a city that symbolically identified with its professional sports teams. Fans had a reputation for devotion to local teams. For many of them, the triumphs and setbacks of teams like baseball's Phillies and football's Eagles took on cultural and social meanings that far surpassed a leisure activity.[69] For blue-collar Philadelphians, fandom became part of their cultural and civic identity. By the 1970s, after the Phillies and Eagles had suffered years of losing records, a new team rose to capture the attention and devotion of blue-collar fans. Professional hockey's Philadelphia Flyers became a source of intense fan devotion and epitomized the traits of a "blue-collar team" for a "blue-collar city" in the 1970s.[70]

The Philadelphia Flyers entered the National Hockey League (NHL) in 1967. Hockey had yet to become a staple of American sports culture and the NHL wanted to expand into a growing professional sports market. Though bringing professional hockey to Philadelphia was a gamble, Ed Snider, a part owner of the Philadelphia Eagles, saw the sport's potential. He convinced the city to help construct the Philadelphia Spectrum, a $12 million stadium near the intersection of Broad and Pattison Avenues in South Philadelphia that soon housed both the Flyers and professional basketball's 76ers. While the Flyers performed poorly in their first few seasons in the NHL, they still built a loyal fan base that grew in size and intensity when the team's fortunes turned around in the early 1970s. Beginning in the 1972–1973 season, the team recruited new players that redefined the Flyers for the remainder of the decade. The new squad was fast and tough. They intimidated its opponents through hard and frequent hits. Hockey was already a violent sport, but the Philadelphia Flyers played with an aggressiveness that made the team stand out above their competitors. After a particularly brutal game against the Atlanta Flames in early January 1973, two local sports journalists gave the team a nickname that stuck with them for the rest of the era, the "Broad Street Bullies."[71]

No team represented Philadelphia's resurgent blue-collar culture more than the Broad Street Bullies. While they were highly trained, talented, and relatively well-paid professional athletes, their style of play earned them a distinction as a "blue-collar" team. They worked hard to compete with more established franchises. They doled out bruising punishment to their opponents. The team soon became the most popular professional sports franchise in Philadelphia, especially among blue-collar whites that could identify with the Broad Street Bullies and their style of play. Hockey's players and fans were almost entirely white. It was also an ultramasculine sport that rewarded violence, and the Flyers played more ferociously than most. The Broad Street Bullies exhibited an amplified version of the city's blue-collar cultural populism. More than that, they became real-life blue-collar heroes when they twice won the Stanley Cup championship trophy in 1974 and 1975. Although Frank Rizzo was not a hockey fan, he could not ignore a successful team with a predominantly white, blue-collar fan base. He accompanied the team on their victory parade after their first championship. The Stanley Cup victories were validations of the Flyers' blue-collar style of play. The team helped create a sense of blue-collar pride that marked the cultural populism of a blue-collar city.[72]

Popular culture offered Philadelphia triumphant symbols of blue-collar culture and bolstered the city's blue-collar identity, first with the Broad Street Bullies and then with the movie *Rocky*. Released in 1976, *Rocky* visually captured the feel of blue-collar Philadelphia. It established the image most readily associated with the city in the 1970s. Philadelphia was more than the film's setting, it was a character in and of itself. The movie's title character was an indelible product of the city and its white ethnic, working-class neighborhoods. *Rocky*'s Philadelphia was dirty. Its citizens were down on their luck, but they refused to give in to the economic decline and physical decay that surrounded them. It was a perfect backdrop for Rocky Balboa, a similarly down-but-not-out boxer given an unbelievable chance at the heavyweight boxing championship. Balboa, furthermore, was a walking, talking white ethnic and blue-collar stereotype. He lived in a never-specified working-class neighborhood. In reality, Rocky's neighborhood was an amalgam of South Philadelphia and Kensington. The fictionalized neighborhood played an essential role in the main character's development, where Rocky fought for survival and tried to parlay those skills into a professional boxing career. The blue-collar neighborhoods that helped create *Rocky* were as central to the film as its supporting characters. Although the real-life boxer that inspired the film grew up and trained in Bayonne, New Jersey, Philadelphia proved a more appropriate setting for the tale of a blue-collar fighter given an incredible chance to rise to the height of his profession.[73]

While the movie offered a snapshot of mid-1970s working-class Philadelphia, its protagonist perfectly captured the rise of white ethnic, blue-collar culture. Rocky Balboa openly celebrated his white ethnic heritage, fighting under the nickname the "Italian Stallion." Rocky did not have access to the most advanced technology or training techniques. He worked hard to overcome his physical shortcomings and make himself a contender in the boxing ring. When not boxing, the struggling fighter surrounded himself with blue-collar archetypes and found work as a dock worker and as muscle for a local loan shark. His friend Paulie worked in a meat packing plant, which allowed Rocky a venue for his unconventional training regimen of using a frozen beef slab as a makeshift punching bag. Rocky and his allies were the fictional personification of blue-collar culture in the 1970s. He also captured the racial and ethnic politics ingrained in the rise of blue-collar cultural populism at the tail end of the civil rights era. The heavyweight champion and Rocky's main opponent was Apollo Creed, a loud, brash, overly confident African American boxer cast in the unmistakable mold of real-life heavyweight champion Muhammad Ali. When Rocky fought Apollo in the film's final sequence—staged at the Philadelphia Spectrum—he not only fought for the championship, but for all of Philadelphia and embattled white ethnics nationwide. Rocky offered redemption to white ethnics who felt they had been on the losing end of the civil rights revolution. He ultimately lost the bout, but not before giving Apollo Creed the fight of his career in a contested decision. By going fifteen brutal rounds with the champion, Rocky won a moral victory for himself and for everything he represented.[74]

Both *Rocky* and the Philadelphia Flyers offered blue-collar Philadelphians vicarious triumphs in the 1970s. Despite the obvious difference between the fictional character and real-life professional sports franchise, moreover, Rocky Balboa and the Broad Street Bullies shared a lot in common. Both took on greater cultural meaning than average professional sports teams or major motion pictures.[75] Admirers cheered both for working their way up to the height of their respective fields. Both also represented decidedly white and male versions of blue-collar cultural populism. Fans celebrated both for their violent, hypermasculine representation of blue-collar whiteness. In

Philadelphia, where both the character and the team symbolized the city on a broader scale, Rocky and the Broad Street Bullies were blue-collar heroes.

There was nothing inherently conservative, or even necessarily political, about the rise of blue-collar cultural populism represented by *Rocky* and the Broad Street Bullies. While *Rocky* certainly engaged the conservative racial politics of the mid-1970s, as the challenges to affirmative action and desegregated education gained legal traction, the production of blue-collar popular culture rarely had an explicit political agenda.[76] Instead, it captured a moment when popular culture in the United States celebrated white, working-class aesthetics. In Philadelphia, that resulted in the recasting of the city's civic and cultural identity in a distinctly blue-collar mold. The politics of blue-collar cultural populism came from those that consumed and imbued it with a conservative meaning. Frank Rizzo, therefore, was able to capitalize on the city's blue-collar identity and direct it toward his own political ends. He ensured that even apolitical expressions of blue-collar culture in Philadelphia maintained conservative connotations.

Whenever Rizzo faced charges of corruption or ineffective governance, he returned to his law-and-order roots. It was a centerpiece of his blue-collar populism and an issue that he knew his supporters would rally behind. He said, for example, that he only ran for mayor in the first place because liberal politicians and lenient judges threatened to ruin the city. Although the claim was disingenuous, the narrative catered to the Philadelphians that championed toughness and sacrifice as blue-collar values. The campaign against liberal judges that Rizzo started as police commissioner remained one of his more popular platforms as mayor.[77] When, in 1974, United States Attorney General William Saxbe called for keeping criminals in longer prison sentences, Rizzo cheered the turn toward a more punitive criminal justice system as a victory for him and his blue-collar supporters. "I've been saying the same thing for twenty years," Rizzo said. Along with Rizzo, the FOP, organized police wives, and the blue-collar Philadelphians that had worked to protect the police could point to Saxbe's position as a validation of their long movement for law-and-order conservatism.[78]

Rizzo both helped create Philadelphia's blue-collar civic identity and reaped the benefits of the city's blue-collar identity politics. His identification with blue-collar Philadelphians helped him survive a tumultuous first term in office that made him a frequent target of the liberals who were never comfortable with his presence in City Hall. New political enemies he created with his divisive politics and personality joined the effort to oust him from office.

In 1975, they waged a challenge to Rizzo in the Democratic primary election. Rallying liberals and civil rights activists behind the candidacy of liberal lawyer and Richardson Dilworth's stepson Louis Hill, Rizzo's critics and enemies hoped they could bring together the traditionally Democratic factions Rizzo had alienated. The threat was real enough. Some of Rizzo's advisers briefly considered switching parties before deciding to wage the fight against liberal Democrats. But Louis Hill and his backers also seriously misjudged Rizzo's enduring popularity. While Hill sought the backing of disaffected Democrats, Rizzo again campaigned in white, blue-collar neighborhoods. He easily held together the coalition of organized labor and white ethnics that elected him in 1971. He won the Democratic primary with a greater margin of victory than he had four years earlier.[79]

Rizzo overcame the primary challenge relatively easily, but he was still livid at the attempt to remove him from office. He vowed revenge after the general election. His retaliation, furthermore, would be severe. On the campaign trail, with victory in the general election all but assured, Rizzo repeatedly told reporters that he would "make Attila the Hun look like a faggot" when dealing with those that he thought had double-crossed him.[80] The comment, which became one of the most famous of Rizzo's entire career, stood apart from the outlandish rhetoric that Rizzo employed on a regular basis.[81] It was emblematic of his blue-collar populism and spoke volumes about his character. The hyperbolic assertion of aggressive manhood promised quick and violent retribution. For liberals and civil libertarians—especially those in or with ties to the homosexual community—the comment confirmed that Rizzo represented the worst of brutish, boorish populist conservatism. They hoped it would sink his campaign.

Blue-collar Philadelphians, however, saw a politician unafraid to speak his mind. As they had in 1971, blue-collar neighborhoods came out in droves to support Rizzo in the general election of 1975. The Republican Party weakly tried to defeat Rizzo with its own appeal to white ethnic politics. They nominated city councilman and fellow Italian American Thomas Foglietta. He simply could not compete against Rizzo for blue-collar, white ethnic votes. Charles Bowser, who was James Tate's city manager and the highest-ranking African American official in the city during the late 1960s, created the Philadelphia Party to wage a third party challenge to Rizzo. While Bowser came in second and marked another notch in the effort to create a new political coalition, he had no chance of defeating the mayor. Rizzo won with 65 percent of the vote and won in blue-collar wards by a four-to-one margin.[82]

The blue-collar populism that carried Frank Rizzo through his early political career appealed to broader popular culture that depended on strong, tough women protectors, but privileged a primarily white and male cultural identity. Rizzo wielded this popularity in the elections of 1971 by contrasting his own blue-collar authenticity with effete liberals that allegedly threatened traditional neighborhoods, schools, and institutions. As he did, Rizzo adopted and exemplified a key trait in the emerging blue-collar conservatism. In 1975, he relied again on his masculine blue-collar identity and politics to remain in office. Supported almost entirely by white, blue-collar voters, Rizzo's victories signaled changes in white, working-class politics as well as a broader rebuke of an urban liberalism based in central planning and the promotion of equal opportunity. Rizzo and his supporters rejected the liberal reform agenda that dominated most of the postwar era. They also ushered in a new era in the city's political and cultural history. By 1977, Rizzo felt confident in declaring that Philadelphia was "now a blue-collar city."[83]

For the entirety of the postwar era, even after James Tate moved his administration away from the liberal reform politics that defined the Clark-Dilworth years, nonwhites and liberals used the municipal government as a means to end discrimination and settle other grievances. From the Police Advisory Board to the efforts to end blackface in the Mummers Parade, from trying to implement school reform and desegregation to support for the Philadelphia Plan and equal employment opportunity, city agencies maintained the hope that powerful Philadelphians were working to ensure equal rights. While many of those agencies began failing or disbanding by the late 1960s, urban liberalism's promise to alleviate structural inequalities and promote opportunity still seemed plausible. Blue-collar whites who felt increasingly burdened by liberalism found a new political outlet in Frank Rizzo. Their engagement with the politics of equal opportunity education, employment, and housing in the 1970s was changed by having an ally like Frank Rizzo in City Hall.

CHAPTER 6

Neighborhood Politics

South Philadelphia's Grays Ferry neighborhood did not remain quiet for long after Police Commissioner Frank Rizzo's tuxedo-clad heroics at the Tasker Homes public housing project in June 1969. In the years thereafter, trouble routinely erupted between the white, mostly Irish Catholic Grays Ferry community and the largely African American residents of the housing project and the Kings Village neighborhood that bordered Grays Ferry to the north. Sandwiched between the Tasker Homes to the south and the Schuylkill River to the west, Grays Ferry whites felt surrounded. They were also determined to keep their neighborhood from being taken over by "outsiders." Problems with Kings Village residents primarily stemmed from African American children passing through Grays Ferry on their way to and from school. Black parents feared sending their children through the hostile white community. Although most of the white parents sent their children to Catholic schools, they still resented the influx of black schoolchildren passing through the neighborhood. The racial battles over neighborhood space were even more pitched over access to the Lanier Playground that sat between the Tasker Homes and Grays Ferry. The confrontations over the playground often turned violent, as residents from both the housing project and white neighborhood fought over recreational space in an area with limited resources. Between the late 1960s and mid-1970s, the combined racially charged clashes over neighborhood access and recreational space led to nine near riots, several assaults, and three murders. By the mid-1970s, the entire area encompassing Grays Ferry, Kings Village, and the Tasker Homes became one of the most volatile in the city.[1]

To make matters worse, despite white residents' intense pride in their homes and community, their neighborhood was on the decline. Like much of South Philadelphia, Grays Ferry was once a testament to Philadelphia's urban industrial might. Its scattered warehouses and industrial plants intermixed with its row-house architecture immediately marked Grays Ferry as a classic urban, white ethnic, working-class neighborhood. For generations, residents shared cramped city streets, church pews, and bar stools as they created the kind of close-knit community that made Philadelphia a city of neighborhoods.[2] Like so many other working-class neighborhoods in deindustrializing cities, however, Grays Ferry in the 1970s showed the signs of age and economic downturn. City-owned vacant houses and boarded-up corner stores littered the neighborhood, providing constant reminders of an urban renewal plan that never quite panned out. Although residents had once embraced urban renewal, they now held past liberal failures responsible for the area's condition.[3] They likewise held the Tasker Homes project and the influx of African Americans in the communities surrounding Grays Ferry responsible for the neighborhood's deterioration. Both were the result of liberal social engineering, Grays Ferry whites said. By the 1970s, the community felt besieged on all sides, but emboldened to defend their neighborhood. Francis Rafferty, a self-proclaimed "working stiff with five kids" and president of the Grays Ferry Community Council (GFCC), captured the overwhelming feeling of the community's residents in an interview with a local reporter. "These jerk liberals come in here and try to tell us how to live," he said. "Nobody tells us how to live," he continued. "This is a good neighborhood and we're going to keep it that way. We're going to fight."[4]

Mid-1970s Grays Ferry residents had earned a reputation for defending their community by any means necessary, including violence. Franny Rafferty, in fact, was a former amateur boxer. Neighbors said the GFCC president would never back down from a physical confrontation. Rafferty and the community's reputation also led to widespread indictments of vigilantism against African Americans by the media, but residents dismissed the accusations as liberal propaganda. Although repeated violence in the Grays Ferry-Tasker Homes area was an undeniable result of racial tensions, Rafferty and the GFCC still tried to claim the aggressive defense of their neighborhood was not racially motivated. "Hell, we fight anybody," another Grays Ferry resident told a reporter before offering the story of a recent tussle with a motorcycle gang. He suggested their violent methods were not limited to African Americans and public housing tenants.[5] In an era and a city that celebrated tough, blue-collar men like Rafferty and the GFCC, their efforts to defend their community were a testament to the sense of loyalty that defined neighborhood politics in 1970s Philadelphia. It was unsurprising, then, that

Rafferty and Frank Rizzo made easy allies. Indeed, all of Grays Ferry was Rizzo country.[6]

The mayor, in turn, gave special attention to white, blue-collar neighborhoods like Grays Ferry. He had increased the police patrols in the Grays Ferry-Tasker Homes area as police commissioner. As mayor, he made sure that police kept a watchful eye on the area. But the police often exacerbated the tensions and made it clear whose side they were on. Black residents and public housing tenants complained about mistreatment from the police as well as their unwillingness to investigate their claims or arrest white assailants. At the same time, police mingled freely with white residents and passed the time by chatting with their fellow blue-collar Philadelphians. Rizzo also visited the neighborhood and promised to keep it safe. Under order from his Recreation Department, the city padlocked the entrance to Lanier Playground facing the Tasker Homes, thereby marking it as a preferred white space. Rizzo made it clear that neighborhoods like Grays Ferry would receive preferential treatment from his administration.[7]

Grays Ferry was not the only community to adopt violent means of neighborhood defense in the 1970s. In Kensington, where white rioters forced African Americans to leave the area in the 1960s, violence once again became a method of chasing off newcomer blacks.[8] In neighborhoods like Whitman in South Philadelphia and Morrell Park in the Far Northeast, culturally blue-collar whites defended their neighborhoods knowing that the mayor was on their side. Rizzo's ascendancy emboldened blue-collar whites, and their years of neighborhood protectionism resulted in a number of legal and legislative victories in the early to mid-1970s. It was the social and political high point of blue-collar politics. In 1975, for example, Francis Rafferty parlayed his community leadership and confrontational reputation into a political career when he won election as a Democratic at-large city councilman. Rafferty took his fighting reputation into municipal government, quite literally at times, as he got into more than one fistfight in city council chambers. Rafferty also became one of Rizzo's greatest allies and biggest boosters. Having Rizzo on their side marked a key difference between the blue-collar battles over space and privilege in the 1960s and those of the 1970s.

Battles over blue-collar neighborhoods in areas like Grays Ferry were not new, but they took on renewed intensity and meaning in the Rizzo era. Having a mayor that vowed to defend white ethnic, blue-collar neighborhoods altered the city's political landscape. As Franny Rafferty's transition from neighborhood leader to municipal government illustrated, the mid-1970s were a high point for white, blue-collar politics. In neighborhoods like Grays Ferry, Kensington, and scores of others, Frank Rizzo's presence in City Hall emboldened the defense of blue-collar traditions and institutions. Throughout the early to mid-1970s, just as the decade's blue-collar cultural populism reached its peak, blue-collar whites won significant victories in key battles over neighborhoods and schools. They did not win all their battles. In fact, most victories were fleeting. But combined with the era's blue-collar cultural populism, political victories signaled an apex of blue-collar influence and power in the 1970s.

The mid-1970s height of local blue-collar power and influence heralded the economic populism of the emerging blue-collar conservatism. As blue-collar whites engaged in pivotal battles over desegregation and welfare state liberalism, they exhibited two of the most important and interwoven prongs of their developing politics. The first was a willingness to accept and even defend some aspects of welfare liberalism, provided that the beneficiaries of government entitlements earned their rights through their loosely defined notion of "hard work." The second was a mutually reinforcing defense of their own "color-blind" class privilege.

The populist aspects of blue-collar politics did not reject all redistributive efforts for social and urban benefit. Instead, blue-collar whites selectively rejected liberal programs—like public housing—while encouraging programs that benefited communities similar to their own, like urban renewal or state funding for parochial schools. They distinguished who deserved government entitlements by drawing a sharp dichotomy between earned privilege and unearned advantage, between those that earned what they had through "hard work" and those that received or expected "handouts." While the discourse on hard work and entitlement was indisputably linked with the politics of racial integration and equal opportunity, blue-collar whites learned to avoid racial dialogues. In their place, they championed blue-collar identity politics. Many blue-collar whites understood how the civil rights movement altered the political discourses surrounding race and desegregation. While they often adopted a racially coded discourse—equating public housing or integration with crime, for example—they carefully avoided explicitly racist denunciations of perceived threats to their neighborhoods, schools, and communities. While many expressions of color blindness turned out to be hollow after blue-collar power and influence began to fade, the emergence of these arguments reinforced the sense of blue-collar class privilege that undergirded their selective rejection of welfare liberalism.

Although the climax of blue-collar politics that accompanied Frank Rizzo's early mayoral tenure helped white Philadelphians win several crucial battles, the power and influence would not last. It was also limited by the efforts of the civil rights, welfare rights, and education reformers that regrouped after earlier political losses. Few examples exemplify these battles over neighborhood and welfare liberalism as clearly as the early to mid-1970s controversies over the construction of new public housing in South and Northeast Philadelphia.

"No One Subsidized Us"

In spring of 1971, as Frank Rizzo campaigned for mayor, the neighborhood politics that encapsulated the height of blue-collar class privilege got an early start in the small white working-class Whitman neighborhood in South Philadelphia. Early on the morning of March 23, a group of about thirty Whitman residents arrived at Whitman Park, a vacant lot on the edge of the neighborhood where the city planned to build a new public housing project. The protesters were mostly women with their young children. They climbed on top of bulldozers and blocked the path of construction crews that had come to begin their workday. They remained there, unmoved, until police officers forced them from the site. Undeterred, they returned to protest the construction site the following morning, and for several weeks thereafter. When the city-contracted Multicon Construction Company obtained an injunction against the protesters, the pickets grew in size and intensity. Protesters created human chains to block traffic. They targeted the construction workers, calling them "scabs" for crossing their picket line. Others disparaged the potential residents of the new housing project and demanded that the city "Think of Our Welfare."[9] Although the Philadelphia Housing Authority attempted to mediate a solution, the residents could not be swayed. The blue-collar Whitman women continued protesting the site until Multicon agreed to halt construction at the end of April. The protestors scored a victory for the women's protectionism that had shaped blue-collar protest and politics for a decade.[10]

The renewed interest in public housing of the 1960s led to plans for several new low-income, federally subsided housing projects throughout Philadelphia.[11] Critics of past attempts to provide a publicly supported alternative to the private housing market protested that public housing construction exacerbated ghettoization by building almost exclusively in already poor neighborhoods with limited resources. The result was cities like Philadelphia, Chicago, and Detroit that showed signs of worsening economic and spatial inequality. Housing reformers also began viewing failed public housing exper- iments as part of the systemic causes of racial segregation.[12] That recognition grew out of larger changes in Philadelphia's housing reform movement. The city's largest and most influential housing reform organization, the Philadel- phia Housing Association, had been a bulwark of white, middle-class pro- gressivism for decades. In the late 1960s, however, the organization merged with the suburban-based Fair Housing Council of the Delaware Valley. The creation of the new Housing Association of the Delaware Valley (HADV) effectively brought private market fair housing advocacy and public hous- ing reform into a single movement. More importantly, the HADV took cues from the changing politics of the civil rights movement. New HADV direc- tor Shirley Dennis was active in the Fair Housing Council and civil rights organizations throughout the 1960s. Influenced by the Black Power move- ment's battles for neighborhood services, housing, and jobs, Dennis tied the problems of poverty, spatial discrimination, racial segregation, and urban- suburban inequality into a single metropolitan crisis. Under her leadership in the 1970s, the HADV became more action oriented and race conscious. She led the organization toward a broader advocacy of welfare rights and race-conscious welfare liberalism. With the HADV leading the movement to reform the city's public housing program, moreover, housing reformers determined to end the cycle of ghettoization by seeking new construction in stable neighborhoods like Whitman.[13]

The protests at Whitman Park captured the depths and ferocity of blue- collar neighborhood politics in the 1970s. Despite the emergence of the con- troversy in 1971, the city had long-standing plans to erect a public housing complex as part of Whitman's extensive conservation program.[14] Plans for the Whitman Park project had undergone extensive changes since city planners first proposed public housing in the neighborhood in the mid-1950s, how- ever. The city originally planned the construction of high-rise buildings, but opposition from housing reformers and community leaders resulted in an altered plan. Throughout the 1960s, the Whitman Area Improvement Coun- cil cooperated with city planners to draft an alternative, eventually agreeing to the construction of 120 individual townhouses. Unlike the Tasker Homes and other troubled housing developments, the renamed Whitman Park would blend into the neighborhood's built environment by matching the architectural plans for the new private housing.[15] Additionally, Whitman Park would be an altogether different type of public housing project called Turnkey III. The new program not only provided residents with individual homes and more privacy than other projects, it also included a provision whereby residents of the rent-subsidized townhouses would have the option to purchase their homes after a period of years. Whitman Park's design was an attempt to rectify the problems associated with public housing. The HADV cheered the plan as the start of a new era of low-income housing construction.[16]

Even though Whitman community leaders in the late 1960s enthusiastically backed Turnkey III policies, the revamped Whitman Council Inc. (WC) claimed they had not been informed about plans to build public housing. Many of the community leaders that had negotiated with the city in the 1960s were part of a small group of the neighborhood's lawyers, doctors, and white-collar workers. They began moving out of the neighborhood by the end of the decade. Although they were involved in the planning of Whitman Park, they had little contact with the wider community. As a result, both the community council and the community changed drastically before the start of the protests against Whitman Park.[17] Under the direction of new president Fred Druding, the newly aroused Whitman Council organized the construction site pickets and neighborhood protectionist movement. Directing the opposition to Whitman Park and stewarding the WC through its legal battles, the soft-spoken Druding created the council's "color-blind" defense of their neighborhood. Although his efforts hid deeper racial antipathies within the community, Druding's attempt to stress the community's blue-collar class identity over its racial identity guided the Whitman Council's neighborhood protectionism. He and the Whitman Council then politicized and united the neighborhood as it had never been before.

Fred Druding won the presidency of the Whitman Council in 1970 and held the position for the next fifteen years. While he worked for several community planning firms throughout the 1970s, he had his eye on a political career from an early age. Preceding his community leadership work, he helped found the Philadelphia Young Democrats, a short-lived youth auxiliary of the local Democratic Party.[18] A self-proclaimed liberal and civil rights sympathizer, Druding campaigned against Frank Rizzo in the Democratic primary election of 1971. "What we need today in the Mayor's office is a personal commitment to reason: rational ideas, not storm-trooper confrontation," Druding said in a statement endorsing William Green III. Rizzo's promise that he would not allow public housing in any neighborhood that opposed it changed Druding's mind. In the election, furthermore, Rizzo earned his highest margin of victory in Whitman's ward.[19] Druding then found an outlet for his political ambitions in the Whitman Council's crusade against public housing and the connections he made within the Rizzo administration. He also became one of the mayor's most vocal supporters. The relationship he developed with City Hall showed how much blue-collar neighborhoods like Whitman benefited under Rizzo.

While Druding pursued legal options to halt the construction of Whitman Park, neighborhood protesters continued picketing the construction site. The press exulted in stories of Whitman women taking to the picket lines, lying down in front of bulldozers, and physically halting construction. "Ordinary housewives," they reported, were compelled to take drastic action in defense of their neighborhood.[20] Protest organizer Gert Hogan received the most attention. Although she often worked with Druding, Hogan preferred a more direct approach. Living adjacent to the construction site, Hogan joined the pickets every day and, on several occasions, donned a Plains Indian headdress and rode a horse through the community to stir up neighbors against the "invasion." Her antics made her stand out to journalists. Conservative *Philadelphia Evening Bulletin* columnist Adrian Lee made her a community icon. In a series of articles defending the Whitman protests, Lee put Hogan at the center of the neighborhood's crusade.[21] Other reporters discussed her behavior, her neighborhood pride, and her ethnicity. "Gert is Irish," quipped one columnist. "Boy, is she Irish." Like Fred Druding, Hogan also denied that race influenced her community's opposition. "When people get something free, they treat it like junk," she said. "We're not racists," she continued. "Why, we had good colored people living here until the city took their houses. I wish they were back."[22] Protesters and sympathetic reporters presented the Whitman pickets as a working-class, white ethnic crusade. The picketers also deflected accusations that their protests were racially motivated by invoking their roles as wives and mothers driven to take extraordinary measures. Hogan and the women that joined her became symbols not only of the blue-collar political ascendancy, but also of blue-collar women's toughness and commitment to neighborhood protectionism.

Fred Druding and Gert Hogan expressed two varieties of the neighborhood's defense, but both displayed the community's overarching discontent with liberal city planners, building companies receiving government subsidies, and the welfare recipients who expected "something for nothing."

Some residents said that Whitman Park would bring crime and blight into their neighborhood. Others claimed it was unfair for the housing authority to sell the units to low-income families receiving federally subsidized mortgages, free utilities, and tax waivers. Although many of their complaints were unfounded—the Turnkey III program, for example, deemed residents responsible for their taxes and utilities—the protestors argued that housing subsidies went to people who had not earned them and punished people who had "worked hard."[23] Another woman, who believed that housing for the "irresponsible poor" would create an "instant slum," said that public housing helped the wrong people. Public housing did not help the poor, she said, "but the builders who are taking advantage of the subsidy." Those that did deserve the benefits were like the people of Whitman: "the real poor, the fellow who has sweated, alongside his wife, to save and struggle to pay for a home, and now is to be taxed to death to pay for the homes of others."[24] The woman's critique harkened back to the labor-based vision of public housing in the 1930s. In the context of the 1970s, however, the economic populism expressed by Whitman protesters relayed a sense of vulnerability. Residents described themselves as a class caught in the middle between out-of-touch liberals and the undeserving poor.[25]

Whitman protesters made targets of welfare state liberalism and welfare recipients themselves, but they carefully avoided explicit discussions of race in their protests against Whitman Park. Instead, they relied on denunciations of "crime" and "blight" that in the context of public housing in the urban North almost always referred to African American criminality and communities. The Whitman Council effectively concealed the racial implications of their opposition in the popular and ostensibly color-blind language of aggrieved blue-collar authenticity. More importantly, their blue-collar populism articulated a dichotomy between their hard-working community that earned what little they had and prospective public housing tenants. Blue-collar residents of neighborhoods like Whitman argued that, compared to the poor and public housing tenants, they were a more privileged social class. But they did not point to their higher incomes or economic status as a means of differentiation. Instead, they adopted a notion of class privilege based upon their view of how they "earned" their homes and incomes. By their own definition, they deserved what they had because they earned it through "hard work." They used this same discourse of blue-collar authenticity to justify their entitlement to federal and city funding for programs like urban renewal and neighborhood development. In 1973, Fred Druding sent the Philadelphia Redevelopment

Authority a lengthy list of improvements the community still demanded and promised to continue working "until the goals that have been set are achieved to the satisfaction of our people."[26] Working hard, saving, and maintaining their own homes had earned them the right to government benefits. Public housing tenants were not similarly entitled. The Whitman Council insisted upon the unfairness of providing "giveaways" to the poor.[27] Their discourse on hard work simultaneously celebrated their own work ethic while denigrating the supposed failings of public housing tenants and welfare recipients.

Like all blue-collar neighborhoods in Philadelphia, the Whitman community gained a powerful ally when Frank Rizzo took office in 1972. With the Whitman Council's backing, the Rizzo administration challenged Whitman Park in court. Construction ended when the city reached an out-of-court agreement with the Multicon Construction Company in December 1972. The Rizzo administration then ignored requests by the federal Department of Housing and Urban Development (HUD) to restart the project. Although Rizzo cost the city a multimillion-dollar settlement, and HUD threatened to cut off funds for urban renewal and other federally funded projects, the residents of Whitman thought it was a small price to pay.[28] At a victory celebration near the abandoned construction site, they cheered Rizzo and vowed their continued support of his political career. Fred Druding thanked the mayor as well, but credited the efforts of the community activists and picketers. "It's Gert's victory," he said. "And Multicon knows that if they show up again Gert will meet them at the gate."[29]

The Whitman community celebrated, but the battle for Whitman Park was far from over. Organizations like the HADV were determined to see the project built and waged an intense campaign to restart construction. Instead of attacking the Whitman community, however, the HADV and tenants' rights organizations like the Residents Advisory Board (RAB) targeted the Rizzo administration. While Rizzo had long been a target of liberals and civil rights activists, his housing policies came under similar attacks shortly after he became mayor. The HADV and RAB immediately worried about Rizzo's commitment to plans for new low-cost housing. Their fears were confirmed when his administration brokered the deal to end construction on Whitman Park. Immediately thereafter, an ad hoc Citizens Committee for Tenants' Rights issued a statement explicitly linking the mayor's racist reputation to his administration's opposition to public housing in Whitman and the denial of federal resources to the black poor.[30] Philadelphia housing activists made Rizzo a symbol of the perpetuation of housing inequality in the city.

In 1973, the Residents Advisory Board filed a federal suit demanding the restart of construction on Whitman Park. The RAB charged the Rizzo administration with violating antidiscrimination laws. By charging the Rizzo administration with breaking equal opportunity housing laws, they forced the court to consider Whitman Park as a civil rights case.[31] Proponents linked Whitman Park to the larger poverty politics in urban America, especially in Frank Rizzo's Philadelphia. They also feared that a Whitman victory would send a signal to other white neighborhoods.[32] Indeed, Whitman was not the only community in Philadelphia fighting the construction of public housing. On the other end of the city, in the Far Northeast, the Morrell Park community was engaged in a similar battle.

Like their counterparts in Whitman, the white residents of Morrell Park publicly protested the construction of federally subsidized low-rent housing in their neighborhood. They similarly enlisted many of the same tactics and much of the same rhetoric as their South Philadelphia compatriots. Like Whitman residents, they too claimed that race had nothing to do with their opposition to public housing and engaged a discourse of blue-collar color blindness and class privilege. Also like Whitman, the class politics of public housing opposition were an attempt to avoid a public dialogue on the racial politics of public housing, but helped create the neighborhood populism that residents employed in defense of their community. But while Morrell Park shared much in common with the battle for Whitman Park, it also represented a different set of challenges to city planners and public housing advocates that stemmed from the unique spatial characteristics of the Far Northeast. The fight against Morrell Park showed how broadly white Philadelphians employed the politics of blue-collar class privilege across economic and spatial boundaries.

The massive growth of Northeast Philadelphia continued into the 1970s. In fact, the Far Northeast was the only section of the city that had gained population since 1960. Many older sections of the city succumbed to the massive exodus of whites that marked the predominant population trends in American cities in the postwar era.[33] But Philadelphia's white flight took a somewhat different tack. While many whites left Philadelphia's inner-city neighborhoods, their relocation was not necessarily or only to the suburban counties beyond the city limits. The newly developed neighborhoods and relatively open space of the Far Northeast was like a suburb in the city that acted as one of the main landing sites for the white exodus. By the 1970s, most inhabitants of the Far Northeast were upwardly mobile white ethnics that had only recently left inner-city enclaves. Although they held on to their sense of blue-collar class privileges and sensibilities, their homes and surrounding area resembled a middle-class American suburb.

Like the suburbs, the Far Northeast also remained almost entirely white. A few areas with long-standing African American populations and planned integrated developments like Greenbelt Knoll were exceptions, but the architects of Northeast Philadelphia's great postwar population explosion intentionally excluded nonwhites. For civil rights and housing activists, then, the effort to erect a public housing complex in Morrell Park was as much about integrating the Far Northeast as it was about alleviating overcrowding in the city's other housing projects.[34]

When plans to build 324 low-income, federally subsidized apartments adjacent to Morrell Park emerged, community leaders fought the plan on the grounds that such a complex represented the exact reasons they left the inner city in the first place.[35] Unlike South Philadelphia neighborhoods like Whitman and Grays Ferry, Morrell Park did not have the kind of long-standing traditions that older neighborhoods called upon to reinforce a sense of community. Although most of the residents were of some white ethnic heritage and Christian church, there was no singular or predominant ethnic or religious background to draw upon for community cohesion, as Irish Catholics did in Grays Ferry. As a result of the suburb-like environment and only recent establishment of the neighborhood, Morrell Park's community protectiveness developed differently than in older, inner-city neighborhoods.[36]

In June 1972, the Morrell Park Civic Association followed the example of the Whitman Council and began picketing the proposed construction site. As in South Philadelphia, Morrell Park residents blocked workers from commencing with construction and said public housing would overburden their schools. Also like Whitman, they ignored the preferential zoning ordinances and other ways their community benefited from the actions and funding of the municipal and federal governments. Most importantly, Morrell Park residents also denied that their opposition to public housing had anything to do with race. Instead, Morrell Park residents depended upon the hard work and collective sacrifice it took for them to move to the area. "Most people in this development have gone out on a financial limb to get away from deteriorating neighborhoods all over the city," one resident wrote to Frank Rizzo in the hope of convincing him to help them block the public housing project.[37] More importantly, they also saw the potential residents of a public housing project as undeserving of sharing in the benefits of living in the Far

Northeast. "The residents and tax payers had to work hard and spend a lot of money to settle in this area," wrote another Morrell Park resident. "No one subsidized us," he continued. It was unfair, he claimed, for residents to have to share urban space with people who had not similarly sacrificed and therefore did not deserve to live in the neighborhood.[38]

As in Whitman, Rizzo remained the key to stopping the public housing project in Morrell Park. Many Morrell Park residents wrote the mayor. One "humble taxpayer" asked Rizzo to think about the schools before allowing apartment construction. "This is not racial," he insisted, but a matter of "overcrowding." He begged Rizzo to "stop man's greed on the Zoning commission, for people who have moved to this area looking for a better life and some green space."[39] Others simply reminded Rizzo of his campaign promise to disallow public housing in neighborhoods that opposed it. Rizzo responded to the white Philadelphians who ensured his political future. Ever the populist, he reassured Morrell Park residents that he would make sure they participated in planning their community. He promised he would advocate for neighborhood self-determination.[40] As he did in Whitman, Rizzo ensured at least a temporary stoppage of construction. Morrell Park residents thanked Rizzo profusely. "You truly are the peoples' mayor," wrote one woman.[41] With Frank Rizzo on their side, both Whitman and Morrell Park residents won early battles against public housing construction.

The contests over public housing in Whitman and Morrell Park marked some of the most important struggles for working- and middle-class white ethnics in 1970s Philadelphia. The backing of the Rizzo administration proved to be a critical factor in their early success. But the battles over neighborhood space and invocation of class privilege were not limited to the controversies over public housing. Morrell Park residents also worried that the influx of new, low-income residents would put a strain on their schools. Many of the same blue-collar politics emerged in the ongoing controversies over the integration of Philadelphia's public schools.

Neighborhood Schools and Neighborhood Politics

When Morrell Park residents protested against the construction of public housing, one of their most oft-repeated arguments was that the influx of population would be a burden on their already inadequate schools. They feared that more students in the local public schools would force the board of education to develop a transfer program for students in Northeast Philadelphia.[42] Their protests against the prospect of forced busing revealed how thoroughly entangled the politics of neighborhood and public housing were with the equally fraught controversies over public education in the 1970s. In the case of public housing and public schools, however, blue-collar neighborhoods had the backing of Frank Rizzo. His opposition to both busing and public housing gave blue-collar whites hope that they would triumph in their battles against unpopular liberal programs.

Like the controversies over public housing and city planning, the late-1960s blue-collar revolt against public school educational policy continued into the 1970s. Frank Rizzo once again added a critical difference to the tenor and direction of the ongoing struggles for public education in Philadelphia. Even more immediately than he addressed his campaign promises regarding public housing, Rizzo made good on another centerpiece of his mayoral campaign when he oversaw the addition of several new members to the board of education. The mayor's office did not actually have the power to remove the unpopular superintendent Mark Shedd, as Rizzo promised during his 1971 election campaign. But, as mayor, Rizzo could help appoint new board members and recommend a replacement for recently retired board president, Richardson Dilworth. Rizzo made certain that his appointees represented a direct challenge to Shedd's progressivism. Even before Rizzo officially took office, he consulted with outgoing mayor James H. J. Tate to choose new appointees. Echoing Rizzo during the campaign, the new board members emphasized the need for basic education in neighborhood schools and a greater emphasis on discipline.[43] The new appointments to the board signaled a response to the blue-collar protests against Mark Shedd and the board of education. Already in a bitter feud with the teachers' union and sensing the forthcoming education changes Rizzo's election signaled, Shedd resigned before Rizzo's inauguration. The new appointments to the board of education ended Shedd's brief push for progressive, integrated education in Philadelphia public schools.[44]

Rizzo also rewarded those who helped him get elected when he made his appointments. He recommended the election of former labor leader and current board member William Ross to replace Richardson Dilworth as president. Ross was the manager of the Dress Joint Board of the International Ladies Garment Workers Union before his appointment to the board of education. He had attended Philadelphia public schools and battled with Dilworth over most of the educational controversies in the 1960s. He especially disapproved of Shedd's hiring, believing that Dilworth and Shedd jeopardized the education of blue-collar children and traditional neighborhood schools. Ross also had the full support of Frank Rizzo. He hoped to restore faith in the public education system through a program of "conservatism and austerity." The promotion of William Ross represented a clear change of direction for the board of education.[45]

The new appointments and leadership at the helm of the public school system signaled an official response to the blue-collar protests against the board of education in the late 1960s. Rizzo intended them to show that the school board in the 1970s would not attempt to overhaul the system as Dilworth, Shedd, and the progressives on the board attempted to do just a few years earlier. But some impending changes were beyond Rizzo's authority. The dictates to integrate the city's public schools, for example, came from the State of Pennsylvania and federal court rulings. Even without Dilworth and Shedd, the board of education was still under orders to implement a desegregation plan.[46]

Responding to the blue-collar effort to protect neighborhood schools and minimize student transfer plans, the Rizzo administration refused to make public school integration a high priority.[47] The board of education faced no repercussions from the Rizzo administration for delaying the exploration and execution of workable plans. The mayor also had what he considered more pressing educational matters to deal with. Philadelphia, like many major American cities in the struggling 1970s economy, faced a fiscal crisis. Rizzo had promised not to raise taxes during his campaign for mayor. Attempting to maintain that promise while weathering a reduction in federal spending in urban areas caused city finances to reach a critical state in nearly all areas. The Rizzo administration and board of education worried about having enough revenue to keep the schools operating and gave those concerns precedence over the order to desegregate the schools. Resulting from the budget crisis, the school district endured a prolonged teachers' strike during the 1972–1973 academic year. Among other issues, the teachers' union sought wage increases and smaller class sizes in contract renegotiations. When negotiations with the board of education turned toxic, teachers walked out and stopped classes for eight weeks. The resolution of the strike not only stretched city finances, it sapped parental confidence in the public school system. William Ross, the longtime labor leader, was censured by the Philadelphia AFL-CIO. Some members of organized labor threatened a general strike in support of the teachers. Ross's relationship with Rizzo soured as well and a period of open feuding followed the teachers' strike.[48] The city budget crisis, the teachers' strike, and the controversies resulting from both added hurdles to any attempt to desegregate the public schools.

Advocates of desegregation worked for a new integration plan against the backdrop of the city budget crisis and the growing resentment toward the public school system.[49] Combined with Rizzo's indifference, implementing a plan to desegregate the public school system faced tremendous odds in the mid-1970s. But champions of integrated education continued pressuring the board of education to use any and all resources to achieve the goal. As with school districts under order to desegregate in cities like Boston, Detroit, and Charlotte, the most controversial and bitter battles derived from attempts to implement student transfer programs.[50]

By the early 1970s, the Philadelphia School District bused over seventeen thousand students to relieve overcrowding and accommodate students with special needs or extraordinary talents. Students were not bused for purposes of desegregation alone. The local educational policy compromises in the 1960s forbade busing solely for integration. They also completely banned so-called reverse busing, the transfer of white students into schools with predominantly African American or Latino student populations. The battles for neighborhood schools in the 1960s ensured that the vast majority of bused students came from the overcrowded school districts of North and West Philadelphia. For many of these pupils, the transfer program was a success. "Most of the kids don't bother you," said one student who rode a bus from his home in West Philadelphia to the Sharswood Elementary School in South Philadelphia. Although he complained that some of his white classmates told him that George Wallace was "going to bus us all back to Africa" if he won the presidential election of 1972, he still preferred going to school at Sharswood. "The education is worth it," he said.[51] Even as the greater burden of busing fell on African American students and their parents, many still considered the school bus a safer and more educationally sound alternative to poor schools in their home districts. Philadelphia had one of the few student transfer programs in the nation that seemed to work.

While integration was not the stated goal of the school board's busing program, the practical result was more African American school children going to schools in predominantly white neighborhoods. Even with its minimal impact, however, parents in those neighborhoods protested the influx of students and potential strain on the resources of their children's schools. At the beginning of the 1973–1974 school year, for example, 380 students from South Philadelphia High School began attending classes at Southwark

Elementary School facilities. They were part of a special program for exceptionally bright, college bound students. About 60 percent of them were African American.[52] With a 98 percent attendance rate, the program was one of the most educationally productive in the city. Despite the program's accolades, however, students faced twice daily protests from local residents who did not want them bused into the neighborhood. The parents of white students that attended Southwark complained of "increased student traffic" in the area and the drain on the school's resources. One protester claimed the area was already overcrowded with students. "There are 10,000 students in a six-block square here," he said. "We don't want any more—black, white, Chinese," he continued, denying that they protested because of the African American students.[53]

Parents with children in the program threatened legal action if the school district eliminated or moved the program.[54] William Ross said he would not give in to the white protester's demands. Making Ross's position more difficult and furthering the rift with the mayor that opened during the teachers' strike, Frank Rizzo backed the South Philadelphia parents and scolded Ross for "trying to make a racial issue" out of Southern High's college motivation program. "That neighborhood has been integrated for 35 years," Rizzo told a reporter, exaggerating the area's demographics. Rizzo lent credence to the protesters' claims of color blindness. He encouraged their sense of victimization and indignation at being labeled racists, saying that the school board "dumped" unwanted policies on South Philadelphia.[55] Blue-collar whites always claimed that their protests against education programs like the college preparation courses at Southwark Elementary were driven by ostensibly color-blind concerns about neighborhood space and resources. While their complaints targeted and affected nonwhite schoolchildren, they maintained that their objections had nothing to do with the students' race. They made similar arguments when the board of education made official plans to address the order to desegregate the public schools.

In cooperation with the city's Commission on Human Relations, the board of education unveiled a new desegregation plan in 1974. The plan called for voluntary measures to desegregate the public schools and the introduction of a transfer program that would transport pupils from their neighborhood school to an integrated academy with specialized subject learning on a weekly basis. While the plan stated an intention to retain neighborhood schools, the board also proposed closing many older schools and transferring students to updated facilities. By shutting down older neighborhood schools, they could also foster integration by populating the newer schools with schoolchildren from different areas of the city.[56] In areas like South Philadelphia, where parents maintained a deep interest in neighborhood schools, the desegregation plan created an uproar.[57]

Connie McHugh, president of the Pennsport Civic Association, was one of the more vocal opponents of the plan. McHugh also knew she could rely on Frank Rizzo. In addition to fighting for the preservation of neighborhood schools, she hounded the mayor for urban renewal and community improvement funding. She once confronted the mayor at one of his favorite Center City lunch spots. Throwing his hands up in mock disgust and pointing to McHugh, Rizzo told a reporter that he "can't even go to lunch without running into this broad." Coming from Rizzo, that was a compliment. McHugh took it as one. For a woman from a blue-collar river ward neighborhood in South Philadelphia, Rizzo's playful antagonism was proof of her tenacity, toughness, and ability to tangle with anyone, whether the mayor or the board of education.[58]

When McHugh testified against the board's recently released desegregation plan, which included plans to close Pennsport's Abigail Vare Elementary School, she said the plan violated blue-collar neighborhood sanctity. Vare Elementary School, she said, had "served the children of longshoremen, firemen, policemen and other working people for four generations." She implored the board to see the value in her neighborhood's "closely-knit community," where "doors go unlocked, even at night, neighbors visit back and forth, and children walk to school and home again for lunch." Closing Vare Elementary would jeopardize all of that, she insisted. Keenly aware of accusations that communities like hers were racist, she explained that her community did not object to black children attending Vare. Rather, much like their neighbors in the bordering Whitman community, she argued that the introduction of such a major change in the neighborhood would disrupt their close-knit community.[59] As he was with Whitman's crusade against public housing, Frank Rizzo was responsive to Pennsport's invocation of blue-collar neighborhood sanctity. He personally petitioned Pennsylvania governor Milton Shapp for an alternative to the desegregation plan that threatened neighborhoods like Pennsport.[60]

In areas like Pennsport and other white neighborhoods in South Philadelphia, the threat of closing older schools prompted parents and community leaders to take action against the board of education's desegregation plan. In other areas of the city, like Northeast Philadelphia, the main incitement of parental outrage was the familiar fear of reverse busing.[61] Part of the board of education's desegregation plan included a provision to introduce a limited student transfer program in order to meet a Commission on Human Relations order to create a "racial balance" in the public schools. The provision was, in part, a response to parents' complaints about the limited facilities in the Northeast. The area's population growth put a strain on the area's schools. Area parents wanted the board of education to build new schools, but the city budget crisis and a depletion in federal funding made new construction untenable.[62] As a temporary measure to relieve the stress on overburdened facilities and teaching staffs—who had waged their strike against the school district partly because of excessive class sizes—the school board planned to bus Northeast Philadelphia schoolchildren. Parents who wanted their children to attend neighborhood schools immediately protested the plans. Northeast Philadelphia state assemblyman Hank Salvatore introduced a bill into the state legislature to remove the Human Relation Commission's authority over the board of education. Salvatore stoked broader fears that the introduction of reverse busing would lead to even more unwanted programs in Northeast Philadelphia.[63] One angry resident told Frank Rizzo that "there will be one hell of a war here in the Northeast" if the busing plan goes forward. He then threatened that "there will be a great exodus from the area which will cost the city its last strong economic base."[64]

The protests against busing in Northeast Philadelphia revealed more than white parents' opposition to the controversial educational policy. They also reflected a growing sense of separateness from the rest of the city and a feeling that their hard-earned class privileges and relatively higher incomes made them targets of unfair legislation. Many opponents of the busing program expressed the widespread belief among the area's residents that their tax payments helped to keep the rest of the city afloat. The belief was inaccurate. Northeast Philadelphia was not the only middle-income section of the city and other, far wealthier areas served as important tax bases as well. Nevertheless, Northeast Philadelphia residents often tried to use their higher incomes and the threat of leaving the city as leverage in protests against many municipal policies. The school busing controversies in the mid-1970s exacerbated those threats. Northeast Philadelphia parents worried that the board of education planned to send their children to far off and potentially dangerous schools in crime-ridden neighborhoods.[65]

The controversy over the board of education's desegregation plan reached its height as Frank Rizzo began his campaign for reelection. During the election year he received hundreds of letters demanding he use the power of his office to block any attempt to introduce a reverse busing program. From Northeast Philadelphia, a couple wrote Rizzo and called busing "a violation of [our] civil rights."[66] Another Northeast Philadelphian said she "moved from a North Philadelphia neighborhood to the Frankford section because of what my child had to put up with everyday in school" and threatened to "go to jail before I go through that again thru busing." She begged Rizzo to "please help the parents and children."[67] As in his first mayoral campaign, Rizzo proved receptive to issues that animated blue-collar whites. He even reinforced and lent credence to Northeast Philadelphia taxpayers' complaints that they alone would have to foot the bill for a busing program that they vehemently opposed. As mayor, he could not reverse the State of Pennsylvania's order, but he did use his considerable political clout to advocate for a change in the state's desegregation order and blocked the implementation of the board of education's plan. He also used his position against busing as fodder in his reelection campaign. Rizzo won the election with an even greater margin of victory than he did in 1971, especially in areas of the city like Northeast Philadelphia. His promise to fight any attempt to introduce reverse busing helped ensure his victory in 1975.

The desegregation plan proved so massively unpopular that the board of education abandoned it in early 1976. In its place, the board introduced a new plan that called for no student transfers and relied on voluntary measures to induce integration. Advocates of desegregation considered the plan a means of circumventing the state's order and a capitulation to the opponents of busing and desegregation.[68] Parents in Northeast and South Philadelphia were thrilled. They credited Frank Rizzo for helping defeat the measure. In the mid-1970s, blue-collar whites were winning their battles against unwanted policies that they felt threatened their neighborhoods. Having one of their own in City Hall seemed to provide the critical advantage they needed and they rewarded him with their political loyalty. When, in 1976, Rizzo's opponents launched a recall effort to oust him from office, the mayor painted the leaders of the effort as advocates of reverse busing. Although the Recall Rizzo movement received a lot of publicity, it never gained the political or popular support it needed. With Rizzo's strength in areas like Northeast and South Philadelphia, the organizers of the recall drive could not even get the necessary number of signatures to force a vote.[69]

The combined efforts of neighborhood protectionists in South and Northeast Philadelphia, local politicians, and Frank Rizzo forced the board of education to adopt a desegregation plan without any real means of enforcing or realizing an integrated education system. Opponents of busing all insisted that race played no role in their opposition to various desegregation plans. As a result of their efforts, Philadelphia maintained one of the most segregated public school districts in the United States.[70] The white, blue-collar parents of public school children won a major victory in the battle with liberal and government policies over educational and neighborhood politics in the 1970s. But, as in many major American cities, the decade's educational crises and politics were not limited to public schools. Over a third of all school children in Philadelphia attended Catholic schools, and their parents faced similar battles for the maintenance of their educational institutions.

With a few exceptions, the archdiocesan school system tried to stay aloof from the racial politics that engulfed the public school system. But the steady growth of the vastly whiter suburban Catholic school district and the intense segregation of parish schools contradicted any attempt to distance the Catholic school system from broader racial educational politics. When faced with potential breaches in the racial boundaries of neighborhood and parish, moreover, Catholic parents often reacted with the same animus as their public school counterparts. In 1974, for example, the archdiocese announced plans to change where girls from St. Bartholomew's parish in the blue-collar Wissinoming neighborhood in the Near Northeast attended high school. Before that year, girls who finished St. Bartholomew's Elementary School attended St. Hubert's High School for Girls in the Northeast. Trying to relieve stress on St. Hubert's when population increases outpaced resources, the archdiocese made the decision to have St. Bartholomew's graduates attend Little Flower High School for Girls. The all-girls high school was located in the Huntington Park neighborhood in North Philadelphia, an area that had recently undergone a rapid racial turnover. Many parents protested the transfer, worrying about the safety of their daughters in North Philadelphia. Several asked Frank Rizzo to intervene on their behalf.[71] He had no authority over the situation, but many Philadelphians who felt a connection with the mayor petitioned him for assistance with any grievance. The archdiocese plans continued despite the parents' protests. Their effort to fight the student transfer reveals how thoroughly Philadelphia's neighborhoods shaped parental concerns about education, both public and private.

"Think of the Thousands and Thousands of Catholics"

The rising costs of education and the budget crisis that threatened the School District of Philadelphia did not solely affect taxpayers with children in public schools. Parents that sent their children to parochial schools bore the brunt of economic downturn as well. Many of them watched the teachers' strike, desegregation plans, and other costly measures with a sense of consternation. For Catholic parents who paid for their own children's education through tuition and for public schools through their taxes, the city's mounting fiscal problems seemed to present a double burden. Like other blue-collar Philadelphians, however, they felt they had an ally in City Hall that could help them weather their financial troubles. Frank Rizzo was a Roman Catholic, after all. They implored him to "think of the thousands and thousands of Catholics who have to pay two school taxes."[72]

While the financial problems of Philadelphia's public school system reached crisis levels, the cost of Catholic education rose concomitantly. Between 1971 and 1974, the cost of running the archdiocesan schools in the five-county Philadelphia area rose by $5 million. Among other factors, the archdiocese blamed the cost increase on land acquisitions for new school construction in the suburbs and a successful unionization effort by Catholic school teachers that came with a contract for higher salaries. The archdiocese passed the costs on to parents through increased tuitions. In many cases, the higher tuitions placed a tremendous burden on blue-collar Catholic parents.[73] For working-class Catholics, they were almost insurmountable. The rising costs forced many Catholics of lesser means to sacrifice even further or abandon their cherished parish and Catholic high schools. For the middle-class Catholic parents already incensed by the taxes used to cover the costs of the public school system, the rising tuitions were an insult. "Why must I pay for public school education and receive nothing for my money and then pay again for Catholic education if that's where I want my children schooled," asked one Northeast Philadelphia woman. Her husband worked forty-eight hours a week and his paycheck was only enough to afford their mortgage, utilities, and essentials, she said. She wrote Frank Rizzo in the hope that "something will be done one day soon to help the 'little guys.'"[74] While others acknowledged that the cost of educating the young was a societal necessity, they thought the cost of educating both public and Catholic schools should be shared. Archdiocesan researcher John T. Gurlash prepared a report on the financial crisis facing Philadelphia's Catholic schools and concluded that they helped relieve overburdened public schools by offering an alternative. As a result, he told Rizzo, the cost of meeting the financial burden "must be borne by all citizens."[75]

Small public steps had been made toward relieving the rising costs of parochial school education. Catholic parents that had rallied for state aid in the 1960s scored a minor victory when their efforts led to the passage of Pennsylvania's Mullen Act, making the state one of the earliest to grant public funding for religious education.[76] Continued pressure on local and federal governments forced similar measures in the 1970s. Republican Pennsylvania senators Richard Schweiker and Hugh Scott introduced legislation into Congress seeking a program to provide federal aid directly to parochial school parents.[77] While stiff opposition from liberals and advocates of the separation of church and state forced the most expansive proposals to fail, the combined efforts of organized Catholics and sympathetic politicians culminated in an unprecedented use of tax dollars for parochial school education.[78]

Blue-collar Catholic parents appreciated the politicians and legislation that helped ease their financial burdens, but provisions like Pennsylvania's Mullen Act were not enough to confront the financial crisis in the Catholic schools. The archdiocese continued raising tuitions throughout the early 1970s. For working-class Catholics, the possibility of sending their children to the same schools they had attended became increasingly less likely.[79] In 1974, over five thousand fewer students attended Catholic schools than had the previous year, marking the first time the Catholic school system lost student population in the long postwar era. Catholic schools maintained enrollments in Northeast Philadelphia and suburban counties because the archdiocese concentrated on expanding and improving facilities in those areas. Instead, the heaviest losses came from older, inner-city parishioners who could no longer afford the steep tuitions. "We're going to people who are already hard-pressed and asking for greater sacrifice," said the Reverend Paul F. Curran, the assistant superintendent of archdiocesan schools. "They will have to sacrifice even more in the years to come," he warned.[80] Even though the public funds provided by the Mullen Act were not enough to ease the burden of rising tuitions, blue-collar Catholics still valued the small amounts of state aid that allowed them to keep sending their children to parish and Catholic high schools.[81]

In Pennsylvania as in other states, however, the legislative measures aroused proponents of the separation of church and state who opposed the diversion of state funds to sectarian education. They also protested that in

places like Philadelphia, the funding effectively elevated Catholic education to a privileged status among private education options. Additionally,
because the Catholic school system was largest in all-white Northeast Philadelphia and the suburbs, the Mullen Act effectively provided state funding
for segregated schools. In 1973, a coalition of Jewish organizations, civil libertarians, public education reformers, and civil rights leaders filed a federal
suit to have aid to nonpublic schools declared unconstitutional. Leading
the case was Sylvia Meek, a longtime educational and civil rights activist.
Meek, a member of the NAACP and several education reform organizations,
had focused much of her earlier activism on public school integration. The
quality of Philadelphia's public education system had occupied the majority
of her work since the mid-1960s.[82] While adding her voice to the protests
over violations of the separation of church and state that induced organizations like the Philadelphia branch of the American Civil Liberties Union
to file suit with her, Meek's primary concern about state aid to parochial
schools was that it diverted much-needed funding from the already financially unstable public school system.[83] Her argument won her widespread
support throughout the state of Pennsylvania. Two years after the initial suit,
the Supreme Court of the United States agreed to hear Meek's case. In 1975,
the court decided in *Meek v. Pittenger* that state aid to nonpublic schools was
unconstitutional.[84]

Many Catholic parents were outraged. They also held Sylvia Meek and liberal Jewish organizations responsible for leading a legal effort to cripple their
school system.[85] In June 1975, a month after the court outlawed state aid to
parochial schools, Catholic parents organized a march to protest the decision.
Around fifty thousand area Catholics marched through Center City Philadelphia for "educational freedom." They carried signs saying that the Supreme
Court penalized them for their religious beliefs, called the decision "Another
Middle Class Rip-Off" and asked if Catholic children were "second class citizens." One South Philadelphia warehouse worker told a reporter how he had
sent seven of his eight children to their parish elementary school, but was
unsure he could continue to do so. The court's decision, he said, was unfair to
parents like him that had sacrificed in order to send their children to Catholic
school.[86] He and other blue-collar Catholic parents were truly vulnerable to
the economic downturns of the 1970s and their impact on urban education.
At the same time, however, their white, blue-collar class privilege made them
feel they had earned the right to state assistance. To deny them these benefits
was tantamount to robbing them of their hard-earned class privileges.

Catholic parents again petitioned for Frank Rizzo's assistance, but the court's decision was beyond his control. Rizzo had endorsed aid to nonpublic schools and expressed disappointment in the Supreme Court, but he could not offer substantive help. He opted not to spend political capital on an issue he could no longer influence.[87] Indeed, the controversy over aid to parochial schools revealed the limits of what Rizzo could do for his blue-collar supporters as well as the limits of blue-collar political power in the mid-1970s. For area Catholics, the tangible result was the loss of $33 million in state funding. In the years following the Supreme Court's decision, the archdiocesan school system faced even greater financial struggles. In 1976, the Catholic teachers' union went on strike seeking higher salaries and smaller class sizes. After the resolution of the strike, the archdiocese again passed the increasing costs on to parents.[88] For hard-pressed, blue-collar Catholics, the end of state funding for their schools fueled their sense of victimization at the hands of liberal politicians and policies.

The battle over state aid to parochial schools illustrated how blue-collar whites at the height of their power and influence selectively rejected the welfare state. As with the politics underpinning public housing and education, culturally blue-collar whites supported welfare state entitlements that benefited those who had earned them through their narrow definition of hard work. Those who had sacrificed to send their children to a specific school or move their family to a nice neighborhood felt they had earned the right to benefits like urban renewal, preferential zoning codes, fully funded neighborhood schools, and government-assisted private education. The emerging blue-collar conservatism espoused by Frank Rizzo's supporters was neither an immediate nor complete break with the liberalism of the postwar era. Instead, blue-collar whites wanted the benefits of the welfare state, so long as those benefits went to those they felt deserved them. Their selective rejection of welfare state liberalism was a qualified means of using blue-collar class distinctions to determine entitlement. The controversies over public housing and education also revealed the economic underpinnings of blue-collar populism.

Blue-collar whites entered the Rizzo era with a series of victories that signaled the height of blue-collar politics in the long postwar era. The failure to secure state aid to parochial schools, however, offered blue-collar whites one of their first losses after Rizzo's ascendency. It highlighted both their vulnerability and their fleeting influence. As their opponents in the battles over public housing, education, and equal opportunity politics won even more victories in the late 1970s, blue-collar whites' color-blind veneer began to fade. Few of them lost faith in their mayor, but as their opponents began winning victories in new battles over welfare state entitlements, their politics—and Rizzo's—turned further to the social and cultural right and fueled more overt hostility to the agents of progressive change.

CHAPTER 7

The Limits of Color Blindness

The suit by the Resident Advisory Board (RAB) against the Rizzo administration for blocking the Whitman Park public housing project reached federal
district court in 1976. Presiding over the case was Raymond Broderick, a Nixon
appointee, former lieutenant governor of Pennsylvania, and 1970 Republican
Party nominee for governor of Pennsylvania. Broderick was a staunch conservative and the press predicted that he would side with Rizzo and the Whitman
Council (WC). But lawyers for the RAB produced ample evidence that Whitman community leaders participated in Whitman Park's planning in the 1960s.
They also relied on lengthy testimonies that highlighted the structural impediments to integration and brought the inequality of Philadelphia's housing
market to the forefront of the Whitman Park dispute. The arguments swayed
Broderick. He ruled that the Rizzo administration violated federal antidiscrimination law and contributed to the city's racial segregation. Broderick ordered
construction on Whitman Park to recommence immediately. The RAB and
Housing Association of the Delaware Valley successfully made racial housing
equality the central issue in the Whitman Park controversy.[1]

Whitman Council president Fred Druding hoped to steer the organization's opposition toward further negotiation, compromise, and legal recourse,
but the WC had mounting legal debts and could no longer afford their lawyers. Trying to keep the fight in the courts, the WC held fundraisers and
reached out to other community organizations for financial help. Only organizations from Grays Ferry and Pennsport publicly supported the Whitman
Council. Residents of Whitman felt betrayed by their government and the
courts for "forcing" public housing into their neighborhood, and angry at the
movements that called the courts into action.[2]

Anger boiled over into the streets of Whitman and into the community newsletter, the *Whitman News*. Since he took over as president, Fred

Druding had successfully made the WC more responsive to the community. The community newsletter furthered that end. In addition to keeping
neighbors abreast of developments concerning Whitman Park, it advertised
WC-sponsored events and delivered birth, marriage, and death announce-
ments. By communicating a common identity, the newsletter helped create
the close-knit community that Druding and the WC claimed the housing
project threatened. In order to project a sense of common identity through
common cause, Druding also reprinted letters he received from sympathetic
politicians and residents. In June 1976, for example, while the case was still
in federal court, the following letter from resident Barry Mitchell appeared in
the *Whitman News*:

> I am writing to express my anger at some statements made
> recently—in the newspapers—by CLS [Community Legal Services]
> spokesmen.
>   How can they ignore the fact that in South Phila projects—Wil-
> son Park, Tasker Homes, etc.—it is young toughs who beat and rob
> the tenants forcing them to flee.
>   Isn't anyone honest enough to admit what has happened to these
> once fine projects? Why aren't the Project Managers speaking out
> that it is the tenants who are responsible for the broken elevators,
> crime, dirt, vandalism, etc.
>   As I said, the young toughs and bad tenants force the good
> to flee.[3]

The letter echoed many of the sentiments trumpeted by the WC since
the beginning of their opposition to Whitman Park. It made the correlation
between public housing and crime, blight, and neighborhood deterioration
that avoided explicit race-baiting. It struck the chords of civility and color
blindness that Fred Druding and the WC adopted early on. The letter in the
Whitman News, however, was not the letter Druding received. Barry Mitchell
originally wrote:

> Am sending you a copy of these articles (you may have seen already)
> to express my anger at some of the statements made by CLS lawyers.
>   How could they ignore the FACT that in So[uth] Phila[delphia]
> alone, Shipyard Homes, Wilson Park and Tasker Homes were
> once <u>all white</u> projects and are now all Black—in their attempt to

"desegregate" Public Housing. Where were they 30 or more years ago! Are they aware how black toughs intimidate white tenants, forcing them to flee (<u>Shipyard</u>, <u>Wilson</u>, <u>Tasker</u> & <u>Schuylkill</u> Homes—to name a few) and that these are projects NOW cited as examples to <u>force</u> integration in virgin, new areas as Whitman? These poor whites tried, oh <u>how</u> they tried—to make it with the newcomer Blacks and eventually were forced to flee by crime and intimidation.

It's unfair, grossly unfair—to now charge that Blacks are being "segregated" and to point to <u>these</u> projects, yet, isn't anyone honest enough to admit what has happened. Why haven't Project Managers, like [Philadelphia Housing Authority director Gordon] Cavanaugh and others complained bitterly that some black tenants are responsible for busted elevators, crime, filth, graffiti <u>and vandalism</u> again and again in answer to <u>Black complaints</u>, to conditions there.

The fact is, they (the toughs) segregate themselves by forcing others to flee.[4]

Fred Druding carefully edited Mitchell's letter before printing it in the *Whitman News*. Most importantly, he removed any mention of race. Both the original and the edited version demonstrate how thoroughly concepts like "crime" and "blight" became stand-ins for race. Furthermore, Mitchell was not the only Whitman resident sending similar letters. He was, however, the most prolific. Mitchell sometimes sent one or two letters a week, often with newspaper clippings, photographs, or his own hand-drawn maps. By the late 1970s, when Whitman Park's completion seemed inevitable, Mitchell began sending maps of where he wanted African Americans placed in the project. He chose the row of townhouses along the easternmost edge of the site, facing Front Street. It was the farthest point from the rest of the neighborhood. Mitchell also believed, mistakenly, that the city planned to build an on-ramp to the adjacent Delaware Expressway that would require a widening of Front Street. Mitchell hoped on-ramp construction would force new African American residents out of the neighborhood.[5]

The WC never gave much credence to Mitchell's wilder suggestions. Fred Druding maintained his own color blindness and liberalism well into the late 1970s.[6] He was also savvy enough to understand that a white protectionist defense of neighborhood was no longer politically viable. By actively hiding the racism underlying some of the opposition to Whitman Park, he showed how well he understood the ways the civil rights movement had changed the racial discourse on rights and poverty. Druding wanted to deflate accusations of racism and redirect the debate to a color-blind discourse on earned privilege and unearned advantage, but a racially neutral debate over Whitman Park became untenable in the late 1970s.[7] While the WC maintained their class-based neighborhood protectionism, the neighborhood's color-blind veneer began to wear thin. So did their patience with the legal system. Although the Rizzo administration slowed construction with a series of legal appeals, they all failed. In 1979, upon learning that Raymond Broderick denied their final appeal, Whitman residents emptied into their narrow South Philadelphia streets to protest. They burned Judge Broderick in effigy.[8]

As the Whitman community's reaction to their legal defeats attests, the blue-collar reaction to liberal policies like public housing grew increasingly hostile as the 1970s wore on. From the mid-1970s to the end of the decade, blue-collar whites felt they lost more often than not. Their opponents made successful use of the federal and local courts, winning important decisions about housing policy and equal opportunity programs. In response, blue-collar whites became even more hostile to liberal politics and policy-making. By the end of the decade, their legal defeats caused the final transition to a more conservative blue-collar populism.

Civil rights and welfare rights organizations not only waged successful efforts to restart projects like Whitman Park, their persistent advocacy for race-conscious equal opportunity programs eroded the façade of blue-collar color blindness. While equal opportunity advocates maintained their focus on old targets like Whitman Park and the construction industry, they also expanded their goals to include the forging of equal opportunity in one of the most cherished blue-collar institutions: the Philadelphia Police Department. The politics of law enforcement and affirmative action combined forcefully as nonwhites and women tried to open one of the most exclusively white, male, and blue-collar institutions in the city. At the same time, the politics of law and order reinvigorated one of the pillars of the emergent blue-collar conservatism as police engaged in the first of many violent confrontations with the small, mostly African American back-to-nature collective known as MOVE. In both the politics of affirmative action and the MOVE conflict, the protection and safety of police officers returned as one of blue-collar Philadelphians' most pressing concerns. Blue-collar whites held MOVE and equal opportunity advocates in contempt for threatening the sanctity and security of police work. Their efforts to rally behind the police revealed how thoroughly the politics of urban law enforcement intersected with the liberal policies of housing and affirmative action.

Legal victories for race-conscious programs like neighborhood deseg-regation through public housing and affirmative action also showed that the defense of white privilege remained central to blue-collar conservatism. The persistence of race-conscious welfare and civil rights activists caused the color-blind rhetoric employed by blue-collar Philadelphians in the mid-1970s to falter. In its place, they began employing an often forceful defense of their white ethnicity. Frank Rizzo, especially, invoked an aggressive white ethnic politics when regrouped liberals and African Americans presented formidable challenges to his political future.

Affirmative Action and "Reverse Discrimination"

In the mid-1970s, Philadelphia journalists Joseph Daughen and Peter Binzen began work on a biography of Frank Rizzo. The result was their 1977 book *The Cop Who Would Be King*. It was both a scathing indictment of Rizzo's mayoral record and a genuine attempt to understand his brand of "one of us" populism. Daughen and Binzen found both in Rizzo's ethnic politics. In addi-tion to the general divisiveness of the mayor's politics, Daughen and Binzen concentrated on the Rizzo administration's distribution of patronage jobs and appointments. They detailed how the mayor used his position to reward friends and punish enemies, showing how Rizzo doled out city jobs through ward leaders and ethnic organizations. His brand of patronage harkened to an era of urban machine politics common to many American cities, but Daughen and Binzen compared it to an even earlier era of Italian immigrant politics. When the massive waves of Italian immigrants arrived in the decades bookending the turn of the twentieth century, many of them found work through an established and well-connected local immigrant leader called a *padrone*. In Italian immigrant communities, the *padrone* was like a political boss. He was a man of the community, but also above it. Patriarchal and mas-culine, he was a man of means that used jobs as currency. Italian immigrants sought work from the *padrone* in exchange for their loyalty. Daughen and Binzen equated Rizzo with the ethnic politics that shaped immigrant com-munities like the one his own parents settled in decades earlier. In fact, before they settled on *The Cop Who Would Be King*, "The Padrone" was the working title of Daughen and Binzen's manuscript.[9]

Daughen and Biznen's description of Rizzo was an indictment of the mayor's brand of politics. It also pointed to the way white ethnic politics saturated cities like Philadelphia in the 1970s. Rizzo, for instance, was intensely proud of being Philadelphia's first Italian American mayor. He took every opportunity to offer reminders not only of his ethnic heritage, but also the hardships his ancestors faced when they arrived in the United States. While Italian Americans took a special pride in Rizzo, his invocations of immigrant heritage resonated throughout white ethnic Philadelphia, especially as controversies over affirmative action captured local and national attention. By the mid- to late 1970s, Rizzo began using his brand of aggressive ethnic politics as an argument against equal opportunity policies. Referring to a near mythic immigrant past characterized by hard work, sacrifice, and self-improvement, he frequently said that no one ever gave white ethnic groups any "special privileges."[10]

Rizzo's attacks on equal opportunity programs tapped into the established blue-collar distinction between hard work and handouts. His rhetoric resonated so widely because he seemed to confirm the suggestion that recipients of federal civil rights legislation had not earned the right to advantages and entitlements. White ethnics and their immigrant parents, by contrast, had worked their way up. Although white ethnics, including those Rizzo directly addressed, had received many state-sponsored advantages in the years since the establishment of the New Deal–era welfare state—federal home mortgage protections and federally funded local initiatives like urban renewal, for example—the rhetoric of white ethnic self-sufficiency was an attractive cudgel against equal opportunity programs.[11] In a populist argument characterized by the artificial dichotomy between the hardworking and those that received handouts, the ethnic memory of ancestral hardships powerfully reinforced claims to earned privileges.

Rizzo's ethnic politics also reflected the broader "white ethnic revival" of the 1970s. The cultural phenomenon was most visible in a spate of books like Michael Novak's *The Rise of the Unmeltable Ethnics*, popular films like *Rocky*, and efforts to promote the study and appreciation of white immigrant heritage.[12] Through his frequent writings and the establishment of his Ethnic Millions Political Action Committee (EMPAC), Novak helped redirect the repopularization of widespread white ethnic consciousness to the center of the nation's political debates over school desegregation and affirmative action.[13] For most working-class white ethnics, however, the so-called revival of white ethnicity was hardly a renewal at all. In white, blue-collar Philadelphia neighborhoods, ethnic consciousness was in no need of reviving. Ethnic traditions like the Mummer's Parade had never lost importance or stopped reinforcing ethnic identity.[14] Nevertheless, the politicization of white ethnic identity and memory helped redirect blue-collar politics. In Philadelphia, white ethnic revival took an already strong sense of identity and imbued it with political imperative. Rizzo's invocation of ethnic memory and claims that white immigrant groups never received any special assistance reflected and refueled the blue-collar engagement with equal opportunity policy-making.

Blue-collar whites in the 1970s increasingly appealed to their ethnic identities and immigrant heritage in their appeals for political patronage. Organizations like the Polish American Citizens Club of Pennsylvania (PACCP), for example, used the popularization of ethnic heritage to swell their numbers in the Philadelphia area. They then used the organization's growing numbers to exert pressure on city and state governments for Polish American appointments and jobs.[15] Led by Philadelphians Joseph Zazyczny—a Democratic city councilman from Bridesburg—and Near Northeast realtor Theodore Dydak, the PACCP attempted to force the Rizzo administration to recognize the importance of Polish Americans to his Democratic coalition. In most cases, the Rizzo administration responded to the demands of white ethnic organizations like the PACCP. Showing that his administration planned to look after its white ethnic constituencies, Rizzo appointed Dydak to the Commission on Human Relations, the agency responsible for overseeing and enforcing the city's equal opportunity policies.[16]

The resurgent politics of white ethnicity intersected with the promotion of equal opportunity most clearly in debates over affirmative action. Not all white ethnic political organizations immediately opposed affirmative action programs, however. Many organizations felt that white ethnics were left out of equal opportunity hiring programs, and instead of opposing them outright, wanted white ethnicity to have the same eligibility as racial or gender minority status. Progressive white ethnic organizations that sought the broader application of equal opportunity policies often clashed with other white ethnic groups that viewed affirmative action policies as a potential threat to their own employment opportunities.[17] Although the statistics pointed toward a much more dire employment outlook for African Americans, white ethnic organizations and some labor unions continued protesting that equal opportunity hiring programs amounted to "reverse discrimination."[18]

Despite the implementation of the Philadelphia Plan, affirmative action was slow to deliver on the promise of equal opportunity in the workplace. Working-class African Americans in Philadelphia still occupied the lowest rungs of the labor market. Due in part to the stagnant economy and reduced federal investments in urban American under Presidents Ford and Carter, the construction industry targeted by the Philadelphia Plan was no longer operating at its 1960s peak. Combined with union hostility to the program, it failed to fully integrate the building and construction trades. By 1976, only 60 percent of contractors operating in the Philadelphia area were compliant with federal guidelines. The percentage fell far short of the goals the framers of the Philadelphia Plan intended. Voluntary efforts undertaken by individual unions also failed to increase the membership of underrepresented groups and federal contract agencies never fully enforced the Philadelphia Plan.[19] By 1977, African American unemployment in Philadelphia reached 18 percent. Nevertheless, predominantly white labor unions and white ethnic civic groups fought the implementation of affirmative action at nearly every juncture. Their recalcitrance was at least partially responsible for the continued low performance of the Philadelphia Plan.[20]

While labor leaders and union organizing bodies worked against the Philadelphia Plan through legal means, they maintained negotiations with otherwise liberal allies. On the jobsite, however, rank-and-file union men belied the efforts of labor leaders to keep the racial peace. White union men resented the "forced" entry of nonwhite members into their unions and often reacted violently to their presence. Members of the Operating Engineers Local 542, for example, attacked African American workers as they arrived at their union hall.[21]

In 1976, the opening of a federal court case against the union brought by the Commonwealth of Pennsylvania and Community Legal Services—the same legal organization representing the RAB in its effort to restart construction on Whitman Park—reignited the controversy over affirmative action in the building trades. The suit charged the union, construction firms, and contractors associations with deliberately engaging in a hiring pattern based on favoritism, nepotism, and racial discrimination. Former president of the Philadelphia NAACP and federal district judge A. Leon Higginbotham presided over the case. Local 542 lawyers wanted Higginbotham to recuse himself, fearing they could not get a fair trial from the longtime civil rights leader. Higginbotham refused to step down. Instead, he heard months of testimony detailing union and contractor efforts to discourage black hiring and create hostile work environments for African Americans. One black operating engineer testified that after receiving training to operate the construction equipment with federal and state funds allocated through the Philadelphia Plan, his first referral was to a job site two hundred miles away, during the night shift, in the rain. Another African American told Higginbotham that working with Local 542 was "as tough as being in Vietnam."[22]

Suits against other Philadelphia building-trades unions found similar patterns of intimidation and discrimination.[23] The lawyers and blue-collar workers in these unions claimed that programs like the Philadelphia Plan denied qualified whites employment and promotion. Unions protested that affirmative action programs jeopardized their hard-earned seniority rights. Representatives for the Operating Engineers said the only reason that Judge Higginbotham even agreed to hear the testimonies was because he was black. When the judge ruled against the Operating Engineers and ordered the union to hire more African American workers, union lawyers continued fighting the ruling. The appeals process lasted until the end of the decade, making the case against the Operating Engineers the longest in US history at that point. In 1979, Higginbotham ruled that the union had to hire one minority member for every white operator hired to work under a federal contract.[24]

The suit against the Operating Engineers showed that full desegregation and equal opportunity in blue-collar employment proved to be a formidable task well into the late 1970s. It became even more difficult, and even more fraught with the social and cultural politics of the Rizzo era, when equal opportunity advocates set their sights on one of the most blue-collar institutions in the city, the Philadelphia Police Department. The efforts to increase diversity on the police force produced some of the most hostile reactions to affirmative action and reinforced the already volatile politics of law enforcement. Supporters of the police saw the effort to diversify the police force not only as an attack on a blue-collar tradition, but also as a threat to personal security and the safety of the police. The politics of affirmative action and law enforcement combined powerfully in 1974, when white policewoman Penelope Brace filed a gender discrimination lawsuit against the city.

Brace was an eight-year veteran of the police department with an exemplary record. She spent most of her time on the force with the Juvenile Aid Division, where all of the department's sixty-six women police officers received assignment.[25] But Brace had higher ambitions. When the department announced the opening of new detective positions, she applied for a promotion. The Philadelphia police had no women detectives, however. After applying, Brace received a letter from the department saying that the announced positions were "for policemen." As she was a policewoman, the letter explained, she did not meet the requirements.[26] This was not Brace's first encounter with discriminatory promotion procedures. She had previously filed two other complaints against the department. After filing in 1974, however, Brace reported harassment and intimidation from her superiors. Days after she went public with her suit and charges of harassment, the department fired her for "neglect of duty."[27]

Brace continued her suit against the city and quickly became a local feminist icon. The Philadelphia branch of the National Organization for Women (NOW) was especially supportive of Brace's efforts to force the gender desegregation of the police department.[28] But while the effort to increase the number of women on the police force focused intensely on Penelope Brace, her promotion was not the only issue that animated women's rights groups. The organization most responsible for backing Brace and other women seeking entrance into the police department was Women Organized Against Rape (WOAR), a support organization for rape victims, as well as an advocacy group for education about sexual violence and the prosecution of crimes against women. They were disturbed by the poor treatment of rape victims by male police officers. Many women, they said, had trouble speaking with men about the crime. Making matters worse, the men belittled the victims and accused them of lying or provoking the attack. In the mid-1970s, WOAR organized around the goal of getting the police department to hire women officers specifically to handle rape cases.[29] The Rizzo administration tried to placate their protests by announcing plans to hire twenty-two women officers by middecade. In a department of nearly one thousand officers, it was a paltry number. Women's organizations considered it little more than a token gesture. Instead, NOW and WOAR promoted Penelope Brace's equal opportunity lawsuit in an effort to change the ultramasculine culture of the police department and challenge the perception of police work as "a man's job."

The police department wanted precisely the opposite. The Fraternal Order of Police was especially vocal against the idea of a quota plan for women recruits. Police commissioner Joseph O'Neill flatly called women "too weak" to serve as full-fledged police officers.[30] One inspector suggested that opening the police department to women would lead to "rampant lesbianism."[31] NOW responded by awarding O'Neill and FOP president Charles Gallagher—who replaced John Harrington as head of Local 5 in 1972—their satirical "barefoot and pregnant" award for reinforcing gender norms and holding back women's equality.[32]

Men in the police department were not alone in their opposition to the hiring and promotion of women. One of the largest groups of opponents of gender equality in the police department were the wives of policemen. Many of them argued that putting women on patrol would endanger their husbands. Some argued that women officers were physically incapable of protecting themselves or their husbands.[33] The wife of one police officer told Frank Rizzo that she would fear for her husband's safety if he were assigned a female partner. "I love my husband and I trust him completely," she said. But, she added, "I want him to stay alive and healthy. If he patrols with a woman, he will constantly feel as though he must protect her."[34] She worried that her husband's sense of chivalry would cause him to forsake his own well-being. Even more than individual officers' wives, however, organized police wives politicized the opposition to women in the police department.

After Police Wives and Interested Citizens for Action (PWICA) organized for stricter criminal punishments and against lenient judges in the late 1960s, they became a civilian-led advocacy group for a whole range of "policemen's rights" issues. In addition to fighting against the hiring and promotion of women, they also challenged accusations of police brutality and corruption. PWICA's Marie Ann Mackley said that their opposition to women's promotions was just another of their efforts to protect policemen's rights. "We are strong adherents of equal rights and we are for the employment of women by the Police Department," she said. "However," she continued, "we do recognize the fact that certain individuals, whether they are men or women, are better qualified to do certain jobs or perform certain duties than other individuals." Jobs like patrol officers and detective were better suited to men, she said. Blue-collar police wives first organized as protectors of a male-dominated profession. In their campaign against Penelope Brace, they continued that mission by trying to block a woman's promotion in the police department.[35]

Brace's case continued in court throughout the mid-1970s. In 1978, after years of harassment and legal battles, a court order made Penelope Brace the first woman detective in the Philadelphia Police Department. Male police officers grumbled and the Rizzo administration promised to appeal the decision, but Brace had won her long-fought battle to force gender equity in police work.[36] Although she was the subject of periodic harassment from her fellow officers, Brace went on to serve a distinguished and decorated career. For the blue-collar whites and police wives that maintained a culture of reverence for the department, however, Brace remained a symbol of liberal social engineering and a threat to the tradition of police work in the city.[37]

Women were not the only ones targeting the police department for a lack of representation. Racial minorities also sought more positions and promotions

on the police force. Like women activists, their demands for more representation in the police department also went beyond employment. Getting more
African American police officers to patrol black neighborhoods had been a
goal of civil rights organizations for decades. The campaigns received new
intensity and attention in the 1970s, largely due to renewed concerns about a
lack of reprisals for charges of police misconduct from the Rizzo administration. Equally important in bringing equal opportunity in police employment
to the forefront of the affirmative action debate was the advocacy of North
Philadelphia NAACP president Alphonso Deal. He became one of the most
vocal critics of the department's hiring and recruiting practices. He also was
in a unique position to critique the police department. In addition to heading
the city's largest branch of the NAACP, Alphonso Deal was also a Philadelphia police officer.

As a child growing up in Jacksonville, Florida, Deal witnessed firsthand
how police unjustly treated people of color. He then settled in Philadelphia
after serving as a member of the military police during World War II. After
the war, he worked at the Edward G. Budd Company, where he became the
first African American to hold office in the United Automobile Workers
Local 813 and chaired the union's Fair Employment Anti-Discrimination
Committee. He left the Budd Company to join the police force in 1954 to
help change discriminatory actions and hostile relations between African
American communities and the police. Two years later, Deal organized the
Guardian Civic League (GCL), an African American policemen's association
dedicated to fostering improved police-community relations. In the mid-
1960s, Deal merged his police work with his growing civil rights activism.
As president of Philadelphia's Fair Housing Council in 1966, for instance,
he protested against housing discrimination in Northeast Philadelphia, saying "I'm a police officer, and my duty is to protect a neighborhood, but then
people in that neighborhood can still refuse to sell me a house because God
made me a black police officer."[38] Deal remained president of the GCL into
the 1970s and only resigned when he became president of the North Philadelphia branch of the NAACP in 1973.

While Deal was a decorated police officer, he was also an open critic of
law enforcement policy and poor police treatment of African Americans. In
the 1960s, he criticized Police Commissioner Frank Rizzo and clashed with
FOP president John Harrington. In 1972, he ran for president of the FOP in
protest of the union's discrimination against African American officers. He
lost the election handily, but firmly established himself as the loudest internal

critic of the police department.[39] Deal's most constant complaint, and one that made him a target of white officers, was the lack of African American representation on the police force. He said that the greatest impediment to improved police-community relations in black neighborhoods was the presence of white, often hostile police officers. His answer to the problem was more black officers. Deal's requests never received much attention from Police Commissioner Joseph O'Neill. Worse, white police officers and administrators were hostile to black officers' complaints. A brawl between white and black officers at the FOP meeting hall in August 1977 shone a spotlight on the racial division in the police force. The Guardian Civic League attempted to meet with FOP leadership to address the racial tensions in the department, but found the white officers unresponsive. More than eight hundred black police officers threatened to picket the meeting hall and leave the FOP in protest. Instead, the GCL filed a class-action discrimination suit against the Fraternal Order of Police with the Commission on Human Relations.[40]

Alphonso Deal and GCL were not alone. In 1977, Isabelo Alvarez led a group of Latino applicants that had been denied positions in the police department by filing a class-action complaint against the City of Philadelphia in federal district court. The case would not be settled until the 1980s and only after considerable protest from the FOP. Nevertheless, it led the city to adopt an affirmative action plan for the police hiring.[41] Like the legal effort to increase nonwhite representation in the building trades, the controversy over affirmative action in the police department challenged the racial composition of one of Philadelphia's blue-collar institutions. The efforts to force racial integration brought cries of "reverse discrimination" from white ethnics that felt unfairly targeted by the legal maneuvering. One Northeast Philadelphia applicant denied a position on the police force said that the only problem he faced was "being a white male."[42]

The effort to win racial and gender integration of the police department, like the continued push for more representation in the building and construction trades, reinforced the belief that "reverse discrimination" was an impediment to white ethnic and blue-collar men. White ethnics, like those Frank Rizzo so aggressively defended, protested that they never received the kind of "special privileges" that now led to the hiring of women and non-whites in jobs previously populated primarily by white men. Additionally, the movements for equal opportunity in the police department combined the politics of affirmative action and law enforcement. The police department was again at the center of blue-collar politics in Frank Rizzo's Philadelphia.

They remained there throughout the late 1970s, as the politics of law and order resurfaced under renewed allegations about systemic police brutality. Forcing the issue to the fore—and beginning one of the most harrowing periods in the city's history—was the emergence of the radical, mostly African American back-to-nature collective known as MOVE.

The Police Department and MOVE

Nearly three hundred police officers gathered in the West Philadelphia neighborhood of Powelton Village in the predawn hours of August 8, 1978. They surrounded a heavily fortified house on the corner of North Thirty-Third and Pearl Streets, the home and headquarters of MOVE. About twenty men, women, and children occupied the house. Reports stated that they were heavily armed. For the past few years, MOVE had staged a number of confrontations with neighbors, city officials, and police officers. Months earlier, they agreed to end the mounting community tensions by surrendering to police and vacating Powelton Village for another location outside of the city. MOVE had recently changed their minds, however. They were now over a week late for a scheduled court date. Frank Rizzo decided that the city had been patient enough and ordered the police to remove the organization from their West Philadelphia headquarters. On May 8, after a few hours of pleading with MOVE to surrender peacefully—punctuated by profanity-laced responses and threats from the MOVE house—police forced their way into the compound with smoke and high-powered water cannons. Shots of indeterminate origin rang out shortly after 8:00 a.m. They wounded several officers, one of them fatally. Police responded by unloading hundreds of rounds into the MOVE house. When the shooting stopped, MOVE members began climbing out of the basement. Children begged the police not to shoot. When MOVE member Delbert Orr Africa attempted to escape, police officers quickly surrounded him and forced him to the ground in full view of gathered crowds and the press. Swift, booted kicks repeatedly struck Delbert's midsection as he lay on the ground with outstretched arms well above his head and a policeman's rifle pressed against his temple. Witnesses then watched as the police forcefully dragged Delbert Africa by his long dreadlocks into a waiting patrol wagon.

The outcry of "police brutality" was immediate. Within days, organizers led marches and rallies in support of MOVE. Alphonso Deal addressed a crowd gathered at City Hall to protest Rizzo and the police. He demanded the immediate dismissal of the officers responsible for beating and detaining Delbert Africa. "Whether or not we agree with Delbert Africa is not the issue," he said. "As long as I have breath in my body, I will not stand by and watch anyone abuse someone on the street."[43] Brutality like that meted out at the showdown with MOVE headquarters only caused more people to lose faith in good police officers, Deal said. Although Police Commissioner Joseph O'Neill later claimed that Delbert Africa was armed when he tried to escape the MOVE house, the police department's latest confrontation with MOVE reignited the controversy over police brutality that had dogged the department throughout the 1970s and helped galvanize a growing coalition of anti-Rizzo activists.

Accusations of police brutality were nothing new in 1978. Before the MOVE confrontation, charges aimed at the police had grown in prevalence and intensity.[44] Many people believed that former police commissioner Rizzo allowed the police department a free hand in dealing with crime and disorder. He did claim to stand behind the department, right or wrong. He often said that if a good cop made a mistake in the process of upholding the law, he should not face repercussions for doing what was an objectively difficult job. Rizzo's respect for the difficulty of police work and steadfast defense of those he continued to call "his men" reflected blue-collar Philadelphians' culture of reverence for the police. But Rizzo was not alone in deflecting criticism of the police department. Police wives were once again instrumental in defending their husbands. They publicly denounced reports of widespread corruption and systemic patterns of police abuse. Police Wives and Interested Citizens for Action feuded with Alphonso Deal, the American Civil Liberties Union, and the press when they lobbed accusations of abuse at the department.[45] But all their efforts could not stop the emergence of evidence of systemic brutality. In 1977, the *Philadelphia Inquirer* published a series of articles that chronicled the deep roots of police corruption as well as patterns of abuse and torture used by police officers. By the late 1970s, the Philadelphia Police Department was also under investigation by the United States Commission on Civil Rights.[46] For critics of the police, the August 1978 raid on MOVE headquarters was a confirmation of the allegations they had long waged against the police department and Frank Rizzo. It also made MOVE seem like a sympathetic victim of longstanding patterns of police misconduct.

That was no small task. MOVE did not garner easy sympathy. The organization was a mystery to most Philadelphians. Most people were bewildered by, afraid of, or outright hostile to MOVE. Even the organization's name caused confusion. Always capitalized, it was no acronym. It was just MOVE. At various points, the press called them anarchists and a cult. They called them black nationalists, radicals, naturalists, and revolutionaries. But no single descriptor was capable of accurately capturing the MOVE philosophy. Despite a resemblance to a number of social and political movements, they did not fit in easily with the history of American radicalism, black militancy, or countercultural movements. Although they preached a kind of black liberation, the organization was never made up solely of African Americans. It was multiracial and members came from various backgrounds that included high school dropouts and PhDs. Early coverage reported that the organization included former members of street gangs and defunct organizations as varied as the Black Panthers and the American Nazi Party. To outsiders, their belief system was a muddled and inconsistent mix of Black Nationalism, natural utopianism, antimodernism, and millennialism. They refused to clothe their children or send them to school. They advocated the abolition of all technology and modern lifestyles. MOVE members rejected medical care and modern amenities like indoor heat, manufactured soap, and waste disposal. They were also radical animal rights activists that rejected any substantive difference between human beings and animals. Their use of profanity was another way of showing their contempt for social norms. Summed up, MOVE's philosophy rested upon a conviction that all of the modern world was hopelessly faulty and the only thing capable of delivering society from its own destruction were the teachings of MOVE founder, John Africa.[47]

MOVE's rejection of Western versions of linear time made the organization's founding almost impossible to ascertain. When asked, members typically said that MOVE had no beginning and no end. Sometime in the early 1970s, however, a charismatic, unemployed West Philadelphia handyman named Vincent Leaphart founded a small organization he called a community action movement after being evicted from a Powelton Village co-op. Though uneducated, Leaphart spoke eloquently about philosophy. His Powelton Village community was also more cosmopolitan than most Philadelphia neighborhoods. Not far from Drexel University and the University of Pennsylvania, Powelton Village was home to college students and professors, counterculturalists and New Left radicals. Leaphart was an eccentric in Powelton Village, but not a threat. To help get his organization off the ground, Leaphart enlisted the help of Donald Glassey, a former white student activist and professor of social work at the Community College of Philadelphia. Glassey became Leaphart's first follower and the home he owned at North Thirty-Third and Pearl Streets became their base of operations. Together, they wrote the document that laid out MOVE's philosophy. Later members simply called it "The Book" or "The Teachings of John Africa," Leaphart's self-appointed new name. Shortening the name of the organization to MOVE, John Africa instructed all subsequent members of the organization to adopt his new surname. He then left Philadelphia and disappeared into self-exile. Although his followers repeatedly invoked his name and teachings, John Africa would not return to Philadelphia until the early 1980s. For the next few years, MOVE carried on and brashly announced their presence without their founder.[48]

Most of Philadelphia's introduction to MOVE came in 1974, when the organization began disrupting school board and community meetings. With the heavy use of profanity and threats of violence, MOVE members attacked the meeting organizers. Referring to themselves as "violent revolutionaries," MOVE protested just about everything. They criticized politicians like Frank Rizzo and Richard Daley as well as antiwar activist Jane Fonda and national NAACP president Roy Wilkins. They demonstrated against human rights activist and comedian Dick Gregory as well as Dr. Ralph Abernathy when they toured Philadelphia. They protested the Philadelphia Zoo and Barnum and Bailey's circus for keeping animals in captivity.[49] From visiting speakers to local politicians, MOVE targeted almost everyone. But they reserved their deepest animosity for the Philadelphia police. They blamed every problem facing the city on a corrupt and brutal police force backed by an equally brutal system of law enforcement.[50]

MOVE's frequent demonstrations and criticisms of the police made them targets. The police repeatedly arrested MOVE members during the mid-1970s. Generally, however, MOVE members reveled in the arrests. Although they had nothing but contempt for the legal system, their court appearances gave them a public platform. MOVE members always acted as their own counsel and mocked the legal system by diverting from the case at hand in order to say whatever they had in mind. In one case they cross-examined police officers for hours and asked them to discuss philosophical topics like the meaning of "truth." Very few MOVE members received convictions for the crime they were accused of, however. In most cases their courtroom behavior ended the trial before a judge or jury could reach a verdict. Throughout the 1970s, MOVE members spent more time in jail for contempt of court, disorderly conduct, and other courtroom charges than any other cause. In a cycle of outrage, jailed members' imprisonment then gave free MOVE members another issue to protest against the police and criminal justice system.[51]

The years of poor police-community relations that plagued black neigh-borhoods in Philadelphia played a critical role in MOVE's emergence. Their protests of police brutality and injustices within the legal system also provided MOVE with some of their more prescient issues. Even when they made valid criticisms or highlighted serious urban problems, however, their methods all but ensured that relatively few others would be swayed by their arguments. Even people that shared political opinions with MOVE found difficulty reach-ing common ground with the organization. Claude Lewis, for example, was one of the first African Americans with a regular column in the *Philadelphia Evening Bulletin*. He was specifically hired to comment on civil rights issues and urban race relations from an African American perspective. Lewis quickly became a relentless critic of Frank Rizzo and the police department. He had spent a career defending militant black activists like the Black Panthers, but he could not get past MOVE's methods. "What they proffer, if listened to, is easy to take," Lewis wrote, "too bad much of it is buried in language that loses the very people they are trying to attract."[52] Shortly after the *Bulletin* published his column criticizing MOVE, seven members of the organization arrived at the newspaper's building to protest. They forced their way into Lewis's office and verbally harassed him until security guards removed them from the building. By 1978, before the raid on MOVE headquarters, even Claude Lewis—one of Frank Rizzo's biggest media critics—came to agree with the mayor's handling of the situation in Powelton Village.[53]

MOVE's immediate neighbors bore the brunt of their nontraditional lifestyle more than most. Powelton Village was economically mixed. Mainly populated by working- and middle-class African Americans, it was also undergoing a process of gentrification by higher-income whites attracted to its large Victorian homes—like the one occupied by MOVE—and students and faculty from the nearby universities. MOVE made life uncomfortable for all of them. In addition to the twenty-plus men, women, and children that occupied their house, MOVE also shared their home with at least twenty stray dogs. They left loose garbage and dog waste across their property in order to replenish the nutrients in the soil. Sanitation violated natural laws, they said. Their belief in uniform life, whereby there was no distinction between humans and animals, also prevented them from harming or remov-ing the rats, roaches, and other vermin that inevitably found their way to MOVE's—and their neighbors'—property. Their radical back-to-nature philosophies might not have caused such a problem in a rural setting or low-population area, where similar countercultural collectives in the 1960s and

1970s lived in opposition to modern materialistic lifestyles. But in a densely populated neighborhood like Powelton Village, MOVE created a nuisance at best, and, at worst, a serious health hazard. Combined with their propensity for verbally harassing and threatening neighbors and passersby, very few of the people that shared close urban space with MOVE responded positively to their presence.[54]

Few people sympathized with MOVE. In a city as racially, socially, and politically divided as Philadelphia in the 1970s, one of the few points of agreement among most people—black and white, blue-collar and white-collar—was that they did not understand or agree with MOVE. If not for Frank Rizzo and the police department's aggressive efforts to extricate MOVE from Powelton Village, the radical organization might never have garnered the broader sympathy, publicity, and notoriety they received in the late 1970s.

By 1976, after complaints and requests from Powelton Village residents, the police put MOVE under a constant state of surveillance and investigation. One shouting match between MOVE and the police led to a scuffle that left several MOVE members injured. They also claimed that the confrontation caused the death of Life Africa, the three-week-old child of two of the commune members. Few believed MOVE at first. Many doubted whether or not the child even existed. Their penchant for over-the-top antics made them difficult for a lot of people to trust. But their insistence on the child's death and the police's responsibility led to a highly publicized invitation for local media to tour the MOVE home. It was the first time anyone outside the organization had seen the inside of the MOVE house. Once the journalists were inside, MOVE members led them through their sparsely furnished home to a room covered with straw, where women gave birth. In the corner, MOVE members led them to a small cardboard box that contained the remains of a lifeless newborn. MOVE refused attempts to investigate the incident with the police or perform an autopsy. Although one officer later testified that he saw a MOVE woman holding a baby at the melee, the police's culpability was never definitively proven. Nevertheless, after the incident and accusation, the already hostile relationship between MOVE and the police steadily deteriorated.[55]

After the death of Life Africa, MOVE began wearing military fatigues and brandishing automatic weapons outside their home. Armed members patrolling the commune led to several tense standoffs with police. Scared neighbors begged Rizzo to intervene. The parents of Drexel University students pleaded with Rizzo to remove the organization from the neighborhood.[56] By 1977, Rizzo promised to get MOVE to leave Powelton Village.

He ordered round-the-clock surveillance of the MOVE house and had police stationed throughout the neighborhood for months. MOVE responded by building a six-foot fence around their house, making it look more like a fortified garrison than a West Philadelphia residence. They then installed loudspeakers to broadcast their message to neighbors and patrolling police officers.[57] News that the cost of heavy police surveillance rose into the millions of dollars unleashed a further torrent of criticism. People accused Rizzo and the city of coddling criminals and wasting taxpayer money.[58]

Rizzo was no stranger to criticism. Throughout his mayoralty he had been accused of fiscal mismanagement, operating a patronage system, and using the police as his personal means of getting retribution on his political enemies. But, before MOVE, no one had ever accused Frank Rizzo of being soft on crime.

Meanwhile, two MOVE members that did not live in the Powelton Village house were convicted of a bomb plot to blow up hotels and embassies in the United States and Western Europe. The star witness against them was Donald Glassey, the former community college professor that helped John Africa write MOVE's founding document. Glassey turned government informant after his own arrest on drug charges. In addition to the bomb plot, Glassey also testified that MOVE was building an arsenal of automatic weapons and explosives. Unsubstantiated rumors claimed MOVE was building an atomic bomb. MOVE had no such technology. But they seemed so out of step and strange to some Philadelphians that even the most outlandish rumors seemed plausible. MOVE was, however, stockpiling weapons for an impending showdown with police. Rizzo decided to erect a blockade of the MOVE house and a four-block radius around it. His plan was to quarantine MOVE into submission.[59]

Combined with the heavy police presence, Rizzo's plan to erect a blockade in Powelton Village eventually engendered sympathy for an otherwise unsympathetic organization. The mayor's actions provoked protesters who decried what they called the establishment of a "police state."[60] Watchdog organizations familiar with the police's recent history with black activists—like the raid on Black Panther headquarters in 1970—began monitoring the police. Few people agreed with MOVE's words or actions. Instead, they worried about the perpetuation of unfettered police abuse. Other sympathizers viewed MOVE members like unwilling participants or brainwashed members of a cult. The national news of Patty Hearst's involvement in the Symbionese Liberation Army was a fresh memory, and many observers found eerie similarities between MOVE members and the country's most famous victim of

"Stockholm Syndrome."[61] The belief that MOVE members were acting against their will intensified when Consuela Africa escaped the barricade with her infant son in February 1978. Sympathizers agreed that MOVE did not fit in urban society, but they objected to the kind of retribution the Philadelphia police were known for, especially when dealing with radical black activists.[62]

The history of poor police-community relations in heavily African American areas over the past two decades helped establish the battle lines as Rizzo amped up the city's efforts to rid Powelton Village of MOVE. Supporters were especially concerned about the fate of the children being starved along with the adult members of the organization. As the blockade continued, MOVE gained more supporters than they otherwise would have. Those already opposed to Rizzo's law enforcement politics considered the blockade inhumane. It also was affecting more than just MOVE members. The blockade stopped deliveries from reaching not only the MOVE house, but also the homes and businesses in the immediate Powelton Village vicinity.[63]

In May 1978, almost a year since heavy surveillance began and two months into the blockade, MOVE members began surrendering. They accepted a deal with the city that included facing weapons charges and leaving Powelton Village. In exchange, they would win their freedom and that of other imprisoned members. MOVE began turning over their arsenal of weapons. Albeit briefly, it appeared as if Rizzo's blockade had worked. He received praise from unusual places, including the chair of the Citywide Black Coalition for Human Rights.[64] Months after MOVE agreed to the deal, however, they refused to make their court appearances and vacate their Powelton Village home. On the morning of August 8, under orders from Frank Rizzo, the police organized the raid on MOVE headquarters. Snipers took to the nearby rooftops and firefighters aimed water cannons at the MOVE house. Via bullhorn, Police Commissioner O'Neill ordered MOVE to surrender. MOVE responded with taunts and insults, calling the police murderers and baby killers. The first officers breached the MOVE house shortly after dawn and confirmed that MOVE was armed. Soon thereafter, the police were under fire.

After the police unloaded into the MOVE house, police sharpshooter James Ramp lay dead. Although MOVE maintained that no one inside their house fired the fatal shot, later investigations revealed that Ramp died of a bullet wound to the front of his neck. Police also claimed they recovered the rifle that killed James Ramp inside the MOVE house, but in a city where the trustworthiness of the police was suspect, whether or not MOVE members actually opened fire on the police and killed James Ramp remained a subject of debate for years. The inability to trust police officers' testimony became one of the longer legacies of the poor police-community relations that plagued Philadelphia for decades. The controversy notwithstanding, in addition to the charges they already faced, the police charged the MOVE members apprehended on August 8, 1978, with the murder of James Ramp.[65]

Blue-collar supporters of the police never had much tolerance for MOVE. To them, there were hardly any crimes worse than harming a police officer. They had no doubt that MOVE was guilty. Their militancy, their dreadlocked hairstyles, their foul language, their unkempt-by-Western-standards living arrangements, and especially their contempt for authority made MOVE a confusing and possibly dangerous Other in the eyes of many Philadelphians. Blue-collar Philadelphians, including the families and friends of police officers, usually denied the existence of widespread police brutality. But if there were ever a case in which they thought brutality was justified, it was against MOVE. Delbert Africa was responsible for the death of a police officer, they thought. Blue-collar supporters of the police simply thought he got what he deserved.[66]

Within hours of MOVE members being taken into custody, bulldozers and cranes arrived in Powelton Village to tear down their headquarters. Police Commissioner O'Neill said it was to erase the symbol of a sad part of the city's history.[67] But the city's long engagement with MOVE was far from over. Instead, the leveling of the MOVE home marked the conclusion of the first act of the three-part tragedy that became Philadelphia's history with the MOVE organization. The second act began shortly thereafter, when the MOVE members arrested on August 8, 1978, faced trial. For the next few years, MOVE members mocked the courts and caused long delays. Worse, the second act failed to rectify or bring closure to the underlying conflict exposed during the first. The hostility between MOVE and the Philadelphia police continued until May 13, 1985, one of the darkest days in the city's history. The third and definitive confrontation between MOVE and the city ended in almost unimaginable horror. The seeds of May 13, 1985, however, were sown well before, in the politics of law enforcement established in Frank Rizzo's Philadelphia.

The inconclusiveness and controversy surrounding the end of the first MOVE confrontation also had a more immediate impact. Rizzo's opponents—especially African American organizers that viewed the MOVE debacle in the context of police-community relations in Philadelphia—organized against the mayor. Most of the protesters that heard Alphonso Deal call for the dismissal of the officers responsible for beating Delbert Africa were gathered at City Hall in opposition to Frank Rizzo. The showdown with MOVE took place against the backdrop of one of the more tumultuous periods of Frank Rizzo's already divisive mayoralty. He was nearing the end of his second term and eyeing his political future. By August 1978, as the police ended the confrontation with MOVE, Frank Rizzo campaigned for an amendment to the city's charter that would allow him to seek a third term as mayor.

Charter Change and the Limits of Color Blindness

In March 1978, as Philadelphia police maintained the blockade against MOVE, Frank Rizzo called a meeting in Whitman, South Philadelphia. The community was still reeling from recent losses in the legal battles over Whitman Park. As long as Frank Rizzo was mayor, however, the neighborhood held out hope that he could help them stop construction of the public housing project. As Rizzo was nearing the end of his second term, many in attendance hoped that Rizzo would announce his intention to attempt changing the city charter so that he could run for a third term. Whitman residents greeted the mayor with chants of "four more years." Rizzo disappointed his audience when he announced he would not seek a charter change amendment, but he reassured them he would continue fighting on their behalf. "It's not only Whitman Park the liberals want to destroy," he said, "but all neighborhoods." He then told his audience that they had the right to "neighborhood purity" and that they needed to "join hands" with other white ethnics. "I'm willing to do battle for every neighborhood of Philadelphia, for all the ethnic groups that came here and got nothing free and asked for nothing," he said. He then continued on a tirade against liberal programs that gave "special privileges" to nonwhites. "My parents and your parents got no special treatment," he said to thunderous applause. He then said he planned to become a "national spokesman" for "white ethnic rights" when his mayoral term ended.[68]

In the late 1970s, Rizzo's aggressive ethnic politics combined with his support of blue-collar neighborhoods and opposition to equal opportunity programs. Rizzo made his comments in Whitman while the Supreme Court heard arguments in *Bakke v. Regents of the University of California* and prepared to hand down a decision in the nation's battle over affirmative action in higher education. Rizzo was outspoken about the *Bakke* case and applied his objection to "special privileges" broadly. Because Rizzo conflated local and national issues in his call for a white ethnic political movement, his address to

Whitman residents became national news. President Jimmy Carter criticized the Philadelphia mayor in an interview. A Louisiana-based branch of the Ku Klux Klan called Frank Rizzo their "racist hero of the month." Rizzo was livid at the Klan's endorsement and said that their beliefs were contrary to everything he had ever been taught. He reiterated that his opposition to public housing and affirmative action had nothing to do with race.[69] Rizzo's supporters agreed with him. Within days, letters from across the country came pouring into his office. Most of them complained about "special treatment" for African Americans. One said that past racial discrimination was not a reason for "junking the Constitution to give a single minority preferential treatment." The outpouring of support convinced Rizzo he had the political capital to launch a campaign to change the city's charter.[70]

Attempting to change the city charter was nothing new in Philadelphia. It came under review every few years after its adoption in 1951. Removal of mayoral term limits had come up for debate before, but restricting mayors to two consecutive terms remained a popular provision.[71] The difference with the charter change amendment proposed in 1978 was that it would allow Rizzo to run for a third term. Rizzo's opponents—the liberals, civil libertarians, and civil rights activists who had been reorganizing throughout the 1970s—immediately focused on Rizzo's shaky mayoral record. In addition to his divisive rhetoric, charges of political corruption continued to take a toll on Rizzo's credibility. As well, several high-profile political failures gave his opponents plenty of fodder. The Rizzo administration had completely bungled the national bicentennial celebration in 1976, for example. In response to a nonexistent threat of political subversion, Rizzo called in the National Guard to assist Philadelphia police. Rizzo scared off tourists and made Philadelphia a national embarrassment when law enforcement personnel outnumbered revelers at the bicentennial celebration.[72] Even worse among city voters, Rizzo had reneged on one of his key promises when the city budget crisis forced him to advocate successive city wage tax hikes in 1976 and 1977. Combined with Rizzo's poor record, his opponents ran an anti-charter-change campaign that warned of an amendment that would allow Rizzo to become "mayor for life."[73]

Rizzo's advisers knew better than to run on his weak mayoral record. Instead, they concentrated on rallying supporters in Northeast and South Philadelphia. He continually reiterated his role as the protector of blue-collar neighborhoods and traditions. All the racial controversies of the past two decades—from police-community relations to school desegregation, from public housing to neighborhood politics—came back during the charter change campaign. After the *Bakke* decision, Rizzo added affirmative action to the list of issues his continued mayoralty would tackle. He promised that the Supreme Court decision would mean an end to quotas in the building trades and police department.[74] In South Philadelphia, he conflated liberals' attempts to build Whitman Park with other attempts to enforce equal opportunity hiring and promotions. In the Northeast, Rizzo told crowds that liberals wanted to erect public housing in their neighborhoods. Without him, he said, there would be public housing projects instead of recreation centers.[75] In another Far Northeast appearance, Rizzo told an audience that local and national black leaders were telling Philadelphia's African American communities to "vote black" against charter change. Outlining his own campaign, he said, "I'm going to say to the people of this city, 'Vote White,' and the black people who think like me, and there are a lot of them . . ." Rizzo never had the opportunity to finish his sentence. The crowd had erupted into applause at the directive to "Vote White."[76]

The words "vote white" reverberated throughout Philadelphia. It became the primary focus of the charter change campaign. Although Rizzo maintained that he never meant the words as the press reported them, to many Philadelphians, especially in African American communities, what Frank Rizzo did or did not mean was unimportant. Opponents of programs like public housing and affirmative action had spent most of the 1970s cultivating color-blind arguments against liberal integration policies. Despite their often concealed racial antipathies, their efforts helped create a race-neutral and blue-collar class conscious conservative discourse. Frank Rizzo belied those efforts when he told one audience to organize for white ethnic rights and another to "vote white." Rizzo revealed the limits of his and his constituents' color blindness when he made the charter change amendment indelibly about race.

The vote on the charter change became a referendum on Frank Rizzo's political career and the racial politics he represented. Rizzo's opponents organized a massive voter registration drive that led to 170,000 new voters, 90,000 of them African American. In November, the amendment failed by a vote of 472,493 to 237,814, a margin of nearly two to one. African American voter turnout was the highest in the city's electoral history, with 96 percent voting against charter change. Support for charter change was strongest in heavily blue-collar, white ethnic wards and Rizzo's amendment won 52 percent of the overall white vote. But with only wards in South Philadelphia and Northeast Philadelphia voting to pass the amendment, it was not enough.[77] Rizzo made his aggressive white ethnic politics and the sanctity of blue-collar neighbor-hoods the centerpieces of his attempt to change the city charter. When it failed, his immediate political future in Philadelphia was effectively over. His mayoralty ended a little over a year later. Rizzo's final political downfall set the stage for the politics that endured well past his mayoral tenure. He left the city almost irreparably divided. As Claude Lewis observed during the campaign to change the city charter, "race in the '70s is more an issue in Philadelphia, Pennsylvania than it is in Philadelphia, Mississippi."[78]

Months before he left office, Frank Rizzo received a number of letters from supporters. They thanked him for all he had done for the city and encouraged him to stay involved in local politics. Most of them told him that he would always be their mayor.[79] They also explained how they feared for the future of the city. "I for one was never afraid while you are in office," wrote a woman from South Philadelphia. Without Rizzo, however, she was "beginning to get that scary feeling that later on things aren't going to be safe."[80]

As long as Rizzo remained mayor, blue-collar Philadelphians felt they still had options. But much as Rizzo's victory in 1971 felt like a victory for them and their institutions, the charter change fight proved that blue-collar tri-umphs in Frank Rizzo's Philadelphia were more of a last gasp than a political ascendancy. In the long term, blue-collar culture was on the losing end of a larger struggle, not to working-class African Americans, but to the eco-nomic restructuring and generational changes in the 1970s that did far more to undermine traditional blue-collar neighborhoods and institutions than liberal policy-making. Nevertheless, Rizzo's defeat seemed like an assault on blue-collar values. In response, blue-collar whites turned even further away from the politics of liberalism. As the 1970s turned into the 1980s, blue-collar whites found their interests increasingly represented by conservative politics. The resultant blue-collar conservatism became one of the key elements of the rightward turn in American political history.

CHAPTER 8

Post-Rizzo Philadelphia

Early on the morning of May 13, 1985, much as they had done eight years before in Powelton Village, Philadelphia police massed around a compound belonging to the radical organization MOVE. In the years since the shootout in 1978, several MOVE members not incarcerated for the murder of Officer James Ramp relocated to Cobbs Creek, a working-class African American neighborhood in West Philadelphia. Thirteen MOVE members, including six children, took up residence in a center row home at 6221 Osage Avenue. As in Powelton Village, MOVE's strict adherence to animal rights and unconventional sanitation habits attracted rats and other vermin. Cobbs Creek's row-home architecture made the pest problem much worse. Exacerbating tensions with Osage Avenue residents, MOVE set up another loudspeaker to deliver late-night denunciations of American materialism and the Philadelphia police. On several occasions they threatened to kill Wilson Goode, the city's first African American mayor. Area residents begged the Goode administration and the police to intervene.[1]

As police stepped up surveillance and patrols, MOVE converted the house into a fortress with boarded-up windows and a rooftop bunker. Warning of an impending confrontation, they armed themselves, stocked their home with sandbags, and placed several drums of gasoline on the roof. On May 1, 1985, after MOVE amped up their usual broadcasted message with threats to kill neighborhood children, Osage Avenue residents held a press conference saying they could no longer coexist with the organization. MOVE fortified their rooftop bunker. On May 11, a judge issued arrest warrants for six adult MOVE members on charges of riot, possession of explosives, and making terroristic threats. Before sunrise on May 13, police arrived outside 6221 Osage Avenue to carry out the warrants.[2]

After evacuating neighbors from the surrounding area, Police Commissioner Gregore Sambor grabbed a bullhorn and addressed the occupants of 6221 Osage Avenue. "Attention MOVE," he said, "This is America! You have to abide by the laws of the United States."[3] Sambor gave them an opportunity to surrender, but MOVE had no intention of leaving their compound. A daylong standoff ensued. Police shot intermittent gunfire at the MOVE compound throughout the day. High-powered fire hoses doused the house for hours in hope the water would force them to evacuate. Though they filled the house with tear gas and water, the police feared getting caught in a crossfire if they attempted to enter the front door. Attempts to enter the MOVE house through adjoining row homes failed. In the late afternoon, with no end in sight, Mayor Goode gave the police permission to take drastic action. Around 5:00 p.m., a police helicopter began circling the 6200 block of Osage Avenue. Half an hour later, Commissioner Sambor gave the order to take out the rooftop bunker. An officer then dropped a satchel filled with three and a half pounds of Tovex and C-4 explosives on a forty-five-second fuse from the helicopter. The bomb exploded with a devastating impact and ignited the drums of gasoline on the roof. Clouds of thick, black smoke darkened all of Cobbs Creek. Police took cover for fear of MOVE gunfire. Commissioner Sambor gave the final order: "Let the bunker burn."[4]

The fires burned through most of the night. By the time firefighters began dousing the blaze, it was too late. The flames spread from the MOVE compound to the surrounding community. They engulfed houses extending in a two-block radius. By the following morning, the fire had destroyed fifty-three homes and left over two hundred people homeless. The bombed-out 6200 block of Osage Avenue looked more like Dresden in 1945 than West Philadelphia forty years later. Only two members of MOVE survived. The rest—including MOVE founder John Africa, five other adult members, and five children—died in the fire, their bodies so badly charred that it took weeks for authorities to reach conclusive identifications.[5]

The MOVE conflagration was an almost incomprehensible tragedy, made worse because blame cannot be attributed to any single party involved. The bombing was a complete failure for the city. The police department, the Goode administration, and every official involved allowed two full city blocks to burn to the ground. It was one of the greatest travesties in Philadelphia history and a complete breakdown of the public trust. The actions against MOVE were utterly unjustifiable, but they were not mere victims of

Figure 9. Two city blocks lie in ruins in the aftermath of the MOVE bombing. The fires destroyed fifty-three homes and left over two hundred people homeless, 1985. Courtesy of Special Collections Research Center, Temple University, Philadelphia, PA.

the police. For over a decade they harassed neighbors in two different areas. Their role in the lead-up to the final confrontation cannot be ignored. Neither can the history of the preceding decades. The polarization over the police department, the politics that promoted law and order over law and justice, as well as anyone willing to turn a blind eye toward police abuses that took place outside their own urban spaces helped create the environment that made the events of May 13, 1985 possible. The MOVE bombing was a product of the politics of the urban crisis in Frank Rizzo's Philadelphia.

The MOVE debacle was an unusual and, in many ways, unprecedented event. Yet it was also symptomatic of the problems that beset post-Rizzo Philadelphia. It was born of the racial and spatial politics of the postwar era. The destruction of an entirely African American community offered a stark example of the consequences wrought by the spatial divisions that had main- tained a hypersegregated metropolis since the 1950s. Like the MOVE disas- ter's long roots, the post-Rizzo city as a whole bore the imprint of the previous decades' spatial and political realignments. The challenges that marked the city's travail in the 1980s grew out of the politics of the urban crisis in Frank Rizzo's Philadelphia. Indeed, Philadelphia in the 1980s showed the continued influence of the spatial politics that had shaped the interconnected and intractable politics of law enforcement, education, employment, and housing in the long postwar era. In the 1960s and 1970s, those politics led to the rise of blue-collar conservatism. The 1980s secured blue-collar conservatism's longevity and lasting influence.

Philadelphia faced both lingering effects and new challenges as it wrestled with the aftermath of the postwar urban crisis. The MOVE bombing heralded a renewed interest in law and order in post-Rizzo Philadelphia, but it was not alone. Before the confrontation, a series of police conflicts had triggered long-standing divisions over police conduct and law enforcement policy. Likewise, the battles over the welfare state continued as blue-collar whites' selective rejection of liberal policies reached new levels of political enactment. At the same time, rising crime rates and shrinking city populations thrust urban America into a new era of crisis. The decline in manufacturing that had already robbed Philadelphia of much of its previous industrial strength continued as capital relocation transferred jobs and economic stability away from the city. Rising poverty rates and inadequate housing compounded urban decay just as the federal commitment to American cities dwindled. As one urban crisis bled into another, blue-collar whites fled Philadelphia in droves. Blue-collar suburbanization in the 1980s had profound consequences for the city and its former mayor, as Frank Rizzo attempted a series of political comebacks throughout the decade. Rizzo's last stand highlighted both the lasting impact of blue-collar conservatism and its limitations in a modern urban political landscape.

Police Politics and Post-Rizzo Philadelphia

Officer Daniel Faulkner worked the overnight shift patrolling "the strip" in F Sector, a three-by-two-block area of Center City. Located only a few blocks southeast of City Hall, the strip was one of the worst sections in downtown Philadelphia. Like the scores of similar areas that succumbed to disrepair by the 1980s, the strip bore the clear signs of urban decay: adult movie theaters, dive bars, prostitution, and crime. Police officers called the overnight patrol of the strip the "worst time and worst place."[6] Several hours after he started his shift on December 8, 1981, Faulkner made a routine traffic stop near the corner of Thirteenth and Locust Streets. The driver, William Cook, had been driving the wrong way on a one-way street. Faulkner stopped Cook and ordered him out of the car. An argument ensued and ended in a scuffle. As Faulkner and Cook struggled, witnesses said they saw someone run toward them from Faulkner's blind side, firing a gun at the officer. Wounded, Faulkner fell to the ground, where he fired one shot from his service revolver. The assailant shot him four more times. Witnesses later identified the gunman as William Cook's brother, journalist and former Black Panther Mumia Abu-Jamal. When reinforcements arrived they found Abu-Jamal sitting on a curb, armed with a pistol, and injured by the shot from Faulkner's gun. Both were rushed to a nearby hospital, where Faulkner died and the police charged Mumia Abu-Jamal with his murder.[7]

In the Philadelphia police's long history of conflict with black radicalism—including the Columbia Avenue uprising, the board of education demonstration, the raids on the Black Panther Party, and the confrontations with MOVE—none remained as divisive as the murder of Daniel Faulkner. Questions over Abu-Jamal's guilt swirled immediately. They intensified after a jury unanimously found him guilty and sentenced him to death. The doubts about Abu-Jamal's culpability combined with the legacy of police brutality in the preceding decades to create a movement of anti-death-penalty advocates who raised funds to appeal his conviction. As Abu-Jamal sat on death row, furthermore, he won the support of liberals, celebrities, academics, and more. On the other side, however, supporters of the police decried that Abu-Jamal had yet to be executed. They demanded "Justice for Daniel Faulkner."[8] Questions about Abu-Jamal's guilt or innocence, whether he received a fair trial, and his death sentence may never be answered adequately. They were products of the politics of policing in the urban crisis. As such, they carried with them the weight of the previous twenty years of Philadelphia law enforcement politics and policy. The politics of race and class that immediately surrounded the controversy were deeply rooted in the polarization over the police department in Frank Rizzo's Philadelphia.

The murder of Daniel Faulkner took place at a critical point in Philadelphia's post-Rizzo politics of law enforcement. Rizzo's immediate successor, William Green III, promised a direct repudiation of the Rizzo era. As Rizzo's Democratic primary opponent in 1971 and the son of a longtime Democratic Party leader, Green harkened back to the reform liberalism that initiated the city's political transformation in the 1950s. When he took office in 1980, he immediately took aim at undoing Rizzo's legacy in city politics and law enforcement. In an attempt to solve the still-pressing city budget crisis that he inherited from Rizzo, Green initiated steep cuts in municipal spending, which included reducing the size of the police department. Like many liberals, Green also believed the leeway Rizzo granted the police had fostered a pattern of abuse. Damning investigations from the United States Civil Rights Commission confirmed liberal suspicions about widespread malpractice and misconduct.[9] Green campaigned on a promise to curb police abuses. Once in office, he proposed the reinstitution of a civilian review process and initiated reduction in personnel.[10]

The Fraternal Order of Police (FOP) and their blue-collar allies immediately attacked the changes, saying they would endanger both police officers and the public.[11] But shortly after Green's proposed reforms and only a year before the murder of Daniel Faulkner, white police officer John Ziegler shot and killed William Howard Green, an unarmed African American teenager, for allegedly stealing a car and evading arrest. Like the killing of Willie Philyaw almost twenty years earlier, the incident led to several nights of unrest in North Philadelphia.[12] The protests only calmed after African American civic leaders, brothers Milton and John Street, assured crowds that Mayor Green would punish Ziegler. Proving that his administration represented a break from his predecessor, Green not only announced that the police department must follow guidelines for the use of deadly force, but that Ziegler would be dismissed and charged with murder. He issued a statement saying "police misconduct will not be tolerated."[13]

The incident in North Philadelphia was uncannily similar to a killing in Liberty City, Miami, that had led to days of urban rioting in South Florida only a few months earlier. Nationally, Mayor Green and Philadelphia's African American leadership earned praise for defusing a potentially volatile situation with limited disorder.[14] At home, however, blue-collar Philadelphians were outraged at Green's clear shift in law enforcement politics. As in the aftermath of the Willy Philyaw shooting, the FOP and blue-collar whites declared their support for Officer Zeigler. Again, the most vociferous responses came from Northeast and South Philadelphia. Allies of the police responded as if the department was under attack. From South Philadelphia, a letter writer concerned about the "plight of the policemen in this city" asked "How come a common criminal (juvenile or adult) can become a martyr while the police officer doing his duty becomes the convicted guilty one?"[15] A woman from the Northeast was incensed at Green because "Much too often the Protectors (Police Officers) of decent, taxpaying, law abiding citizens are injured or killed by hoodlums and other criminals." Defending Ziegler, she asked "the so called teenager was a thief, wasn't he?"[16] Another simply stated that William Howard Green "deserved what he got."[17] Others accused Mayor Green of having a vendetta against the police department and reminded him that Frank Rizzo would never turn his back on the police.[18]

Not since the FOP's crusade against the Police Advisory Board had white, blue-collar Philadelphia responded so fervently to perceived threats to police officers. Twenty years after the similar killing of Willie Philyaw, the blue-collar reverence and protectionism for the police had not waned. In fact, their angry responses to Mayor Green's law enforcement politics signaled that they had intensified and would continue to play a central role in blue-collar politics. By the time of Daniel Faulkner's death, then, blue-collar supporters of the police had come to believe that Green's reforms signaled a dangerous departure from the Rizzo years. They blamed Green's reforms and reductions in law enforcement personnel for putting Faulkner at risk and allowing Mumia Abu-Jamal to murder a police officer.

Abu-Jamal's case was primed to be a local media spectacle. Born Wesley Cook, he had joined the Black Panther Party as a teenager and led an unsuccessful movement to rename his high school after Malcolm X. After leaving the Black Panthers, Cook changed his name and embarked on a career in journalism. By the late 1970s, Abu-Jamal established himself as an impressive young journalist and a gifted writer with a burgeoning radio career.[19] He was also an unrelenting critic of the police. He followed the police's early confrontations with MOVE closely and continued to report on the organization's ensuing court cases. Abu-Jamal viewed the MOVE confrontations through the prism of his own radical education and the recent history of police-community relations. Like many Philadelphians, he came to empathize with an organization that might never have garnered sympathy without the actions of the police department. Although Abu-Jamal never joined MOVE, he began wearing his hair in dreadlocks, which further confused his loyalties and confounded his fellow journalists. Nevertheless, after his arrest, his peers expressed shock and disbelief. He was president of the local Association of Black Journalists and members of the organization described him as "brilliant," "compassionate," and "peace-loving."[20]

Despite his journalistic success, Abu-Jamal struggled financially. To make ends meet, he worked part-time driving a graveyard-shift taxicab, which is what put him near the corner of Thirteenth and Locust at 4:00 a.m.

on December 9, 1981. Within hours, the story broke and a clear narrative emerged: a radical black journalist killed a white cop. Yet conflicting eyewitness accounts and an inconclusive ballistics test muddied the official account and offered Abu-Jamal's supporters evidence of his innocence. Abu-Jamal also claimed that police had beaten him while he was in custody, which further fueled the belief that he had been wrongfully accused.[21] Police denied Abu-Jamal's charges and claimed he confessed to the murder while in the hospital. The conflicting stories made the emerging controversy bigger than the tragic murder of a police officer and the trial of his accused killer.[22] It pit those who maintained the culture of reverence for the police against those who questioned whether they were a protective or an oppressive force. Neither position was the sole result of this case or the evidence involved. Both grew out of the politics of law enforcement in a city where spatial separation had shaped attitudes toward the police for decades.

The supporters of Mumia Abu-Jamal were not without reason to be suspicious of the charges. For the past twenty years—especially with Frank Rizzo at the helm—police acted with near impunity. With the aid of their blue-collar supporters, the police moved steadily away from the city's postwar law enforcement liberalism based on effective police-community relations to a law-and-order conservatism that advocated more punitive law enforcement procedures. African American communities disproportionately bore the brunt of that shift. With the death of William Howard Green only a year old, it was no stretch of the imagination for Abu-Jamal's supporters to question the official story.[23] For supporters of the police, however, the evidence was clear. The police found Abu-Jamal at the scene and vouched for his confession. Although area newspapers eventually ran editorials contextualizing and questioning the official story, all their initial reports pointed toward Abu-Jamal's guilt. Those that learned of the murders from the mainstream Philadelphia media, especially in places like Northeast and South Philadelphia where the culture of reverence for the police was strongest, were given no reason to doubt the official story. "Wesley Cooke a/k/a Mumia Abu Jamal decided a short time ago that a police officer's life was worthless so he brutally and for no reason took that life," wrote one white Philadelphian to a *Philadelphia Evening Bulletin* forum on Faulkner's murder. Like so many others, he needed little convincing that a black radical with a history of criticizing the police and sympathizing with MOVE was guilty. Others were resentful of media attempts to complicate the official story, to discuss race, or focus on anything other than Faulkner. "The issue is not black or white," said another letter writer, "it is blue." They blamed Mayor Green and his reforms for endangering Faulkner by making him patrol Center City alone. "Had Officer Faulkner had a partner we would not be writing to this forum," wrote another woman. Above all, however, they believed Abu-Jamal deserved swift retribution for the sake of all police, their neighbors, and their families. "He should burn in the electric chair," wrote another man. "A murderer is an animal who does not have the right to live."[24]

Faulkner became a martyr in blue-collar Philadelphia. Just as importantly, like Frank Rizzo and thousands of white police officers before him, Faulkner became the city's blue-collar culture personified. His wife and family knew him as Danny. Soon, too, did legions of Philadelphians introduced to Faulkner after his death. Newspapers recounted how, after two years in the army, he followed his two older brothers into police work in 1976. They told how Faulkner distinguished himself as an aggressive cop who received several commendations.[25] Readers also learned that Danny Faulkner was a hardworking Catholic who lived with his wife in a modest row home in a blue-collar Southwest Philadelphia neighborhood. They learned that he had only been married to his wife Maureen for a year and they had yet to have children, so "Uncle Danny" reveled in playing Santa Claus for his nieces at Christmas.[26] Neighbors recalled how he always greeted them with a smile or how he threw a party when the Philadelphia Phillies won the World Series in 1980. Faulkner's emerging image and memory encapsulated the toughness, sacrifice, and tradition that marked Philadelphia's blue-collar culture. Police had epitomized blue-collar culture for decades. They were symbols of blue-collar authenticity in the face of rising crime and disorder. Frank Rizzo exploited the blue-collar culture of reverence for the police to transition from law enforcement to municipal politics. By the 1980s, there were still few blue-collar Philadelphians more blue-collar than police officers. In death, Daniel Faulkner became a slain symbol of white, blue-collar Philadelphia's decline in the post-Rizzo years.[27]

Faulkner's fellow officers, including those who served with him and those who joined the force after his death, helped maintain that image. But no one did more to sustain and politicize Faulkner's memory than his widow, Maureen Faulkner. She initially grieved privately. At her husband's funeral, Maureen Faulkner stayed close to family. The only public figure she embraced was Frank Rizzo, who attended the services but remained uncharacteristically quiet.[28] She did not immediately seek a public role. In her first media interview, she kept the attention on her husband's life and lamented that most of the media coverage had focused on Mumia Abu-Jamal.[29] In the years that followed, however, she became a key figure in an effort to win retribution for her husband. After Abu-Jamal's conviction and death sentence, Maureen Faulkner responded to the movement that sought his freedom by pushing to have his sentence carried out. Faulkner assumed a role that had long been established by police wives before her. Like Bonnie Whalen, Marie Ann Mackley, and the other women that worked through police wives organizations in the 1960s and 1970s, Maureen Faulkner became an advocate for a more punitive criminal justice system. She embraced the long tradition of police wives engaging the blue-collar culture of reverence by acting as a protector of the police. Maureen Faulkner sought to protect both her husband's memory and his fellow officers so that they would not have to make a similar sacrifice.[30] In 1995, she established Justice for Daniel Faulkner, an organization founded to combat Abu-Jamal's allies. She helped maintain her husband's memory until it became part of the institutional history of the Philadelphia Police Department and the collective memory of Philadelphia's blue-collar supporters of the police.[31]

The divide that remained over the murder of Daniel Faulkner and the conviction of Mumia Abu-Jamal was indicative of one of the most long-standing legacies of the politics of law enforcement in Frank Rizzo's Philadelphia. The residual anguish that circulated through the police department also surrounded the events that led to the MOVE bombing. In the years between the death of Daniel Faulkner and the confrontation with MOVE, the Philadelphia police took jurisdiction over the situation on Osage Avenue. The department would not allow civilian agencies like the Commission on Human Relations to try to ease tensions between MOVE and the community.[32] They bore the responsibility for the events leading to the final confrontation and, as a result, questions about culpability in the aftermath of tragedy largely focused on what the police did and did not do. Were MOVE members killed by the fire or by police bullets? Did the police make escape from the MOVE compound impossible? Did MOVE members attempting to escape the burning row home get forced back into the house to succumb to the smoke and flames? What more could have been done to save the MOVE children?

Mayor Green's successor Wilson Goode established the Philadelphia Special Investigation Commission (MOVE Commission) to address these questions. The police, however, felt under attack. The Fraternal Order of Police filed suit against the Goode administration in an attempt to stop the MOVE Commission's formation. When their efforts failed, many police came to believe that the investigators were "out to get them." The FOP encouraged them to remain evasive under questioning and most cited their Fifth Amendment rights to avoid offering answers.[33] The FOP also organized support for recently retired police commissioner Gregore Sambor when he came under scrutiny for his decision to let the fires burn. They were not alone. The commission received letters from blue-collar Philadelphians accusing them of targeting the police. A woman from Far Northeast Philadelphia chastised the commission for using their position to "ruin the careers of men who had put their lives on the line to follow the mayor's orders."[34]

Despite the accusations waged at Goode, the MOVE Commission did not spare him or his administration. They blamed the mayor for not confronting MOVE sooner, for not using civilian negotiators, and for following a policy of appeasement with MOVE.[35] Yet Goode's decision to organize the MOVE Commission—a move that would have been unthinkable for a mayor like Frank Rizzo—helped build retroactive support for his actions. Goode took ultimate responsibility for the bombing. "The buck stops with me," he told the MOVE Commission. By contrast, former commissioner Sambor and most police involved in the confrontation expressed no remorse for their actions or decisions. "No one was killed on Osage Avenue," declared an FOP spokesman about six adults and five children. "Eleven people committed suicide."[36]

Like the controversy surrounding Mumia Abu-Jamal, the aftermath of the MOVE confrontation and investigation left an unresolved legacy of division between supporters and critics of the police. Moreover, the inseparable controversies lingered long after the 1980s. Supporters of the police objected to any investigation of the police for the MOVE bombing and demanded Abu-Jamal's execution. They likewise equated Abu-Jamal's supporters with precisely the kind of "liberal elites" that blue-collar conservatism rose in opposition to. As late as December 2011, thirty years after Daniel Faulkner's murder, the *Northeast Times* ran an editorial titled "Die, Mumia, Die" that denounced Abu-Jamal for committing the "dirtiest deed of all." A court had recently commuted Abu-Jamal's death sentence to life in prison and the newspaper's editorial staff blamed the decision on "bleeding-heart, liberal cowards from Hollywood and other know-nothing big mouths who despise the death penalty" as well as journalists and others who "find racism in every fiber of life."[37] The lengthy dispute laid bare the most long-lasting consequences of postwar law enforcement politics. The culture of reverence for the police and the politics of law and order continued to animate blue-collar whites. Protection of the police and punitive criminal justice remained central to their politics. The politicized culture of reverence for the police continued to shape blue-collar conservatism long after the era of the urban crisis.

(Sub)urban Space and the Rejection of Liberalism

The blaze that consumed the 6200 block of Osage Avenue reverberated throughout the city, but it was practically a world away from the former centers of Frank Rizzo's Philadelphia. Fires of a different sort burned throughout the racially and spatially separate neighborhoods of South Philadelphia and Northeast Philadelphia as they wrestled with lingering politics of the urban crisis. In South Philadelphia's Whitman neighborhood, the loss of Frank Rizzo as a political ally made an immediate impact in the fight against the construction of the Whitman Park public housing project. Even when Rizzo had no authority over the controversy, his Whitman supporters still felt they had political options left. Once he was gone, the Whitman Council (WC) overwhelmingly voted to go "back to the streets." As in 1971, they blocked traffic and stopped construction crews. Stressing their neighborhood's blue-collar identity, they carried signs demanding construction workers respect the "Whitman Picket Line." When workers ignored the protesters, one resident set up a loudspeaker to blast polka music and verbally harass the workers, calling them "scabby scumbo" for breaking the picket line. Protesters hung ribbons around the neighborhood and staged a mock funeral for Gert Hogan. Lying in a coffin, she clutched a copy of the United States Constitution while passing neighbors mourned the collective loss of their neighborhood. While a few local politicians tried to halt the project, Whitman residents no longer had the backing of City Hall. William Green ensured that construction continued. It was clear that the brief ascendancy and power of blue-collar politics had ended. Stinging from their loss of political clout, frustrated Whitman residents hung a large sign across the street from the construction site. It read: "The Boy Blunder Bill Green and the U.S. Govt. Bring Yous Whitman Park: A 10 Million Dollar Housing Failure."[38]

Construction on Whitman Park concluded in 1982. Before tenants moved in, however, Whitman Council president Fred Druding worked behind the scenes to determine the project's demographics. He helped broker a deal for a racial balance whereby 50 percent of Whitman Park residents had to be white, publicly contradicting claims of the color blindness they

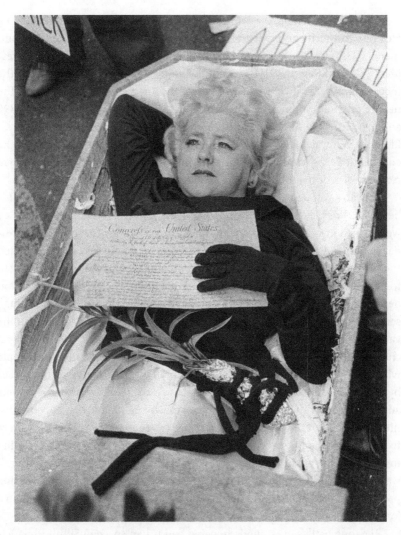

Figure 10. Protesting the plans to open the Whitman Park public housing complex, Gert Hogan lies in a coffin clutching a copy of the US Constitution, 1980. Courtesy of Special Collections Research Center, Temple University, Philadelphia, PA.

maintained throughout the 1970s. The WC also pressured the Philadelphia Housing Authority and federal Department of Housing and Urban Development (HUD) to raise minimum income requirements of Whitman Park residents. Ronald Reagan's HUD responded to the WC's requests and raised the income requirements to make "moderate income people more eligible." The new regulations stipulated that tenants earn between $11,760 and $25,895 and mandated that they could not receive any other form of welfare. The residents of Whitman Park would have incomes closer to those of the rest of the community. By excluding the poorest Philadelphians, the Whitman Council reinforced their neighborhood's blue-collar class politics.[39]

The first residents of Whitman Park moved into the complex in October 1982. Local residents did not protest the move-in, but neither did they welcome their new neighbors with open arms. Wounds from the extraordinarily long battle of Whitman Park were slow to mend. Yet, two years later, the relationship between the neighborhood and the housing complex began to change. Residents who had long protested and picketed the construction began to appreciate the development. "I personally think it's a nice thing," said former protester Evelyn Fayne. "The homes are a far sight better than the vacant land. The land was rat-infested and garbage-strewn." Even Gert Hogan changed her mind, because, she said, "We have good people in there. People who are paying their own way." Hogan maintained her protectionist impulses by sitting on the screening committee that selected Whitman Park tenants and upheld fifty-fifty racial balance. But she also maintained that her community's opposition to the housing project was never about race. "As God is here to judge me," she told a reporter, "it was never, never racial." Fred Druding insisted that they had actually won their long fight because Whitman Park was not traditional public housing. In fact, he did not think of it as a housing project at all. "It's really a middle-income housing development, rather than a low-income housing project," he said.[40]

The long battles over public housing and urban space in South Philadelphia ended with far less rancor than they began, due in part to the racial and income restrictions that the Whitman Council negotiated. The blue-collar politics forged in the early opposition to public housing continued to shape Whitman Park. They also had broader consequences. Whitman's populist revolt against liberal planners and welfare recipients that expected "something for nothing" established their selective rejection of welfare liberalism. Despite the advantages their own community had reaped from federal spending since the 1950s, the white South Philadelphians cheered the changes in the nation's shift away from the welfare state under Ronald Reagan.[41]

At the other end of Frank Rizzo's Philadelphia, the culturally blue-collar residents of Morrell Park fared differently, but Northeast Philadelphians still harbored a growing resentment toward the city. The planned public housing project in Morrell Park was never built. In fact, after the extended fight in Morrell Park, the city planned no more public housing construction in the Far Northeast. The Philadelphia Housing Authority shifted priorities from public housing complexes to rent-assisted scattered site housing, so-called Section 8 housing. Under orders from HUD to expand Section 8 housing in "non-impacted" areas—those not already designated poor or overcrowded—or risk losing federal funding, housing officials began looking to the less densely populated Northeast in the late 1970s. Any kind of public housing in Northeast Philadelphia remained as unpopular, however. Residents raised the same protests against Section 8 that Morrell Park protesters raised before: that rent-assisted tenants would not care for their homes and would destabilize tight-knit communities. The uproar over Section 8 housing pulled the Greater Northeast together in a common cause.[42] The anxieties over public housing also combined with Northeast Philadelphians' continued belief that they bore the brunt of liberal policies. More than anyone in the 1980s, Republican state representative Hank Salvatore sought to capitalize on that resentment and harness the area's blue-collar conservatism.

First elected to the state legislature in 1972, Frank "Hank" Salvatore was the son of Italian immigrants and a lifelong resident of Northeast Philadelphia. Before his entry into politics, Salvatore served in the Marine Corps during World War II and founded a wholesale beer distributorship in 1958. Although he had long been a Republican, as a member of the Sons of Italy, Salvatore supported Frank Rizzo's Democratic candidacy for mayor in 1971. He rose to prominence, however, as an opponent of busing in the 1970s. In 1974, Salvatore introduced legislation to prevent any student transfer program from affecting Northeast Philadelphia. By the 1980s, he became a critic of Mayors Green and Goode. He fought Green's police department reforms and threatened to form a state committee to take authority over the MOVE Commission because he believed it would treat the police unfairly.[43] Salvatore also spent the 1980s attacking the tenets of welfare liberalism. In 1980, he introduced a bill into the state legislature to punish welfare fraud. Two years later he backed Republican governor Richard Thornburg's signature application of Reagan-era austerity, the Pennsylvania Welfare Reform Act of 1982 (WRA).[44]

The WRA restructured Pennsylvania's welfare program so that it encouraged "self-reliance" through work incentives and attempted to eliminate fraud among welfare recipients. Nicknamed "Thornfare," it became a model for later programs known nationwide as "workfare."[45] By encouraging the able-bodied to choose hard work over handouts, it directly appealed to the blue-collar values that animated white working- and middle-class Philadelphians. Unlike measures in states that simply cut their assistance programs, Thornfare was a selective rejection of welfare liberalism. By 1988, however, sociologist Anthony P. Halter found that Thornfare had failed. Halter studied 113 former general-assistance recipients in Philadelphia between 1985 and 1986. Only forty-two found work in their first year off the welfare rolls and only three of those maintained their employment.[46] Nevertheless, when Hank Salvatore supported Thornfare, as he did when he opposed busing and supported the police, he showcased a keen sense of the issues that energized his blue-collar constituency.

Salvatore made his most audacious attempt to exploit Northeast Philadelphia's blue-collar conservatism in 1983, after William Green won a property tax increase to meet the city's budget shortfall. Northeast Philadelphians felt specifically targeted. Although by the 1980s Northeast Philadelphia boasted some of the city's best public schools, playgrounds, and street maintenance, residents complained that they received fewer city services in return for their tax dollars. The myth that Northeast Philadelphia taxes kept the rest of the city afloat combined with opposition to Section 8 housing and the area's sense of separateness from the rest of the city. Fed by Salvatore and the *Northeast Times*, the combination of spatial separation and overburdened taxpayer rhetoric reached a breaking point. Many began threatening to leave the city if their taxes rose.[47] Salvatore upped the ante by suggesting that all of Northeast Philadelphia leave the city. In 1983 he introduced a bill into the state legislature that, if passed, would have made all the land northeast of Frankford Creek a Philadelphia suburb called "Liberty County."[48]

Despite widespread support for his secession bill, it was little more than a political grandstand. Most Northeast Philadelphians realized it was unrealistic, even when they cheered Salvatore's efforts.[49] The Republican's proposal faced stiff opposition in the Democrat-controlled state house. More importantly, Northeast Philadelphia was still home to a large percentage of police officers and other municipal employees. Secession would have created too many problems for the area's police, firefighters, and other city employees bound to live within the city limits by the city charter. But secession maintained an appeal among aggrieved Northeast Philadelphians. Even though few people outside the Northeast took it seriously, Salvatore reasserted the Liberty County proposal every few years to remind lawmakers that Philadelphia's most conservative neighborhoods were separate and distinct from "the city."[50]

Salvatore's crusade underscored the area's separate spatial and political development. In fact, Northeast Philadelphia was different from the rest of the city.[51] When community opposition forced the abandonment of plans to expand the subway and highway systems into Northeast Philadelphia in the late 1960s, they effectively cut off large sections of the area. Even by the 1980s, the Far Northeast remained geographically distant and less accessible than other areas. While it was more ethnically and economically diverse than it had ever been before, residents and community activists emphasized what separated them from the rest of the city. John Fitzpatrick, a consumer activist that spoke of dispelling myths about the Northeast's homogeneity, nevertheless said that shared whiteness brought the various peoples of the Northeast together. "It's the common denominator, the only common denominator. It's white," he explained. Emphasizing the area's blue-collar character, state senator James Lloyd said it was more than whiteness. "It's something else," he said. "I sense that these are people who fought in the wars. I sense that they are people who built buildings, who stand between order and disorder—police and firemen. They're people who pay taxes."[52] Race and class combined in Northeast Philadelphia to reinforce its blue-collar culture and politics. By the 1980s, the blue-collar values born in the row-house neighborhoods of South Philadelphia and Kensington found their clearest representations in the suburb-like neighborhoods of the Greater Northeast. Unlike the suburbs, however, the Northeast was still a part of the city and embroiled in its politics. Locally, the area's blue-collar conservatism became a counterweight to the urban Democratic politicians and coalitions that arose in the post-Rizzo years.

Blue-collar culture and politics also began expanding beyond Philadelphia's borders and seeping into its working- and middle-class suburbs. Northeast Philadelphia had been like a suburb in the city since the 1950s, where upwardly mobile white ethnics and blue-collar transplants found refuge from their former inner-city neighborhoods. By the 1980s, however, Northeast Philadelphia was no longer the primary destination for white flighters. Bucks, Chester, Delaware, and Montgomery Counties began planning for the influx in the 1970s. By the next decade, more Philadelphians began taking advantage of new housing construction beyond the city's borders and across the Delaware River in suburban New Jersey.[53] They cited rising crime rates and the loss of Frank Rizzo as reasons for abandoning the city.[54] "Frank Rizzo prevented crime in Philadelphia," one Northeast Philadelphia woman wrote. "Under Rizzo there were no gang wars, no organized mob killings, no racial violence, no brutal rapes, and no murders of senior citizens," she continued. "The people of Philadelphia felt safe because they WERE safe."[55] Without Rizzo, she said, people were bound to leave the city. Crime had actually risen during Rizzo's mayoralty, but the belief that he kept the city safe remained strong. Younger Philadelphians, especially those who came of age in South Philadelphia, Kensington, and the Near Northeast, increasingly started their adult lives with a suburban address. Even the Far Northeast, which was the only section of the city to continually gain population over the course of the long postwar era, reported its first population loss by the end of the 1980s.[56]

As in most of the cities in the United States, Philadelphia's white middle-class population steadily declined over the course of the postwar era. Suburbanization exploded as Northeast Philadelphians joined South Philadelphians and others already looking beyond the city's borders. By the late 1990s, the number of home sales in South Philadelphia and the Near Northeast were near the top in the city. Over 43,000 whites left South Philadelphia in the last two decades of the twentieth century. The Greater Northeast maintained the city's largest white population, but 50,991 whites had left the Near Northeast and 23,739 left the Far Northeast by the end of the century.[57] In the process, the white, blue-collar culture and politics that shaped the city for a generation shifted to the suburbs. Those suburbs, moreover, became increasingly important in state and national elections. As Pennsylvania turned into a key swing state in presidential elections, with solidly Democratic bases in Philadelphia and Pittsburgh and Republican strongholds throughout the state's hinterland, the Philadelphia suburbs held a disproportionate influence over the state's Electoral College votes. In 1988, for example, the Philadelphia suburbs gave George H. W. Bush 205,000 more votes than Michael Dukakis. The Bush campaign's infamous "Willie Horton ad" was specifically designed to appeal to the advocates of law and order like those that had recently left Philadelphia. Bush's boost in the Philadelphia suburbs allowed him to carry Pennsylvania and win the election. As well, Arlen Specter—Philadelphia's former law-and-order district attorney and 1967 Republican mayoral candidate—won election to the US Senate in 1980, where he served as a Republican until 2009, largely through his popularity in the Philadelphia suburbs.

The blue-collar conservatism forged over the course of the 1960s and 1970s informed suburban Philadelphia voting habits into the 1980s and beyond.[58]

The realignment of urban space in Northeast and South Philadelphia had remade white, blue-collar politics since the 1950s. By the 1980s, as those politics shifted to suburban spaces, the blue-collar conservatism born out of the urban crisis made its indelible mark on modern American political development. Blue-collar conservatism, with its constitutive selective rejection of welfare liberalism and promotion of law and order, remained a powerful force in American politics. As well, the continued centrality of urban and suburban spatial politics in the 1980s showed that post-Rizzo metropolitan Philadelphia bore the ineffaceable imprint of the politics of the urban crisis. So, too, did the man himself.

Rizzo's Last Stand

In September 1981, not even two years out of office, Frank Rizzo served as the grand marshal of a parade to support a South Philadelphia youth athletic association. Taking place on "Two Street," Mummers strutted and played for crowds in order to sell buttons and balloons to benefit youth sports, but Frank Rizzo was the main attraction. One woman waited more than three hours to see him. "I'd wait forever for that man," she said. "So would everyone up and down this street, and 1983 isn't forever," she said of the city's next mayoral election. Other South Philadelphians greeted the ex-mayor with signs saying "Save our City Frank" and "Frank, Make Our City Safe." A reporter covering the event said that Rizzo spent the afternoon shaking hands, hugging his supporters, kissing women, saluting police officers, and doing "everything a candidate would do, except admit that he was, indeed, a candidate." Rizzo said he was flattered, but his participation in the parade was only to help the community fundraiser. His longtime political ally Al Pearlman was less coy. When asked if Rizzo would run for mayor again in 1983, Pearlman replied, "Absolutely. I'd bet my life on it. What do you think he's doing here? He's meeting the people— his people—and he's showing the people he's still with them."[59]

Frank Rizzo was restless in his postmayoral career. Even if he failed to say so publicly, he kept a close watch on the city politics that he and his supporters helped shape. He also desperately wanted to reclaim his former office. Part of it was his desire to secure a positive legacy. He never wanted to be remembered poorly. Rizzo was also infuriated with William Green's attempt to unmake his mayoralty. But Green was also a disappointment to the anti-Rizzo coalition that had come together in the 1970s. The new mayor was a throwback to Philadelphia's reform era, but the coalition of liberals and African Americans that made up his base wanted a new direction in city leadership. In late 1982, William Green announced that he would not seek a second term. His departure left the door open for a contested primary between the Rizzo and the anti-Rizzo factions of the city's Democratic Party.[60]

Green's managing director Wilson Goode quickly became a top Democratic contender. Goode had been a West Philadelphia community organizer and a founder of the Black Political Forum, an organization that sought to elect African American politicians that would be accountable to African American communities rather than white-led Democratic organizations. Throughout the 1970s, Goode's West Philadelphia–based Philadelphia Council for Community Advancement focused on developing and securing economic development programs for impoverished city neighborhoods. In 1978, Pennsylvania governor Milton Shapp appointed Goode to the state Public Utilities Commission. Because of his community leadership and administrative experience, Green then appointed Goode as the city's managing director. By the time Green announced his decision not to seek reelection, Goode had earned a reputation as an effective organizer, a talented administrator, and a political bridge builder. He had the best chance to be the city's first African American mayor. Former members of the Black Political Forum and other African American empowerment organizations rallied behind Goode. But Rizzo, knowing that an African American would be vulnerable in the city's white, blue-collar neighborhoods, staged a political comeback to challenge Goode for the nomination.[61]

Rizzo was determined to remake his image in his 1983 primary election campaign. He resented his reputation as a racist and a bully. He promised to run a positive campaign and largely avoided attacking Wilson Goode personally. He also admitted to making mistakes in his career, including some of his divisive rhetoric in the 1970s and his attempt to change the city charter. He said that he now wanted to reach out to all Philadelphians. He wanted to be the mayor of "all the people," he said. "I mean just that—the young, the old, rich, poor, black, white."[62] Rizzo even reached out to African American communities for the first time in his career. Trying to siphon votes from Goode, he visited a West Philadelphia church and told its congregation not to believe everything they had heard about him. "I come from humble beginnings like most of you," he added.[63] Throughout the primary campaign he called his racist reputation a "bum rap" and attempted to introduce the city to the "new Rizzo." Regardless of his rhetoric or sincerity, too many people—especially liberals and people of color—remembered the old Rizzo far too well. There was also no ignoring the fact that the Democratic primary pitted a symbol of African American political ascendency against white Philadelphia's old savior. Rizzo's only real chance to capture the nomination was to appeal to his former blue-collar strongholds.[64]

To Rizzo's disappointment, the city had changed since he left office and he struggled to pull together his former supporters. Organized labor, for instance, divided over Rizzo's primary bid. The building-trades unions and the Fraternal Order of Police declared their support, but almost all others endorsed Wilson Goode. Rizzo's campaign rested on turning out the vote in the city's white, blue-collar neighborhoods that supported him the 1970s. White South Philadelphians once again turned out to support their native son and Rizzo campaigned hardest in Northeast Philadelphia.[65] The *Northeast Times* endorsed Rizzo, touting his support for the police and calling him "a controversial ex-mayor who, while being deficient in fiscal matters, is a leader who makes things happen."[66] Rizzo's campaign figured that he needed to win 70 percent of the vote in Northeast Philadelphia to defeat Goode. He won 90 percent. He swept every ward in Northeast and South Philadelphia, but it was not enough.[67]

Wilson Goode's candidacy was the culmination of the new coalition of African Americans and liberals that opposed Rizzo throughout the 1970s. The nascent coalition had been responsible for challenging Rizzo in the 1975 primary election and 1976 recall drive. They built a grassroots structure based upon black political empowerment that posed a challenge to both Rizzo's blue-collar constituency and the local Democratic Party's older reform liberalism. Goode's campaign had roots in nearly fifteen years of political mobilization and community organizing. He dominated in North Philadelphia, West Philadelphia, and Center City. Overall, Goode won 90 percent of the African American vote and, despite Rizzo's continued strength in South and Northeast Philadelphia, 20 percent of the white vote. Goode's victory signaled the start of a new era of Philadelphia politics. As well, in a city where Republicans were outnumbered by more than two to one, Goode's triumph in the Democratic primary was tantamount to a coronation. After a contested but relatively easy general election campaign, Goode became the first African American mayor of Philadelphia.[68]

Rizzo's new demeanor quickly faded after the election. In the years that followed he became an unrelenting critic of the Goode administration.

Sympathetic media figures continually sought out Rizzo to deliver sound bites about Goode's mayoralty. After the MOVE bombing, Rizzo thought Goode was vulnerable. The Osage Avenue tragedy tarnished Goode's longtime reputation as an administrator and bridge builder. Shortly after the release of the MOVE Commission's final report that held Goode accountable and still a year from the 1987 election, rumors circulated that a host of challengers would seek the Democratic mayoral nomination, Rizzo included.[69] Rizzo, however, was contemplating switching parties to challenge Goode in the general election. He had grown up a Republican and remained one until he became Mayor James Tate's police commissioner in 1967. As Wilson Goode appeared weakened he openly and publicly toyed with the idea of switching back. He claimed that rank-and-file Democratic workers, Democratic ward leaders, and Republican officials were behind the effort to get him to switch parties. He even bragged that if he were to switch parties he could convert fifty thousand Democrats to the Republicans. Talking like a candidate in 1986, Rizzo reminded crowds of the city's rising crime rate and his law-and-order reputation.[70] He finally stopped fueling speculation in early 1987. Rizzo not only announced the start of his campaign for his former position, but that he would also seek to become the first Republican mayor of Philadelphia in over forty years.[71]

Rizzo opened his campaign with a vow to serve Northeast Philadelphia and received enthusiastic support from its white, blue-collar residents. Abandoning his 1983 image reinvention, he promised a far more negative campaign. "I was too subdued," Rizzo said of his 1983 run for mayor. "I wasn't the real Rizzo."[72] In addition to attacking Goode for the MOVE bombing, his campaign hammered home his old strengths, law and order in particular. In the Northeast, playing to the culture of reverence for the police, he lamented the state of the police department. "Today you can't walk the streets in safety" because "[police] morale is down," he said.[73] Rizzo did not try to hide from his record or present a "new Rizzo" in 1987. Instead, he pointed to rising crime rates, a growing homeless population, and a number of other urban ills that struck American cities in the 1980s. He blamed them all on the Goode administration. He also pointed out that city streets looked far better when he was mayor. He was not entirely wrong, but the new urban crisis of the 1980s had much deeper roots than Rizzo granted. Continued deindustrialization and suburbanization drained cities of jobs and tax revenue. Federal policy changes in the Ford, Carter, and Reagan eras crippled aid to American cities. Philadelphia, like most large urban areas, succumbed to widespread decline.

Nevertheless, the Rizzo campaign ran a series of advertisements with the former mayor standing on rundown street corners, decrying the state of the city and promising a return to law and order. A direct-mail campaign letter more explicitly engaged Rizzo's law-and-order background. "When I was mayor of Philadelphia we were at the bottom of the FBI's crime statistics for the nation's 10 largest cities," it proclaimed. "But not anymore. Today we are at the bottom of everything else but the crime statistics."[74]

Playing to his strengths, Rizzo energized the white, blue-collar Philadelphians that remained in Northeast and South Philadelphia, but he underestimated Mayor Goode's popularity in the rest of the city. Wilson Goode showed immense leadership when he took ultimate responsibility for the bombing of the MOVE compound. His public apology helped resurrect his image. Rizzo's candidacy also played well into Goode's reelection strategy. Even before Rizzo entered the race, Goode believed that he would galvanize African American voters. Rizzo's candidacy also meant that the likelihood of Goode facing a white Democratic challenger shrank. The city's first black mayor was unpopular in the vestiges of Frank Rizzo's Philadelphia. Northeast and South Philadelphia were unlikely to go for Goode under any circumstances. Any white Democrat hoping to pull votes from those areas in a potential primary challenge would be neutralized by Rizzo's Republican candidacy.[75] Furthermore, once Rizzo began running as a law-and-order candidate, his old foes organized against him. The remnants of the Recall Rizzo movement from 1976 reorganized to oppose his 1987 candidacy. They republicized Rizzo's controversies and fiscal failures.[76] The 1987 mayoral race reignited the political fights between blue-collar whites on one side and liberals and African Americans on the other. Rizzo's political legacy hung in the balance. He was able to rally his supporters to overcome similar challenges in the 1970s. By the late 1980s, however, his political base of support had dissipated. Rizzo's aggressive campaign and Goode's renewed popularity made for an incredibly close race. In the end, however, while Rizzo performed well in the city's remaining blue-collar white neighborhoods, he lost handily in African American and liberal wards.

Rizzo completely swept Northeast and South Philadelphia with dominant margins. He caused a massive turnout in South Philadelphia's Thirty-Ninth Ward—which included Whitman, Pennsport, and several other white, blue-collar neighborhoods—where 78 percent of voters turned out. Rizzo earned 90 percent of the vote in the traditionally Democratic ward. Likewise, he won 86 percent of the vote in the Near Northeast Bridesburg and Mayfair neighborhoods. Citywide, Rizzo won 83 percent of the white vote. He won in his

traditional strongholds because he ran on his reputation. He lost the rest of
the city, especially in African American wards, for precisely the same reason.
Goode won an estimated 97 percent of the African American vote. Nevertheless, the results were so close that Rizzo refused to immediately concede. It
took Rizzo another day to admit that he had lost by less than 3 percent of the
vote. It was a bitter pill for Rizzo to swallow. But too many of his supporters
had left the city. White flight and blue-collar suburbanization had sapped his
urban base of support enough to cost him the election. His political career
became the latest casualty of the aftermath of the politics of the urban crisis
in Frank Rizzo's Philadelphia.[77]

Despite the electoral loss, Rizzo's 1987 mayoral campaign neatly encapsulated the broader changes in white, blue-collar politics since the 1950s. His
ultimate conversion from Democrat to Republican symbolized the culmination of blue-collar conservatism in the 1980s. Moreover, he was not alone in
switching his party affiliation. Many of his strongest former supporters followed him into the Republican fold. In South Philadelphia, Whitman community leader Fred Druding—founder of the Young Democrats and once a
self-proclaimed liberal—ran in his last campaign for public office as a Republican candidate for state representative and later served as a Republican ward
leader.[78] Connie McHugh, leader of the nearby Pennsport Civic Association
in the 1970s and another Rizzo ally, made her first foray into electoral politics
as a Republican candidate for city council in 1987. Even more than Druding and McHugh, former Grays Ferry community leader Francis Rafferty
emerged as one of Philadelphia's most controversial politicians. In the years
after winning election as at-large city councilman in 1975, the former amateur boxer got in two fistfights in the council chambers. In solely legislative
battles over public housing, welfare, and, especially in the 1980s, gay rights,
Rafferty earned a reputation as one of the city's most conservative politicians.
His openly homophobic politics eventually cost him reelection in 1991, when
a gay-led movement succeeded in ousting him. Yet Rafferty remained a loyal
Democrat until 2004, when he broke with the party to endorse George W.
Bush for president. Citing a "radical left wing" takeover of the Democratic
Party, Rafferty lamented that "What was a party associated with the blue-
collar workers is now the party of blue-blooded elitists who use the real working class as pawns to help push their liberal agenda."[79]
    As Rafferty's political career suggests, party conversion was not the only
sign of blue-collar conservatism's ascendancy. Even when Rizzo's supporters

remained Democrats longer than he did, they represented a broader shift in blue-collar politics. That was especially true in Northeast Philadelphia, where registered Democrats continued to outnumber Republicans by a margin of two to one. In October 1984, the *Northeast Times* declared Northeast Philadelphia "the bailiwick of Democrats who, when it comes to pulling the lever, vote predominantly with the Grand Old Party."[80] A few weeks later, they overwhelmingly voted to reelect Ronald Reagan.[81] Rather than shift their voter registration, Democrats in areas like Northeast Philadelphia shifted the Democratic Party. Blue-collar conservatives in the Democratic Party represented a new breed of Democrats that helped shift the party away from the welfare liberalism of the 1960s. They were Reagan Democrats in the 1980s and the blue-collar arm of Bill Clinton's New Democrats in the 1990s. In Philadelphia and its surrounding suburbs, they started out as Rizzocrats.

Both those that remained in the former centers of Frank Rizzo's Philadelphia and those that left the city joined the conservative coalition that thrust Ronald Reagan into the White House and altered American politics for the ensuing decades. By the closing decades of the twentieth century, their blue-collar conservatism found currency throughout the nation. As a center-right, populist variant of modern conservatism with a clear class emphasis and color-blind veneer, the blue-collar conservatism that developed in the 1960s and matured in the 1970s reached its final culmination in the 1980s. The end of the twentieth century witnessed its full transformative effect on modern American political history. Philadelphia's continued engagement with the politics of law enforcement and welfare liberalism further illustrated blue-collar conservatism's long-term consequences and lasting legacies for the city, metropolitan America, and the nation. As blue-collar suburbanization indicates, the rise of blue-collar conservatism in postwar Philadelphia was indicative of a broader political movement with profound effects on American political development. More than join the counterrevolution, blue-collar whites helped shape modern American history's rightward political turn.

Blue-Collar Conservatism
and Modern America

Frank Rizzo died in 1991. At the time, he was once again seeking to become mayor of Philadelphia. He spent the years after his 1987 campaign hosting a daily radio talk show that allowed him to comment regularly on Philadelphia politics, keep in contact with his loyal supporters in the metropolitan area, and position himself for another shot at City Hall. He had recently won the Republican primary, and after four more years of a lackluster Goode administration, Rizzo biographer S. A. Paolantonio thought the city would elect its first Republican mayor since 1947. Rizzo crisscrossed the city, campaigning on his greatest strength: law and order. He especially campaigned against the spiking crime rates and the crack epidemic that ravaged urban America in the 1980s.[1] By midsummer, polls showed Rizzo in a dead heat with Democratic candidate and former district attorney Ed Rendell. Several local media outlets started predicting a Rizzo victory. But, at seventy-one years of age, Rizzo's heavy campaign schedule took its toll. Following a massive heart attack, Frank Rizzo died on July 16, 1991.[2]

Two days later, thousands of onlookers filled the streets along the route of Rizzo's funeral procession. Lines formed outside the Basilica of Saints Peter and Paul, the city's largest Roman Catholic church in Center City Philadelphia. They waited over three hours in the sweltering July heat until Rizzo's open casket became available for public viewing. Philadelphia reporter Bill Baldini then captured the mood inside the basilica. Baldini listed those attending the services. He emphasized Rizzo's close relationship with his family. He named the fellow politicians that came to pay their respects. But those that would have really mattered to Rizzo, he said, sat in the church's first few pews. "The real dignitaries here are the policemen," he went on. Occupying the front pews were "chauffeurs, former policemen, firemen, working peo-ple. The dignitaries that normally would take the front rows are sitting in the back: the lawyers, the doctors, the Indian chiefs. That's Frank Rizzo. If he ever had a legacy, the legacy would be, he was, definitely, a man of the people."[3]

Baldini was only partly correct. Rizzo was never a man of all the people. He could rightfully claim identification and representation of Philadelphia's white, blue-collar urban neighborhoods, but his divisiveness ensured that his legacy would remain as controversial as his police and political career. Instead, Rizzo was a symbol for an era. He was a transitional figure that repre-sented legions of white, working- and middle-class Philadelphians and their counterparts across urban America. Together they initiated a blue-collar rev-olution that thoroughly transformed modern American politics. The effects of that revolution continue today.

The rise of blue-collar conservatism represented by Rizzo and his support-ers was a long process shaped by the restructuring of urban space and urban politics in the 1950s, forged in the urban crisis of the 1960s, and matured during the policy debates of the 1970s. It was also one of the most consequen-tial political turns in modern American history. It did not result simply from a blue-collar reaction against the perceived shortcomings of liberal politics and policies. As working-class and middle-income whites engaged the inter-secting politics of the urban crisis, they carefully and proactively negotiated their place within the changing politics of the era. Two decades of navigat-ing the politics of crime, housing, education, and employment culminated in blue-collar whites finding more commonality with conservatives than liber-als. Along with the conservative movements that remade the South, Sunbelt, and West, the blue-collar whites in the urban North helped usher in the con-servative ascendency that has dominated recent American political history.

The qualified, populist, center-right conservatism espoused by blue-collar whites in Frank Rizzo's Philadelphia became one of the most domi-nant modes of political thought in the modern United States. Even as Ronald Reagan symbolized the national shift to the right in the 1980s, blue-collar urbanites never fully rejected liberal economic policies like progressive taxa-tion, urban renewal, and state funding for education. Although they cheered when Reagan vilified welfare recipients or when Bill Clinton vowed to "end welfare as we know it," their acceptance of welfare state programs for peo-ple they deemed deserving proved more widespread and long lasting.[4] Blue-collar conservatives did not view the liberal governance of the 1960s as a failure. Instead, blue-collar whites' selective rejection of liberalism grew out of a belief that liberalism succeeded too well for the wrong people. How they determined who deserved the benefits of the welfare state, moreover, thoroughly imbued their nascent conservatism with the racial and class politics of the 1960s and 1970s.

Blue-collar whites made class a central aspect of their conservative politics, even as the racial fissures of the era marked every aspect of their political evolution, including their blue-collar identity politics. As well, many of those that claimed race did not matter to them genuinely were "color-blind." Some of them really did not think about race. For them, however, their color blindness was the ultimate luxury of their white privilege. They were the products of segregated environments that allowed them to mask their social privilege behind blue-collar identity politics and their veneer of color-blind values like toughness and hard work. The kind of white privilege they possessed was so intractable because it masqueraded as identity. Those with structural privilege were unwilling to admit that those privileges existed or recognize the disadvantages faced by those without structural privilege. Blue-collar whites like those in Frank Rizzo's Philadelphia believed they had earned rights through hard work that others—usually poor people of color—had not similarly earned. By engaging the politics of welfare and liberalism through the lens of hard work and handouts, blue-collar whites thoroughly conflated their white privilege with class privilege. That way of imagining privilege and disadvantage was by no means limited to postwar Philadelphia. But Frank Rizzo and his supporters created a time and place that allowed it to flourish. They also foreshadowed the antiwelfare policies that began in earnest during the Reagan era. Few blue-collar conservatives objected to the partial repeal of the New Deal welfare state because they had already deemed the poor undeserving of government assistance.

The selective rejection of the American welfare state was one arm of blue-collar conservatism's long influence. The militarization of police and rise of the carceral state was another. The white, blue-collar promotion of law enforcement conservatism laid the groundwork, and lent the political support, for the turn toward a more punitive criminal justice system and mass incarceration in modern America. Blue-collar whites reinforced and condoned the shift in law enforcement policy in the 1960s and 1970s. When police unions, police wives, and their blue-collar supporters clamored for law and order, harsher punishments, and greater legal protections for police officers, they not only demanded conservative criminal justice reform, they also prepared themselves to accept broader changes in American carceral policy. Policies and laws like Ronald Reagan's War on Drugs and Bill Clinton's Violent Crime Control and Law Enforcement Act dramatically increased the prison population in the United States, making it the largest in the world. These antidemocratic policies ultimately rested upon the kind of tacit and explicit approval that developed in places like Frank Rizzo's Philadelphia. The politicization of the white, blue-collar culture of reverence for the police represents a grassroots origin for the modern American carceral system and law enforcement conservatism.[5]

In addition to the policy implications of blue-collar conservatism, the blue-collar populism espoused by Frank Rizzo and his supporters also prefigured a dominant sensibility of modern American politicking. Rizzo's "one of us" populism was genuine, but the broader turn toward the politics of relatability in recent American history played on politicians' similar abilities to play the part of blue-collar populist. The veneration for hard work, support for law and order, and rhetorical turn toward color blindness and blue-collar identity at the heart of blue-collar conservatism were malleable and easily appropriated across class boundaries. Ronald Reagan understood this especially well. Reagan was adept at appropriating the rise of conservative populism that grew not only in Frank Rizzo's Philadelphia, but throughout blue-collar America. Before his presidency, in 1977, Reagan grounded his appeal to blue-collar whites in their class identity when he told a convention of conservative activists that the Republican Party needed to reach beyond the upper classes and big-business men. "The New Republican Party," he said, "is going to have room for the man and woman in the factories, for the farmer, for the cop on the beat and the millions of Americans who may never have thought of joining our party before, but whose interests coincide with those represented by principled Republicanism." Reagan said he wanted not only to "make room" for disaffected members of the working class, but make certain they "have a say in what goes on in the party."[6] After his election to the presidency, in 1981, he gave another speech before a convention of the United Brotherhood of Carpenters and Joiners in Chicago. He told the labor unionists that "working people in America value family, work, and neighborhood. These are things we have in common socially and politically."[7] Later in his presidency, when Reagan attacked welfare programs, he followed the blue-collar conservative formula. He did not engage in direct racial dialogues. Instead, he invoked the more indirect and subtle demonization of "welfare queens." The connotations were racialized and gendered, but the language spoke to the beleaguered working and middle classes that struggled in tough economic times through hard work. The antipoverty discourses of the 1980s played on a sense of class unfairness where those on the bottom dishonestly worked the system to reap advantages they did not earn.

Reagan's speeches showed a deep understanding of the way class and identity mattered to blue-collar Americans. The so-called Reagan Democrat responded to Reagan's welfare state reforms because he so successfully tapped into the blue-collar discourses on hard work and the undeserving poor. For Reagan, antipoverty politics worked not only to demonize the poor, they also enabled populist relatability. Reagan appealed to the same sense of blue-collar authenticity championed by Rizzo and his supporters. More recently, the politics of racially saturated class-forward populist conservatism found renewed currency in Donald Trump's 2016 campaign for the presidency.

Trump drew several comparisons to Frank Rizzo throughout his campaign, highlighting their similar political style and appeal to white, blue-collar voters.[8] Of course, there were countless differences between them. Most notably, Rizzo's blue-collar background was authentic, while Trump—the real estate mogul and reality television star—inherited much of his fortune. Even more than Reagan, Trump showed how far blue-collar populist sensibilities could be stretched beyond class barriers. Nevertheless, Trump and Rizzo shared a similar appeal to blue-collar whites. Like Rizzo, Trump's populism depended not just on what he said, but how he said it. Trump's campaign and debate styles were unpolished. He made a series of provocative statements and seemed to speak his mind regardless of the consequences. When Trump attacked his opponents with churlish nicknames or made exaggeratedly confrontational statements, his supporters rallied further behind him. They said they liked that he "told it like it is."[9] In Frank Rizzo's Philadelphia they might have said he sounded like "one of us." Indeed, despite his wealth and lavish lifestyle, Trump assumed the role of a blue-collar populist. Donald Trump Jr. even called his father a "blue-collar billionaire" at campaign stops in Des Moines and Pittsburgh.[10] As with Rizzo, "blue-collar" was less an indicator of Trump's class status than it was a statement of cultural identity and association. His "blue-collar billionaire" persona helped elevate him over more traditional Republican contenders in the primary election and illustrated the continued centrality of class politics and identities in modern conservatism.

The campaign stylings that helped Trump win the presidency in 2016 were born out of the rise of blue-collar conservatism in urban America during the 1960s and 1970s. Trump intentionally made provocative statements designed to capture the attention and energize blue-collar conservative sensibilities. His campaign also engaged the politics that had long animated blue-collar whites. As the Black Lives Matter movement spurred renewed national protests over police abuses and misconduct, Trump declared himself the "law-and-order" candidate. His invocation of 1960s-era law enforcement conservatism won him the endorsement of national police unions and supporters of the police that rallied around the slogan "Blue Lives Matter."[11] Like Rizzo, Trump capitalized on the widespread belief that urban police forces were under attack. Of course, urban America had changed dramatically between Rizzo and Trump. Despite being from New York City, Trump's greatest appeal in the 2016 election was in rural and suburban areas. He lost in almost all major American cities, including Philadelphia.[12] Yet he still engaged the politics of the urban crisis by repeatedly painting cities as mired in chaos and decline. He referred to inner cities as "a disaster" and racialized urban America by saying that "Our African-American communities are absolutely in the worst shape they've ever been in before. . . . You take a look at the inner cities, you get no education, you get no jobs, you get shot walking down the streets."[13] Trump's dire descriptions of urban America ignored steadily rising living standards and declining crime rates in the previous two decades.[14] Yet by stoking fears of urban America, he capitalized on the politics of the urban crisis that had animated blue-collar whites since the mid-twentieth century.

Trump's rehashing of law and order and the urban crisis made clear that his popularity rested on underlying racial resentments. Like Rizzo and his blue-collar supporters, however, Trump was loath to admit it. Much like Rizzo, Trump bragged and exaggerated on the campaign trail. For example, when confronted with accusations of racism for comments he made regarding Muslim and Mexican Americans, Trump replied with the hyperbolic claim that he was "the least racist person."[15] He adopted a color-blind veneer cloaked in blue-collar identity politics to avoid questions about his inflammatory rhetoric. Furthermore, as deindustrialization continued into the twenty-first century and the rise of globalization led to anxieties over economic uncertainty and national security, Trump exploited blue-collar grievances by lambasting the loss of manufacturing jobs and the fear of nonwhite immigrants. His campaign tapped into a wellspring of resentment that combined the politics of racial and class privilege. Yet there was more than just resentment behind Trump's appeal to blue-collar voters. Trump also extolled the virtues of blue-collar work like coal mining and promised an impossible return of industrial jobs that had succumbed to a combination of global competition, technological change, and automation. It was not simply an empty promise, however. Like Rizzo in the 1970s, Trump celebrated blue-collar pride, tradition, and hard work.

Shortly after Trump's victory, focus turned toward his ability to court the "white working class." In fact, not all, or even most, of Trump's voters were traditionally "working class."[16] While no one class was responsible for Trump's victory, he did engage the malleable blue-collar politics that propelled working- and middle-class populism since the 1960s. Even still, two competing narratives emerged to explain Trump's success with these blue-collar politics. One focused on racial resentment and the other on economic anxiety. The example of Frank Rizzo's white, blue-collar supporters shows that dichotomy to be false. White, blue-collar Philadelphians in the 1960s and 1970s were motivated both by racial resentment and by perceived economic anxiety. They were both economically vulnerable and opposed to liberal policies designed to aid people of color. One did not preclude the other. Race and class were not mutually exclusive in Frank Rizzo's Philadelphia. Nor were they during the 2016 election. The combination of race, class, and urban politics created blue-collar conservatism. In the ensuing decades it grew beyond its urban spaces. Donald Trump's 2016 campaign showed that a similar politics rooted in racially bound class identities still resonated. Indeed, it suggested that blue-collar conservatism had become more than one of many American conservatisms. In 2016, it became a dominant variant of modern American conservatism.

ABBREVIATIONS

ADAP   Americans for Democratic Action, Southeastern Pennsyl-
            vania Chapter Papers, Special Collections Research Center,
            Temple University Libraries, Philadelphia, Pennsylvania
ATC   Arlene Tyner Collection, Special Collections Research Cen-
            ter, Temple University Libraries, Philadelphia, Pennsylvania
BBMAP   Bridesburg Business Men's Association Papers, Special
            Collections Research Center, Temple University Libraries,
            Philadelphia, Pennsylvania
CCCPP   Citizens Committee on City Planning Papers, Special
            Collections Research Center, Temple University Libraries,
            Philadelphia, Pennsylvania
CCPEP   Citizens Committee on Public Education Papers, Special
            Collections Research Center, Temple University Libraries,
            Philadelphia, Pennsylvania
CCPR   Crime Commission of Philadelphia Records, Special Collec-
            tions Research Center, Temple University Libraries, Phila-
            delphia, Pennsylvania
CFFR   City Fire Fighters, International Association of Fire Fight-
            ers Local 22 Records, 1929–1978, Special Collections
            Research Center, Temple University Libraries, Philadelphia,
            Pennsylvania
CHRT   Commission on Human Relations, Public Hearing Tran-
            scripts, 1959–1974, Philadelphia City Archives, Philadel-
            phia, Pennsylvania
CLSR   Community Legal Services Records, Special Collections
            Research Center, Temple University Libraries, Philadelphia,
            Pennsylvania
DN   *Philadelphia Daily News*

EMPAC   Ethnic Millions Political Action Committee, Collection 3094, Historical Society of Pennsylvania, Philadelphia, Pennsylvania

ENBP   Edmund Norwood Bacon Papers, Architectural Archives, University of Pennsylvania, Philadelphia, Pennsylvania

FCR   Fellowship Commission Records, Special Collections Research Center, Temple University Libraries, Philadelphia, Pennsylvania

FLP   Floyd Logan Papers, Special Collections Research Center, Temple University Libraries, Philadelphia, Pennsylvania

FLR   Mayor's Correspondence and Files, Administration of Frank L. Rizzo, Record Group 60-2.6, City of Philadelphia, Department of Records, City Archives, Philadelphia City Archives, Philadelphia, Pennsylvania

GJSM   Giordano J. Scopinich Memoirs, Collection 3113, Historical Society of Pennsylvania, Philadelphia, Pennsylvania

GPC   General Pamphlet Collection, Special Collections Research Center, Temple University Libraries, Philadelphia, Pennsylvania

HADVR   Housing Association of the Delaware Valley Records, Special Collections Research Center, Temple University Libraries, Philadelphia, Pennsylvania

HSCPR   Home and School Council of Philadelphia Records, Special Collections Research Center, Temple University Libraries, Philadelphia, Pennsylvania

JCAP   John C. Anderson Papers, Special Collections Research Center, Temple University Libraries, Philadelphia, Pennsylvania

JHJT   Mayor's Correspondence and Files, Administration of James H. J. Tate, Record Group 60-2.5, City of Philadelphia, Department of Records, City Archives, Philadelphia City Archives, Philadelphia, Pennsylvania

JLCR   Jewish Labor Committee Collection, Special Collections Research Center, Temple University Libraries, Philadelphia, Pennsylvania

JLZP   Joseph L. Zazyczny Papers, MSS 136, Historical Society of Pennsylvania, Philadelphia, Pennsylvania

LPR   Latino Project Records, MSS 117, Historical Society of Pennsylvania, Philadelphia, Pennsylvania

NAACP-6   National Association for the Advancement of Colored People, Philadelphia Branch Records, URB 6, Special Collections Research Center, Temple University Libraries, Philadelphia, Pennsylvania

NOW-PC   National Organization for Women, Philadelphia Chapter Records, Historical Society of Pennsylvania, Philadelphia, Pennsylvania

NPCCR   Northeast Philadelphia Chamber of Commerce Records, Special Collections Research Center, Temple University Libraries, Philadelphia, Pennsylvania

NT   *Northeast Times*

NYT   *New York Times*

PABR   Police Advisory Board Records, Special Collections Research Center, Temple University Libraries, Philadelphia, Pennsylvania

PAHRC   Philadelphia Archdiocesan Historical Research Center, Wynnewood, Pennsylvania

PBCC   *Philadelphia Bulletin* Clippings Collection, Special Collections Research Center, Temple University Libraries, Philadelphia, Pennsylvania

PBP   Peter Binzen Papers, Special Collections Research Center, Temple University Libraries, Philadelphia, Pennsylvania

PBRR   Philadelphia Board of Realtors Records, Special Collections Research Center, Temple University Libraries, Philadelphia, Pennsylvania

PC   *Philadelphia Courier*

PCA   City of Philadelphia, Department of Records, City Archives, Philadelphia City Archives, Philadelphia, Pennsylvania

PCAFL-CIO   Philadelphia Council, American Federation of Labor and Congress of Industrial Organizations Records, Special Collections Research Center, Temple University Libraries, Philadelphia, Pennsylvania

PCPCF   Philadelphia City Planning Commission Files, Record Group 145.2, City of Philadelphia, Department of Records, City Archives, Philadelphia City Archives, Philadelphia, Pennsylvania

PEB   *Philadelphia Evening Bulletin*

PFTP   Philadelphia Federation of Teachers, American Feder-
                ation of Teachers Local #3 Papers, Special Collections
                Research Center, Temple University Libraries, Philadelphia,
                Pennsylvania
PI   *Philadelphia Inquirer*
PILCP   Public Interest Law Center of Philadelphia Oral History
                Project, Special Collections Research Center, Temple
                University Libraries, Philadelphia, Pennsylvania
PJT   *Philadelphia Jewish Times*
PM   *Philadelphia Magazine*
PPD-DB   Philadelphia Police Department, Detective Bureau, White
                Papers, Nov. 1983–Dec. 1984, RG 79.43, Philadelphia City
                Archives, Philadelphia, Pennsylvania
PSICR   Philadelphia Special Investigation (MOVE) Commission
                Records, Special Collections Research Center, Temple
                University Libraries, Philadelphia, Pennsylvania
RDP   Richardson Dilworth Papers, Collection 3112, Historical
                Society of Pennsylvania, Philadelphia, Pennsylvania
RRC   Ruben Reina Collection: Student Papers in Anthropology,
                MSS 83, Historical Society of Pennsylvania, Philadelphia,
                Pennsylvania
RSSP   Richard S. Schweiker Papers, Historical Collections and
                Labor Archives, Special Collections Library, Pennsylvania
                State University, University Park, Pennsylvania
SCRC   Special Collections Research Center, Temple University
                Libraries, Philadelphia, Pennsylvania
SPR   *South Philadelphia Review*
SSP   Stefan Solokowski Papers, MSS 176, Historical Society of
                Pennsylvania, Philadelphia, Pennsylvania
TLUP   Tile Layers Union Local 6 Papers, Special Collections
                Research Center, Temple University Libraries, Philadelphia,
                Pennsylvania
WC-332   Whitman Council Records, Accession 332, Special Collec-
                tions Research Center, Temple University Libraries, Phila-
                delphia, Pennsylvania
WC-523   Whitman Council Records, Accession 523, Special Collec-
                tions Research Center, Temple University Libraries, Phila-
                delphia, Pennsylvania

WC-632   Whitman Council Records, Accession 632, Special Collec-
           tions Research Center, Temple University Libraries, Phila-
           delphia, Pennsylvania
WC-638   Whitman Council Records, Accession 638, Special Collec-
           tions Research Center, Temple University Libraries, Phila-
           delphia, Pennsylvania
WJG   Mayor's Correspondence and Files, Administration of Wil-
           liam J. Green III, Record Group 60-2.7, City of Philadelphia,
           Department of Records, City Archives, Philadelphia City
           Archives, Philadelphia, Pennsylvania
WOARR   Women Organized Against Rape Records, Special Collec-
           tions Research Center, Temple University Libraries, Phila-
           delphia, Pennsylvania
WP   *Washington Post*
WPOHP   Walter Phillips Oral History Project, Special Collections
           Research Center, Temple University Libraries, Philadelphia,
           Pennsylvania
WSJ   Wall Street Journal

NOTES

Introduction

1. Joseph F. Lowry, "2,000 Cheer Columbus and Rizzo in South Phila.," *PEB*, October 12, 1971, PBCC; Sandy Grady, "Rizzo Hailed, Intellectuals Rapped in S. Phila. Bar," *PEB*, October 12, 1971, PBCC.

2. S. A. Paolantonio, *Frank Rizzo: The Last Big Man in Big City America*, 10th anniversary ed. (Philadelphia: Camino Books, 2003); Daniel J. McKenna, "Rizzo Defends Tough Stand on Criminals," *PEB*, October 11, 1967, PBCC.

3. Paolantonio, *Rizzo*, 229.

4. Sandra Featherman, *Jews, Blacks and Ethnics: The 1978 "Vote White" Charter Campaign in Philadelphia* (New York: American Jewish Committee, 1979).

5. Joseph R. Daughen and Peter Binzen, *The Cop Who Would Be King: Mayor Frank Rizzo* (Boston: Little, Brown, 1977); Bill Biggin, *Rizzo and the Police State* (Philadelphia: Freedom Press, 1971); Fred Hamilton, *Rizzo: From Cop to Mayor of Philadelphia* (New York: Viking Books, 1973); Paul Lyons, *The People of This Generation: The New Left in Philadelphia* (Philadelphia: University of Pennsylvania Press, 2003).

6. Paolantonio, *Rizzo*; Daughen and Binzen, *The Cop Who Would Be King*; Hamilton, *Rizzo*.

7. Mary C. Brennan, *Turning Right in the Sixties: The Conservative Capture of the GOP* (Chapel Hill: University of North Carolina Press, 1995); Dan T. Carter, *From George Wallace to Newt Gingrich: Race in the Conservative Counterrevolution, 1963–1994* (Baton Rouge: Louisiana State University Press, 1996); Donald T. Critchlow, *The Conservative Ascendency: How the GOP Right Made Political History* (Cambridge, MA: Harvard University Press, 2007); Godfrey Hodgson, *The World Turned Right Side Up: A History of the Conservative Ascendency in America* (New York: Houghton Mifflin, 1996).

8. Nancy MacLean, *Freedom Is Not Enough: The Opening of the American Workplace* (Cambridge, MA: Harvard University Press, 2008), 101–102; Rick Perlstein, *Nixonland: The Rise of a President and the Fracturing of America* (New York: Scribner, 2008), 497–499.

9. Thomas J. Sugrue, *Origins of the Urban Crisis: Race and Inequality in Postwar Detroit* (Princeton, NJ: Princeton University Press, 1996).

10. James Wolfinger, *Philadelphia Divided: Race and Politics in the City of Brotherly Love* (Chapel Hill: University of North Carolina Press, 2007); Guian A. McKee, *The Problem of Jobs: Liberalism, Race, and Deindustrialization in Philadelphia* (Chicago: University of Chicago Press, 2008); Stefano Luconi, *From Paesani to White Ethnics: The Italian Experience in Philadelphia* (Albany: State University of New York Press, 2001).

11. Thomas Byrne Edsall and Mary D. Edsall, *Chain Reaction: The Impact of Race, Rights, and Taxes on American Politics* (New York: W.W. Norton, 1991); Jonathan Rieder, *Canarsie: The*

Jews and Italians of Brooklyn Against Liberalism (Cambridge, MA: Harvard University Press, 1985); Jim Sleeper, *The Closest of Strangers: Liberalism and the Politics of Race in New York City* (New York: W. W. Norton, 1999). On shifts in conservative movement historiography see Darren Dochuk, "Revival on the Right: Making Sense of the Conservative Movement in Post–World War II American History," *History Compass* 4, no. 5 (2006): 975–979; Kim Phillips-Fein, "Conservatism: A State of the Field," *Journal of American History* 98, no. 3 (December 2011): 723–743.

12. Sugrue, *Origins of the Urban Crisis*; Wolfinger, *Philadelphia Divided*; Arnold Hirsch, *Making the Second Ghetto: Race and Housing in Chicago, 1940–1960* (Cambridge: Cambridge University Press, 1983); Ronald P. Formisano, *Boston Against Busing: Race, Class, and Ethnicity in the 1960s and 1970s* (Chapel Hill: University of North Carolina Press, 1991); Kenneth D. Durr, *Behind the Backlash: White Working-Class Politics in Baltimore, 1940–1980* (Chapel Hill: University of North Carolina Press, 2003).

13. Jefferson Cowie, *The Great Exception: The New Deal and the Limits of American Politics* (Princeton, NJ: Princeton University Press, 2016); Steve Fraser and Gary Gerstle, eds., *The Rise and Fall of the New Deal Order, 1930–1980* (Princeton, NJ: Princeton University Press, 1989).

14. Lisa McGirr, *Suburban Warriors: The Origins of the New American Right* (Princeton, NJ: Princeton University Press, 2001); Kevin M. Kruse, *White Flight: Atlanta and the Making of Modern Conservatism* (Princeton, NJ: Princeton University Press, 2005); Matthew Lassiter, *The Silent Majority: Suburban Politics in the Sunbelt South* (Princeton, NJ: Princeton University Press, 2006).

15. Kevin M. Kruse, *One Nation Under God: How Corporate America Invented Christian America* (New York: Basic Books, 2014); Darren Dochuk, *From Bible Belt to Sunbelt: Plain-Folk Religion, Grassroots Politics, and the Rise of Evangelical Conservatism* (New York: W. W. Norton, 2012).

16. Jennifer Burns, *Goddess of the Right: Ayn Rand and the American Right* (New York: Oxford University Press, 2011).

17. Andrew Hartman, *A War for the Soul of America: A History of the Culture Wars* (Chicago: University of Chicago Press, 2015), 5–6, 21–28.

18. Matthew Frye Jacobson, *Roots Too: White Ethnic Revival in Post–Civil Rights America* (Cambridge, MA: Harvard University Press, 2006).

19. Jefferson Cowie, *Stayin' Alive: The 1970s and the Last Days of the Working Class* (New York: New Press, 2010). As Cowie argues elsewhere, "While the reality of the working class in the 1970s was increasingly multiracial and multicultural by any objective measure, the *idea* of the working class in the popular idiom had, by the 1980s, devolved even further into a repository for patriarchy and racism." See Jefferson Cowie and Lauren Boehm, "Dead Man's Town: 'Born in the U.S.A.,' Social History, and Working-Class Identity," *American Quarterly* 58, no. 2 (June 2006): 353–378, 357.

20. Lassiter, *The Silent Majority*; Kruse, *White Flight*; Joseph Crespino, *In Search of Another Country: Mississippi and the Conservative Counterrevolution* (Princeton, NJ: Princeton University Press, 2007); Michael K. Brown et al., *Whitewashing Race: The Myth of a Color-Blind Society* (Berkeley: University of California Press, 2003); Christopher Bonastia, *Knocking on the Door: The Federal Government's Attempt to Desegregate the Suburbs* (Princeton, NJ: Princeton University Press, 2006).

21. MacLean, *Freedom Is Not Enough*, 225–236, 230.

22. Peter Binzen, *Whitetown USA* (New York: Vintage Books, 1971), 27–29.

23. Michael W. Flamm, *Law and Order: Street Crime, Civil Unrest, and the Crisis of American Liberalism in the 1960s* (New York: Columbia University Press, 2005).

24. Dan T. Carter, *The Politics of Rage: George Wallace, the Origins of the New Conservatism, and the Transformation of American Politics*, 2nd ed. (Baton Rouge: Louisiana State University Press, 2000); Michael Kazin, *The Populist Persuasion: An American History*, rev. ed. (Ithaca, NY: Cornell University Press, 1998).

25. Michael B. Katz, "Why Don't American Cities Burn Very Often?" *Journal of Urban History* 34, no. 2 (January 2008): 185–208, 200.

26. Elizabeth Hinton, *From the War on Poverty to the War on Crime: The Making of Mass Incarceration in America* (Cambridge, MA: Harvard University Press, 2016).

27. Matthew Countryman, *Up South: Civil Rights and Black Power in Philadelphia* (Philadelphia: University of Pennsylvania Press, 2006); Thomas J. Sugrue, *Sweet Land of Liberty: The Forgotten Struggle for Civil Rights in the North* (New York: Random House, 2008); Robert O. Self, *American Babylon: Race and the Struggle for Postwar Oakland* (Princeton, NJ: Princeton University Press, 2003); Jacquelyn Dowd Hall, "The Long Civil Rights Movement and the Political Uses of the Past," *Journal of American History* 94, no. 1 (March 2005): 1233–1263.

28. Formisano, *Boston Against Busing*; Dennis DeSlippe, *Protesting Affirmative Action: The Struggle over Equality After the Civil Rights Revolution* (Baltimore: Johns Hopkins University Press, 2012).

29. Karen Benjamin, "Suburbanizing Jim Crow: The Impact of School Policy on Residential Segregation in Raleigh," *Journal of Urban History* 38 (March 2012): 225–246. Ira Katznelson argues that urban working-class culture was distinctive because of the separation of work and neighborhood. As Benjamin shows, however, the politics of school and housing were too closely tied to consider separately. See Ira Katznelson, *City Trenches: Urban Politics and the Patterning of Class in the United States* (Chicago: University of Chicago Press, 1981).

30. J. Joseph Huthmacher, "Urban Liberalism and the Age of Reform," *Mississippi Valley Historical Review* 49, no. 2 (September 1962): 231–241; John D. Fairfield, *The Public and Its Possibilities: Triumphs and Tragedies in the American City* (Philadelphia: Temple University Press, 2010); Christopher Klemek, *The Transatlantic Collapse of Urban Renewal: Postwar Urbanism from New York to Berlin* (Chicago: University of Chicago Press, 2011), 6–13.

31. While this book follows a standard periodization of civil rights movement history—from gradualism to Black Power—because that is how white, blue-collar Philadelphians experienced it, recent scholarship finds the Black Power movement far more complex and deeply rooted. See Peniel Joseph, *Waiting 'til the Midnight Hour: A Narrative History of Black Power in America* (New York: Henry Holt, 2006).

32. Howard Gillette Jr., "The Emergence of the Modern Metropolis: Philadelphia in the Age of Its Consolidation," in William W. Cutler III and Howard Gillette Jr., eds., *The Divided Metropolis: Social and Spatial Dimensions of Philadelphia, 1800–1975* (Westport, CT: Greenwood Press, 1980).

33. Wolfinger, *Philadelphia Divided*, 16–18; Meredith Savery, "Instability and Uniformity: Two Philadelphia Neighborhoods, 1880–1970," in Cutler and Gillette, *The Divided Metropolis*, 193–194.

34. Frederic Miller, Morris J. Vogel, and Allen F. Davis, *Philadelphia Stories: A Photographic History, 1920–1960* (Philadelphia: Temple University Press, 1988), 3–6.

35. Ibid., 191–193.

36. William J. Speers, "Rizzo for Mayor? Not Running, but Walking Fast," *PI*, February 8, 1970.

37. Paolantonio, *Rizzo*, 155.

Chapter 1

1. Charles Shaw, "The Jungle: Seven Square Miles That Shame—and Menace—Our City," *PEB*, February 3, 1957, PBCC.

2. Anne E. Hellyer, "Kensington and Richmond Are Proud of Their Homes," *PEB*, February 17, 1957, PBCC.

3. Hellyer, "Kensington and Richmond Are Proud of Their Homes."

4. Ibid.

5. Ibid.; "Bridesburg: Where Everybody Knows and Helps His Neighbor," *PEB*, March 11, 1951, PBCC; Philip B. Schaeffer, "Mayfair Grew Up Rapidly, but Civic Pride Kept Pace," *PEB*, March 25, 1951, PBCC; "Port Richmond—a Proud Neighborhood Where Big Industry Hums," *PEB*, June 3, 1951, PBCC; Rex Polier, "People Take Intense Pride in Their Homes," *PEB*, August 12, 1951, PBCC; Adolph Katz, "The Silk Stocking Wealth Is Gone but New Plants Bustle in Northeast," *PEB*, March 10, 1961, PBCC; "Kensington Says It Is NOT a Slum Area," *PI*, August 16, 1964, PBCC.

6. Julilly Kohler-Hausman, "Miltarizing the Police: Officer Jon Burge, Torture, and the War in the 'Urban Jungle,'" in Stephen J. Hartnett, ed., *Challenging the Prison-Industrial Complex: Activism, Arts, and Educational Awareness* (Urbana: University of Illinois Press, 2011), 47–57.

7. Guian A. McKee, *The Problem of Jobs: Liberalism, Race, and Deindustrialization in Philadelphia* (Chicago: University of Chicago Press, 2008).

8. Ibid., 20–22.

9. Charles L. Crangle, "Philadelphia Tomorrow," *U.S.A. Tomorrow*, October 1954, Folder 9, Box 507, GPC.

10. Ibid.; City Planning Commission, *The Better Philadelphia Exhibition* (Philadelphia: City Planning Commission, 1947); John Bauman, *Public Housing, Race, and Renewal: Urban Planning in Philadelphia, 1920–1970* (Philadelphia: Temple University Press, 1987), 100; Carolyn Teich Adams, *The Politics of Capital Investment: The Case of Philadelphia* (Philadelphia: Temple University Press, 1988), 30–32.

11. Crangle, "Philadelphia Tomorrow."

12. Joseph D. Crumlish, *A City Finds Itself: The Philadelphia Home Rule Charter Movement* (Detroit: Wayne State University Press, 1959), 12–14.

13. Bauman, *Public Housing*, 100, 119–121; Kirk Petshek, *The Challenge of Urban Reform: Policies and Programs in Philadelphia* (Philadelphia: Temple University Press, 1973).

14. Crumlish, *A City*, 84–85.

15. Ibid., 79–96.

16. James Wolfinger, *Philadelphia Divided: Race and Politics in the City of Brotherly Love* (Chapel Hill: University of North Carolina Press, 2007), 212–241; Matthew J. Countryman, *Up South: Civil Rights and Black Power in Philadelphia* (Philadelphia: University of Pennsylvania Press, 2005), 58–59.

17. Joseph S. Clark Jr. and Dennis J. Clark, "Rally and Relapse," in Russell F. Weigley, ed., *Philadelphia: A 300 Year History* (New York: W. W. Norton, 1982), 650–661.

18. Abigail Perkiss, *Making Good Neighbors: Civil Rights, Liberalism, and Integration in Postwar Philadelphia* (Ithaca, NY: Cornell University Press, 2014), 38–39; Thomas J. Sugrue, *Origins*

of the Urban Crisis: Race and Inequality in Postwar Detroit (Princeton, NJ: Princeton University Press, 1996), 224–225.

19. Interview with George Schermer, May 2, 1976, Box 4A, WPOHP.

20. Hannah Lees, "How Philadelphia Stopped a Race Riot," *Reporter*, June 2, 1955, Box 184, Folder 12, GPC; Wolfinger, *Philadelphia Divided*, 183–184; Stanley Keith Arnold, *Building the Beloved Community: Philadelphia's Interracial Civil Rights Organizations and Race Relations, 1930–1970* (Oxford: University Press of Mississippi, 2014), 97–98.

21. Lees, "How Philadelphia Stopped a Race Riot."

22. Ibid; Wolfinger, *Philadelphia Divided*, 185.

23. Christopher Klemek, *The Transatlantic Collapse of Urban Renewal: Postwar Urbanism from New York to Berlin* (Chicago: University of Chicago Press, 2011), 68–77.

24. "Philadelphia's New Problem," *Time*, February 24, 1958; Peter Binzen and Jonathan Binzen, *Richardson Dilworth: Last of the Bare-Knuckled Aristocrats* (Philadelphia: Camino Books, 2014), 145–146.

25. Richardson Dilworth to Time, Inc., February, 1958, Folder 4, Box 42, FLP.

26. United States Commission on Civil Rights, *Housing: 1961 Commission on Civil Rights Report*, Report (United States Commission on Civil Rights), 1961, book 4 (Washington, DC, 1961); Robert O. Self, *American Babylon: Race and the Struggle for Postwar Oakland* (Princeton, NJ: Princeton University Press, 2003), 256–290, 370n.; Thomas J. Sugrue, *Sweet Land of Liberty: The Forgotten Struggle for Civil Rights in the North* (New York: Random House, 2008), xxiv.

27. Wolfinger, *Philadelphia Divided*, 178–179, 191–197.

28. Philadelphia was primarily a black and white city in the postwar era. By 1960, African Americans made up 99 percent of all nonwhites. Latinos, especially Puerto Ricans, were a rising minority. As were Asian immigrants after 1965. But combined they made up less than 1 percent of the population until the 1970s. As a result, most Philadelphians conceived of urban space in black and white terms. See Commission on Human Relations, "These Are the Facts about Negroes and Puerto Ricans in Philadelphia," 1960, Box 555, GPC.

29. David M. Freund, *Colored Property: State Policy and White Racial Politics in the Suburbs* (New York: New Press, 2009); Christopher Bonastia, *Knocking on the Door: The Federal Government's Attempt to Desegregate the Suburbs* (Princeton, NJ: Princeton University Press, 2006).

30. Klemek, *Transatlantic Collapse*, 21–78.

31. Bauman, *Public Housing*, 93–95.

32. Gregory L. Heller, "Salesman of Ideas: The Life Experiences That Shaped Edmund Bacon," in Scott Gabriel Knowles, ed., *Imagining Philadelphia: Edmund Bacon and the Future of the City* (Philadelphia: University of Pennsylvania Press, 2009), 28–34.

33. Heller, "Salesman of Ideas," 42–44.

34. Henry S. Churchill et al., "A Statement on Housing and Urban Renewal Policy for Philadelphia," October 1955, Box 729, GPC.

35. Bauman, *Public Housing*, 181–182; Klemek, *Transatlantic Collapse*, 70–74; Heller, "Salesman of Ideas," 42–44.

36. S. A. Paolantonio, *Frank Rizzo: The Last Big Man in Big City America*, 10th anniversary ed. (Philadelphia: Camino Books, 2003), 25–32, 44–50.

37. Guian McKee, "Liberal Ends Through Illiberal Means: Race, Urban Renewal, and Community in the Eastwick Section of Philadelphia, 1949–1990," *Journal of Urban History* 27 (2001): 547–583.

38. Timothy J. Lombardo, "The Battle of Whitman Park: Race, Class, and Public Housing in Philadelphia, 1956–1982," *Journal of Social History* 47, no. 2 (Winter 2013): 401–428.

39. Redevelopment Authority Planning Division, South Philadelphia Area, Summary of Housing Characteristics, April 29, 1957, Folder: Housing, Box 1, WC-332; "Southeast Phila. Area Set for Redevelopment," *PEB*, December 4, 1957, PBCC; "City Seeks Survey Funds to Redevelop 264 Acres," *PEB*, February 13, 1958, PBCC.

40. Francis J. Lammer to Edmund N. Bacon, November 20, 1957, Folder: Redevelopment—Whitman 1957-1964, Box A-2953, PCPCF; Edmund N. Bacon to Francis J. Lammer, December 6, 1957, Folder: Redevelopment—Whitman 1957-1964, Box A-2953, PCPCF; City Planning Commission, Whitman Redevelopment Area, December 10, 1957, Folder: Redevelopment—Whitman 1957-1964, Box A-2953, PCPCF.

41. Redevelopment Authority Planning Division, South Philadelphia Area, Summary of Housing Characteristics, April 29, 1957, Folder: Housing, Box 1, WC-332; Lewis J. Carter, "Urban Renewal and Non-White Families in Philadelphia," A Statement of Facts and Opinions to be presented to the National Urban League's Renewal Institute, April 16, 1956, Box 74, GPC.

42. Southwark Community Council, Copy of Letters Sent to William Rafsky, Paul D'Ortona, and Thomas M. Foglietta, April 9, 1957, Folder: Southwark Community Council, Box 3, WC-332; Conservation Program of the Redevelopment Authority of the City of Philadelphia, January 1962, Box 80, GPC.

43. Community Council General Meeting Minutes, May 7, 1957, Folder: Southwark Community Council, Box 3, WC-332; Minutes, Urban Renewal Committee, Southwark Community Council, July 25, 1957, Folder: Jacob, Morris, Box 1, WC-332.

44. "Great Strides by Northeast Made in 5 Years," *Public Ledger*, January 9, 1927, PBCC; Harry C. Silcox and Frank W. Hollingsworth, *Northeast Philadelphia: A Brief History* (Charleston, SC: History Press, 2009); Stephen G. Kidd, "Design of Markets: Social Division and the Progressive Design of Northeast Philadelphia, 1900–1960" (PhD diss., George Washington University, 2002).

45. Kidd, "Design of Markets," 153–184; Harry Harris, "Three-Quarters of All City Construction Going On in Northeast—Room for at Least Half-Million Seen," *PEB*, August 30, 1947, PBCC; Charles W. Biddle, "Huge Growth Forecast for Mayfair Section," *PEB*, November 5, 1949, PBCC.

46. "Meaning of 'Greater Northeast,'" *PEB*, August 1, 1947, PBCC; Adolph Katz, "The Northeast: A Boom Town Is Growing Up," *PEB*, March 9, 1961, PBCC.

47. Torresdale Delaware River Report, January 23, 1956, Folder: Planning—Neighborhood—Northeast, Box A-2905, PCPCF; Resume of Development in the Far Northeast, March 13, 1956, Folder: Planning—Neighborhood—Northeast, Box A-2905, PCPCF; Larry Reich, Memorandum for Files, January 16, 1957, Folder: Planning—Neighborhood—Northeast, Box A-2905, PCPCF.

48. McKee, *Problem of Jobs*, 41–82.

49. Ibid; Katz, "The Silk Stocking Wealth Is Gone but New Plants Bustle in Northeast," *PEB*, March 10, 1961, PBCC; Adolph Katz, "The Northeast: A Boom Town Is Growing Up," *PEB*, March 9, 1961, PBCC. On deindustrialization, see Sugrue, *Origins of the Urban Crisis*, 125–152.

50. Torresdale Delaware River Report, January 23, 1956, Folder: Planning—Neighborhood—Northeast, Box A-2905, PCPCF.

51. Kidd, "Design of Markets," 172; Heller, "Salesman of Ideas," 39–42; Guian A. McKee, "A Utopian, a Utopianist, or Whatever the Heck It Is," in Scott Gabriel Knowles, ed., *Imagining*

Philadelphia: Edmund Bacon and the Future of the City (Philadelphia: University of Pennsylvania Press, 2009), 53–58; Klemek, *Transatlantic Collapse*, 70–80.

52. Morrell Park Map, undated, Folder B.13, Box 53, Series IV, Collection 292, ENBP; Mr. Irving Pitchnick to E. H. Bacon, February 16, 1957, Folder: Planning—Neighborhood— Northeast, Box A-2905, PCPCF; David F. Luithlen to Richardson Dilworth, February 21, 1957, Folder: Planning—Neighborhood—Northeast, Box A-2905, PCPCF.

53. Adolph Katz, "The Kitchen Is at the Front Door in Northeast's Gift to Row Housing," *PEB*, March 12, 1961, PBCC; Heller, "Salesman of Ideas," 39–42; Kidd, "Design of Markets," 171–173.

54. "Space Is a Big Feature of Morrell Park Homes," *PEB*, January 20, 1963, PBCC.

55. Katz, "The Northeast: A Boom Town Is Growing Up"; Kidd, "Design of Markets," 185–187.

56. Lewis J. Carter, "Urban Renewal and Non-White Families in Philadelphia," A Statement of Facts and Opinions to be presented to the National Urban League's Renewal Institute, April 16, 1956, Box 74, GPM; McKee, "A Utopian," 58–61; Bauman, *Public Housing*, 149–151; Lisa Levenstein, *A Movement Without Marches: African American Women and the Politics of Poverty in Postwar Philadelphia* (Chapel Hill: University of North Carolina Press, 2009), 11.

57. "U.S. Approves Phila. Program to Clear Slums," *PEB*, February 9, 1955, PBCC; "2,000 Families Must Move for Phila. Projects," *PEB*, March 20, 1955, PBCC.

58. Countryman, *Up South*, 52–71; Carter, "Urban Renewal and Non-White Families in Philadelphia"; Characteristics of the Residential Relocatee, 1958–1962, City of Philadelphia Community Renewal Program, 1964, Box 599, GPC.

59. Leon H. Sullivan, *Build Brother Build* (Philadelphia: Macrae Smith, 1969), 57–58.

60. Commission on Human Relations, "These Are the Facts about Negroes and Puerto Ricans in Philadelphia"; Countryman, *Up South*, 51–57.

61. Countryman, *Up South*, 53–71.

62. Katz, "The Northeast: A Boom Town Is Growing Up."

63. "Bridesburg: Where Everybody Knows and Helps His Neighbor," *PEB*, March 11, 1951, PBCC.

64. John Lukacs, *Philadelphia: Patricians and Philistines, 1900–1950* (New York: Farrar, Straus, Giroux, 1980), 310–313.

65. "Port Richmond—a Proud Neighborhood Where Big Industry Hums," *PEB*, June 3, 1951, PBCC; Katz, "The Silk Stocking Wealth Is Gone but New Plants Bustle in Northeast," *PEB*, March 10, 1961, PBCC.

66. "People Take Intense Pride in Their Homes," *PEB*, August 12, 1951, PBCC; Philip B. Schaeffer, "Mayfair Grew Up Rapidly, But Civic Pride Kept Pace."

67. Moran quoted in Kidd, "Design of Markets," 168–169.

68. Katz, "The Northeast: A Boom Town Is Growing Up."

69. Hugh E. Flaherty, "Old Men Fight to Save the Old Life, but Their Sons Move to the Suburbs," *PEB*, August 14, 1962, PBCC.

70. Commission on Human Relations, "These Are the Facts about Negroes and Puerto Ricans in Philadelphia."

71. Memorandum from George Schermer to Community, Civic, and Religious Leaders RE: Subject Matter, Purposes and General Plan for a Clinical Inquiry into Incidents of Intimidation and Mob Pressure Forcing Minority Families to Vacate their Homes, December 8, 1960, Folder 36, Box 12, PBRR.

72. Ibid.

73. Pennypack Woods Home Ownership Association Information Sheet, no date, Folder 106, Box 12, CCCPP; Sugrue, *Sweet Land of Liberty*, 236.

74. Andrew W. Nix & Calvin Hall v. Morrell Park Homes, Investigative Hearing before Philadelphia Commission on Human Relations, December 18, 1959, Box A-2843, RG148.8, CHRT.

75. "Builder Admits Issuing Order Banning Sale of New Homes to Negroes," *PC*, January 2, 1960.

76. Statement of Policy issued by the Philadelphia Northeast Realty Board, 1960, Folder 36, Box 12, PBRR.

77. "Civil Rights and the White Majority," *NT*, August 1, 1963; "Plan to Move Negroes to NE Subject of Talks," *NT*, October 17, 1963.

78. Bauman, *Public Housing*, 127–130.

79. "Oxford Village Ban Is Asked," *PEB*, January 10, 1958, PBCC; "300 Protest Oxford Project," *PEB*, February 26, 1958, PBCC; Edward J. Tyburski, "Summerdale Threatens Vote Reprisal Unless Green Halts Low-Rent Project," *PEB*, April 2, 1958, PBCC; "Housing Limit 'Promised' in NE," *PEB*, April 10, 1959, PBCC; "Green Joins Opposition to Oxford Village Project," *PEB*, May 6, 1958, PBCC; Joseph M. Guess, "98 Row Homes May Make History: Fast, Cheap, Livable Public Housing," *PEB*, October 18, 1959, PBCC; Commission on Human Relations, Johnson Report, 1957, Box 439, Folder 3, GPM.

80. Commission on Human Relations, Johnson Report, 1957, Box 439, Folder 3, GPM.

81. Ibid.

82. Sugrue, *Origins of the Urban Crisis*; Arnold Hirsch, *Making the Second Ghetto: Race and Housing in Chicago, 1940–1960* (Cambridge: Cambridge University Press, 1983).

83. Conrad Weiler, *Philadelphia: Neighborhood, Authority, and the Urban Crisis* (New York: Praeger, 1974), 166–168; Clark and Clark, "Rally and Relapse," 685–686.

84. Martha and Del Molarsky to Representative W. J. Green, June 7, 1963, Folder: Commission on Human Relations, Box A-6359, JHJT; Daniel B. Sevick to Mayor James Tate, June 7, 1963, Folder: Commission on Human Relations, Box A-6359, JHJT; Dorothy S. Montgomery to James H. J. Tate, June 7, 1963 and Dorothy S. Montgomery to Sadie T. M. Alexander, June 6, 1963, Folder: Commission on Human Relations, Box A-6359, JHJT; Martin S. Barol to James H. J. Tate, June 14, 1963, Folder: Commission on Human Relations, Box A-6359, JHJT; Dorothy Anderson to James H. J. Tate, June 9, 1963, Folder: Commission on Human Relations, Box A-6359, JHJT; Jimmy Jones to James H. J. Tate, June 6, 1963, Folder: Commission on Human Relations, Box A-6359, JHJT.

Chapter 2

1. Lenora E. Berson, *Case Study of a Riot: The Philadelphia Story* (New York: Institute of Human Relations Press, 1966), 15; Matthew J. Countryman, *Up South: Civil Rights and Black Power in Philadelphia* (Philadelphia: University of Pennsylvania Press, 2006), 156–157; Memorandum from Lary Groth to Community Leaders and Intergroup Health & Welfare Agencies, "Disturbances in North Philadelphia," September 3, 1964, Folder: Human Relations, Commission on (1), Box A-4113, JHJT.

2. Memorandum from Lary Groth, "Disturbances in North Philadelphia"; S. A. Paolantonio, *Frank Rizzo: The Last Big Man in Big City America*, 10th anniversary ed. (Philadelphia:

Camino Books, 2003), 74–75; Fred Hamilton, *Rizzo: From Cop to Mayor of Philadelphia* (New York: Viking Books, 1973), 66–70.

3. Paolantonio, *Rizzo*, 74–75; Memorandum from Lary Groth, "Disturbances in North Philadelphia."

4. Berson, *Case Study*, 20; Countryman, *Up South*, 159.

5. The use of the term "riot" to describe the urban uprisings that struck American cities in the 1960s has become a contentious argument among historians. Many rightly argue that the term denotes a sort of aimless lawlessness, rather than targeted and political acts of rebellion. This book uses the terms "riot," "uprising," and "rebellion" somewhat interchangeably, but favors "riot" only in an effort to present the events as they were experienced by blue-collar whites. On the debate over terminology, see Heather Thompson, "Urban Uprisings: Riots or Rebellions?" in David Farber and Beth L. Bailey, eds., *The Columbia Guide to America in the 1960s* (New York: Columbia University Press, 2003).

6. Ibid., 154–156; Michael W. Flamm, *In the Heat of the Summer: The New York Riots of 1964 and the War on Crime* (Philadelphia: University of Pennsylvania Press, 2016).

7. Michael W. Flamm, *Law and Order: Street Crime, Civil Unrest, and the Crisis of Liberalism in the 1960s* (New York: Columbia University Press, 2005).

8. The police department was not exclusively made up of white men. African Americans and other nonwhites made up around 20 percent of the force. But police work in the civil rights era contrasted forcefully with the Black Freedom Struggle, and police officers became symbols of the white power structure. Women also held positions in divisions set aside for female officers—like the juvenile affairs—or in clerical posts, but no woman rose to the rank of detective until after a legal battle in 1978. For police demographics, see David Alan Sklanky, "Not Your Father's Police Department: Making Sense of the New Demographics of Law Enforcement," *Journal of Criminal Law and Criminology* 96, no. 3 (2006): 1209–1243.

9. Philadelphia Council for Community Advancement, Summary of Model Police District, Demonstration Project, "A Community Education Program for Police and Citizens in North Philadelphia," December 5, 1963, Folder: Police Department (2), Box A-6363, JHJT.

10. Countryman, *Up South*, 154–155.

11. Maurice Fagan to Editor, *Evening Bulletin*, October 31, 1963, Folder 17, Box 23, JLCR; Confidential Memorandum from Richard H. Buford to James H. J Tate, "Advisory Committee on Civil Rights Meeting on Philyaw Investigation," December 12, 1963, Folder: Advisory Committee on Civil Rights, Box A-6353, JHJT.

12. Edward S. Hollander on Behalf of the Executive Committee of Philadelphia CORE, Statement of Membership Withdrawal from the Citizens Advisory Committee on Civil Rights, November 1, 1963, Folder: Congress on Racial Equality, Box A-6355, JHJT.

13. Paolantonio, *Rizzo*, 72–75.

14. Joseph E. Clark to Mayor Tate, October 30, 1963, Folder: Police Department, Box A-6364, JHJT; Harriet Malamud to Mayor Tate, no date [received October 31, 1963], Folder: Police Department (2), Box A-6364, JHJT; Thomas K. Buntz to James H. J. Tate, October 30, 1963, Folder: Police Department, Box A-6364, JHJT.

15. Robert G. Rosen to Mayor Tate, October 29, 1963, Folder: Police Department, Box A-6364, JHJT.

16. Mrs. Thomas McGee to Mayor Tate, October 29, 1963, Folder: Police Department (2), Box A-6364, JHJT.

17. Regina L. Lobin to Office of the Mayor, October 30, 1963, Folder: Police Department (2), Box A-6364, JHJT.

18. James H. J. Tate, "In Praise of Politicians," unpublished memoir, 1973, SCRC; Guian A. McKee, *The Problem of Jobs: Liberalism, Race, and Deindustrialization in Philadelphia* (Chicago: University of Chicago Press, 2008), 72–73.

19. Confidential Memorandum from Richard H. Buford to James H. J Tate, "Advisory Committee on Civil Rights Meeting on Philyaw Investigation," December 12, 1963, Folder: Advisory Committee on Civil Rights, Box A-6353, JHJT.

20. Joseph D. Lohman and Gordon E. Misner, *The Police and the Community: The Dynamics of Their Relationship in a Changing Community*, vol. 2 (Washington, DC: Government Printing Office, 1966), 62–63; Statement of the Mayor, December 20, 1963, Folder: Police Department (2), Box A-6364, JHJT; Paolantonio, *Rizzo*, 73.

21. Paolantonio, *Rizzo*, 37–52, 60–61; Marc Stein, *City of Sisterly and Brotherly Loves: Lesbian and Gay Philadelphia, 1945–1972* (Chicago: University of Chicago Press, 2000), 157–161.

22. Martin R. Freeman to James H. J. Tate, December 24, 1963, Folder: Police Department (2), Box A-6364, JHJT; Lohman and Misner, *The Police*, 64–65.

23. Karl E. Johnson, "Police-Black Community Relations in Postwar Philadelphia: Race and Criminalization in Urban Social Spaces, 1945–1960," *Journal of African American History* 89, no. 2 (2004): 118–134.

24. Reba O. Bowie et al. to James H. J. Tate, November 9, 1962, Folder: Police Advisory Board, Box A-6338, JHJT.

25. Lohman and Misner, *The Police*, 51–52.

26. Memorandum from the Police Commissioner to Chief Inspector, Administration, December 7, 1962, Folder: Police Department, Box A-337, JHJT.

27. "'Scurrilous, Dirty and Vicious,'" *NT*, July 6, 1961.

28. George E. Sokolsky, "Let's Not Disarm the Cops," *NT*, December 7, 1961.

29. Patrick Geraghty to James H. J. Tate, August 8, 1963, Folder: NAACP, Box A-6361, JHJT.

30. James H. J. Tate to Patrick Geraghty, September 5, 1963, Folder: NAACP, Box A-6361, JHJT.

31. Kennedy quoted in Rick Perlstein, *Nixonland: The Rise of a President and the Fracturing of America* (New York: Scribner, 2008), 16; "The Far Country," *Time*, September 24, 1965.

32. Memorandum from Fred T. Corleto to James H. J. Tate, December 11, 1963, "Community Education Program for Police and Citizens in North Philadelphia," Folder: Police Department (2), Box A-6364, JHJT.

33. Philadelphia Council for Community Advancement, Summary of Model Police District, Demonstration Project, "A Community Education Program for Police and Citizens in North Philadelphia," December 5, 1963, Folder: Police Department (2), Box A-6363, JHJT.

34. Louis S. Smith to James H. J. Tate, March 21, 1964, Folder: Committee on Racial Equality, Box A-4410, JHJT.

35. Moore quoted in Countryman, *Up South*, 160.

36. "Our Hands Are Tied, Cries Police Sergeant," *PI*, August 30, 1964. A friend of the mayor sent a copy of the article to James Tate, along with a note saying, "This Republican bum will cost the Democrats a lot of votes. He should be made to retract his statement in the newspapers and should be reprimanded." Frank Busillo to Jim, August 31, 1964, Folder: Police-North Philadelphia (1), Box A-4420, JHJT.

37. Richard T. Lane to Howard R. Leary, October 30, 1964, Folder: Police—North Phila-delphia Letters (1), Box A-4420, JHJT; Rev. William B. Toland to James H. J. Tate, September 7, 1964, Folder: Police—North Philadelphia Letters (2), Box A-4420, JHJT.

38. James O. Williams to James H. J. Tate, September 15, 1964, Folder: Police—North Phila-delphia Letters (2), Box A-4420, JHJT.

39. Countryman, *Up South*, 160–162; Fellowship Commission, Committee on Commu-nity Tensions, Special Meeting on North Philadelphia Rioting and Looting, September 3, 1964, Folder 17, Box 23, JLCR.

40. Cecil B. Moore to James H. J. Tate, September 8, 1964, Folder: Police-North Philadelphia (2), Box A-4420, JHJT.

41. Edna C. Wells to James H. J. Tate, November 10, 1964, Folder: North Philadelphia Let-ters, Box A-4420, JHJT; Francis J. White, William T. Bode, and John McNelis to James H. J. Tate, September 15, 1964, Folder: North Philadelphia Letters, Box A-4420, JHJT; Max I. Cohen to Mr. Mayor, September 2, 1964, Folder: North Philadelphia (1), Box A-4420, JHJT.

42. Fellowship Commission, Committee on Community Tensions, Special Meeting on North Philadelphia Rioting and Looting, September 3, 1964, Folder 17, Box 23, JLCR; Report on Meeting with Committee of Columbia Avenue Business Men's Association, December 4, 1964, Folder: Police Department (1), Box A-4419, JHJT; Howard R. Leary to James H. J. Tate, December 7, 1964, Folder: Police Department (1), Box A-4419, JHJT; Berson, *Case Study*, 20.

43. Memorandum from Captain Pawley to Commissioner of Police, September 2, 1964, Folder: General Information re: Operation Columbia, Box A-4597, JHJT; Report on Meeting with Committee of Columbia Avenue Business Men's Association, December 4, 1964, Folder: Police Department (1), Box A-4419, JHJT; Howard R. Leary to James H. J. Tate, December 7, 1964, Folder: Police Department (1), Box A-4419, JHJT. This was not an occurrence limited to Philadelphia. See Lizabeth Cohen, *A Consumer Republic: The Politics of Mass Consumption in America* (New York: Vintage Books, 2003), 374–376.

44. Lester Krieger to James H. J. Tate, September 3, 1964, Folder: Police—North Philadel-phia Letters (2), Box A-4420, JHJT; Morris Gorin to Mayor Tate, September 1, 1964, Folder: Police—North Philadelphia Letters, JHJT; Memorandum from Tony Zecca to James H. J. Tate, January 29, 1965, Folder: Columbia Avenue Riot, Box A-4491, JHJT.

45. Report on Meeting with Committee of Columbia Avenue Business Men's Association, December 4, 1964 Folder: Police Department (1), Box A-4419, JHJT; Howard R. Leary to James H. J. Tate, December 7, 1964, Folder: Police Department (1), Box A-4419, JHJT.

46. Alex Wollod to Emanuel Muravchik, Report of Activities, August 15 to September 15, 1964, Folder AD 33, Box 4, JLCR.

47. Brant Coopersmith to Philadelphia ADL Regional Board, B'nai B'rith Lodge and Chap-ter Presidents and ADL Chairman, September 2, 1964, Folder 16, Box 22, FCR; Memorandum from Terry C. Chisholm to James H. J. Tate, "North Philadelphia Merchant-Community Pro-gram," February 4, 1965, Folder: Columbia Avenue Riot, Box A-4491, JHJT.

48. Alex Wollod, Jewish Labor Committee Activities Review, November 1964, Folder 14, Box 7, JLCR.

49. Joseph D. Walsh to James H. J. Tate, September 2, 1964, Folder: Police-North Philadel-phia (2), Box A-4420, JHJT; Board of Directors Meeting Minutes, September 1, 1964, BBMAP; Regular Monthly Meeting Minutes, September 8, 1964, BBMAP.

50. Paolantonio, *Rizzo*, 75–78; Countryman, *Up South*, 164.

51. Lohman and Misner, *The Police*, 48–51.

52. John J. Harrington to James H. J. Tate, FOP News Release, August 31, 1964, Folder: Police—North Philadelphia Letters (2), Box A-4420, JHJT.

53. John J. Harrington to James H. J. Tate, October 20, 1965, Folder: Fraternal Order of Police, Box A-4482, JHJT.

54. Maurice M. Lewis Jr., "Head of FOP Faces Fight for Reelection," *PEB*, March 3, 1964, PBCC.

55. "Candidate for Head of FOP Wants 'Image' for Police," *PEB*, March 10, 1964, PBCC.

56. Lohman and Misner, *The Police*, 48–49.

57. "President Harrington Says," *Peace Officer*, Vol. 24, No. 2, March-April, 1965, Folder 94, Box 34, CFFR; "Harrington Defeats O'Leary in FOP Election Upset," *PEB*, April 8, 1964, PBCC.

58. Mrs. Helen E. Shaw to James J. Tate, no date, Folder: Police-North Philadelphia (2), Box A-4420, JHJT.

59. Irene B. Muzslay to James H. J. Tate, Folder: Police Department Miscellaneous Complaints (2), Box A-4420, JHJT.

60. Memorandum from John F. Driscoll to Howard R. Leary, August 8, 1964, "Meeting with Mr. William Devlin and Mr. William Meehan of the Republican City Committee," Folder: Police-North Philadelphia (2), Box A-4420, JHJT.

61. Ruth Scott to James H. J. Tate, September 9, 1964, Folder: Police Department Miscellaneous Complaints (2), Box A-4420, JHJT; Bill Allen to Mayor, no date, Folder: Police Department Miscellaneous Complaints (2), Box A-4420, JHJT; F. L. Benson Jr. to Mayor, September 8, 1964, Folder: Police Department Miscellaneous Complaints (2), Box A-4420, JHJT.

62. Flamm, *Law and Order*, 44–45.

63. Elizabeth Hinton, *From the War on Poverty to the War on Crime: The Making of Mass Incarceration in America* (Cambridge, MA: Harvard University Press, 2016), 55–57.

64. "Second Class Citizens," *Peace Officer*, Vol. 24, No. 2, March-April 1965, Folder 94, Box 34, CFFR.

65. Maurice B. Fagan to Winn Newman, Esq., May 10, 1960, Folder 24, Box 22, FCR; Peter Binzen and Jonathan Binzen, *Richardson Dilworth: Last of the Bare-Knuckled Aristocrats* (Philadelphia: Camino Books, 2014), 198. On the PAB's creation, see Eric C. Schneider, Christopher Agee, and Themis Chronopoulos, "Dirty Work: Police and Community Relations in the Limits of Liberalism in Postwar Philadelphia," *Journal of Urban History*, May 1, 2017, https://doi.org/10.1177/0096144217705497.

66. Clarence Picket, Regulations and Procedures, The Police Review Board of the City of Philadelphia, September 15, 1959, Folder: Rules of Practice 1959-66, Box 1, PABR.

67. "Police Board Cases Pile Up, Pending Suit," *PEB*, January 11, 1966, PBCC.

68. Lohman and Misner, *The Police*, 258–264.

69. Orrin Evans, "Police Advisory Board Remains a Controversial Agency After 4 Years," *PEB*, September 4, 1962, PBCC.

70. Countryman, *Up South*, 95.

71. Reba O. Bowie et al. to James H. J. Tate, November 9, 1962, Folder: Police Advisory Board, Box A-6338, JHJT.

72. Nicholas deB. Katzenbach to James H. J. Tate, May 14, 1965, Folder: Attorney General, Box A-4475, JHJT.

73. Evans, "Police Advisory Board Remains a Controversial Agency After 4 Years."

74. Francis J. Zoltowski to Mayor Tate, January 7, 1964, Folder: Police Advisory Board, Box A-4421, JHJT.

75. William J. Storm, "Advisory Board Harasses Police, FOP Says," *PEB*, July 19, 1964, PBCC.

76. Flamm, *Law and Order*, 76–80.

77. John J. Harrington, "Cry of Police Brutality," *PEB*, October 5, 1964, PBCC.

78. "President Harrington Says," *Peace Officer*, Vol. 24, No. 2, March-April, 1965, Folder 94, Box 34, CFFR.

79. "Phila. FOP Leader Seeks National Post," *PEB*, August 22, 1965, PBCC; William Storm, "Harrington Takes Over National GOP with Call for Police Dogs at Girard," *PEB*, August 29, 1965, PBCC.

80. James H. J. Tate to Francis J. Zoltowski, January 10, 1964, Folder: Police Advisory Board, Box A-4421, JHJT; "Police to Get Overtime Pay by Year's End," *PEB*, December 6, 1965, PBCC; "Tate Appoints 2d Policeman to Advisory Unit," *PEB*, May 5, 1966, PBCC.

81. Mercer D. Tate to Robert F. Reid, January 13, 1966, Folder: Correspondence—Chairmen 1966, Box 1, PABR.

82. Lary Groth to Ephraim Gomberg, March 23, 1966, Folder: Leary, Howard, Box 4, CCPR; Paolantonio, *Rizzo*, 77–78.

83. Albert V. Gaudiosi, "Police Morale Sinks to New Low; Some Blame 'Appeasement' Policy," *PEB*, September 7, 1965, PBCC.

84. "FOP Reelects Harrington by 3-to-1 Margin," *PEB*, April 6, 1966, PBCC.

85. "FOP Chief Retires from Force, Says Court Shackles Police," *PEB*, July 1, 1966, PBCC.

86. "FOP Secretary Says Advisory Board Precludes 'Good Law Enforcement,'" *PEB*, September 20, 1966, PBCC.

87. "Harrington Rips Review Boards," *PEB*, August 31, 1966, PBCC.

88. "FOP Says Police Quelled Riot Only After Getting Immunity," *PEB*, September 19, 1966, PBCC.

89. Philadelphia Police Department, Crime in the Nation, January to September 1966, Folder: Police, Box A-4525, JHJT.

90. "Board Brand FOP President 'a Demagogue,'" *PI*, October 25, 1966, PBCC.

91. Mercer D. Tate, "Chairman of Police Advisory Board Refutes Charges by FOP's Harrington," October 24, 1966, Folder: Committee on Community Tensions, Box 2, PABR.

92. "Pattern of Police Brutality Charged by Mrs. Alexander," *PEB*, September 29, 1966, PBCC; "Masses Fear Phila. Police, Prof Testifies," *PEB*, October 15, 1966, PBCC; Harmon Y. Gordon, "Citizens' Police Advisory Board Ordered Abolished by Weinrott," *PEB*, March 29, 1967, PBCC.

93. Paolantonio, *Rizzo*, 87; Petition to James H. J. Tate, November 22, 1967, Box 37, Folder: Rizzo, JHJT.

94. Kos Semonski, "Tate Abandons Fight to Save Police Board," *PEB*, November 15, 1967, PBCC.

Chapter 3

1. Giordano J. Scopinich, "Everyone is Important," unpublished memoir, November 1979, p. 1, Folder 4, Box 1, GJSM.

2. Giordano J. Scopinich, "Letter From a Mummer's Journal," unpublished memoir, undated, p. 1, Folder 4, Box 1, GJSM.

3. Ibid.

4. Charles E. Welch, *Oh! Dem Golden Slippers: The Colorful Story of the Philadelphia Mummers* (New York: Thomas Nelson, 1970), 124–136. For photos and descriptions of the Mummers

Parade, see Murray Dubin, *South Philadelphia: Mummers, Memories, and the Melrose Diner* (Philadelphia: Temple University Press, 1996); E. A. Kennedy III, *Life, Liberty, and the Mummers* (Philadelphia: Temple University Press, 2007).

5. "Mummers Bar Insulting Antics in Annual Frolic," undated newspaper clipping, Memorandum, Case 54-1-38, February 2, 1954, NAACP-6; James O. Williams to Terry Chisholm, November 9, 1964, Folder: Human Relations, Commission on (1), Box A-4113, JHJT; Copy of Letter by J. Charles Short to Lewis H. Van Dusen Jr. and Lawrence Pratis, November 3, 1964, Folder 13, Box 64, FCR; Welch, *Golden Slippers*, 137.

6. "Blackface Banned at Mummers Parade," news clipping, Folder: Mummers, Box A-4414, JHJT.

7. Welch, *Golden Slippers*, 139.

8. Memorandum from Terry C. Chisholm to James H. J. Tate, "CORE Threat to Protest New Year's Parade," December 11, 1964, Folder: Mummers, Box A-4414, JHJT; Memorandum from Richard L. Olanoff to Fred T. Corleto, "Televising of the 1965 Mummers," December 21, 1964, Folder: Mummers, Box A-4414, JHJT; Statement by Mayor James H. J. Tate, November 12, 1964, Folder: Mummers, Box A-4414, JHJT.

9. Robert W. Crawford to Robert Hall, November 16, 1964, Folder 13, Box 64, FCR.

10. Orrin Evans, "Mrs. Wright Tells of Move into All-White Section," *PEB*, October 4, 1966, PBCC.

11. Memorandum from Lary Groth to Tom Hadfield and Joe Cronin, October 3, 1966, Folder: Negroes, Box 5, PBP.

12. "500 Battle Policemen 3 Hours in Kensington," *PEB*, October 4, 1966, PBCC; "Police Chase 3 New Crowds in Kensington," *PEB*, October 5, 1966, PBCC.

13. "Youths Burn Negro Effigies in Kensington," *PEB*, October 6, 1966, PBCC.

14. "Clergy Groups Deplore 'Mob' in Kensington," *PEB*, October 6, 1966, PBCC.

15. "36 More Arrested on Kensington Street," *PEB*, October 8, 1966, PBCC; Police Coverage—Area—2474 Coral Street, Saturday, October 8, 1966, Folder: Police, Box A-4525, JHJT.

16. Police Coverage—Area of 2474 Coral Street, Tuesday, October 11, 1966, Folder: Police, Box A-4525, JHJT; Police Coverage—Area of 2474 Coral Street, Wednesday, 12 October 1966, Folder: Police, Box A-4525, JHJT.

17. Fair Housing Council of Delaware Valley, "Mayor Tate—Speak Out on Kensington!" October 7, 1966, Folder: Kensington, Box A-4518, JHJT; Arnold P. Abbot to James H. J. Tate, October 16, 1966, Folder: Kensington, Box A-4518, JHJT; Marion H. Scull and Lawrence Scott to James H. J. Tate, October 11, 1966, Folder: Kensington, Box A-4518, JHJT; Stephan B. Narin to James H. J. Tate, October 14, 1966, Folder: Kensington, Box A-4518, JHJT; Richard K. Taylor to James H. J. Tate, October 9, 1966, Folder: Kensington, Box A-4518, JHJT; Lonnie Spain to The Editor, *PI*, October 18, 1966.

18. Sadie T. M. Alexander to James H. J. Tate, October 13, 1966, Folder: Human Relations, Box A-4517, JHJT; Commission on Human Relations to James H. J. Tate, October 13, 1966, Folder: Human Relations, Box A-4517, JHJT.

19. Peter Binzen, *Whitetown, U.S.A.* (New York: Random House, 1970); Murray Friedman, "Kensington, U.S.A.," in Murray Friedman, ed. *Overcoming Middle Class Rage* (Philadelphia: Westminster Press, 1971).

20. Friedman, "Kensington, U.S.A."

21. Binzen, *Whitetown*, 81.

22. Paul Green to James H. J. Tate, February 13, 1964, Folder: City Planning Commission, Box A-4409, JHJT.

23. Friedman, "Kensington," 57–60; Binzen, *Whitetown*, 110–111.

24. Friedman, "Kensington," 58–59.

25. Murray Friedman, "The Kensington Riot of 1966: A Look at the Underlying Factors Behind White Rioting Against Negroes," Remarks before a workshop of social workers of the Lighthouse and Lutheran Settlement House at the Lutheran Settlement House in Kensington, February 3, 1967, Folder: Kensington, Box 3, PBP. Friedman later published a different version of his talk as "Kensington, U.S.A."

26. Binzen, *Whitetown*, 80–81.

27. "Kensington Says It Is Not a Slum Area," *PI*, August 16, 1964, PBCC.

28. Binzen, *Whitetown*, 100–101.

29. Peter Binzen, Fishtown interview, 1967, p. 1, Folder: Kensington, Box 3, PBP.

30. Police Intelligence Report, 2474 N. Coral Street, October 1966, Folder: Kensington, Box A-4518, JHJT; Police Coverage—Area—2474 Coral Street, Saturday, October 8, 1966, Folder: Police, Box A-4525, JHJT; Police Coverage—Area of 2474 Coral Street, Monday October 10, 1966, Folder: Police, Box A-4525, JHJT; Police Coverage—Area of 2474 Coral Street, Tuesday, October 11, 1966, Folder: Police, Box A-4525, JHJT.

31. Peter Binzen, Fishtown interview, p. 2-4, Folder: Kensington, Box 3, PBP.

32. Peter Binzen, Oliver interview, October 24, 1967, p. 5-6, Folder: Fishtown, Box 3, PBP.

33. Peter Binzen, Fishtown interview, p. 5, Folder: Kensington, Box 3, PBP.

34. Peter Binzen, Oliver interview, October 24, 1967, p. 5-6, Folder: Fishtown, Box 3, PBP.

35. Joe McGinnis, "Empty Victory for Kensington," *PI*, March 29, 1967, PBCC.

36. Peter H. Binzen and J. William Jones, "1500 Negro Pupils Will Be Bused to 15 White Schools Starting Friday," *PEB*, September 8, 1964, PBCC.

37. "125 March in Protest of Student Busing," *PEB*, May 13, 1965, PBCC; "Suit to Halt Pupil Busing Is Dismissed by Judge," *PEB*, December 17, 1964, PBCC.

38. Charles C. Becket, Statement presented to Mayor's Citizen Advisory Committee on Civil Rights, July 14, 1964, Folder: Integration, Box 24, PFTP.

39. City of Philadelphia, Community Renewal Program: Major Policies and Proposals, Confidential Draft, November 1966, 54-55, Folder: Community Renewal Program, Box A-4511, JHJT.

40. Charles C. Becket, Statement presented to Mayor's Citizen Advisory Committee on Civil Rights, July 14, 1964, Folder: Integration, Box 24, PFTP.

41. Ronald P. Formisano, *Boston Against Busing: Race, Class, and Ethnicity in the 1960s and 1970s* (Chapel Hill: University of North Carolina Press, 1991), 35–37; Matthew Lassiter, *The Silent Majority: Suburban Politics in the Sunbelt South* (Princeton, NJ: Princeton University Press, 2006), 23–25, 131–137.

42. David B. Bernhardt et al. to John F. Lewis and Ralph W. Pitman, December 11, 1963, Folder: Committee on Non-Discrimination, Box 24, PFTP.

43. A. Leon Higginbotham Jr. to Floyd L. Logan, January 30, 1961, Folder 5, Box 4, FLP.

44. Notes on Meeting of Citizens Advisory Committee on Civil Rights, July 1, 1964 Folder: Citizens Advisory Committee on Civil Rights, Box 4408, JHJT; Thomas D. McBride and Rev. Henry H. Nichols to Committee, July 7, 1964, Folder: Citizens Advisory Committee on Civil Rights, Box 4408, JHJT.

45. "Federation Maps Plan to Fight School Busing," *NT*, July 23, 1964; Barbara Murphy, "Civic League Sets Plan to Lead Busing Protest," *PEB*, June 18, 1964, PBCC; "Civic League to Go to Court to Halt Busing," *PEB*, July 19, 1964, PBCC.

46. Paul D'Ortona, Remarks to City Advisory Committee on Civil Rights, July 14, 1964, Folder: Integration, Box 24, PFTP.

47. Conrad Weiler, *Philadelphia: Neighborhood, Authority, and the Urban Crisis* (New York: Praeger, 1974), 63.

48. Floyd L. Logan to James H. J. Tate, July 13, 1964, Folder: Citizens Advisory Committee on Civil Rights, Box 4408, JHJT.

49. Formisano, *Boston Against Busing*; Lassiter, *The Silent Majority*; Matthew F. Delmont, *Why Busing Failed: Race, Media, and the National Resistance to School Desegregation* (Berkeley: University of California Press, 2016).

50. Mrs. Raymond Berkowitz, Northeast Town Meeting on Quality Education and Integration, Discussion Group Summary, May 7, 1964, CCPEP.

51. Binzen and Jones, "1500 Negro Pupils Will Be Bused to 15 White Schools Starting Friday"; Edith Moses to Mrs. Clinton Thon, October 20, 1965, Folder 42, Box 4, Series IV, HSCPR.

52. Peter Binzen and Jonathan Binzen, *Richardson Dilworth: Last of the Bare-Knuckled Aristocrats* (Philadelphia: Camino Books, 2014), 186–187.

53. Statement of Mrs. Sadie T. M. Alexander at Public Hearings of the Board of Public Education on the Report of the Task Forces, February 1,1966, Folder 47, Box 4, Series IV, HSCPR.

54. Testimony of JOINT at Public Hearings of Board of Education on Report of Task Forces, January 31, 1966, Folder 47, Box 4, Series IV, HSCPR; John A. Ryan, Philadelphia Federation of Teachers Statement to the Board of Education, February 1, 1966, Folder 48, Box 4, Series IV, HSCPR.

55. Mrs. Pauline Feldmen to Dr. C. Taylor Whittier, January 8, 1965, Folder 20, Box 1, Series II, HSCPR; Lillian Seltzer to Beatrice Marks, January 7, 1965, Folder 20, Box 1, Series II. HSCPR; Philadelphia Home and School Council, Statement on the Task Forces Report, January 31, 1966, Folder 44, Box 4, Series IV, HSCPR.

56. Gertrude Gubin to Richardson Dilworth, September 30, 1965, Folder 42, Box 4, Series IV, HSCPR; Board Members of F. S. Edmonds Home and School Association to Richardson Dilworth, October 20, 1965, Folder 42, Box 4, Series IV, HSCPR.

57. Statement by Mrs. Clinton Thon before Task Force—Dilworth's Obulci Hearing, October 26, 1965, Folder: 44, Box 4, Series IV, HSCPR; Statement of District 7 to Board of Education, February 1, 1966; Folder: 44, Box 4, Series IV, HSCPR; Testimony offered by parents from District 3 at Public Hearings on Reports of Task Forces to Board of Education, January 31, 1966, Folder: 44, Box 4, Series IV, HSCPR; Mildred G. Ragnow and Dorothy F. Smith, District 8 Statement Made at Public Hearings Sponsored by Board of Education on the Task Force Reports, February 1, 1966, Folder: 44, Box 4, Series IV, HSCPR.

58. Mildred Poole to Richardson Dilworth, January 28, 1966, Folder 46, Box 4, Series IV, HSCPR.

59. Miriam Biddle to Richardson Dilworth, February 22, 1966, Folder 11, HSCPR; "Taxation Without Representation," *NT*, June 22, 1967.

60. Marilyn Slawsky to Mrs. Marks, September 21, 1964, Folder 18, Box 1, Series I, HSCPR; Mrs. Earl Slosberg to Mrs. David Q. Ewing, November 19, 1966, Folder 20, Box 7, Series VII, HSCPR; Harold Rosenthal to Richardson Dilworth, December 23, 1965, Folder 43, Box 4, Series IV, HSCPR.

61. Marion Blum, Clara Barton Home and School Association Statement to the Task Force, 1966, Folder 46, Box 4, Series IV, HSCPR.

62. Mayfair Home and School Association Statement to Board of Education Task Force, January 31, 1966, Folder 46, Box 4, Series IV, HSCPR.

63. Miriam M. Biddle to Mrs. David Q. Ewing, December 7, 1966, Folder 20, Box 1, Series II, HSCPR.

64. Neighborhood School Association flier, 1966, Folder 11, Box 7, HSCPR.

65. Neighborhood School Association, Statement to Board of Education, January 31, 1966, Folder 48, Box 4, Series IV, HSCPR; Robert E. Holcombe and Mrs. Pat Holcombe to Mrs. Jean Thon, January 25, 1966, Folder 51, Box 4, Series IV, HSCPR; Mrs. Theodore L. Adams to Mrs. Clinton Thon, December 5, 1965, Folder 51, Box 4, Series IV, HSCPR; On the Charlotte busing crisis, see Lassiter, *The Silent Majority*, 121–123.

66. Florence Cohen to C. Taylor Whittier, January 15, 1966 and C. Taylor Whittier to Mrs. Florence Cohen, January 24, 1966, Folder 11, Box 7, HSCPR.

67. S. A. Paolantonio, *Frank Rizzo: The Last Big Man in Big City America*, 10th anniversary ed. (Philadelphia: Camino Books, 2003), 76–77; Matthew Countryman, *Up South: Civil Rights and Black Power in Philadelphia* (Philadelphia: University of Pennsylvania Press, 2006), 178–179.

68. Countryman, *Up South*, 168; Report of Girard College Emergency, Philadelphia Police Department, July 8, 1965, Folder: Girard College, Box A-3094, FLR; Paolantonio, *Rizzo*, 73–76.

69. William White Jr., Confidential Memorandum, August 18, 1965, Folder: War on Crime, Box A-4491, JHJT.

70. John J. Harrington to James H. J. Tate, July 14, 1965, Folder: Fraternal Order of Police, Box A-4482, JHJT; Paolantonio, *Rizzo*, 76–77.

71. Countryman, *Up South*, 178.

72. Martin R. Freeman to James H. J. Tate, December 24, 1963, Folder: Police Department (2), Box A-6364, JHJT.

73. Paolantonio, *Rizzo*, 76–77.

74. Michael W. Flamm, *In the Heat of the Summer: The New York Riots of 1964 and the War on Crime* (Philadelphia: University of Pennsylvania Press, 2016).

75. Lary Groth to Ephraim Gomberg, March 23, 1966, Folder: Leary, Howard, Box 4, CCPR; Paolantonio, *Rizzo*, 76–77. Leary did not last long in New York City. Scandal hit the NYPD shortly after he took over when Officer Frank Serpico began exposing widespread corruption on the force. John Lindsay demanded Leary's resignation after federal Knapp Commission investigations into police corruption determined that he failed to exercise effective leadership. Leary's takedown was a further blow to the philosophy of law enforcement liberalism nationally.

76. Mayor's Advisory Committee to James H. J. Tate and Fred C. Corleto, April 29, 1966, Folder: Police Commissioner Appointment, Box, A-4524, JHJT.

77. Statement of James H. J. Tate, May 6, 1966, Folder: Police Commissioner Appointment, Box A-4524, JHJT; Edward F. Toohey to James H. J. Tate, May 12, 1966, Folder: Police Commissioner Appointment, Box A-4524, JHJT.

78. Paolantonio, *Rizzo*, 84–85; Countryman, *Up South*, 214–217; "SNCC Leader Says Police 'Planted' Dynamite in Home," *PEB*, August 20, 1966, PBCC; "SNCC Director Assails Rizzo as a 'Racist,'" *PEB*, August 30, 1966, PBCC.

79. Emil F. Goldhaber and Charles G. Simpson to Maury Fagan, May 26, 1967, Folder 27, Box 64, FCR.

80. Paolantonio, *Rizzo*, 87–91.

81. Mark R. Shedd to Mrs. David Q. Ewing, November 6, 1967, Folder 31, Box 7, HSCPR; Countryman, *Up South*, 223–230.

82. "Black Schools Unite," flier, 1967 Folder 15, Box 140, RDP; "Attention Brothers and Sisters," flier, 1967, Folder 15, Box 140, RDP; "Aide Says Shedd Backs Most Negro Demands," *PEB*, November 24, 1967, PBCC.

83. Paolantonio, *Rizzo*, 92.

84. John T. Gillespie, "Dr. Shedd Sets 'Reason' as Goal in Race Relations," *PEB*, November 26, 1967, PBCC.

85. Judge Raymond Pace Alexander's Statement in Reduction of Bail of William Mathis and Walter Palmer and Criticism of Police Commissioner Rizzo, November 20, 1967, Folder 17, Box 140, RDP; "D'Ortona Raps Shedd's Action in Disorder," *PEB*, November 23, 1967, PBCC; Gillespie, "Dr. Shedd Sets 'Reason' as Goal in Race Relations."

86. Kensington and Fishtown, Seventy Foot Petition and Holiday Greeting, December 1967, Box 42684, JHJT; Petition to James H. J. Tate, November 22, 1967, Folder: Rizzo, Box 42684, JHJT; Citizens Who Support Law and Order Support Philadelphia Police Commissioner Frank L. Rizzo, Petition, no date [received January 31, 1968] Folder: Rizzo, Box 42684, JHJT; Petition to the Honorable Mayor James H. Tate, no date [received January 4, 1968], Folder: Rizzo, Box 42684, JHJT.

87. Margaret Moran to James Tate, January 6, 1968, Folder: Rizzo, Box 42864, JHJT.

88. One Who Wants to Save Philadelphia to Mayor Tate, December 17, 1967, Folder: Rizzo, Box 42684, JHJT.

89. North City Congress, "The Double Standard: A Comparison of Police Action in the Kensington Riots, October 1966, and the school board Demonstration, November 1967," November 29, 1967, Folder: 31, Box 7, HSCPR.

Chapter 4

1. Richardson Dilworth to Roy E. Moor, November 21, 1967, Folder: Richardson Dilworth, Box 3, CCPEP.

2. John P. Corr to Richardson Dilworth, November 28, 1967, Folder 1, Box 158, RDP.

3. Henry Aubin, "D'Ortona Raps Shedd's Action in Disorder," *PEB*, November 23, 1967, PBCC.

4. Ruth L. Bylone to Richardson Dilworth, November 30, 1967, Folder 1, Box 158, RDP.

5. Mark R. Shedd to Mrs. David Q. Ewing, November 6, 1967, Folder 31, Box 7, Series VII, HSCPR.

6. John P. Corr, "Prospects for City's Schools: Shedd—A 'Cool Young Tiger,'" *PI*, May 14, 1967, PBCC; John T. Gillespie, "Shedd Takes Office as Superintendent of Schools," *PEB*, September 1, 1967, PBCC.

7. Mark Shedd, Speech to the Principals, December 12, 1967, Folder: Student Demonstration at Administration Building, Box 5, CCPEP.

8. John T. Gillespie, "Dr. Shedd Sets 'Return to Reason' as Goal in Race Tensions," *PEB*, November 26, 1967, PBCC.

9. Statement of Crime Commission of Philadelphia Following Demonstration at Board of Education Headquarters, November 18, 1967, Folder: Paul Maloney, Box 4, CCPR.

10. Petition to the Honorable Mayor James H. Tate, no date [received by office of the Mayor, January 4, 1968], Folder: Rizzo, Box 42864, JHJT.

11. Philadelphia Council for Community Advancement, Houses, Schools and Jobs in the Philadelphia Metropolitan Area, 1965, Box 507, Folder 4, GPC.

12. Archdiocese of Philadelphia, Report of the Parish Schools, 1963–1964, PAHRC; Archdiocese of Philadelphia, Report of the Parish Schools, 1964–1965, PAHRC; Archdiocese of

Philadelphia, Report of the Parish Schools, 1965–1966, PAHRC; Archdiocese of Philadelphia, Report of the Parish Schools, 1966–1967, PAHRC; Archdiocese of Philadelphia, Report of the Parish Schools, 1967–1968, PAHRC. Although the schools shared the same grounds, they maintained the tradition of single-sex education found in all archdiocesan secondary schools until 1988, when Archbishop Ryan merged into a coeducational facility.

13. Testimony offered by parents from District 3 (South Phila. Section) at Public Hearings on Reports of Task Forces to Board of Education, January 31, 1966, Folder 44, Box 4, Series IV, HSCPR.

14. Philadelphia Parish Demographic Book, PAHRC; and the Archdiocese of Philadelphia's Reports of the Parish Schools, PAHRC.

15. Peter Binzen, *Whitetown, U.S.A.* (New York: Random House, 1970), 240–251.

16. John Krol to Peter Binzen, March 29, 1965, Folder: Catholics, PBP.

17. John T. Gurash et al., *The Report on the Archdiocesan Advisory Committee on the Financial Crisis of the Catholic Schools in Philadelphia and Surrounding Counties* (Philadelphia, 1972), Box 11, Folder 11, GPC.

18. Binzen, *Whitetown*, 238–239.

19. Edward T. Hughes to Richardson Dilworth, June 14, 1967, Folder 4, Box 76, RDP.

20. Binzen, *Whitetown*, 244–246. See also Thomas J. Donaghy, *Philadelphia's Finest: A History of Education in the Catholic Archdiocese, 1692–1970* (Philadelphia: American Catholic Historical Society, 1972).

21. Memorandum from Allan R. Howe and Roy E. Moor to All Discussion Leaders, November 1, 1967, Folder 7, Box 1, CCPEP; Richardson Dilworth to Right Reverend Edward T. Hughes, February 26, 1969, Folder 4, Box 76, RDP; Richardson Dilworth to William D. Valente, Esquire, August 22, 1969, Folder 4, Box 76, RDP; Joint Statement by Richardson Dilworth, William D. Valente, Rt. Rev. Msgr. Edward T. Hughes, and Dr. Mark Shedd, November 24, 1969, Folder 5, Box 76, RDP; Peter H. Binzen, "Aid Bills Mark a Milestone in Education," *PEB*, May 5, 1965, PBCC; Archdiocese of Philadelphia, Report of the Parish Schools, 1965–1966, PAHRC.

22. "Non-Public School Bill Gets Support by Area Trustees," *NT*, June 29, 1967; Mrs. James Batts to PHSC President, "Extract of House Bill #1136," November 1, 1967, Folder 31, Box 7, HSCPR.

23. "Nonpublic School Aid a Necessity," *NT*, August 3, 1967.

24. "Rep. John D. Pezak," *Bridesburg Bulletin*, June 1968, Folder: Bridesburg Bulletin 1968, Box 1, BBMAP; "Catholics Send 100,000 Wires on School Aid," *PEB*, November 27, 1967, PBCC.

25. Jewish Community Relations Council of Greater Philadelphia Statement on Project "Get Set," 1965, Folder 2, Box 10, JLCR; Alex Wollod to Emanuel Muravchik, Report of Activities, August 15 to September 15, 1965, Folder AD 33, Box 4, JLCR.

26. Mrs. Elmer Shamwell and Mrs. James A. Batts, PHSC Fact Sheet on House Bill #1136 (Mullen Bill), 1967, Folder: 31, Box 7, HSCPR; Rev. H. Francis Hines to Norman S. Berson, August 10, 1967 and Rev. Robert C. S. Deacon to George K. Haudenshield, July 28, 1967, Folder 7, Box 1, CCPEP.

27. Mrs. Elmer Shamwell and Mrs. James A. Batts, PHSC Fact Sheet on House Bill #1136 (Mullen Bill), 1967, Folder: 31, Box 7, HSCPR.

28. Binzen, *Whitetown*, 238.

29. "Racial Conflict Is Blamed for Stab Slaying," *PEB*, February 13, 1961, PBCC; Chas. E. Montgomery, "Stabbing Led to Outbreak in 'Rec' Room," *PEB*, September 21, 1966, PBCC; "10 Boys Held in Shooting at S. Phila. High," *PEB*, September 22, 1966, PBCC.

30. John T. Gillespie, "More Police Demanded by S. Phila. High Parents," *PEB*, November 28, 1967, PBCC; "More Trouble Seen at S. Phila. High," *SPR*, November 30, 1967; Matthew Countryman, *Up South: Civil Rights and Black Power in Philadelphia* (Philadelphia: University of Pennsylvania Press, 2006), 248.

31. Carrol Innerst, "3,000 Try to Enter Technical Highs; Only 1,500 Will Meet Qualifications," *PEB*, February 5, 1967, PBCC; Carrol Innerst, "Bok Trains Pupils for Industry Jobs; 95% of Enrollment Are Negroes," *PEB*, February 6, 1967, PBCC.

32. Memorandum from C. Taylor Whittier to Members of the Board of Education, December 14, 1966, Folder 1, Box 21, FLP.

33. Frederick A. McCord, "Ten Days of Disorders: Pupils, Neighbors and Faculty Describe the Crisis," *PEB*, October 20, 1968, PBCC.

34. Countryman, *Up South*, 248–250; Memorandum from Commission on Human Relations, "Bok School Incidents and Related Events," Folder 4A, Box 28, JLCR; Barry Freeman, Incidents in the Community, Report of the Crisis Committee, October 14, 1968, Folder: Phila. Crisis Committee, Box 57, HADVR; "Bok Is Closed Early as Student Clashes Continue Second Day," *PI*, October 6, 1968, PBCC; Fletcher Clarke, "Police Pledge Protection to Bok Negroes," *PEB*, October 8, 1968, PBCC.

35. Countryman, *Up South*, 251; "Close It or 'We'll Burn It,'" *PI*, October 10, 1968, PBCC; "Bok School Closed After Racial Disorders," *PEB*, October 10, 1968, PBCC.

36. "1000 in South Phila. March to Demand Stay Closed," *PEB*, October 13, 1968, PBCC; "Shedd Asks Peace; 1200 Hold March for 'White Power,'" *PI*, October 14, 1968, PBCC.

37. Jack Smyth, "Silver's Comments on Bok Incident Called 'Bad Taste' at H&S Meeting," *PEB*, October 13, 1968, PBCC.

38. "Whites, Negroes Disagree on Causes of Tension," *PEB*, October 15, 1968, PBCC.

39. "Mayor Says He'll Propose a Solution," *PEB*, October 16, 1968, PBCC.

40. John T. Gillespie, "Board Pledges to Keep Order in South Phila.," *PEB*, October 18, 1968, PBCC.

41. McCord, "Ten Days of Disorders: Pupils, Neighbors and Faculty Describe the Crisis."

42. John G. McGullough, "Whites Who Stayed Feel Hard-Pressed," *PEB*, October 18, 1968, PBCC.

43. Martin J. Herman, "Board Denying School Use to 2 Unions," *PEB*, November 24, 1968, PBCC; Guian A. McKee, *The Problem of Jobs: Race, Liberalism, and Deindustrialization in Philadelphia* (Chicago: University of Chicago Press, 2008), 226–227.

44. Joseph F. Burke to Richardson Dilworth, July 24, 1968, Folder 6, Box 153, RDP; Joseph F. Burke to Richardson Dilworth, August 14, 1968, Folder 6, Box 153, RDP.

45. Peter Binzen, Interview at the home of Nick Paonessa, 867 E. Thompson St. Present: Mr. and Mrs. Paonessa, Mr. and Mrs. Goloff, Mrs. Barrineau, Mrs. Loncki, Mr. and Mrs. Plant, no date, p. 2-4, Folder: Kensington, Box 3, PBP.

46. Thomas J. Sugrue, "Affirmative Action from Below: Civil Rights, the Building Trades, and the Politics of Racial Equality in the Urban North, 1945–1969," *Journal of American History* 91 (June 2004): 145–173.

47. James H. J. Tate to Norman Blumberg, January 22, 1964, Folder: City Planning Commission, Box A-4409, JHJT; James H. J. Tate to Norman Blumberg, April 13, Folder: City Planning Commission, Box A-4409, JHJT; James H. J. Tate to Dean G. Holmes Perkins, December 23, 1964, Folder: City Planning Commission, Box A-4409, JHJT.

48. Minutes, Philadelphia Council of Industrial Organizations, April 5, 1967, Folder: Phila Council of Industrial Organizations 1967 Minutes, Box 1, PCAFL-CIO; "Labor's Goal to Aid Tate Is $1 Million," *PEB*, June 16, 1967, PBCC; "Building Trades Unions to Back Tate, Seek Other Union Support for Reelection," *PEB*, November 30, 1966, PBCC.

49. Interview with Edward Toohey, January 17, 1979, Box 5, WPOHP.

50. Memorandum from Terry C. Chisholm to James H. J. Tate, August 9, 1965, "Apprenticeship Training Opportunities in the Building and Construction Trades," Folder A-4483, JHJT.

51. Joseph B. Meranze and James J. Jones, "Jewish Labor Committee—Negro Trade Union Leadership Council, announcement," no date, Folder AD 11, Box 3, JLCR; Minutes on JOINT Meeting, February 16, 1966, Folder AD12, Box 3, JLCR.

52. Interview with Joseph Burke, March 15, 1979, WPOHP.

53. Robert Self, *All in the Family: The Realignment of American Democracy Since the 1960s* (New York: Hill and Wang, 2012).

54. U.S. Conference of Mayors, Community Relations Service, "Changing Employment Practices in the Construction Industry," Experience Report 102, September 1965, Folder: AFL-CIO + Hospital, Box A-4507, JHJT.

55. Minutes, Third Philadelphia AFL-CIO Meeting, June 12, 1963, Folder Phila Council Misc. 1964–1965, Box 1, PCAFL-CIO; Statement of Joseph F. Burke, President Local Union No. 19, Sheet Metal Workers' International Union, Delivered by Daniel Gravensteene, August 19, 1963, Folder: Commission on Human Relations (2), Box A-6359, JHJT; "Agency Prods Drug Firms to Hire Negroes," *PEB*, October 7, 1967, PBCC.

56. Sugrue, "Affirmative Action," 155–157; McKee, *Problem of Jobs*, 213–216.

57. McKee, *Problem of Jobs,* 213–216; Hugh Davis Graham, *The Civil Rights Era: Origins and Development of National Policy* (New York: Oxford University Press, 1990).

58. Wage Rates (*Including Fringes) for Various Trades 1960–1970, Philadelphia and Vicinity, Folder 139, Box 18, TLUP.

59. Martin J. Herman, "Engineers Union Raps U.S. Decree, Says It Has Sought Negro Members," *PEB*, April 28, 1968, PBCC.

60. Nicholoas W. Stroh, "U.S. to Require Builders to Hire Negroes," *PEB*, October 26, 1967, PBCC.

61. Ibid.

62. "U.S. Upholds Phila. Hiring Plan," *PI*, April 21, 1968, PBCC; "Building Unions May Walk Out in Bias Dispute," *PI*, April 26, 1968, PBCC; McKee, *Problem of Jobs*, 218–219.

63. "Mint Contractor Gets Ultimatum on Negro Jobs," *PI*, April 25, 1968, PBCC; "McCloskey Plans Increase in Negro Workers at Mint Job," *PEB*, April 30, 1968, PBCC; "Drive to Hire Negroes for U.S. Project Hits Snag," *PI*, May 1, 1968, PBCC; Martin J. Herman, "2 of 11 Negroes Qualify for Jobs at Mint; Unions Protest 'Union Busting,'" *PEB*, May 3, 1968, PBCC; McKee, *Problem of Jobs*, 221–223.

64. Herman, "2 of 11 Negroes Qualify for Jobs at Mint; Unions Protest 'Union Busting;'" "Trade Unions Hit Job Quotas in Phila. Plan," *PEB*, May 22, 1968, PBCC; McKee, *Problem of Jobs*, 220–221.

65. Martin J. Herman, "Building Unions Vote to Take More Negroes," *PEB*, May 2, 1968, PBCC; Kos Semonski, "Trade Unions Agree on Plan of Recruitment," *PEB*, May 18, 1968, PBCC; McKee, *Problem of Jobs*, 222–223.

66. Sugrue, "Affirmative Action," 170–172; McKee, *Problem of Jobs*, 231–233.

67. Graham, *Civil Rights Era*, 289; S. A. Paolantonio, *Frank Rizzo: The Last Big Man in Big City America*, 10th anniversary ed. (Philadelphia: Camino Books, 2003), 105–122.

68. Philadelphia Urban League, A Statement on a "Philadelphia Plan" for the Board of Education, July 22, 1968, Folder 6, Box 153, RDP; Commission on Human Relations Press Release, August 13, 1968, Folder 6, Box 153, RDP; McKee, *Problem of Jobs*, 218–222.

69. "U.S. to Revise and Reinstate 'Phila. Plan' on Minority Hiring," *PEB*, June 12, 1969, PBCC; Sugrue, "Affirmative Action," 170–172; McKee, *Problem of Jobs*, 231–233.

70. Martin J. Herman, "'Philadelphia Plan' Remains Quota System, Builders Say," *PEB*, July 6, 1969, PBCC; "Phila. Plan Ruled Illegal by Comptroller," *PEB*, August 6, 1969, PBCC; Martin J. Herman, "Opponents Win Delay of Phila. Plan," *PEB*, August 9, 1969, PBCC; McKee, *Problem of Jobs*, 233–235.

71. Department of Labor, *Public Hearing: The Philadelphia Plan, August 26–28* (Washington, DC: Department of Labor, 1969), 239–312; McKee, *Problem of Jobs*, 235–237.

72. Graham, *Civil Rights Era*, 331–345.

73. "Labor Aide Tells Unions to Accept Philadelphia Plan," *PEB*, October 14, 1971, PBCC.

74. City of Philadelphia, Community Renewal Program: Major Policies and Proposals, Confidential Draft, November 1966, Folder: Community Renewal Program, Box A-4511, JHJT.

75. John Bauman, *Public Housing, Race, and Renewal: Urban Planning in Philadelphia, 1920–1970* (Philadelphia: Temple University Press, 1987).

76. Recommendations to the Mayor of the City of Philadelphia by the Citizens Committee on Minority Housing of the Council for Equal Housing Opportunities, of the Fellowship Commission, February 18, 1966, Folder: Fellowship Commission, Box A-4515, JHJT; Jefferson B. Forman to James H. J. Tate, February 18, 1966, Folder: Fellowship Commission, Box A-4515, JHJT.

77. Memorandum from John J. O'Shea to James H. J. Tate, "Housing Problems—North Philadelphia Area," January 11, 1966, Folder: Housing Association, Box A-4517, JHJT.

78. Philadelphia Housing Authority, Public Housing Site Information, 1964, Box 599, Folder 9, GPC; Philadelphia Housing Authority, Biennial Report, 1965–1966, October 1, 1967, Folder: Phila. Housing Authority, Box A-4560, JHJT.

79. Bauman, *Public Housing*; Lisa Levenstein, *A Movement Without Marches: African American Women and the Politics of Poverty in Postwar Philadelphia* (Chapel Hill: University of North Carolina Press, 2009), 87–119; James Wolfinger, "The Limits of Black Activism: Philadelphia's Public Housing in the Depression and World War II," *Journal of Urban History* 35 (2009):787–813.

80. Tasker Homes Pamphlet, no date [1950s], Box 470, GPC; Barbara Barnes, "First Housing Projects Here Pay Dividends in Happiness," *PEB*, June 11, 1949, PBCC. On crime and poor conditions at the Tasker Homes housing project, see "Tenants Press Repairs Fight with 2 Groups," *PEB*, November 1, 1968, PBCC; Charles Montgomery, "Tasker Homes People Live in 'Island of Fear,'" *PEB*, November 24, 1969, PBCC; Charles Montgomery, "Woman Grocer Beaten, Robbed near Tasker Homes," *PEB*, November 25, 1969, PBCC; "Troubled Neighborhood," *PEB*, June 12, 1970, PBCC.

81. Timothy J. Lombardo, "The Battle of Whitman Park: Race, Class, and Public Housing in Philadelphia, 1956–1982," *Journal of Social History* 47, no. 2 (Winter 2013): 401–428.

82. Conservation Program of the Redevelopment Authority of the City of Philadelphia, January 1962, Box 80, GPC; Francis J. Lammer to Edmund N. Bacon, November 20, 1957 and Edmund N. Bacon to Francis J. Lammer, December 6, 1957, Folder: Redevelopment—Whitman 1957-1964, Box A-2953, PCPCF; Summary Report to the Whitman Area Improvement Council, December 1965, Folder 172, Box 16, CCCPP.

83. Edmund N. Bacon to Sol Schrago, August 8, 1962, Folder: Redevelopment—Whitman 1957-1964, Box A-2953, PCPCF; Philadelphia Redevelopment Authority, Whitman Urban Renewal Area: Fact Sheet, 1965, Box 443, GPC; "300 to Be Cited for Renewal in Whitman Area," *PEB*, January 25, 1965, PBCC; "An Emblem for Whitman Area," *PEB*, January 26, 1965, PBCC; "300 South Phila. Families Honored for Fixing Homes," *PEB*, January 29, 1965, PBCC; Carol Innerst, "$1,500 Grant from Uncle Sam Works a Miracle on Tree Street," *PEB*, November, 13, 1966, PBCC.

84. "Community Efforts Get 120 New Homes at Whitman Place," *PEB*, May 2, 1969, PBCC; William J. Storm, "Protests Halt Whitman Park Housing Work," *PEB*, March 23, 1971, PBCC; "PHA Refuses to End Job at Whitman Park," *PEB*, April 7, 1971, PBCC; Harmon Y. Gordon, "Builder Agrees to Halt Job at Whitman Park," April 30, 1971, PBCC.

85. Mrs. Betty Volkman, Public Letter, April 21, 1971, Folder: Community Letters 1917, Box 2, WC-332.

86. "Public Housing Plan Denounced by Homeowners," *NT*, December 11, 1968; Fritz Dysart, "Far NE Area Invaded by 'Public Housing,'" *NT*, July 22, 1970; Jack Smyth, "Apartment Plan Opposed by Morrell Park Group," *PEB*, December 5, 1968, PBCC; Margaret Eisen, "Morrell Park Residents Oppose Federal Housing Project," *PEB*, March 24, 1972, PBCC.

87. Edmund N. Bacon to Walter E. Alessandroni, March 26, 1965, Folder: City Planning Commission, Box A-4477, JHJT; G. Holmes Perkins to James H. J. Tate, May 5, 1965, Folder: City Planning Commission, Box A-4477, JHJT; Memorandum from Anthony P. Zecca to James H. J. Tate, May 11, 1965, Folder: City Planning Commission, Box A-4477, JHJT; Memorandum from Robert W. Crawford to Anthony P. Zecca, "Report on Recreation in the Northeast," October 31, 1966, Folder: Far Northeast Clergy, Box A-4514, JHJT.

88. Adolph Katz, "The Kitchen Is at the Front Door in Northeast's Gift to Row Housing," *PEB*, March 12, 1961, PBCC.

89. Minutes, Meeting with Far Northeast Clergy Association, December 21, 1965, Folder: Far Northeast Clergy, Box A-4514, JHJT.

90. Maurice M. Lewis Jr., "'Pulaski' Road Title Surprises Residents," *PEB*, November 21, 1968, PBCC.

91. Eugene L. Meyer, "Northeast Group Opposes Route of Subway Extension," *PEB*, March 20, 1968, PBCC; "Citizen Council Backs Plan to Axe Freeway," *PEB*, January 22, 1970, PBCC; Maurice M. Lewis Jr., "500 Plan to Protest Freeway-Subway Bill," *PEB*, February 22, 1971, PBCC; "800 Protest New Route of Pulaski Highway at Citizens Meeting," *News Gleaner*, September 30, 1971, PBCC.

92. Al Haas, "Ordinary Folks Rebel Against Highways Giant," *PI*, November 9, 1971, PBCC.

93. Maurice M. Lewis Jr., "1,000 Protest Plans for Northeast Roads," *PEB*, March 23, 1972, PBCC; "City Drops Plan to Build 2 Freeways in Northeast," *PEB*, May 23, 1973, PBCC.

94. "The Northeast Is Being Shortchanged," *NT*, April 22, 1970.

95. Peter H. Binzen, "Northeast's Middle Class Feels Neglected by City," *PEB*, October 12, 1969, PBCC.

96. Ibid.

97. "Olney Students Stage Sit-In in Lunchroom," *PEB*, June 4, 1970, PBCC; "Olney Pupils, Shedd to Air Grievances," *PEB*, June 5, 1970, PBCC; "Olney Civic Group Votes to Demand Shedd's Ouster," *PEB*, June 16, 1970, PBCC.

98. Helen Wiley to Richardson Dilworth, June 5, 1970, Folder 54, Box 2, RDP.

Chapter 5

1. Greg Walter, "Frank Rizzo," *PM*, July 1967; "Reporter-Writer Greg Walter," *DN*, May 26, 1989; "Greg Walter, Reporter Who Shook Up the City," *PI*, May 26, 1989; S. A. Paolantonio, *Frank Rizzo: The Last Big Man in Big City America*, 10th anniversary ed. (Philadelphia: Camino Books, 2003), 139–140.

2. Walter, "Frank Rizzo."

3. Ibid.

4. Paolantonio, *Rizzo*, 229; Daniel J. McKenna, "Rizzo Defends Tough Stand on Criminals," *PEB*, October 11, 1967, PBCC.

5. Nancy MacLean, *Freedom Is Not Enough: The Opening of the American Workplace* (Cambridge, MA: Harvard University Press, 2005); Matthew Frye Jacobson, *Roots Too: White Ethnic Revival in Post–Civil Rights America* (Cambridge, MA: Harvard University Press, 2006); Dennis DeSlippe, "'We Must Bring Together a New Coalition:' The Challenge of Working-Class White Ethnics to Color-Blind Conservatism in the 1970s," *International Labor and Working-Class History* 74 (Fall 2008): 148–170; Thomas J. Sugrue and John D. Skrenty, "The White Ethnic Strategy," in Bruce J. Schulman and Julian E. Zelizer, eds., *Rightward Bound: Making America Conservative in the 1970s* (Cambridge, MA: Harvard University Press, 2008), 179–183.

6. Matthew Countryman, *Up South: Civil Rights and Black Power in Philadelphia* (Philadelphia: University of Pennsylvania Press, 2006), 258–294.

7. Charles Montgomery, "Tasker Homes People Live in 'Island of Fear,'" *PEB*, November 24, 1969, PBCC; "Troubled Neighborhood," *PEB*, June 12, 1970, PBCC; Joseph R. Daughen and Peter Binzen, *The Cop Who Would Be King: Mayor Frank Rizzo* (Boston: Little, Brown, 1977), 146–147.

8. Daughen and Binzen, *The Cop Who Would Be King*, 146–147.

9. Fred Hamilton, *Rizzo: From Cop to Mayor of Philadelphia* (New York: Viking Press, 1973), 124–125; Nicole Maurantonio, "Crisis, Race, and Journalistic Authority in Postwar Philadelphia" (PhD diss., University of Pennsylvania, 2008), 117–118.

10. Paul Herbert, "Rizzo Urges 'Swift, Sure' Justice for Criminals," *PEB*, September 21, 1967, PBCC. Before widespread implementation, "stop and frisk" policies had been proposed by different law enforcement analysts since at least the mid-1960s: see Elizabeth Hinton, *From the War on Poverty to the War on Crime: The Making of Mass Incarceration in America* (Cambridge, MA: Harvard University Press, 2016), 82.

11. Bayard Brunt, "FOP President Fears Racial Split on Force," *PEB*, September 15, 1968, PBCC.

12. "Crime Rate Here Lowest of 19 Cities," *PEB*, March 14, 1968, PBCC.

13. "Rizzo Is Given 'Total Praise,'" *PEB*, May 29, 1968, PBCC; James V. Magee, "Mayor, Judges Credit Rizzo with Drop in Crime Rate," *PEB*, March 17, 1968, PBCC.

14. William E. Gordon to James H. J. Tate, September 4, 1969, Folder: Mayor James H. J. Tate, Box 60, HADVR; "Philadelphia Spared Summer Riots; Human Relations Vigil Given Credit," GPC; Thomas S. Logan to Frank Rizzo, April 15, 1968, Folder: Comm. Rizzo, Box A-4596, JHJT; Daughen and Binzen, *The Cop Who Would Be King*, 137–138.

15. North City Congress, Police-Community Relations Program, Summary Final Report, April 8, 1969, Box 635, Folder 7, GPC; Countryman, *Up South*, 285.

16. Jennifer Siebens, Analysis of Philadelphia's Fatal Police Shootings and Their Coverage Through the *Philadelphia Inquirer* and *The Evening Bulletin*, October 1970, Folder 1, Box 20, FCR.

17. Kos Semonski, "Rizzo Asserts U.S. Official Talks Hogwash," *PEB*, June 18, 1969, PBCC; Frank Lenny, "Rizzo Charges Plot Against All Police," *PEB*, September 1, 1970, PBCC.

18. Citizens for the Police Advisory Board, Press Release, October 9, 1969, Folder 22, Box 22, FCR; Mercer D. Tate, Press Release, "Reinstatement of Police Advisory Board," July 2, 1969, Folder: Correspondence, PABR; James H. J. Tate to Mercer D. Tate, September 30, 1969, Folder: Correspondence, PABR.

19. Countryman, *Up South*, 283–284.

20. "Crime," *Bridesburg Bulletin*, October 1970, Box 1, Folder: Bridesburg Bulletin, BBMAP; Daughen and Binzen, *The Cop Who Would Be King*, 149.

21. Daughen and Binzen, *The Cop Who Would Be King*, 149; Maurantonio, "Crisis," 107–110; Paolantonio, *Rizzo*, 100–101.

22. Lenny, "Rizzo Charges Plot Against All Police;" Walter Sucharski to James H. J. Tate, September 2, 1970, Folder 6, Box 23, SSP.

23. Maurantonio, "Crisis," 111–112; Paolantonio, *Rizzo*, 101–102.

24. Countryman, *Up South*, 289.

25. "Rizzo Asks Firm Justice to Reduce Rate of Crime," *PEB*, February 20, 1970, PBCC.

26. Meridee Merzer, "Our Policemen's Wives Learn to Live with Fear," *PEB*, September 1, 1970, PBCC.

27. "Police Wives Ask Increased Jail Sentences," *PEB*, August 9, 1969, PBCC; H. James Laverty, "Police Wives Urge Judges to Give Tougher Sentences," *PEB*, September 30, 1969, PBCC. Originally named Police Wives for Action, the organization incorporated as Police Wives and Interested Citizens for Action in 1969.

28. "Police Wives Start Mail Campaign to Build Support for Their Husbands," *PEB*, June 16, 1970, PBCC; Fred W. Smigelski, "Wives' Mail Drive Reveals Wide Support for Police," *PI*, May 7, 1970, PBCC; "Police Wives Call Judge Levin 'Soft,' Ask for Ouster," *PEB*, September 14, 1970, PBCC; "Over-Lenient Charge Denied by Judge Levin," *PEB*, September 20, 1970, PBCC; Jean Campbell, "Police Wives to Ask Levin's Censureship," *PEB*, September 23, 1970, PBCC.

29. "Levy Assails Judge Levin, Calls Him 'Sick Do-Gooder,'" *PEB*, October 29, 1970, PBCC.

30. Hinton, *From the War on Poverty to the War on Crime*.

31. Frank L. Rizzo to James H. J. Tate, February 2, 1971, Folder: Comm. Frank Rizzo, Box A-3094, FLR.

32. William J. Thompson to James H. J. Tate, undated [1971], Folder: Campaign for Mayor, Box A-3105, FLR.

33. Gene Harris, "Rizzo Blasts Mark Shedd, School Board," *PEB*, April 9, 1971, PBCC; "Discipline Won't Hurt Taxpayer, Shedd Hopes," *DN*, February 19, 1971.

34. "Take a Look at the Man Who Means Business," Rizzo for Mayor Campaign Pamphlet, 1971, SSP.

35. Joseph F. Lowry, "Rizzo Says He Seeks Votes from Middle Ground," *PEB*, February 2, 1971, PBCC.

36. Green for Mayor Committee, Campaign Flier, 1971, Folder 37, Box 14, ADAP; Independents for Green, List of Members, 1971, Folder 30, Box 14, ADAP; Paolantonio, *Rizzo*, 112–114.

37. Paolantonio, *Rizzo*, 112–114. Countryman, *Up South*, 309–315.

38. Richardson Dilworth, Statement, July 6, 1971, Folder: School President Mr. Dilworth, Box A-3101, FLR.

39. "The People Want Rizzo," Campaign Flier, 1971, Folder: Campaign for Mayor, Box A-3103, FLR.

40. "Let's Talk Qualifications," ADA Campaign Flier, 1971, Folder 31, Box 14, ADAP; People for Longstreth, October 19, 1971, Folder 31, Box 14, ADAP; Democrats for Longstreth, 1971, Folder 30, Box 14, ADAP; "Listen to Frank Rizzo," Democrats for Longstreth flier, 1971, Folder 30, Box 13, ADAP.

41. "Longstreth Does Not Care About the Working Man," Rizzo for Mayor Campaign Committee Materials, 1971, Folder: Campaign for Mayor, Box A-3105, FLR. See also W. Thacher Longstreth, *Main Line WASP: The Education of Thacher Longstreth* (New York: Norton, 1990).

42. Warrant T. Corbin to James H. J. Tate, September 16, 1961, Folder: Campaign for Mayor, Box A-3105, FLR; Joseph F. Lowry, "AFL-CIO Unit Backs Rizzo and Foglietta," *PEB*, July 13, 1971, PBCC.

43. Ike Freedman et al. to Concerned Citizen, July 6, 1971, Folder AD 6, Box 3, JLCR.

44. Gene Harris, "Tate Brings Crowd for Rizzo," *PEB*, October 19. 1971, PBCC; Minutes of the Philadelphia Council AFL-CIO, September 8, 1971, Folder: Phila Council AFL-CIO Minutes 1971, Box 1, PCAFL-CIO.

45. Sandy Grady, "Rizzo Draws Union Ire," *PEB*, February 22, 1973, PBCC.

46. Sandy Grady, "Rizzo Hailed, Intellectuals Rapped in S. Phila. Bar," *PEB*, October 12, 1971, PBCC.

47. Joseph F. Lowry, "Crossover Vote Likely in Central City," *PEB*, October 20, 1971, PBCC; Paolantonio, *Rizzo*, 121–122.

48. Paolantonio, *Rizzo*, 116.

49. On Philadelphia's WASP-y reputation, see John Lukacs, *Philadelphia: Patricians and Philistines, 1900–1950* (New York: Farrar, Straus, Giroux, 1980).

50. Copy of *Doonesbury*, *PEB*, August 7, 1972, Folder: Newspapers—Bulletin, Box A-3535, FLR.

51. *Doonesbury*, *WP*, August 8, 1972, Folder: Newspapers—Bulletin, Box A-3535, FLR.

52. *Doonesbury*, *PEB*, August 8, 1972, Folder: Newspapers—Bulletin, Box A-3535, FLR. The *Bulletin* editor warned Rizzo of the forthcoming publication, but it is not clear if the Rizzo administration pressured the newspaper into editing the comic. Memorandum from Al Roberts to Tony Zecca, July 31, 1972, Folder: Newspapers—Bulletin, Box A-3535, FLR.

53. *Doonesbury*, *PEB*, August 9, 1972, Folder: Newspapers—Bulletin, Box A-3535, FLR.

54. Such letters can be found throughout Rizzo's mayoral correspondence, often in miscellaneous folders. Letters regarding abortion can be found in Folder: Abortion, Box A-3540, FLR; letters regarding capital punishment in Folder: Capital Punishment, Box A-3540, FLR; birthday and holiday greetings are in Box A-3416, FLR; letters to Carmella Rizzo are in Folder: Mrs. Rizzo, Box A-3546, FLR.

55. Loretta Crea to Frank L. Rizzo, no date [1972], Folder: Lou Gordon Show, Box A-3536, FLR.

56. Richardson Dilworth to Harvey Jolly, May 29, 1973, Folder 10, Box 211, RDP.

57. Paolantonio, *Rizzo*, 165–167.

58. Anna Rapinesi Houck to Frank L. Rizzo, September 9, 1973, Folder: Polygraph Test, Box A-3401, FLR; Marvin L. Malickson to Frank L. Rizzo, September 5, 1973, Folder: Polygraph

Test, Box A-3401, FLR; more letters of support can be found in Folder: Polygraph Test, Box A-3401, FLR.

59. (Mrs.) Sadie Ellis to Mayor Rizzo, no date, Folder: Lou Gordon Show, Box A-3536, FLR.

60. Mrs. Carmella Caltabiano to Mr. and Mrs. Rizzo, December 16, 1973, Folder: Mayor's House Roxborough, Box A-3417, FLR; Leonard J. Berwick to Mayor Rizzo, May 17, 1973, Folder: Mayor's House Roxborough, Box A-3417, FLR; Mrs. Larkins to the Dear People of Phila., May 18, 1973, Folder: Mayor's House Roxborough, Box A-3417, FLR.

61. "Rizzo Says 'Liberals' Violate Others' Rights," *PEB*, November 3, 1972, PBCC.

62. Frank L. Rizzo to Kenneth R. Cole Jr., September 7, 1972, Folder: Assistant to the President for Domestic Affairs, Box A-3540, FLR.

63. Richardson Dilworth to Robert L. Taylor, December 7, 1972, Folder 2, Box 107, RDP.

64. David Berkowitz to Frank L. Rizzo, no date [received August 1, 1974], Folder: City Planning, Box, A-4860, FLR.

65. Jefferson Cowie, *Stayin' Alive: The 1970s and the Last Days of the Working Class* (New York: New Press, 2010), 192–205.

66. Guian A. McKee, "'I've Never Dealt with a Government Agency Before': Philadelphia's Somerset Knitting Mills Project, the Local State, and the Missed Opportunities of Urban Renewal," *Journal of Urban History* 35 (2009): 387–409.

67. Carolyn Teich Adams, *The Politics of Capital Investment: The Case of Philadelphia* (Albany: State University of New York Press, 1988), 127–151.

68. Charles E. Welch, *Oh! Dem Golden Slippers: The Colorful Story of the Philadelphia Mummers* (New York: Thomas Nelson, 1970).

69. On Philadelphia sports, see Ryan A. Swanson and David K. Wiggins, eds., *Philly Sports: Teams, Games, and Athletes from Rocky's Town* (Fayetteville: University of Arkansas Press, 2016).

70. "Bully Boys," *DN*, January 17, 1992; Jim Jackson and Ed Snider, *Walking Together Forever: The Broad Street Bullies, Then and Now* (Champaign, IL: Sports Publishing, 2005), 3.

71. Jack Chevalier, *The Broad Street Bullies: The Incredible Story of the Philadelphia Flyers* (New York: Rutledge, 1974), 15–23; John Wong, "Making Ice (Hockey) in Philadelphia: Leadership, Organization, and the Tale of Two NHL Franchises," in Swanson and Wiggins, eds. *Philly Sports*, 173–179.

72. Paolantonio, *Rizzo*, 178–179; Chevalier, *Broad Street Bullies*, 15–23.

73. *Rocky*, directed by John G. Avildsen, United Artists, 1976; Cowie, *Stayin' Alive*, 326–329; Jacobson, *Roots Too*, 98–104.

74. Jacobson, *Roots Too*, 98–104; Victoria E. Elmwood, "'Just Some Bum from the Neighborhood': The Resolution of Post-Civil Rights Tension and Heavyweight Public Sphere Discourse in *Rocky* (1976)," *Film and History* 35, no. 2 (2005): 49–59; Clay Motley, "Fighting for Manhood: *Rocky* and Turn-of-the-Century Antimodernism," *Film and History* 35, no. 2 (2005): 60–66.

75. Jaime Schultz, "Philadelphia's Greatest Sports Hero? The Case for Rocky Balboa," in Swanson and Wiggins, eds. *Philly Sports*, 147–159.

76. Jacobson, *Roots Too*, 100–101.

77. "Newsmaker," *PI*, December 12, 1972, PBCC; Jeanette Bisirri to Mayor Rizzo, October 15, 1973, Box A-3403, Folder: Leniency of Judges, FLR; May S. Belle to Frank Rizzo, December 9, 1973, Folder: Leniency of Judges, FLR.

78. Charles F. Thomson and Harmon Y. Gordon, "Rizzo and Packel Disagree on Saxbe View of Jail Terms," *PEB*, August 30, 1974, PBCC.

79. Paolantonio, *Rizzo*, 191–192.

80. Jim Mann, "Rizzo Rules Powerful Coalition," *PI*, November 5, 1975, PBCC.

81. Rizzo's opponents used his well-known propensity for outlandish statements in an attempt to embarrass the mayor. The Philadelphia Chapter of the Americans for Democratic Action published a book of some of his more controversial, insensitive, and bizarre pronouncements. See Americans for Democratic Action, *The Sayings of Chairman Frank: or, I Never Saw My Mother Naked* (Philadelphia: Southeastern Chapter of the Americans for Democratic Action, 1977).

82. Paolantonio, *Rizzo*, 192.

83. Martin J. Herman, "Rizzo's 'Blue-Collar City' Draws Cheers of Labor Union," *PEB*, May 25, 1977, PBCC.

Chapter 6

1. "3 Hurt, 3 Held, Dog Killed in S. Phila. Melee," *PEB*, May 20, 1974, PBCC; Jerome Mondesire, "Officials Talk to Residents," *PI*, May 21, 1974, PBCC; "Tasker Homes Race Strife Takes a Young Life," *DN*, April 2, 1974, PBCC.

2. Joseph Hanania, "Grays Ferry Is Buoyant," *PEB*, April 18, 1976, PBCC. See also Jon Wilson Anderson, "Little Community in the Big City: Social Organization and Community Culture in an Urban Neighborhood" (master's thesis, University of Pennsylvania, 1969). For anonymity, Anderson called Grays Ferry "Bogstown." Jon Anderson, Proposal for a study of the community organization of a stable Working Class Urban Neighborhood, no date, Folder 7, Box 6, RRC.

3. Jack Eisele to Joe Lynn, January 18, 1972, Folder: Redevelopment—Grays Ferry 1970-1972, Box 71, PCPCF; Redevelopment Authority of the City of Philadelphia, Urban Renewal Plan for Grays Ferry Urban Renewal Area, Amended November 1972, Folder: Redevelopment—Grays Ferry 1970-1972, Box 71, PCPCF.

4. John Corr, "They'll Fight Anybody, Anytime," *PI*, March 4, 1974, PBCC.

5. Ibid.

6. Francis W. Rafferty to Frank L. Rizzo, June 28, 1973, Folder: Grays Ferry Community Council, Box A-3424, FLR; *Grays Ferry Community Council Gazette*, Vol I, No. 42, 1976, Folder: Grays Ferry Community Council, Box A-5130, FLR; Hanania, "Grays Ferry Is Buoyant."

7. Corr, "They'll Fight Anybody, Anytime."

8. David Guo, "A Racial Battlefield: Blame Is Exchanged," *PI*, July 22, 1974, PBCC; John Hilferty, "Kensington, Blow by Blow," *PI*, July 30, 1974, PBCC.

9. Philadelphia Police Department, Civil Disobedience Unit, Official Photographs, March 25, 1971, April 5, 1971, and April 20, 1971, Folder: Whitman Park (1), Box A-3532, FLR.

10. Joseph F. O'Neill, "Whitman Area Project," Philadelphia Police Department Report, July 9, 1971, Folder Whitman Area, Box A-3111, FLR; William J. Storm, "Protests Halt Whitman Park Housing Work," *PEB*, March 23, 1971, PBCC; "PHA Refuses to End Job at Whitman Park," *PEB*, April 7, 1971, PBCC; Harmon Y. Gordon, "Builder Agrees to Halt Job at Whitman Park," April 30, 1971, *PEB*, PBCC.

11. Memorandum from Jerry Parker to Bob McMullin, RE: Possible Sites for New Construction, November 14, 1972, Folder: Housing—General 1972, Box A-2961, PCPCF.

12. Arnold Hirsch, *Making the Second Ghetto: Race and Housing in Chicago, 1940–1960* (Cambridge: Cambridge University Press, 1983); Thomas J. Sugrue, *Origins of the Urban Crisis: Race and Inequality in Postwar Detroit* (Princeton, NJ: Princeton University Press, 1996).

13. HADV, Memo to Staff, "Housing the Poor: The Missing Mandate," September 30, 1970, Folder: Public Housing—General, Box 40, HADVR; Margaret Eisen, "Mrs. Dennis Presses for Fair

Housing," *PEB*, April 3, 1969, PBCC; Bernard C. Meltzer, "Urban League Officials Question Housing Policies for the Poor," *PEB*, May 29, 1970, PBCC; "New Chief Sees Housing Unit as 'Advocate,'" *PEB*, October 2, 1971, PBCC; John Bauman, *Public Housing, Race, and Renewal: Urban Planning in Philadelphia, 1920–1970* (Philadelphia: Temple University Press, 1987), 205–206.

14. Conservation Program of the Redevelopment Authority of the City of Philadelphia, January 1962, Box 80, GPC.

15. J. Edward Mitinger to Morris Jacobs, May 12, 1969, Folder: RDA-1957-1971, Box 2, WC-632.

16. Memorandum from Paul F. Noll to Damon Childs, June 4, 1970, Folder: Redevelopment Whitman 1965-1967, Box A-2976, PCPCF; Proposed Turnkey Public Housing Construction Program, Presented to Urban Coalition, September 1968, Folder: Turnkey III, Box 40, HADVR; Memorandum from Robert Hubbard to Cushing N. Dolbeare, "Supporters of Turnkey Proposals," February 20, 1969, Folder: Turnkey III, Box 40, HADVR.

17. Timothy J. Lombardo, "The Battle of Whitman Park: Race, Class, and Public Housing in Philadelphia, 1956–1982," *Journal of Social History* 47, no. 2 (Winter 2013): 401–428.

18. Frederick C. Druding to Dear Friend, June 1966, Folder: Young Democrats of Phila., 1961–1971, Box 2, WC-638; Fred Druding, Address to Young Democrats, October 1966, Folder: Young Democrats of Phila., 1961–1971, Box 2, WC-638; Fred Druding to James H. J. Tate, July 15, 1969, Folder: Tate, James H. J., Box 2, WC-638; Francis E. Gleeson to James H. J. Tate, July 16, 1969, Folder: Gleeson, Frank, Box 2, WC-638; Fred Druding, Remarks at Man of the Year Award Dinner of the Young Democratic Club of Philadelphia, Honoring James H. J. Tate, October 15, 1969, Folder: Tate, James H. J., Box 2, WC-638.

19. Katrina Dyke, "Rizzo, Longstreth Differ on Housing Vote," *PEB*, June 15, 1971, PBCC; Fred Druding to Frank L. Rizzo, May 9, 1976, Folder: Politics: General City, Box A-5128, FLR.

20. Storm, "Protests Halt Whitman Park Housing Work"; "'Whitman Park Phantoms' Picket Cavanaugh's Home," *PEB*, May 20, 1971, PBCC; Raymond C. Brecht, "Can City Revive Whitman Park Homes Plan?" *PEB*, May 25, 1971, PBCC.

21. Adrian Lee, "'The Bulldozers Are Coming…The Bulldozers Are…,'" *PEB*, November 21, 1976, PBCC; Adrian Lee, "Whitman Park Story—A Sorry Chapter," *PEB*, November 23, 1976, PBCC; Adrian Lee, "Echoes at Whitman Park," *PEB*, September 26, 1977, PBCC; Adrian Lee, "Gert Hogan's Story: She's Against Public Housing," *PEB*, January 9, 1977, PBCC; Adrian Lee, "Whitman Ponders the Next Move," *PEB*, June 26, 1979, PBCC.

22. Sandy Grady, "Battling Gert Knocks Down Housing Plan," *PEB*, June 25, 1972, PBCC.

23. Doris B. Wiley, "Free Utilities, No Taxes Gall Whitman Residents," *PEB*, July 18, 1971, PBCC; "Whitman Homes Residents to Pay Taxes, Utilities, Cavanaugh Says," *PEB*, July 18, 1971, PBCC.

24. Sophie F. Horman, Letters to the Bulletin, May 26, 1971, PBCC.

25. On early conceptions of public housing, see Gail Radford, *Modern Housing for America: Policy Struggles in the New Deal Era* (Chicago: University of Chicago Press, 1996).

26. Fred Druding to Dan Margsak, February 14, 1973, Folder: OHCD Housing Program, Box 1, WC-638; Jan Schaffer, "The Whitman Battle Cry: No Housing Project Here," *PI*, January 26, 1976, PBCC.

27. Statement of Whitman Area Improvement Council, December 12, 1972, Folder: Krusen, Evans, and Byrne, Box 1, WC-332; Wiley, "Free Utilities, No Taxes Gall Whitman Residents."

28. Gordon Cavanaugh to James H. J. Tate and Fred T. Corleto, May 24, 1971, Folder: Housing—General 1971, Box A-2961, PCPCF; Richard Deasy, "City to Ignore HUD on Whitman,"

DN, June 10, 1972, PBCC; Dennis Kirkland, "Opponents Are Apparent Victors in Whitman Park Housing Battle," *PI*, June 29, 1972, PBCC; Richard Deasy,"Whitman Fight Won, but the Debts Remain," *DN*, March 23, 1973, PBCC.

29. Grady, "Battling Gert."

30. Memorandum from the Citizens Committee for Tenants Rights to All Philadelphia Media, December 5, 1972, Folder: Philadelphia Housing Authority, Box A-3531, FLR.

31. Ewart Rouse, "Rizzo Public Housing Policy Is on Trial," *PI*, November 10, 1975, PBCC; Joe Davidson, "City Prevents Good Housing, Aide Charges," *PEB*, May 27, 1976, PBCC. See also *Resident Advisory Board v. Rizzo*, 425 F. Supp. 987 (E.D. Pa. 1976).

32. Jonathon Stein to Arthur Lefco, April 30, 1975, Folder: Krusen, Evans, and Byrne, Box 1, WC-332.

33. Kevin M. Kruse, *White Flight: Atlanta and the Making of Modern Conservatism* (Princeton, NJ: Princeton University Press, 2005).

34. Memorandum from Phil Martin to Presbytery Delegates, June 12, 1972, Folder: Site and Project Selection, Box 40, HADVR.

35. Jack Smyth, "Apartment Plan Opposed by Morrell Park Group," *PEB*, December 5, 1968, PBCC; Margaret Eisen, "Morrell Park Residents Oppose Federal Housing Project," *PEB*, March 24, 1972, PBCC.

36. "Life in Morrell Park Earns a Split Verdict," *PEB*, October 5, 1969, PBCC.

37. Mr. and Mrs. John A. Halligan to Frank Rizzo, June 14, 1974, Folder: Knights Road and Clarendon, Box A-3545, FLR.

38. Albert Schoppy to Mayor Rizzo, June 23, 1972, Folder: Knights Road and Clarendon, Box A-3545, FLR.

39. William C. Blacknell to Mayor Rizzo, July 8, 1972, Folder: Knights Road and Clarendon, Box A-3545, FLR.

40. Frank Rizzo to William C. Blacknell, July 12, 1972, Folder: Knights Road and Clarendon, Box A-3545, FLR.

41. Patricia Baumgartner to Frank Rizzo, June 28, 1972, Folder: Knights Road and Clarendon, Box A-3545, FLR.

42. Phil Schieber to Frank L. Rizzo, June 28, 1972, Folder: Knights Road and Clarendon, Box A-3545, FLR; Linda McCutcheon to Mayor Rizzo, June 19, 1972, Folder: Knights Road and Clarendon, Box A-3545, FLR.

43. Joseph F. Lowry, "Rizzo Says Tate May Let Him Fill School-Board Vacancies," *PEB*, September 28, 1971, PBCC; Peter H. Binzen, "He Gambled on Ideas and Lost Out on Allies," *PEB*, November 21, 1971, PBCC.

44. William T. Kennedy, "Board Buys Shedd Pact of $58,500," *PEB*, December 9, 1971, PBCC.

45. William T. Kennedy, "Ross Elected President of School Board," *PEB*, December 6, 1971, PBCC; Charles H. Thomson, "Ross and Dilworth: They Differ in Background, Style, Basic Concepts," *PEB*, January 24, 1972, PBCC.

46. Larry Fields, "I Was a Doer, Not a Dreamer, Ross Recalls," *DN*, January 17, 1973, PBCC.

47. Frank L. Rizzo to Peter Zenser, October 1972, Folder: School Busing, Box A-3532, FLR.

48. James Sanzare, "A Study of Teacher Unionism in Philadelphia, 1941–1973: The Case of Local 3, Philadelphia Federation of Teachers" (Ed.D. diss., Temple University, 1977); Joseph A. Daughen, "Ross: A Story of Conflicting Loyalties," *PEB*, February 15, 1973, PBCC.

49. Concerned Parents to Frank L. Rizzo, September 15, 1973, Folder: Busing, Box A-3398, FLR.

50. Floyd L. Logan Press Release, National Hysteria Over Busing For School Integration, March 20, 1972, Folder 21, Box 7, FLP; Ronald P. Formisano, *Boston Against Busing: Race, Class, and Ethnicity in the 1960s and 1970s* (Chapel Hill: University of North Carolina Press, 1991); Matthew Lassiter, *The Silent Majority: Suburban Politics in the Sunbelt South* (Princeton, NJ: Princeton University Press, 2006); Matthew Delmont, *Why Busing Failed: Race, Media, and the National Resistance to School Desegregation* (Berkeley: University of California Press, 2016).

51. Marci Shatzman, "The Little Riders: A City Busing Program That Works," *PEB*, May 7, 1972, PBCC.

52. "Neighbors and School Clash on Program for Bright Pupils," *PEB*, October 14, 1974, PBCC.

53. Elizabeth A. Williams, "Residents Fight Board Refusal to Move Motivation Class," *PEB*, October 22, 1973, PBCC.

54. Ibid.

55. "Rizzo Says He Backs Protesters at Schools," *PEB*, October 24, 1973, PBCC.

56. Thomas Boonin, Proposed Plan for Programmatic Desegregation, February 1974, Folder: School District, Box A-4857, FLR.

57. Betty Zolo to Frank L. Rizzo, undated, Folder: Busing, Box A-4857, FLR.

58. Larry McMullen, "She's a Whirlwind," *DN*, June 27, 1973, PBCC.

59. Constance McHugh to Frank L. Rizzo, January 18, 1974, Folder: Busing, Box A-4857, FLR.

60. Frank L. Rizzo to Milton J. Shapp, September 20, 1974, Folder: Kurtzman Plan, Box A-4873, FLR.

61. Marc Werlinsky, "'No Busing' NE Tells School Board," *NT*, January 23, 1974.

62. Thomas M. Foglietta to Frank L. Rizzo, December 28, 1972, Folder: City Councilmen, Box A-3533, FLR; "White House Recommends Slashes in U.S. School Aid Budget," *PEB*, December 26, 1972, PBCC.

63. "Salvatore Boasts Support Against Mandated Busing," *NT*, February 20, 1974; "Salvatore Seeks to Stop Forced School Busing," *PEB*, February 12, 1974, PBCC.

64. Joseph D'Arcangelo to Mayor Rizzo, no date, Folder: Busing, Box A-4857, FLR.

65. Barbara L. Geiger to Mayor Frank Rizzo, January 18, 1974, Folder: Busing, Box 1-4857, FLR.

66. Mr. and Mrs. Curtis Carpenter to Mayor Frank Rizzo, July 31, 1975, Folder: Busing, Box A-3857, FLR.

67. Jeanine McGill to Frank Rizzo, September 26, 1975, Folder: Busing, Box A-3857, FLR. Rizzo received hundreds of similar letters in 1975.

68. Carol Rich, "2 Black Leaders Rip Pupil Integration Plan," *PEB*, May 11, 1976, PBCC.

69. John DuBois, "Rizzo Says Recall Move Will Fail," *PEB*, April 1, 1976, PBCC; S. A. Paolantonio, *Frank Rizzo: The Last Big Man in Big City America*, 10th anniversary ed. (Philadelphia: Camino Books, 2003), 193–211.

70. "Boston's School Busing Proves Mostly a Model of How Not to Do It," *WSJ*, October 13, 1976.

71. Mr. and Mrs. Michael Harrop to Frank Rizzo, no date, Folder: Archdiocese of Phila., Box A-4874, FLR; Donald J. Hicks to Frank L. Rizzo, May 2, 1974, Folder: Archdiocese of Phila., Box A-4874, FLR; Mr. and Mrs. Frank Lopinski to Frank Rizzo, March 8, 1974 Folder: Archdiocese of Phila., Box A-4874, FLR.

72. Joseph Stefankiewiz to Mr. Rizzo, September 2, 1976, Folder: Board of Education, Box A-5107, FLR.

73. David C. Hackney, "Catholic Schools Feel the Pinch, May Have to Raise Tuition," *PEB*, November 10, 1974, PBCC.

74. Helen Baker to Mayor Rizzo, October 3, 1972, Folder: Aid to Non-Public Schools, Box A-3540, FLR.

75. John T. Gurash to Mayor Rizzo, June 19, 1972, Folder: Archdiocese of Philadelphia, Box A-3551, FLR; John T. Gurash et al., The Report on the Archdiocesan Advisory Committee on the Financial Crisis of the Catholic Schools in Philadelphia and Surrounding Counties, (Philadelphia, 1972), Box 11, Folder 11, GPC.

76. On tax credits and vouchers for religious education, see Joseph Crespino, *In Search of Another Country: Mississippi and the Conservative Counterrevolution* (Princeton, NJ: Princeton University Press, 2007).

77. Richard S. Schweiker, Press Release, "Schweiker, Scott Ask for Hearings on Catholic School Crisis," June 21, 1972, Folder 53, Box 19, RSSP; "High Court Backs Interim Parochial Aid," *PEB*, March 22, 1971, PBCC.

78. Annual Report of the Superintendent of the Archdiocese of Philadelphia,1971–1972, PAHRC; Annual Report of the Superintendent of the Archdiocese of Philadelphia, 1973–1974, PAHRC; Annual Report of the Superintendent of the Archdiocese of Philadelphia, 1974–1975, PAHRC.

79. Maurice M. Lewis Jr., "Catholic High Schools to Raise Tuition $100," *PEB*, January 16, 1975, PBCC.

80. Hackney, "Catholic Schools Feel the Pinch, May Have to Raise Tuition."

81. Henry R. Darling, "Pupils Shifting to Suburban Catholic Schools," *PEB*, August 26, 1974, PBCC; Annual Report of the Superintendent of the Archdiocese of Philadelphia, 1975-1976, PAHRC.

82. Daniel J. McKenna, "Urban League Asks Schools to Force Staff Integration," *PEB*, March 16, 1966, PBCC; Henry W. Messaros,"Suit Seeks to End State Aid Given to Nonpublic Schools," *PEB*, September 11, 1973, PBCC; Sylvia Meek to Floyd L. Logan, April 7, 1964, Folder 2, Box 4, FLP.

83. Messaros, "Suit Seeks to End State Aid Given to Nonpublic Schools."

84. Meek v. Pittenger, 421 U.S. (1975).

85. Carole Rich, "Suit Divided Catholics, Jews," *PEB*, November 23, 1975, PBCC.

86. Carole Rich and William J. Storm, "Parents March to Protest Aid Cut," *PEB*, June 11, 1975, PBCC.

87. H. Leverne Rosenberger and James L. J. Pie to Frank L. Rizzo, June 4, 1975, Folder: Aid to Nonpublic Schools, Box A-3857, FLR; Frank L. Rizzo to James L. J. Pie, June 9, 1975, Folder: Aid to Nonpublic Schools, Box A-3857, FLR.

88. Carole Rich, "Tuition Raised at Catholic High Schools," *PEB*, February 24, 1976, PBCC; Carole Rich, "Catholic School Strike: Mood Is Sad," *PEB*, September 10, 1976, PBCC.

Chapter 7

1. *RAB v. Rizzo* Exhibit 195, Report of Professor Yale Rabin: "The Whitman Park Townhouse Public Housing Project and Its Relationship to Black Population and the Housing Policies of Government Agencies," 1976, Folder 16, Box 6, CLSR; John F. Morrison and John T. Gillespie, "City Vows to Fight Integrated Housing," *PEB*, November 9, 1976, PBCC; "From Politics to Judiciary, Swirl Surrounds Broderick," *PEB*, November 10, 1976, PBCC.

2. Fred Druding, "Whitman PAC Funding—The Truth is All We Ask," *Whitman News*, Vol. 3, Ed. 2, June 8, 1973, Folder: Whitman News, Box 2, WC-523; Fred Druding to Jimmy Carter, January 31, 1978, Folder: Board Meeting 1977-1978, Box 4, WC-632; Robert E. Taylor, "U.S. Rebuffs Whitman Bid," *PEB*, November 17, 1978, PBCC; Kit Konolige, "Whitman Foes Lose Final Court Battle," *DN*, June 19, 1979, PBCC.

3. "Toughs Blamed for Project Failures," *Whitman News*, Vol. 6, Ed. 1, June 1976, WC-523. "Barry Mitchell" is a pseudonym. Temple University's Special Collections Research Library makes these records available under the condition that researchers protect the anonymity of some council members and neighborhood residents.

4. Barry Mitchell to Fred Druding, May 2, 1976, Folder: B.M., Box 11, WC-632. All punctuation in original.

5. Mitchell's maps are included in: Barry Mitchell to Fred Druding, November 13, 1976; Barry Mitchell to Fred Druding, March 4, 1978, Mitchell titled this map "Transfer of Population"; Barry Mitchell to Fred Druding, August 31, 1979; Barry Mitchell to Fred Druding, July 28, 1981, Folder: B.M, Box 11; WC-632.

6. Fred Druding to Barry Mitchell, November 17, 1976, Folder: B.M., Box 11, WC-632; J. D. McCaffrey, "Whitman Council President: 'I'm a Liberal,'" *PEB*, April 13, 1978, PBCC.

7. Fred Druding to Judge Raymond Broderick, July 31, 1978, Folder: Green, Wm., Box 2, WC-638.

8. Harmon Y. Gordon, "Whitman Project Ordered," *PEB*, September 1, 1977, PBCC; Jim Smith and Stephan Rosenfield, "City to Appeal Whitman Park Housing OK," *DN*, September 1, 1977, PBCC; Bill Keough, "High Court OKs Whitman Park," *PEB*, February 27, 1978, PBCC; "Judge Under Fire in Whitman," *DN*, June 21, 1979, Folder: Whitman Special Vote 1979, Box 4, WC-632 Records.

9. Joseph R. Daughen and Peter Binzen, *The Cop Who Would Be King: Mayor Frank Rizzo* (Boston: Little, Brown, 1977), 36–39.

10. Frank J. Montemuro Jr. to Frank L. Rizzo, October 26, 1972, Folder: Order Sons of Italy in America, Box A-3554, FLR; "Italian Group Hears Rizzo Boast of Ethnics," *PEB*, March 29, 1978, PBCC.

11. Ira Katznelson, *When Affirmative Action Was White: An Untold History of Racial Equality in Twentieth Century America* (New York: W. W. Norton, 2006).

12. Matthew Frye Jacobson, *Roots Too: White Ethnic Revival in Post–Civil Rights America* (Cambridge, MA: Harvard University Press, 2006).

13. Michael Novak, "Busing—the Arrogance of Power," *WSJ*, July 25, 1975; Novak, "Liberal Resistance to Busing," *NYT*, October 16, 1975; Michael Novak to Dear Cousin, no date [1976], Folder 4,Box 1, EMPAC.

14. "'Ethnic Consciousness' Is Growing Among Many Minority Individuals," *PJT*, January 20, 1972.

15. Joseph L. Zazyczny to Peter Camiel, November 30, 1971, Folder 1 ,Box 1, JLZP; Joseph L. Zazyczny to Martin Weinberg, February 3, 1977, Folder 3, Box 1, JLZP; Joseph L. Zazyczny, Polish American Citizens League of Pennsylvania, Report of the President, April 24, 1977, Folder 3, Box 1, JLZP.

16. "Mayor Appoints Commissioner," *Bridesburg Bulletin*, April 1972, Folder: Bridesburg Bulletin 1968, Box 1, BBMAP; Joseph L. Zazyczny, Polish American Citizens' League of Pennsylvania President's Report, April 25, 1976, Folder 2, Box 1, JLZP.

17. James Jones Jr. and Robert Fluehr to Philadelphia Local Unions, March 29, 1971, Folder 5, Box 19, JLCR; Alex Wollod, "A Capsule on JOINT (Jewish Labor Committee and Negro Trade

Union Leadership Council)," Folder 5, Box 2, JLCR; Richard Moss, *Creating the New Right Ethnic in 1970s America: The Intersection of Anger and Nostalgia* (New York: Rowman and Littlefield, 2017).

18. Thomas J. Sugrue and John D. Skrenty, "The White Ethnic Strategy," in Bruce J. Schulman and Julian E. Zelizer, eds., *Rightward Bound: Making America Conservative in the 1970s* (Cambridge, MA: Harvard University Press, 2008), 179–183.

19. "Blacks Feel the Job Squeeze," *PEB*, June 2, 1975, PBCC; Bennett O. Stalvey Jr. to Ernest Soden, October 1, 1976, Folder 1, Box 16, LPR; Bennett O. Stalvey Jr. to Dewey E. Dodds, October 1, 1976, Folder 1, Box 16, LPR.

20. Stephen Franklin, "Minority Job Plan Is a Flop," *PEB*, June 26, 1977, PBCC; Dennis Deslippe, *Protesting Affirmative Action: The Struggle over Equality After the Civil Rights Revolution* (Baltimore: Johns Hopkins University Press, 2012).

21. Henry W. Messaros, "Judge Warns Operating Engineers Against Further Racial Violence," *PEB*, June 21, 1972, PBCC; Henry W. Messaros, "Judge Restrains Union from Harassing Blacks," *PEB*, August 4, 1972, PBCC.

22. Harmony Y. Gordon, "Bias Trial of Unions Begins," *PEB*, January 22, 1976, PBCC; Jim Smith, "2 Sides Brace for Bias Trial," *DN*, January 19, 1976, PBCC.

23. "Judge Orders Union Local to Add Blacks," *PEB*, July 9, 1975, PBCC.

24. Minutes of the Philadelphia Council AFL-CIO, February 12, 1975, Folder: Phila Council AFL-CIO Minutes 1974, Box 1, PCAFL-CIO; Harmon Y. Gordon, "Unions, Firms Told to Hire Minorities," *PEB*, November 8, 1979, PBCC.

25. Harry Gould, "Policewoman Charges Bias," *PI*, February 13, 1974, PBCC; Dct. Sgt. Penelope Brace Interview, October 31, 1984, Box 1, PILCP.

26. "Policewoman Sues City over Alleged Bias," *PEB*, February 13, 1974, PBCC.

27. Patsy Sims, "Nation's Policewomen Are Angry over Firing of Penelope Brace," *PI*, March 6, 1974, PBCC.

28. Joan McClure, "End Sex Discrimination in Philadelphia Police Department," no date, Folder: Brace, Penelope, Box 2, NOW-PC.

29. Women Organized Against Rape, "10 Point Proposal for a Sexual Assault Squad in Philadelphia," August 1975, Folder: Phila. Rape Squad 1974-1975, Box 7, WOARR; "The Case of the Lady Cops," *PM*, February 1976, PBCC.

30. Harmon Y. Gordon, "O'Neill Calls Women Too Weak for Police," *PEB*, February 10, 1975, PBCC

31. Dct. Sgt. Penelope Brace Interview, October 31, 1984, PILCP.

32. Nada Goodman to Charles Gallagher, October 23, 1974, Folder: Barefoot and Pregnant 1974, Box 1, NOW-PC Records; Nada Goodman to Joseph O'Neill, October 23, 1974, 1974, Folder: Barefoot and Pregnant 1974, Box 1, NOW-PC.

33. Mrs. Rita M. Brown to Dear Sir, March 1, 1976, Folder: Law Enforcement, Box A-5117, FLR.

34. Mrs. Janet Harrop to Mayor Rizzo, September 28, 1974, Folder: Police Departments, Box A-4864, FLR.

35. Marie Ann Mackley to Mayor Rizzo, October 9, 1974, Folder: Police Departments, Box A- 4864, FLR; Thomas J. Gibbons Jr., "Police Wives Rip Plan for Women to Patrol," *PEB*, September 26, 1974, PBCC.

36. Bob Warner, "Brace Wins Detective Rank in Court," *DN*, September 15, 1978, PBCC.

37. Dct. Sgt. Penelope Brace Interview, October 31, 1984, PILCP.

38. Richard D. Siegel, "Northeast Is Tagged Worst City Area of Bias Against Negroes," *PI*, July 29, 1966, PBCC.

39. Alphonso Deal Biographical Information, PBCC; Acel Moore, "A Policeman of Principle, Unwavering," *PI*, August 24, 1978, PBCC.

40. Tyree Johnson, "FOP Fight Spurs Bias Protest," *DN*, August 5, 1977, PBCC; Mark S. Guralnick, "FOP Is Insensitive, Black Officers Say," *PEB*, August 5, 1977, PBCC; Clifton O. Lee, "Racism Alleged in FOP," *PEB*, August 9, 1977, PBCC; Laura Murray, "Black Cops Vote to Picket FOP," *PEB*, August 9, 1977, PBCC; Marc T. Henderson,"Black Policemen Cancel Protest," *PEB*, August 13, 1977, PBCC; "Bias Is Charged by Black Policemen," *DN*, August 16, 1977, PBCC.

41. Complaint, *Alvarez v. City of Philadelphia*, Civil Action No. 77-4424, United States District Court for the Eastern District of Pennsylvania, 1977, Folder 1, Box 11, LPR; Ad Hoc Coalition for Affirmative Action Hiring and Promotion in the Philadelphia Police Department, January 26, 1982, Folder: Police Department 1982, Box A-5591, WJG; Report on Increased Minority Employment in the Philadelphia Police Department, March 19, 1982, Folder: Police Department 1982, Box A-5591, WJG.

42. Charles F. Davis to Mayor Green, February 12, 1982, Folder: Police Department 1982, Box A-5578, WJG.

43. "Cop Calls for Firing of Police," *DN*, August 18, 1978, PBCC.

44. Statement of Police Commissioner Joseph F. O'Neill Concerning A National Crime Survey Report: A Comparison of 1972 and 1974 Findings of Criminal Victimization in Chicago, Detroit, Los Angeles, New York and Philadelphia, December 30, 1976, Folder: Police Department, Box A-5117, FLR.

45. Helen Kerns to Frank L. Rizzo, June 14, 1972, Folder: Police Wives-Interested Citizens, Box A-3556, FLR; Marie Ann Mackley to Mayor Rizzo, August 12, 1973, Folder: Police Corruption, Box A-3409, FLR; Helen Kerns to Frank L. Rizzo, August 20, 1975, Folder: Police Wives-Interested Citizens, Box A-3879, FLR; Helen Kerns to Joseph Rhodes, August 10, 1978, Folder: Police Brutality, Box A-5355, FLR; Helen Kerns,"What About Abused Police?" letter to the editor, *PEB*, June 26, 1977, PBCC.

46. United States Commission on Civil Rights, *Hearing Before the United States Commission on Civil Rights: Police Practices and Civil Rights: Hearing Held in Philadelphia, Pennsylvania, February 6, 1979, April 16–17, 1979* (Washington, DC: Government Printing Office, 1979); S. A. Paolantonio, *Frank Rizzo: The Last Big Man in Big City America*, 10th anniversary ed. (Philadelphia: Camino Books, 2003), 218–219.

47. Claude Lewis, "MOVE Stirs Anger," *PEB*, October 25, 1974, PBCC; John T. Gillespie, "MOVE Rejects 'Modern Life-Style," *PEB*, April 8, 1975, PBCC.

48. John Anderson and Hilary Hevenor, *Burning Down the House: MOVE and the Tragedy of Philadelphia* (New York: W. W. Norton, 1987).

49. Lewis, "MOVE Stirs Anger."

50. Sam W. Pressley, "Blacks and Whites Disrupt Gang-Violence Meeting," *PEB*, February 19, 1974, PBCC; Elizabeth A. Williams, "Radical Group Stops School Board Meeting," *PEB*, March 26, 1974, PBCC.

51. Marilyn Schaeffer, "Radical Group Keeps Officer on Stand," *PEB*, November 13, 1974, PBCC; Marilyn Schaeffer, "Radicals Are Given Jail Terms," *PEB*, November 19, 1974, PBCC; Marilyn Schaeffer, "18 Charged in Courtroom After Fracas," *PEB*, January 14, 1975, PBCC; Larry Eichel, "MOVE Members Speak Out—Loudly," *PI*, April 21, 1975, PBCC.

52. Lewis, "MOVE Stirs Anger."

53. Claude Lewis, "MOVE's Day in Court," *PEB*, May 5, 1978, PBCC.

54. Ibid; John T. Gillespie, "MOVE Appeals to Zoning Board over 20 Stray Dogs," *PEB*, April 25, 1975, PBCC; John T. Gillespie, "Neighbors Complain About Threats from MOVE Members," *PEB*, April 29, 1975, PBCC.

55. Marc Schogol and Robert J. Terry, "Commune Members Clash with Police; Six Arrested," *PI*, March 26, 1976, PBCC; Charles Layton, "Body of Baby Seen at MOVE Commune," *PI*, April 10, 1976, PBCC; John T. Gillespie, "MOVE Shows Photos of Dead Tot," *PEB*, April 11, 1976, PBCC; John T. Gillespie, "Officer Saw Mother, Baby at MOVE Melee," *PEB*, April 13, 1976, PBCC.

56. Kitty Caparella, "Armed MOVE Hikes Tension," *DN*, May 23, 1977, PBCC; "MOVE and Police Wait It Out with Guns," *PEB*, May 24, 1977, PBCC; Frederick and Ruth Diengott to Frank Rizzo, September 19, 1977, Folder: MOVE, Box A-5219, FLR; Mrs. M. A. Ardecky to Frank Rizzo, August 11, 1977, Folder: MOVE, Box A-5219, FLR.

57. Bill Keough, "MOVE Is Making Lots of Noise on Loudspeakers," *PEB*, May 26, 1977, PBCC.

58. Mrs. G. Russell to Mayor Rizzo, April 15, 1978, Folder: MOVE, Box A-5356, FLR; Powelton Emergency Human Rights Committee to Frank Rizzo, March 5, 1978, Folder: MOVE, Box A-5356, FLR; David Runkel, "Siege Is Eyed to Starve Out Move," *PEB*, July 11, 1977, PBCC; Bill Keogh, "Irony Taints City's 'Handling' of MOVE Situation," *PEB*, July 25, 1977, PBCC.

59. Runkel, "Siege Is Eyed to Starve Out Move"; Joe O'Dowd, "The MOVE Impasse: $1M Dilemma," *DN*, February 17, 1978, PBCC.

60. Robert J. Terry, "MOVE Supporters Rally in W. Phila.," *PI*, July 10, 1977, PBCC; Elmer Smith and Joe Davidson, "Protesters Liken to Rizzo to Hitler," *PEB*, March 17, 1978, PBCC.

61. Terry, "MOVE Supporters Rally in W. Phila."

62. Bruce Boyle, "Mother Flees MOVE Office with Infant," *PEB*, February 20, 1978, PBCC.

63. "Blockade of MOVE Hurts Merchants," *PEB*, March 19, 1978, PBCC.

64. Alphonso D. Brown Jr., "How They Gave Up," *PI*, May 7, 1978, PBCC; "Rizzo, Police Hailed on MOVE Outcome," *PEB*, May 11, 1978, PBCC.

65. Ronald Goldwyn, "Siege Ended as Predicted: With Blood, Controversy," *PEB*, August 9, 1978, PBCC.

66. Arthur C. Dorrance Jr. to Editorial Office, August 9, 1978, Folder: MOVE, Box A-5356, FLR; Marjorie L. Fougeray to Frank L. Rizzo, August 22, 1978, Folder: MOVE, Box A-5356, FLR.

67. Elmer Smith, "O'Neill Had MOVE House Razed 'to Erase Symbol,'" *PEB*, December 16, 1978, PBCC.

68. J. D. McCaffrey, "Next? Neighborhood Lobbyist," *PEB*, March 16, 1978, PBCC; David Runkel and Joe Davidson, "Rizzo Urges Whites to 'Join Hands,'" *PEB*, March 17, 1978, PBCC.

69. Aaron Epstein, "Carter: Rizzo Would Be Ineffective Crusader," *PEB*, April 7, 1978, PBCC; Joe Davidson, "Rizzo Is Roaring Mad After Plaudits of KKK," *PEB*, April 28, 1978, PBCC.

70. Adrian Lee, "Rizzo's Mail Backs Him Up," *PEB*, April 3, 1978, PBCC.

71. "Two-Term Limit for Mayor Favored by Majority," *PEB*, May 2, 1977, PBCC.

72. Scott Gabriel Knowles, "Staying Too Long at the Fair: Philadelphia Planning and the Debacle of 1976," in Scott Gabriel Knowles, ed., *Imagining Philadelphia: Edmund Bacon and the Future of the City* (Philadelphia: University of Pennsylvania Press, 2009).

73. Committee to Protect the Charter, Campaign Flyer, 1978, Folder: Charter Change—Miscellaneous, Box 2, ADAP.

74. Aaron Epstein, "A Backlash Rises Among White Males," *PI*, May 7, 1978, PBCC; "Mayor Rizzo on Schools," *PEB*, May 16, 1978, PBCC; Dorothy Brown and Ashley Halsey, "Rizzo

Pledges to Challenge Race Quotas," *PEB*, May 15, 1978, PBCC; Bob Frump, "The Mayor Takes Heart from Bakke," *PEB*, June 29, 1978, PBCC.

75. Brian Feldman, "Rizzo Vows to Save Neighborhoods," *PEB*, September 14, 1978, PBCC.

76. Ronald Goldwyn and Joe Davidson, "Rizzo: 'Vote White,' Charter Change," *PEB*, September 22, 1978, PBCC; Sandra Featherman, *Jews, Blacks, and Ethnics: The 1978 "Vote White" Charter Campaign in Philadelphia* (New York: American Jewish Committee, 1979); Paolantonio, *Rizzo*, 229.

77. Paolantonio, *Rizzo*, 229; Featherman, *Jews, Blacks, and Ethnics*, 5–7.

78. Claude Lewis, "Race Is Frank Rizzo's Issue," *PEB*, September 22, 1978, PBCC.

79. Mr. and Mrs. I. M. Rubinstein to Honorable Sir, August 30, 1979, Folder: Police Department, Box A-5478, FLR; Elsie Stevens to Frank L. Rizzo, November 8, 1979, Folder: Police Wives/Interested Citizens, Box A-5483, FLR.

80. Mrs. Sofie Ratkowski to Frank L. Rizzo, August 26, 1979, Folder: Police Department, Box A-5478, FLR.

Chapter 8

1. John Anderson and Hilary Hevenor, *Burning Down the House: MOVE and the Tragedy of Philadelphia* (New York: W. W. Norton, 1987); Information Report, RE: MOVE Organization, June 14, 1984, Folder: MOVE White Papers, Box A-850, PPD-DB; Information Report, RE: MOVE Organization, June 7, 1984, Folder: MOVE White Papers, Box A-850, PPD-DB.

2. Memorandum from Ms. Hanley to Mr. Lytton, July 15, 1985, RE: Chronology of Events involving 'MOVE' from May 1984 to May 12, 1985, Folder: 6, Box 8, PSICR.

3. Anderson and Hevenor, *Burning Down*, 112.

4. Charles W. Bowser, *Let the Bunker Burn: The Final Battle with MOVE* (Philadelphia: Camino Books, 1989).

5. Ibid.; William K. Stevens, "6 Bodies in Ashes of Radicals' Home," *NYT*, May 14, 1985.

6. Richard Esposito, "'The Strip' Called Worst Place, Haunted by Muggers, Prostitutes," *PEB*, December 10, 1981, PBCC.

7. Alphonso D. Brown Jr., Dan Freedman, and Walter F. Naedele, "Suspect, 27, Is Wounded by Officer," *PEB*, December 9, 1981, PBCC.

8. For Mumia Abu-Jamal's role in the Black Panther Party, see Matthew J. Countryman, *Up South: Civil Rights and Black Power in Philadelphia* (Philadelphia: University of Pennsylvania Press, 2006), 286–289. On his arrest, trial, and death sentence, see Amnesty International, *The Case of Mumia Abu-Jamal: A Life in the Balance* (New York: Seven Stories Press, 2000); Daniel R. Williams, *Executing Justice: An Insider Account of the Case of Mumia Abu-Jamal* (New York: St. Martin's Press, 2001); Maureen Faulkner and Michael A. Smerconish, *Murdered by Mumia: A Life Sentence of Loss, Pain, and Injustice* (Guilford, CT: Lyons Press, 2008).

9. United States Commission on Civil Rights, *Police-Community Relations in Philadelphia: A Report to the United States Commission on Civil Rights* (Washington, DC: Government Printing Office, 1972); United States Commission on Civil Rights, *Police Practices and Civil Rights: Hearing Before the United States Commission on Civil Rights, Held in Philadelphia, Pennsylvania, February 6, 1979, April 16–17, 1979* (Washington, DC: Government Printing Office, 1979).

10. Reverend John Gravatt, Statement of the Coalition for a Fair Police Complaint Procedure to the Public Safety Committee, March 24, 1980, Box 1, Folder—Bill #12, JCAP; Lyman C. Ogilby to William J. Green, March 20, 1980, Box 1, Folder—Bill #12, JCAP.

11. "Police and Firemen to Fight Layoffs, City Told," *PEB*, January 24, 1980, PBCC.

12. Fawn Vrazo and Randolph Smith, "Cop Kills Youth After Car Chase," *PEB*, August 25, 1980, PBCC; "Youth's Slaying Protested," *PEB*, August 26, 1980, PBCC.

13. "Green Appeals for Calm," *PEB*, August 26, 1980, PBCC.

14. Eugene Robinson, "North Philadelphia: A Ghetto Defused by Men, Circumstances," *WP*, August 29, 1980.

15. Byron Eskra to Mayor Green, September 12, 1980, Folder—Police Department 1980, Box A-5991, WJG.

16. Erika Grava to W. Green, August 27, 1980, Folder—Police Department 1980, Box A-5991, WJG.

17. Beatrice DeSimone to Mayor Green and Commissioner Solomon, no date, Folder—Police Department 1980, Box A-5991, WJG.

18. William Michetti to William Green, August 29, 1980, Folder—Police Department 1980, WJG; Stephan Staib to Sir, August 31, 1980, Folder—Police Department 1980, Box A-5991, WJG; Roberta Schneider to William J. Green, September 18, 1980, Folder—Police Department 1980, Box A-5991, WJG.

19. Ron Goldwyn, "Cop Is Dead, Radio Man Is Held, but Why Did It Happen?" *PEB*, December 10, 1981, PBCC.

20. "The Accused: Friends Can't Fathom 'Brilliant' Newsman as Murder Suspect," *DN*, December 10, 1981, PBCC.

21. "Cops Beat Him, Abu-Jamal Says," *PEB*, January 5, 1982, PBCC; Stephen Braun, "Jamal Denies Killing Cop; Alleges Brutality," *DN*, January 5, 1982, PBCC.

22. Dave Racher and Maria Gallagher, "Cop: Jamal Admitted Killing Faulkner," *DN*, January 9, 1982, PBCC.

23. Open Letter to Philadelphia News Media Personnel, February 1982, Folder 9, Box1, ATC; Mumia Abu Jamal Defense Committee pamphlet, no date, Folder 9, Box 1, ATC; "You Be the Judge," pamphlet, no date, Folder 9, Box 1, ATC.

24. "Black and White Issues in a Policeman's Death," letters to the editor, *PEB*, December 26, 1981, PBCC.

25. Dan Freedman and Kathy Sheehan, "Aggressive, Young Cop Was a Hero," *PEB*, December 9, 1981, PBCC.

26. Kathy Sheehan, "Kids Loved Uncle Danny…He Played Santa," *PEB*, December 10, 1981, PBCC.

27. Nicole J. Maurantonio, "Crisis, Race, and Journalistic Authority in Postwar Philadelphia" (PhD diss., University of Pennsylvania, 2008), 220–283.

28. Bonnie L. Cook and William J. Nazzaro, "Slain Officer Mourned," *PEB*, December 14, 1981, PBCC.

29. Thomas J. Gibbons Jr., "Officer's Widow Recalls Their Last Goodbye Kiss," *PEB*, December 20, 1981, PBCC.

30. Faulkner and Smerconish, *Murdered by Mumia*.

31. Nicole Maurantonio, "Justice for Daniel Faulkner? History, Memory, and Police Identity," *Journal of Communication Inquiry* 32, no. 43 (2008): 43–59.

32. Berit M. Lakey to William Brown, July 15, 1985, Folder 14, Box 58, FCR.

33. Fraternal Order of Police, *Lodge No. 5 v. City of Philadelphia et al.*, Philadelphia County Court of Common Pleas, No. 2977, July Term, 1985, Box 9, Folder 4, PSICR; James J. Creaturo, Memorandum "Interview of Officer Christopher Cherry, Badge No. 1220," July 31, 1985, Box 16, Folder 14, PSICR; Memorandum from James J. Creaturo to H. Graham McDonald, July 16,

1985, Box 16, Folder 15, PSICR; John Biggins to William H. Brown III, October 23, 1985, Box 10, Folder 6, PSICR.

34. Lyn Colbentson to MOVE Commission, no date [received November 5, 1985], Box 4, Folder 3, PSICR.

35. "What Probers Concluded," *DN*, March 7, 1986.

36. Memorandum from Tino Calabia to Edward Rutledge, June 3, 1985, Box 7, Folder 5, PSICR.

37. "Die, Mumia, Die," *NT*, December 14, 2011, accessed June 21, 2016, http://www .northeasttimes.com/2011/dec/14/4317-editorial-die-mumia-die.html/#.V2lnU6JuMsA.

38. Joe Davidson, "Whitman Project Started," *PEB*, March 18, 1980, PBCC; "Resting in Peace," photograph, *PEB*, April 13, 1980, PBCC; William J. Storm and Joe Reichwein, "Whitman Park Foes Express their Anger with Blaring Music," *PEB*, November 9, 1980, PBCC; "Whitman Cost Rising Through the Roof," *DN*, July 17, 1980.

39. The People of Whitman, Petition to President-elect Ronald Reagan, 1980, Folder: Reagan, Ronald, Box 1, WC-632; Whitman Council, Inc., Memorandum to All Whitman Block Captains, November 1982, Folder: Board Meeting Minutes, Sept. 1982–Aug. 1983, Box 8, WC-632; Harmon Y. Gordon and Joe Davidson, "50-50 Race Ratio for Whitman," *PEB*, March 19, 1980, PBCC; Earni Young, "Whitman Residents Due Soon," *DN*, October 5, 1982.

40. Janet McMillan,"Old Accepts New: A Housing 'Project' Wins Respect in S. Phila.," *PI*, November 23, 1984.

41. "Fred Druding to Quit Whitman at End of Term," *SPR*, September 26, 1985, Folder: Others (Various Politicians, etc.), Box 2, WC-638.

42. Jack Kirkwood, "Huge Crowd Rejects Section 8 Proposal," *NT*, June 11, 1980; Lou Antosh, "Taxing Question: Do the Poor Deserve Luxury Housing?" *DN*, July 15, 1981, PBCC.

43. "Salvatore Tries to Block Police Layoffs," *NT*, February 2, 1980; Hank Salvatore, Statement Announcing Richard Sprague Chief Council to the Senate Urban Affairs and Housing Committee Investigation of MOVE, July 17, 1985, Box 11, Folder 13, MOVE Commission Records.

44. "Salvatore Wants Tougher Penalties," *NT*, May 28, 1980.

45. Michael B. Katz, *In the Shadow of the Poorhouse: A Social History of Welfare in America* (New York: Basic Books, 1996), 294–296; Robert P. Fairbanks II, *How It Works: Recovering Citizens in Post–Welfare Philadelphia* (Chicago: University of Chicago Press, 2009), 66–69; Jennifer Middlestadt, *From Welfare to Workfare: The Unintended Consequences of Liberal Reform, 1945–1965* (Chapel Hill: University of North Carolina Press, 2005).

46. Anthony P. Halter, "The Impact of the Welfare Reform Act of 1982 on the Transitionally Needy in Philadelphia" (PhD diss., University of Pennsylvania, 1986).

47. John F. Fitzpatrick to John C. Anderson, April 30, 1982, Folder—Misc. Correspondence—April 1983, Box 6, JCAP; Dan Rottenberg, "Northeast Phila. Isn't an Island," *PI*, March 19, 1985.

48. Marc Sugarman, "Welcome to ? County," *NT*, November 23, 1983; Walter F. Roche Jr., "Lawmaker's Plan: Let Northeast Quit the City," *PI*, November 16, 1983.

49. Marc Sugarman, "Residents React to Secession Bill," *NT*, November 23, 1983.

50. Tom Infield, "As Northeast Secession Talk Wanes, Leader of the Drive Moves Gingerly," *PI*, May 19, 1985; "Northeast Teased by Idea of Separation," *PI*, April 1, 1987; Bill Miller, "Liberty County Revived for Re-Election Campaign," *PI*, February 4, 1980.

51. Tom Infield, "Strangers, by Choice, to Center City," *PI*, February 9, 1986.

52. Michael Sokolove, "Campaign '83: The Northeast Playing Politics in Philadelphia's Hottest Property," *DN*, May 5, 1983.

53. Bucks County Housing Plan, Part I: Population and Housing Data, 1960–1970, January 1972, Box 587, Folder 10, GPC; Montgomery County Planning Commission, Housing Distribution Plan, 1974, Box 713, Folder 13, GPC.

54. Philadelphia Criminal Justice Coordinating Commission, Description and Analysis of Selected Trends in Reported Crime in Philadelphia, 1972-1982, April 1984, Box 886, GPC.

55. Sandra Freeman, "Rizzo Is the Answer," letter to the editor, *NT*, September 9, 1981.

56. Walter F. Naedele, "S. Phila. Is Aging as Young Depart," *PEB*, January 14, 1980, PBCC.

57. Philadelphia City Planning Commission, City Stats: General Demographic and Economic Data, January 2005, accessed June 21, 2016, http://www.phila.gov/pdfs/citystats.pdf.

58. "The 1988 Elections: Northeast; Pennsylvania," *NYT*, November 9, 1980; Renée M. Lamis, *The Realignment of Pennsylvania Politics Since 1960: Two-Party Competition in a Battleground State* (Philadelphia: University of Pennsylvania Press, 2009). Arlen Specter switched parties in 2009 and finished his final term as US Senator as a Democrat.

59. Mark Fineman, "Rizzo Walks Two St. Like a Man on a Campaign," *PI*, September 21, 1981.

60. S. A. Paolantonio, *Frank Rizzo: The Last Big Man in Big City America*, 10th anniversary ed. (Philadelphia: Camino Books, 2003), 260–272.

61. Countryman, *Up South*, 308, 323–324.

62. Larry Eichel, "It's Official: Rizzo in Race for 3d Term," *PI*, January 13, 1983.

63. Carol Horner, "Rizzo Takes His Case to Black Areas," *PI*, March 21, 1983.

64. Carol Horner, "Rizzo: Simply a Complex Man," *PI*, May 3, 1983.

65. Carol Horner, "Rizzo Goes Marching in South Philly," *PI*, May 16, 1983.

66. "Endorsements," *NT*, May 5, 1983.

67. Mitch Plotnick, "Rizzo, Goode Look to Northeast," *NT*, February 23, 1983; Mitch Plotnick, "Election Predictions Missed Mark," *NT*, May 25, 1983.

68. Countryman, *Up South*, 322–327; Acel Moore, "Why Wilson Goode Won," *PI*, May 19, 1983.

69. Tom Fox, "Rizzo Candidacy? . . . Meanwhile, Some Wait in the Wings," *PI*, March 5, 1986; Claude Lewis, "MOVE's Aftermath: Mayor Goode Is Facing a Time of Testing," *PI*, March 5, 1986.

70. Paul Nussbaum, "Rizzo May Run Again, as Republican," *PI*, May 29, 1986; H. G. Bissinger, "In the Return of Rizzo, Past and Future Collide," *PI*, November 16, 1986.

71. H. G. Bissinger, "The Obvious Is Official: He's in Race," *PI*, February 27, 1987.

72. H. G. Bissinger, "In the Return of Rizzo, Past and Future Collide."

73. Lini S. Kadaba, "Rizzo Opens Race with Vow to Serve Northeast," *PI*, March 1, 1987.

74. H. G. Bissinger, "Rizzo Aims Letter at Law-and-Order Supporters," *PI*, September 2, 1987.

75. H. G. Bissinger, "A Run by Rizzo Might Be Just the Ticket for Goode," *PI*, November 14, 1986.

76. Tom Infield, "Anti-Rizzo Group of '76 Forms Again," *PI*, September 9, 1987.

77. H. G. Bissinger, Tom Infield, and Christopher Hepp, "Goode Wins in Tight Race; Rizzo Refuses to Concede," *PI*, November 4, 1987; "Rizzo Comes to Terms," *PI*, November 5, 1987; Paolantonio, *Rizzo*, 313–325.

78. "Fred Druding to Quit Whitman at End of Term"; Vanessa Williams, "Council Races Are Expected to Yield Something Old and Something New," *PI*, October 4, 1987.

79. Francis Rafferty, "Why I'm Voting for W.," *DN*, October 29, 2004.

80. Lorraine Gengo, "NE Electorate: Closet Voters and Ticket Splitters," *NT*, October 10, 1984.

81. David Zucchino, "In the Far Northeast, a Party Battle," *PI*, October 10, 1984.

Epilogue

1. S. A. Paolantonio, "Rizzo Anti-Drug Stand Garners Black Support," *PI*, June 18, 1991.

2. S. A. Paolantonio, *Frank Rizzo: The Last Big Man in Big City America*, 10th anniversary ed. (Philadelphia: Camino Books, 2003), 362–368.

3. WCAU special report, "Frank Rizzo: The End of an Era," aired July 18, 1991.

4. For a similar argument, see Bethany Moreton, *To Serve God and Walmart: The Making of Christian Free Enterprise* (Cambridge, MA: Harvard University Press, 2010).

5. Elizabeth Hinton, *From the War on Poverty to the War on Crime: The Making of Mass Incarceration in America* (Cambridge, MA: Harvard University Press, 2016).

6. Ronald Reagan, speech to the Fourth Annual Conservative Political Action Committee Convention, February 6, 1977.

7. Ronald Reagan, remarks in Chicago, Illinois, at the Annual Convention and Centennial Observance of the United Brotherhood of Carpenters and Joiners, September 3, 1981.

8. Jake Blumgart, "Donald Trump is Frank Rizzo, Reborn," *PM*, January 31, 2016; Alan Rappeport, "In Philadelphia, a Brash Ex-Mayor Draws Comparisons to Donald Trump," *NYT*, April 24, 2016; Adam Goodman, "Donald Trump's Frank Rizzo Factor—'The Hidden Vote,'" *The Daily Beast*, June 26, 2016, accessed January 3, 2017, http://www.thedailybeast.com/articles /2016/06/26/donald-trump-s-frank-rizzo-factor-the-hidden-vote.html; Brian Hickey, "Is Donald Trump the New Frank Rizzo?" *Philly Voice*, August 10, 2016, accessed January 3, 2017, http:// www.phillyvoice.com/is-donald-trump-the-new-frank-rizzo-the-former-philadelphia-mayors -family-weighs-in/.

9. Elizabeth Markovits, "Trump 'Tells It Like It Is,'" *WP*, March 4, 2016, accessed January 3, 2017, https://www.washingtonpost.com/news/monkey-cage/wp/2016/03/04/trump-tells-it-like -it-is-thats-not-necessarily-a-good-thing-for-democracy/?utm_term=.cbfbcc282e73.

10. "Donald Trump Jr. Refers to Dad as 'the Blue-Collar Billionaire' at Pittsburgh Campaign Stop," *CBS Pittsburgh*, September 14, 2016, accessed January 3, 2017, http://pittsburgh .cbslocal.com/2016/09/14/donald-trump-jr-refers-to-dad-as-the-blue-collar-billionaire-during -pittsburgh-campaign-stop/; "Donald Trump a 'Blue-Collar Billionaire' with a Lot of Money," *USNews.com*, July 18, 2016, accessed January 3, 2017, http://www.usnews.com/news/politics /articles/2016-07-18/donald-trump-a-blue-collar-billionaire-with-a-lot-of-money.

11. Tom Jackman, "Fraternal Order of Police Endorses Trump," *WP*, September 16, 2016, accessed January 3, 2017, https://www.washingtonpost.com/news/true-crime/wp/2016/09/16 /fraternal-order-of-police-union-endorses-trump/?utm_term=.db217e3dd309.

12. Ronald Brownstein, "How the Election Revealed the Divide Between City and Country," *Atlantic.com*, November 17, 2016, accessed January 3, 2017, http://www.theatlantic.com/politics /archive/2016/11/clinton-trump-city-country-divide/507902/.

13. Bryce Covert, "Donald Trump's Imaginary Inner Cities," *The Nation*, November 7, 2016, accessed January 3, 2017, https://www.thenation.com/article/donald-trumps-imaginary-inner -cities/.

14. Elizabeth Kneebone and Steven Raphael, *City and Suburban Crime Trends in Metropolitan America* (Washington, DC: Brookings Institution Metropolitan Policy Program, 2011).

15. Eugene Scott, "Donald Trump: I'm 'the Least Racist Person,'" *CNN.com*, September 15, 2016, accessed January 3, 2017, http://www.cnn.com/2016/09/15/politics/donald-trump -election-2016-racism/.

16. Nicholas Carnes and Noam Lupu, "It's Time to Bust the Myth: Most Trump Voters Were Not Working Class," June 5, 2017, accessed June 27, 2017, https://www.washingtonpost.com /news/monkey-cage/wp/2017/06/05/its-time-to-bust-the-myth-most-trump-voters-were-not -working-class/?utm_term=.df3af58d8a7f.

INDEX

ACKNOWLEDGMENTS

This is a book about people and their relationship to the places they create, inhabit, and cherish. As I reflect on the process of researching and writing it, I see more clearly than ever that this book is also the product of the people and places that inspired and sustained me for the better part of the past decade. I can think of no greater privilege or pleasure than taking the opportunity to publicly thank the people and places that helped make this book happen.

No historian can write a book like this on their own. We are especially indebted to the librarians and archivists who tirelessly guide us through the myriad methods of cataloging and curating the raw materials of historical investigation. I was lucky enough to encounter some truly wonderful people and places in the process of researching this book. I benefited greatly from the expert staffs of the Philadelphia City Archives, Pennsylvania State University's Historical Collections and Labor Archives, the Philadelphia Archdiocesan Historical Research Center, the Mid-Atlantic Region of the National Archives and Records Administration, and the Pennsylvania Historical Society. The latter also granted me an Andrew W. Mellon Visiting Research Fellowship to work with their collections. While they all offered exceptional help, I must single out the incredible staff of what was until recently Temple University's Urban Archives, now rebranded as Temple's Special Collection Research Center. I did the bulk of the research for this book in these collections, often for days on end for more than a month at a time. I was there when the archive outgrew its tiny basement reading room. I returned and persevered as it opened a temporary reading room in what can generously be called a large concrete closet. And I was privileged to be the first researcher to use their impressive new facilities. I was just as fortunate to spend that much time with their generous and talented staff. Brenda Galloway Wright, John Pettit, and their students and volunteers made every research day a great experience. Of all of Temple's staff, however, Ann Mosher deserves special recognition. Ann helped lighten my workload with moments of levity and laughter throughout my months of research. It is common to find professional and helpful staff in the archives. It is somewhat less common to find new friends. To Ann I am grateful for all her help with my research, but I am especially thankful for her friendship.

While most of the research for this book took place in Philadelphia, it first began to take shape at another place seven hundred miles away in Lafayette and West Lafayette, Indiana. At Purdue University, funding and resources from the Department of History and the Purdue Research Foundation helped get the early research and writing for this project off the ground. Even more important than this material support was the intellectual guidance and scholarly community that Purdue offered. I benefited greatly from years of conversations and advice from David Atkinson, Alicia Decker, R. Douglass Hurt, John Larson, and the late Michael Morrison. I am especially indebted to Darren Dochuk, who not only helped spark the earliest idea for this book, but also first put me in touch with Bob Lockhart at the University of Pennsylvania Press. Darren's prompting led me to this project and his enthusiasm for it has not wavered since. Likewise, I owe Jon Teaford a similar debt. He had retired before I even arrived in Indiana, so I am incredibly grateful that he was so willing to work with me as the project moved from idea to manuscript. His willingness to continue reading and critiquing my drafts even after I left Purdue has been more generous than I could have imagined. Finally, Nancy Gabin helped guide this project through more stages than I care to count. Her steadfast support and enthusiasm for both the book and my career has been nothing short of remarkable. I appreciate everything that she and everyone else at Purdue helped make possible.

I was also fortunate to have an exemplary cohort of young scholars, historians, and friends take the journey though Lafayette and West Lafayette with me. So many people read early drafts and provided an environment that made Indiana feel like a second home. I offer my sincere thanks to all those who came and went, but some deserve special appreciation. They include Brian Alberts, Cori and Tim Derifield, Sanket Desai, Brittany Bayless Fremion, Josh Jeffers, Kara Kvaran, Andrew McGregor, Erica Morin, Mark Otto, Tim and Tana Olin, Jeff Perry, Kate Pospisek, Max Rieger, Andrew and Erika Smith, the late Chris Snively, and Karen Sonneliter. Among this illustrious group, Patrick Pospisek, Brandon Ward, and Mauricio Castro deserve special mention. Patrick probably suffered my early chatter about this project more than anyone else at Purdue. Yet most of the time he still managed to do so with his trademark wit and generous spirit. For some reason he even remained my friend at the end of it. So have Brandon and Mauricio. Both became frequent travel companions and roommates as we shared our research on urban history at various conferences and professional settings. More importantly, they both took the time to read the full manuscript at a critical point in its revision process. The book is no doubt better because of their feedback. I am better because of their friendship.

Scholarly places are often less permanent than others. Academic conferences and early career teaching positions are temporary by design. Yet I have been fortunate enough to find a welcoming group of scholars and friends in all these settings. I delivered early parts of this research at the Social Science History Association Annual Meeting, the Pennsylvania Historical Association Annual Meeting, the North American Labor History Conference, and the Midwest Labor and Working Class History Colloquium. The Policy History Conference and Urban History Conference have been especially fruitful. I would like to thank all the co-panelists, audience members, and other attendees that offered their support and critical feedback on papers. I am just as grateful to those who stopped to share a drink or exchange ideas in less formal conference settings. You know who you are. Thanks especially to Chris Agee, Guian McKee, Carol McKibben, Sam Mitrani, Elizabeth Shermer, Shannon King, and Beryl Satter for offering their commentary on various segments of this work.

It seems strange to say that one of the more important places I found support for the later stages of this book has been virtual. While there is no shortage of darkness coming from all corners of the internet, academic Twitter has helped make a sense of community for a lot of early-career academics. As I revised this book I found a number of scholars in various career levels and disciplines willing to offer words of wisdom, consolation, support, solidarity, and enthusiasm. Many of them I have never met in person, although those I have met tend to be just as gracious and friendly as they are online. It would take another book to list all the kind and supportive people that have helped buoy my spirits while finishing this one. Since I cannot name everyone, I must at least acknowledge those who contributed to the #WritePeasant virtual writing group. Our weekly check-ins kept me on pace throughout the final writing and revision process and offered a steady stream of much-needed encouragement and levity. Thanks to you all.

Several others lent their eyes and expertise to this book in various stages. Robert Lockhart at the University of Pennsylvania Press has a growing reputation for his patience and generosity, and for being one of the best editors a historian could ask for. I am happy to confirm that the reputation is well deserved. Thanks as well to the entire staff at Penn Press. Anonymous readers for the *Journal of Urban History* and *Journal of Social History* offered valuable feedback in some of the early stages of my writing. I am also grateful to the *Journal of Social History* for granting permission to publish parts of this book that originally appeared there. Of course, my biggest debts are to those that read the entire manuscript in its later stages. I am grateful to Guian McKee for giving my manuscript such a close and thorough reading. His detailed feedback helped give the book its final form and saved me from making a number of embarrassing errors. Guian's scholarship on Philadelphia liberalism provided an early model for much of my own research. His level of engagement with my work has provided a new model of professional generosity. The late Eric Schneider also offered a critical reading that helped me clarify and strengthen my arguments. He was also enthusiastic about the book's publication and I am deeply sorry that he passed away before I was able to finish it. Eric will be sorely missed by the entire historical community, but especially among urban historians.

In the years since I started writing this book I have been fortunate to find work at a number of institutions where supportive staff, helpful colleagues, and curious students helped this book take shape in one way or another. My friends and colleagues at Indiana University–Purdue University at Indianapolis and Grand Valley State University offered welcoming environments and, most importantly, the ability to stay connected to the field. Just as importantly, every scholar also knows that our students are often the first audience for our new ideas. While all of mine deserve acknowledgement, I must single out those that took my American Urban History course at IUPUI and my America in the 1960s, Post-1945 US History Seminar, and Urban Crucible courses at the University of South Alabama. Whether they know it or not, their questions and conversations helped sharpen my thinking many times over. Finally, it has been my colleagues at the University of South Alabama that have offered the encouragement, time, and resources I needed to finish this work. Funds from the Department of History and the College of Arts and Sciences allowed for the procurement of permissions and materials needed to produce the final manuscript. Thanks especially to my first department chair, the late Clarence Mohr, for his confidence and support of my writing and teaching. Thanks as well to Martha Jane Brazy, Donald DeVore, Robert Faust, Leanne Good, Marsha Hamilton, Will Holmes, Mara Kozelsky, Mel McKiven, David Meola, Dave Messenger, Alex McManus, Harry Miller, Dan Rogers, Michele Strong, and Rebecca Williams for their support and for making me feel welcome. Special thanks to Claire Cage for organizing our informal writing group and taking the time to read and comment on parts of my manuscript at various stages.

My students, friends, and colleagues at the University of South Alabama have also helped make Mobile, Alabama, the latest and perhaps least likely place to shape this book. Mobile is not where I thought my career would take me, but thanks to a number of people I am glad that it did. In addition to Claire, the other members of our writing group have offered critical feedback along with their friendship. Thanks to Shane Dillingham, David Head, Kenny Moss, and Nic Wood. Outside of academia there have been a number of people that have helped lighten the load and make my wife and me feel welcome in a new place. All of those that joined us for brunch, pub trivia, or anything else that made Mobile worth hanging around for a while deserve my sincere gratitude, but I am especially appreciative of Buffy, Heather, and Shane for making it feel a bit more like home.

Mobile may feel like home, but the place that has shaped this book more than any other will always be home. I was born and raised in Philadelphia. I lived in sections of the city I write about in this book. With the exception of my doctorate, all my formal schooling took place in the city. While the vast majority of this book takes place before I was born, much of it remains personal; not because it is the story of my city, but because so much of it is the story of my grandparents, my aunts and uncles, and my broader extended family. Although I have not lived in Philadelphia in many years, the majority of my friends and family still do. I know many of them will not agree with all my arguments, perspectives, and conclusions, but I hope they appreciate my efforts nonetheless. I also hope they recognize their role in helping make this book a reality. The same is true for my non-Philadelphia family. I was also lucky enough to join a West Coast family in the process of researching and writing this book. Jennifer and Robert Venter have given me the pleasure of adding their home in suburban San Diego to the list of places that matter to me. I am equally thankful to Kelsea Venter and Nick Gabriel for welcoming me into their family. They have continued to support my work and my career, even as it has caused their daughter and sister to continue living farther away from home. As anyone interested would, they often greeted my visits with questions about when I would be done with the book. At long last, I am happy to share the finished product with them.

Back in Philadelphia, so many people engaged my mind and spirit during long trips home for research that I am bound to neglect someone. They should know they are in my thoughts even if they are not explicitly thanked here. Of all these friends and family, I reserve my deepest thanks to those who provided me with a place to stay while I was researching. At various points I stayed with my father as well as my best friends, Samantha Nestor and Andrew Haneiko. Sam and Andrew welcomed Franklin and Olive into the world as I was researching and writing this book and I'm glad that all four of them were willing to welcome me back so often. After Sam and Andrew, no one in Philadelphia endured my presence longer or did more to ensure the success of this book than my sister and brother-in-law, Kathryn and William Rhoads. Kate and Bill allowed me to stay with them for two extended research trips, even as they moved from their first home and their family grew. They were joined by Billy and Suzie while I was home researching. One day, when they are old enough, I hope Franklin, Olive, Billy, and Suzie will have an opportunity to read this book, learn more about their hometown, and understand what I was working on all that time. Finally, while I share my deepest thanks and appreciation with their parents, I reserve the lion's share for mine. Thomas and Susan Lombardo have encouraged and supported me throughout this process, and throughout my life. After years of fits and starts and everything else in between, I know that no one will be happier to see this book than my mom and dad. I hope it makes them proud. Thanks so much to all of you.

Last, and most importantly, there is only one person that has been through all of these places with me. Rebecca Venter-Lombardo has been my partner, my best friend, and the best person I know for almost as long as I've been working on this book. From Lafayette to Indianapolis to Grand Rapids to Mobile, she has been there every step of the way. She graciously put her own career on hold as mine took us from one new place to another. When first confronted with the news that I landed a job interview in southern Alabama, the southern California native never hesitated or balked at the possibility. Instead she cheered the news as an exciting new adventure. Beyond her willingness to endure my early career vagaries, Beca also accompanied me on my final research trip, helped choose photographs, and read every word in this book. Twice. She has been my proofreader, my style coach, my critic, and my cheerleader all in one. Dedicating the book to her is the least I can do to thank her for all she did to make it happen. I cannot even begin to imagine what it would take to properly thank her for everything else. But I'll spend as long as it takes trying to figure it out.

CPSIA information can be obtained
at www.ICGtesting.com
Printed in the USA
LVHW092133230719
625103LV00005B/21/P

9 780812 250541